Lecture Notes in Computer Science   12271

More information about this series at http://www.springer.com/series/7408

Jean-Michel Bruel · Alfredo Capozucca ·
Manuel Mazzara · Bertrand Meyer ·
Alexandr Naumchev · Andrey Sadovykh (Eds.)

Frontiers in Software Engineering Education

First International Workshop, FISEE 2019
Villebrumier, France, November 11–13, 2019
Invited Papers

 Springer

Editors
Jean-Michel Bruel
University of Toulouse
Blagnac, France

Alfredo Capozucca ⓘ
University of Luxembourg
Esch-sur-Alzette, Luxembourg

Manuel Mazzara ⓘ
Innopolis University
Innopolis, Russia

Bertrand Meyer
Schaffhausen Institute of Technology
Schaffhausen, Switzerland

Alexandr Naumchev
Innopolis University
Innopolis, Russia

Andrey Sadovykh
Innopolis University
Innopolis, Russia

ISSN 0302-9743   ISSN 1611-3349   (electronic)
Lecture Notes in Computer Science
ISBN 978-3-030-57662-2   ISBN 978-3-030-57663-9   (eBook)
https://doi.org/10.1007/978-3-030-57663-9

LNCS Sublibrary: SL2 – Programming and Software Engineering

This Springer imprint is published by the registered company Springer Nature Switzerland AG
The registered company address is: Gewerbestrasse 11, 6330 Cham, Switzerland

Preface

The First International Workshop on Frontiers in Software Engineering Education (FISEE 2019) (https://www.laser-foundation.org/fisee/fisee-2019/), held during November 11–13, 2019, at the Château de Villebrumier, France, builds on top of the experience gained with previous events run at the same place, for example DEVOPS 2018 and DEVOPS 2019. It aimed at bringing the attention to a topic of great importance and actuality for academia, namely education. The event happened before the global and massive move to online teaching, therefore the emphasis is more on "classic" education, still there is mention of "remote teaching." It can be considered a compendium on best practices in the world pre 2020; a starting point to explore the ongoing changes happening right now, while we are writing.

The event was kicked off by an outstanding introduction to the field by Professor Alexander Tormasov, Founding Rector at Innopolis University, Russia, and Chief Scientist of Parallels. The participants came from diverse organizations, with a representation of both industry and academia. This volume gathers their papers, considerably enhanced thanks to the feedback received during the conference and during two different peer-review phases. We invited an excellent Program Committee as it can be seen on the website. People from different continents allows for a broad and heterogeneous vision about teaching software engineering. This enriches perspectives, experiences, and lessons learnt at the moment of assessing the submitted works. The contributions cover a wide range of problems and are organized in different parts: Course Experience, Lessons Learnt, Curriculum and Course Design, Competitions and Workshops, Empirical Studies, Tools and Automation, and Globalization of Education. The final part Tools Workshop: Artificial and Natural Tools (ANT) contains submissions presented at a different, but related, workshop run at Innopolis University, Russia, in the context of the TOOLS 2019 conference. We realized that these works also deserve adequate dissemination in the context of education since they present research results that are achieved thanks to the work of students, therefore representing a good example of "learning by doing."

FISEE 2019 is part of a series of scientific events held at the new LASER center in Villebrumier near Montauban and Toulouse, France. Inspired by the prestigious precedent of the Dagstuhl center in Germany (the model for all such ventures), but adding its own sunny touch of accent du sud-ouest (the songful tones of Southwest France), the LASER center (http://laser-foundation.org, site of the foundation which also organizes the LASER summer school in Elba, Italy) provides a venue for high-tech events of a few days to a week in a beautiful setup in the midst of a region rich with historical, cultural, and culinary attractions. The proceedings enjoy publication in a subseries of the Springer *Lecture Notes in Computer Science*.

We hope that you will benefit from the results of FISEE 2019 as presented in the following pages and you may join one of the future events in Villebrumier.

July 2020

Jean-Michel Bruel
Alfredo Capozucca
Manuel Mazzara
Bertrand Meyer
Alexandr Naumchev
Andrey Sadovykh

Organization

Program Committee

Yamine Ait-Ameur	INP-ENSEEIHT, France
Hamna Aslam	Innopolis University, Russia
Jean Botev	University of Luxembourg, Luxembourg
Joseph Alexander Brown	Innopolis University, Russia
Jean-Michel Bruel	IRIT, France
Antonio Bucchiarone	FBK-IRST, Italy
Alfredo Capozucca	University of Luxembourg, Luxembourg
Maximiliano Cristia	CIFASIS-UNR, Argentina
Martina De Sanctis	Gran Sasso Science Institute (GSSI), Italy
Carlo A. Furia	Universita della Svizzera Italiana (USI), Switzerland
Nicolas Guelfi	University of Luxembourg, Luxembourg
Mohamad Kassab	Penn State University, USA
Manuel Mazzara	Innopolis University, Russia
Bertrand Meyer	ETH Zurich, Switzerland
Henry Muccini	University of L'Aquila, Italy
Gail Murphy	The University of British Columbia, Canada
Alexandr Naumchev	Innopolis University, Russia
Cecile Peraire	Carnegie Mellon University Silicon Valley, USA
Benoît Ries	University of Luxembourg, Luxembourg
Victor Rivera	The Australian National University, Australia
Andrey Sadovykh	Innopolis University, Russia

Contents

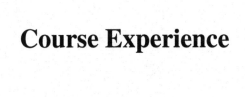

Course Experience

Teaching Formal Methods: An Experience Report

Mehrnoosh Askarpour[1]([✉])[iD] and Marcello M. Bersani[2][iD]

[1] Computing and Software, McMaster University, Hamilton, Canada
askarpom@mcmaster.ca
[2] DEIB, Poltecnico di Milano, Milan, Italy
marcellomaria.bersani@polimi.it

Abstract. The general attitude of students towards formal specification and verification of systems is not exactly what one could call enthusiastic. Generally, software engineering courses at universities include an introduction to specification with formal notations such as Z, Alloy, UML, etc. However, it seems that the importance of formal specification to replicate expected system behavior does not sink in as it should with the students. Moreover, other products of computer science (e.g., machine learning algorithms, robot systems deployment), rather than software, benefit from formal specification as well. This paper is a general report of our observations on teaching formal methods on undergraduate and graduate levels at Politecnico di Milano.

Keywords: Formal methods · Temporal logic · Computer science · Computer engineering · Formal specification

1 Introduction

Formal methods (FM) have been used in hardware and software for a wide range of applications (e.g., aerospace, transportation). Methods such as automated formal verification and model checking are used in many different research and practical areas. Hence, it is paramount for computer scientists and engineers to be aware of their benefits and apply them to problems of the real world.

Formal Methods community is very well-known, and the world congress FM is a landmark worldwide. Their affiliated Formal Methods Teaching Committee (FMTea)[1] gathered a repository of FM university courses around the world,[2] which gives a reliable estimation of the situation globally. As of April 2020, the website displays sixty-two -courses, mainly from European universities (see Fig. 1a), dispensed at the M.Sc. level (see Fig. 1b), the half of which include explicitly Logic in the list of topics of the course. Moreover, only ten of the reported courses include Temporal Logic in their program.

---

[1] fmeurope/teaching.
[2] fme-teaching/courses.

© Springer Nature Switzerland AG 2020
J.-M. Bruel et al. (Eds.): FISEE 2019, LNCS 12271, pp. 3–18, 2020.
https://doi.org/10.1007/978-3-030-57663-9_1

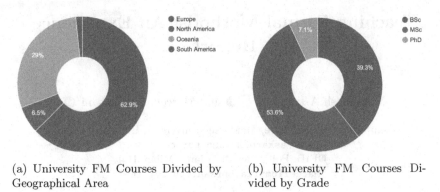

(a) University FM Courses Divided by Geographical Area

(b) University FM Courses Divided by Grade

Fig. 1. A visual representation of the current state of Teaching Formal Methods around the world, based on an study done by Formal Methods Teaching Committee.

To the best of our knowledge, and based on our observations at Politecnico di Milano and our discussions with our colleagues elsewhere, the participation of students in FM courses is decreasing, and their interest in doing thesis or research about FM concepts is alarmingly low. For example Politecnico di Milano has around 200 graduates every year[3] in Master of computer science and engineering of which only on average 30 students participate in our FM course—which we later report in this paper—annually.[4] We asked those 30 attendees via a questionnaire if they are interested in doing their master thesis in this area, and only about 11% of them had positive answers. Based on the same questionnaire, about 33% of students have some background or interest in the subject, which means one third of those who are interested in FM still won't pick it as their thesis topic.

Da Rosal [48] argues that the reason why students find FM courses challenging lies in their mathematical background from high school. This opinion has been raised even before [8,31,48] and highlights the need for a fundamental change in high school education and more focus on discrete and applicable mathematics, instead of pedagogical issues. Gibson [25] blames neglecting case studies and illustrative examples during teaching; Robinson [47] mentions the lack of visibility of industrial use; Mandrioli [38] blames miscommunication, and fuzzy terminology, and suggests the use of "push button" and user-friendly tools; Buote [11] claims that tools could be misleading if mathematical fundamentals and concepts are not clearly understood. Others point out student's desire of achieving quick results and bypassing important design steps [45] or their drift to virtual reality, rather than modeling [27].

Just like FM courses, any other course in computer engineering/Science has its difficulties. Students, though, do not run away from them because they view

---

[3] Average computed by considering the last 5 years.

[4] All the statistics and percentages reported throughout the paper are rounded and therefore are approximate values.

Table 1. The second column categorizes the papers in proceedings of Formal Methods in Computer Science Education 2008, Formal Methods Teaching 2004 - 2009 - 2019, based on the tools and concepts they used. The third column lists the most popular tools listed in FME Education Course Database (fme-teaching/courses).

Tools	Papers	FME course database
JML	[3, 34, 44]	-
Ada	[13, 36]	-
Abstract state machines	[10]	-
Eiffel	[43]	-
B, Event-B	[1, 14, 15, 26, 28, 34, 46, 46]	-
Hoare's Logic	[29, 53, 54]	-
Alloy	[12, 41, 50, 51, 55]	8 entries
Logic	[7, 20, 33, 35, 42, 52]	-
UML	[16, 24]	-
Z, Object-Z	[17, 55]	-
Proof-checking	[4, 9, 40]	-
Model checking	[6, 19, 30, 32]	-
Concurrency theory	[2]	-
Danfy	-	7 entries
SPIN	-	9 entries
Nusmv/Nuxmv	-	3 entries
Mini-sat	-	2 entries
Mcrl2	-	4 entries
Coq	-	7 entries

them as important and necessary for their careers. Students often think of FM courses as too theoretical and not practical. For example, when we teach them about Hoare's Logic, they straight up ask if there is any use of that at all. This shows a serious lack of prospect that will be adjusted by showing the student real-life examples of using FM in the industrial ambient or asking them to do practical projects [58]. Open-source tools such as UPPAAL [57], NuSMV [18], GreatSPN [56] are good examples of means that have industrial purposes and could be used for homework projects as well. Other tools developed for modeling and verifying complex systems, whose behavior combines discrete aspects (e.g., states and transitions) and continuous dynamics (e.g., time, continuous laws, etc.), can be found, for instance, at [23] and [21]. Section 3 explains our experience with Zot [59] on encouraging students to use formal verification for a practical project.

Table 1 envisions the current state of FM courses and their subjects, by integrating the teaching concepts extracted from teaching FM proceedings, and the most popular concepts and tools highlighted in FME course data base. As it is evident from the table, the importance of teaching temporal specification and Temporal Logic to students, seems to be left out of spotlight in FM community. On the Contrary, here at Politecnico di Milano we particularly focus on teach temporal logic in addition to other concepts. Table 2 shows the profile of this course in the last ten years.

Table 2. The profile of FM course tought at Politecnico di Milano over the last ten years.

Title	Formal methods for concurrent and real-time systems
Students level	Second year of Ms.c. in computer engineering and computer science
Average number of students	30
Hours per semester	80
Course type	Not mandatory
Required background	Theoretical computer science and mathematical logic
The syllabus	The basis of FM,
	Bisimulation, abstraction and refinement
	Concurrent, distributed and real-time systems,
	Computation tree logic,
	PetriNets,
	Hoare's logic,
	Timed automata,
	Temporal logic (TRIO),
	Case studies,
Evaluation	Studying and presenting a recently published article with a topic close the material of the course,
	Applying Hoare's logic on an algorithm,
	Modeling a toy example via TRIO and verify a predefined property with a local model-checker

The rest of this paper is structured as follows: Sect. 2 discusses the importance of teaching formal specification and verification to students, Sect. 3 reports our experience at Politecnico di Milano on project-based and lecture-based teaching, and finally Sect. 4 concludes.

2   Teaching Formal Specification: Why and When?

Language

Model based approaches are fundamental for all the academic curricula, not only those belonging to scientific faculties. The act of transferring an abstract representation of facts and their relations demands non trivial capabilities. The problem is even more complex if we consider the case where the language, that supplies all the syntactical structures capturing the facts and their relations, has not been devised yet. This scenario is, of course, far from the reality that professors or lectures face in their everyday academic teaching, which is instead characterized by a different challenge.

Conveying facts and their relations through a predefined (logical) language is the actual challenge that universities try to tackle, and that requires students to learn specific capabilities, and professors and lecturers to develop suitable teaching approaches. The first capability requires the development of specific mental process that allows a subject to encode facts into sentences of the language, by only using a limited number of basic syntactical structures, each providing predefined, and formally stated, semantics. Yielding two different logic formulae that are syntactically different but semantically equivalent is very common when the same reality is analysed by two persons. Transferring an idea into a formula or expressing solutions to problems in an algorithmic manner implicates Computational Thinking, which is envisioning the reality through simpler facts and more basic relationships. Computational thinking dates back to '50, and has been nourishing an interesting debate and research among pedagogues on whether it can be counted as a basic skill that schools should teach with no distinction of study careers and since the beginning of education. The mental path that a subject follows to analyse and decompose the reality is, of course, strongly dependent on the subject's way of thinking. Additionally, the presence of a duality, or a degree of freedom in the language is sometimes a source of problems for students that are learning logics-related subjects. For example, a subject can state the relation between A and B either by using a "future-to-past" direction, or a "past-to-future" one; that is, A will cause B in the future, or B is caused by A occurred in the past.

The presence of a duality, or a degree of freedom in general, in the language is sometimes a source of problems for students that are learning logics-related subjects. This freedom of choice has negative side effects leading to a phenomenon called "Supermarket dilemma". Schwart analysed this phenomenon in [49] by providing the evidence that "Autonomy and Freedom of choice are critical to our well being, and choice is critical to freedom and autonomy". For this reason, a person who stands in front of a supermarket shelf can find the choice of a product difficult, if a decision has not been already taken in her/his mind. The same feeling is experienced by students in learning logic. Despite the formal definition of a logical language, the availability of a number of distinct ways to approach the encoding of the decomposed reality they have in mind, might hamper the construction of the sentence that should be the result of a correct composition of basic syntactical structures.

Abstraction

The correct identification of the facts and relations of the reality that matter, can be attained first by answering the question "What should I say with the formula?" and, then by pulling the essential facts and relations out of the identified answer, by using a possibly iterative process that removes unessential details. Choosing the right facts and relations is another source of problems for the students who come upon the study of logic-related subjects. The lack of capacity for abstraction is the origin and the reason why students perceive the study of logic too difficult.

The causes that might lead to a scarce development of abstraction skills are far from being obvious, though they can be classified into exogenous and endogenous ones. The former are related to the environment that surrounds a subject and where the subject intertwines relationship with other persons, such as the family, friends and the attended schools. It is well known that the environment has a tangible impact on the subjects that live therein. Schools play an important role in this game, because their programs and teaching methodologies can determine the development of abstraction skills in students. The latter ones are strongly dependent on the subject's way of thinking, and can unlikely be studied by only observing the behavior of subjects.

According to Anderson et al. [37], knowledge can be classified into four distinct classes, namely, factual knowledge, conceptual knowledge, procedural knowledge and metacognitive knowledge. Factual knowledge is the first kind of knowledge that students learn at schools, and that schools must provide, and pertains to the basic evidence of a discipline. For this reason, factual knowledge always conveys the terminology and the specific details of a subject, and supplies basic building blocks to understand the higher level relationships among the objects of a given reality. Abstraction capabilities can be nourished through conceptual and procedural knowledge, that focus on the relationship among the pieces of a larger structure and how to solve problems. The pillars characterizing conceptual knowledge are: Knowledge of classifications and categories, Knowledge of principles and generalizations and Knowledge of theories, models, and structures. The lack of abstraction capabilities in students can, therefore, originate from the scarce presence of the conceptual dimension of knowledge, which is not adequately conveyed by suitable teaching program during the school.

Temporal Logic

Students often do not comprehend the meaning of the syntactical structures of the language because they do not grasp the overall context in which the language is defined. Missing the general picture is the main reason of a weak comprehension of the basic evidence conveyed through the factual knowledge.

Logical languages were conceived by humans to capture very diverse aspects of the reality. Modal logic is an example, and is one of the main families of languages that are taught during academic careers at M.Sc. of Computer Science. It includes several distinct languages that can be used to specify the "mode" (or "modality") that qualifies the validity of the sentences. Modalities can be intuitively explained by analogize them to adverbs, as they change the truth value of a sentence as adverbs refine the verbs in natural languages. For instance, the sentence "it will rain tomorrow" does not express how the rain will be and how likely the rain will occur. By using a "modality", or an adverb in this case, the information that the sentence conveys can be refined; for instance, "it will surely rain tomorrow" communicates a more precise information about the rain.

The reception of logic by Computer Science is rather recent, despite Computer Science is tightly connected with Mathematics. Amir Pnueli pioneered the use of a specific class of Modal logic, called Temporal logic, in Computer Science. Temporal logic allows for representing, and reasoning about, facts qualified in terms of time. For this reason, the language is equipped with two modalities that characterize the occurrence of a fact, that are the "eventually" and "always" modalities. The semantics of the language is based on the intuitive order of time, that allows humans to distinguish the notions of "before" and "after", that is, in particular, if an event, or a fact, holds true before or after a different one. Temporal logic includes, in turn, several families, but in its original definition, it allows one to state, for instance, that if something happens now, then in the forthcoming future something else will occur.

Temporal logic in Computer Science is adopted to express the desired properties of systems or to specify entirely their behavior over the time. Writing formulae that specify how a system behaves is fundamental to precisely capture the functionality that the system should exhibit, but also to verify if the designed system can actually behave as intended. For this reason, temporal logic became rapidly one of the baseline tools to perform requirement specification and analysis, during the Requirement Engineering phase of a project, and to verify certain properties of the model of a system through Formal Verification.

The notion of time in Temporal logic has been refined over the years, moving from a simple order to trees of realizable futures, or to dense time. According to Furia et al. [22] there are many issues that temporal specification faces once a system is subject to be modeled. It is important to clarify if a system is more compatible with continuous or non-continuous time models. For example, manifesting the behaviors of a model with certain characteristics is presumably simpler considering continuous time domain. It is also important to figure out if a system may function in a finite, infinite or periodic time window.

Moreover, to choose a suitable formalism for modeling purposes, one need to realise if temporal characteristics of the system concern only order of events (e.g., event A happens before event B) or also metric constraints are important (e.g., event B must happen exactly three time units before event A). One needs to choose between linear (i.e., sequences of states of the model) and branching time (i.e., trees of states of the model) pattern to better describe the system behavior. The granularity (e.g., seconds, minutes, days) and scaling with which the temporal constraints of the system are described, is also another point to be careful about. The nature of the system, in terms of determinism, non-determinism, and probabilistic, is also very crucial in picking the right modeling means and tools.

Considering all the mentioned issues, we advocate the teaching of logic and logical thinking in schools and more emphasis on temporal logic in M.Sc. of Engineering curricula, as it is of utmost importance to the future computer scientists and engineers. We argue that the fundamentals of formal methods need to start being thought at the initial years of university. This is in fact how universities around the world approach to building the logic and discrete mathematical background of students. However, more specific material such as formal modeling of systems, model checking, and formal verification are concepts to be thought during Masters, when students have already passed programming courses and developed an understanding of requirements specification (e.g., by using Alloy, UML diagrams).

3   Experience Report at Politecnico di Milano

In this section, we report our experience of teaching a FM course at our university. The course, as shown in Table 2, has been going on for more than ten years and follows a standard structure. The first part of this section explains our project-based teaching method of temporal logic, and the second part reports our observations from teaching Hoare's Logic.

Project-Based Teaching of Temporal Logic

A part of the evaluation is usually done by a modeling project. In other words, students are required to write a specification of a (complex) system by using temporal logic formulae. This task is demanding but essential to make students aware of the potential of logic and to show how logic goes beyond the abstract examples that are commonly adopted for teaching it. Using logic to specify and verify properties of realistic scenarios is therefore fundamental to motivate Computer Engineering students, as the exercise links abstract notions with tangible and realistic applications that they might encounter in their professional life.

We provide students with description of a safety-critical system. Using the last years's project[5] as an illustrative example, the students were supposed to formalize a scenario in which a human and a robot collaborate in an industrial setting; robot moves workpieces around in a the workcell to suitable places (position p1 and p2) for human to manipulate (at p1) and inspect (at p2) them. Students had to model the dynamics between human and robot and temporal back and forth between the two in a realistic and correct manner. Once they do that, they need to come up with a simple safety property such as "human and robot should never be closer that a certain distance, while robot is moving" and verify if the model they defined satisfy this property or not.

---

[5] polimi/fm2019.

The formula below is an example of what students wrote as safety property. It states that always[6] no same position for human and robot exists when the robot is moving.

$$\mathsf{Alw}(\neg\exists x \in Positions : RobotPosition == x \wedge$$
$$HumanPosition == x \wedge RobotMoving) \tag{1}$$

where $RobotPosition$ and $HumanPosition$ are variables with a limited domain expressing the position of the elements, and $RobotMoving$ is a predicate indicating robot is changing its position.

$$RobotMoving \Leftrightarrow \exists x,y \in Positions :$$
$$(x \neq y \wedge RobotPosition == x \wedge \mathsf{Past}\,(RobotPosition == y, 1)) \tag{2}$$

Students were supposed to use TRIO [22], a metric temporal logic, to build their model, and Zot [59], a bounded satisfiability checker implemented and maintained at Politecnico di Milano, to verify their specified property. Following the "push button tools" indication earlier, the Zot tool is easily accessible through a Docker image and easy to use and readable instruction guides.

Our main observations during supervising the students for their projects follows below.

– It is only by doing the project that students perceive the concept of exhaustiveness of model checking which is its main difference with simulation. They learn how important it is to define constraints that make the model outputs realistic, but at the same time, do not limit the model to propagate only certain outputs (e.g., those that are most probably predictable by students while they imagine the model outputs) and avoid biased results.
– The concept of guaranteeing a property was also better conveyed to students by doing the project. For example, a common mistake by many students was to verify property P by model M with checking formula $M \wedge P$. They are happy when the tool satisfies the formula and pops out a trace of M in which P holds. This again shows the lack of proper understanding of model checking as a concept.
– Again on property verification, it is hard for students to grasp its motivation on a simple toy example; usually they ask "but why not to add the property directly in the model instead of verifying if the model satisfies it or not"? Working on the project allows students to clearly distinguish the model of the system from the specification that renders a specific requirement stated during requirement analysis, and that should be verified.
– Students usually better comprehend automata-based models, such as Timed Automata [5], rather than plain logic formulae, and prefer to practice on graphical modeling tools instead of writing formulae with a text editor. This is not a problem per se, as we could use off-the-shelf tools such as UPPAAL.

---

[6] A TRIO operator formalized as $\mathsf{Alw}\,(\phi) \Leftrightarrow \forall t(\mathsf{Dist}\,(\phi, t))$ which means ϕ occurs d time units in the future, where $\mathsf{Dist}\,(\phi, d)$ holds at time t if, and only if, ϕ holds at time $t + d$.

Lecture-Based Teaching of Hoare's Logic

Another part of the evaluation of the students is the application of Hoare's logic to a sample algorithm. We teach the use of Hoare's logic by applying it on a simple loop-less algorithm, given proper pre and postconditions. The students should learn how to come up with (i) a suitable invariant to prove the partial correctness of the algorithm, and (ii) a variant to prove the termination of the algorithm. After explaining the basics of Hoare, we move on to explain how we can unroll the loops and analyse all the iterations with deductive reasoning. We then see the same thing for conditional clauses. Students then are asked to do the same thing on a new algorithm.

For example, consider the bubble sort algorithm below. Its pre-condition is that array a had no repetition $(D(a))$, and its postcondition is that array a is sorted $(ORD(a))$, has no repetition and has all, and only the elements that it had before the execution of the algorithm. The latter is formalized by $P(a, b)$ that holds if there is an array b which had all and only the elements of a. The

---

Algorithm 1. The bubble sort algorithm used as an example to teach correctness proof.

```
 1: {n ≥ 0 ∧ P(a,b) ∧ D(a) = pre}
 2: i := n-1;
 3: while i > 0 do
 4:     j := 0;
 5:     while j < i do
 6:         if a[j] > a[j + 1] then
 7:             temp := a[j + 1]; a[j + 1] := a[j]; a[j] := temp;
 8:         end if
 9:         j + +;
10:     end while
11:     i − −;
12: end while
13: {P(a,b) ∧ D(a) ∧ ORD(a) = post}
```
---

steps of correctness proof is the following:

There are two while loops in the algorithm, thus students need to come up with two invariants, that are Inv_1 for the outer while and Inv_2 for the inner loop. Here we do not go trough the whole proof which is available in Mandrioli et al. [39] and discuss the parts student find more challenging which are defining Inv_1 and Inv_2, and analysing the effect of $temp := a[j + 1]; a[j + 1] := a[j]; a[j] := temp$; at step three which requires to be unrolled properly. We suggest students to ask themselves two questions in order to discover the proper invariant: (i) what keeps the loop going on? and (ii) what does each iteration do? The answers to these two questions for the outer loop are (i) while goes on for $0 < i < n$, (ii) it decreases i at each iteration so at final iteration $i = 0$ and rearranges the array at each iteration so that every element after position i is larger than every

---

Algorithm 2. The steps of correctness proof for algorithm 1.

1:          $\{pre\}\ i := n - 1; \{Inv_1\}$
2:          $\{Inv_1 \wedge i > 0\}\ j := 0; \{Inv_2\}$
3:          $\{Inv_2 \wedge j < i \wedge a[j] > a[j+1]\}\ temp := a[j+1]; a[j+1] := a[j]; a[j] := temp; j++; \{Inv_2\}$
4:          $\{Inv_2 \wedge j < i \wedge a[j] \leq a[j+1]\}\ j++; \{Inv_2\}$
5:          $\{Inv_2 \wedge j \geq i\}\ i--; \{Inv_1\}$
6:          $\{Inv_1 \wedge i \leq 0\} \Rightarrow \{post\}$

---

element before it. We also make students note that the precondition constraints still hold at line 3. Hence, Inv_1 would be:

$$Inv_1 = \begin{bmatrix} (0 < i < n \vee i == 0) \wedge \\ \forall z(i < z < n \Rightarrow \forall m(0 \leq m \leq i \Rightarrow a[m] < a[z])) \wedge \\ P(a,b) \wedge D(a) \wedge ORD(a,i) \end{bmatrix} \qquad (3)$$

The first line cold be rewritten as $(0 \leq i < n)$.

For the outer loop the answers are (i) the loops goes on for $0 \leq j < i$ while Inv_1 holds, (ii) it increases j at each iteration so at final iteration $j = i$ and it places the largest element between position 0 and j at position j.

$$Inv_2 = \begin{bmatrix} Inv_1 \wedge (0 \leq j \leq i) \wedge \\ \forall z(0 \leq z < j \Rightarrow a[j] > a[z]) \end{bmatrix} \qquad (4)$$

After defining Inv_1 and Inv_2, we guide the students through the deduction they need to make step by step starting from precondition down to postconditions, as described in Algorithm 2. The most challenging step of Algorithm 2 for students is step three, where they have to analyse the manipulation of an array. We try to make it easy to understand as along the following lines. Starting from the constraint on line three of Algorithm 2 and having Inv_2 figured out, we need to replace j in Inv_2 with $j + 1$ (assuming that backwards replacement has been already explained to students with easier examples). Then, we need to study how to apply backwards replacement with $a[j] := temp$. We ask the students to imagine a new and old version for the array a, which correspond to before and after execution of $a[j] := temp$. This would lead to the conclusion that a_{new} is the same as a_{old} except at position j where $a_{new}[j] = temp$. Next, we analyse $a[j+1] := a[j]$. Here again a_{new} is the same as a_{old}, except for positions j and $j+1$ where $a_{new}[j] = temp$ and $a_{new}[j+1] = a_{old}[j]$. Finally, $temp := a[j+1]$ ends to a_{new} be the same as a_{old} except for $a_{new}[j] = a_{old}[j+1]$ and $a_{new}[j+1] = a_{old}[j]$. This in other words mean that the analysed three commands swaps element j with $j+1$ and the rest of a has remained the same.

Our main observations on teaching Hoare follows:

– It is usually very difficult for students to guess an invariant. They usually move along the proof with a wrong invariant and surprisingly get to the end

(of course by mistake). It shows that student still have issues recognizing the edge cases in an algorithm.
- It is particularly difficult for students to deal with algorithms that work with arrays.
- Backwards replacement and deductions from constraints is not always easy for students, and even in best cases one could find errors in their proofs which goes back to their logic background, and imprecision.

4 Conclusions

In this paper we surveyed the current status of teaching formal methods at university and discovered a lack of effort in encouraging students to learn temporal modeling and specification. We analyzed several factors that might hamper an effective learning of logic and advocated the need for more effort in teaching logical thinking from the early stage of students careers. We argued that students lack a correct prospect on the practice of formal specification and verification which could be treated by project-based teaching. We then presented a report on our experience at Politecnico di Milano on teaching temporal and Hoare's logic. We used a project-based teaching method for the first one and a lecture-based for the other. In order to make a comparison between the two methods we asked student's feedback through a questionnaire. From 30 students attending the latest round of the course, of which only about 33% claimed to have some knowledge about FM, approximately 45% reported that the course made them more interested in the topic, only 11% consider to do their master thesis in this area, and 45% evaluated the project as the most interesting and useful part of the course. We received several comments from the students stating that the project helped them to practice temporal logic that otherwise would seem too theoretical and impractical. Additionally, we draw the following few observations:

- Teaching model checking is more productive by practicing it with a realistic system and off-the-shelf tools; Project-based teaching helps students practicing concepts such as exhaustiveness, property verification, and providing guarantee that a certain situation would never happen.
- The tool we provide the students with is well documented and has many available examples. However, not all off-the-shelf tools, which could potentially be very good alternatives to Zot, are well documented and easy for students. We have to consider that students have a limited time for the project and the effort for using the tool and modeling the scenario should be proportional to the credits of the course. Therefore, our options for the tool(s) we suggest to students are limited.
- Logic formulae scares students. It is helpful to use automata notions as the first step of approaching formalization of systems.
- In order to teach either of theorem proving or model-checking, students need a strong initial motivating introduction that demonstrates the practical use of these techniques.

– The questionnaire asked students to pick their favourite part of the course. As we said earlier 45% voted to the project, the other 33% picked the theoretical part of the course on temporal logic (which was necessary for the project as well), and 22% found the student presentations more interesting. That leaves 0% in favor of Hoare's logic! We think that the unpopularity of the Hoare's logic among students is due to the lack of case studies to justify its usefulness in the industry, and little possibility of assigning students with a feasible and meaningful project about it.

Acknowledgements. The credit of the statistics reported on our course goes to its official responsibles, previously prof. emeritus Dino Mandrioli and currently prof. Pierluigi San Pietro.

References

1. Abrial, J.R.: Teaching formal methods: an experience with event-B (invited speaker's extended abstract). In: Formal Methods in Computer Science Education, p. 1 (2008)
2. Aceto, L., Ingólfsdóttir, A., Larsen, K.G., Srba, J.: Teaching concurrency: theory in practice. In: Proceedings of the Inernational Conference on TFM, pp. 158–175 (2009)
3. Ahrendt, W., Bubel, R., Hähnle, R.: Integrated and tool-supported teaching of testing, debugging, and verification. In: Proceedings of the International Conference on TFM, pp. 125–143 (2009)
4. Almeida, A.A., Rocha-Oliveira, A.C., Ramos, T.M.F., de Moura, F.L.C., Ayala-Rincón, M.: The computational relevance of formal logic through formal proofs. In: Dongol, B., Petre, L., Smith, G. (eds.) FMTea 2019. LNCS, vol. 11758, pp. 81–96. Springer, Cham (2019). https://doi.org/10.1007/978-3-030-32441-4_6
5. Alur, R., Dill, D.L.: A theory of timed automata. Theoret. Comput. Sci. **126**(2), 183–235 (1994)
6. Artho, C., Taguchi, K., Tahara, Y., Honiden, S., Tanabe, Y.: Teaching software model checking. In: Workshop on Formal Methods in Computer Science Education, pp. 171–179 (2008)
7. Back, R.J., Mannila, L., Peltomaki, M., Sibelius, P.: Structured derivations: a logic based approach to teaching mathematics. In: FORMED 2008: Formal Methods in Computer Science Education (2008)
8. Back, R.J., Von Wright, J., et al.: Structured derivations: a method for doing high-school mathematics carefully. In: Turku Centre for Computer Science (1999)
9. Bohórquez, J., Rocha, C.: Assisted calculational proofs and proof checking based on partial orders. In: Formal Methods in Computer Science Education, p. 37 (2008)
10. Börger, E.: A practice-oriented course on the principles of computation, programming, and system design and analysis. In: Dean, C.N., Boute, R.T. (eds.) TFM 2004. LNCS, vol. 3294, pp. 65–84. Springer, Heidelberg (2004). https://doi.org/10.1007/978-3-540-30472-2_5
11. Boute, R.: Teaching and practicing computer science at the university level. ACM SIGCSE Bull. **41**(2), 24–30 (2009)
12. Boyatt, R., Sinclair, J.: Experiences of teaching a lightweight formal method. In: Proceedings of Formal Methods in Computer Science Education (2008)

13. Carro, M., Mariño, J., Herranz, Á., Moreno-Navarro, J.J.: Teaching how to derive correct concurrent programs from state-based specifications and code patterns. In: Dean, C.N., Boute, R.T. (eds.) TFM 2004. LNCS, vol. 3294, pp. 85–106. Springer, Heidelberg (2004). https://doi.org/10.1007/978-3-540-30472-2_6

14. Cataño, N.: Teaching formal methods: Lessons learnt from using event-B. In: Dongol, B., Petre, L., Smith, G. (eds.) FMTea 2019. LNCS, vol. 11758, pp. 212–227. Springer, Cham (2019). https://doi.org/10.1007/978-3-030-32441-4_14

15. Dadeau, F., Tissot, R.: Teaching model-based testing with Leirios test generator (2008)

16. Davies, J., Simpson, A., Martin, A.: Teaching formal methods in context. In: Dean, C.N., Boute, R.T. (eds.) TFM 2004. LNCS, vol. 3294, pp. 185–202. Springer, Heidelberg (2004). https://doi.org/10.1007/978-3-540-30472-2_12

17. Duke, R., Miller, T., Strooper, P.: Integrating formal specification and software verification and validation. In: Dean, C.N., Boute, R.T. (eds.) TFM 2004. LNCS, vol. 3294, pp. 124–139. Springer, Heidelberg (2004). https://doi.org/10.1007/978-3-540-30472-2_8

18. FBK-IRST, group at Carnegie Mellon University, T.M.C., the Mechanized Reasoning Group at University of Genova, at University of Trento, T.M.R.G.: NuSMV (2015). http://nusmv.fbk.eu/

19. Fernández-Iglesias, M.J., Llamas-Nistal, M.: An undergraduate course on protocol engineering – how to teach formal methods without scaring students. In: Dean, C.N., Boute, R.T. (eds.) TFM 2004. LNCS, vol. 3294, pp. 153–165. Springer, Heidelberg (2004). https://doi.org/10.1007/978-3-540-30472-2_10

20. Ferreira, J.F., Mendes, A., Backhouse, R., Barbosa, L.S.: Which mathematics for the information society? In: Gibbons, J., Oliveira, J.N. (eds.) TFM 2009. LNCS, vol. 5846, pp. 39–56. Springer, Heidelberg (2009). https://doi.org/10.1007/978-3-642-04912-5_4

21. Filippidis, I.: A catalog of tools for verification and synthesis. github.com/fm-tools

22. Furia, C.A., Mandrioli, D., Morzenti, A., Rossi, M.: Modeling time in computing: a taxonomy and a comparative survey. ACM Comput. Surv. **42**(2), 6:1–6:59 (2010)

23. Garavel, H., Jorgensen, M.: A catalog of tools for the quantitative zoo. http://cadp.inria.fr/faq.html

24. Gibson, J.P., Lallet, E., Raffy, J.L.: How do i know if my design is correct. In: Formal Methods in Computer Science Education, pp. 61–70 (2008)

25. Gibson, P., Méry, D.: Teaching formal methods: lessons to learn. In: 2nd Irish Workshop on Formal Methods, vol. 2, pp. 1–13 (1998)

26. Guyomard, M.: Eb: A constructive approach for the teaching of data structures. In: Formal Methods in Computer Science Education, p. 25 (2008)

27. Habrias, H.: Teaching specifications, hands on. In: Formal Methods in Computer Science Education, pp. 5–15 (2008)

28. Habrias, H., Faucou, S.: Linking paradigms, semi-formal and formal notations. In: Dean, C.N., Boute, R.T. (eds.) TFM 2004. LNCS, vol. 3294, pp. 166–184. Springer, Heidelberg (2004). https://doi.org/10.1007/978-3-540-30472-2_11

29. Hähnle, R., Bubel, R.: A Hoare-style calculus with explicit state updates. In: Formal Methods in Computer Science Education, pp. 49–60 (2008)

30. Hallerstede, S., Leuschel, M.: How to explain mistakes. In: Gibbons, J., Oliveira, J.N. (eds.) TFM 2009. LNCS, vol. 5846, pp. 105–124. Springer, Heidelberg (2009). https://doi.org/10.1007/978-3-642-04912-5_8

31. Hartel, P.H., van Es, B., Tromp, D.: Basic proof skills of computer science students. In: Hartel, P.H., Plasmeijer, R. (eds.) FPLE 1995. LNCS, vol. 1022, pp. 269–283. Springer, Heidelberg (1995). https://doi.org/10.1007/3-540-60675-0_50

32. Jard, C.: Teaching distributed algorithms using spin. In: Formal Methods in Computer Science Education, p. 101 (2008)
33. Kofroň, J., Parízek, P., Šerý, O.: On teaching formal methods: behavior models and code analysis. In: Gibbons, J., Oliveira, J.N. (eds.) TFM 2009. LNCS, vol. 5846, pp. 144–157. Springer, Heidelberg (2009). https://doi.org/10.1007/978-3-642-04912-5_10
34. Kramer, J.: Abstraction and modelling: A complementary partnership. In: Gibbons, J., Oliveira, J.N. (eds.) TFM 2009. LNCS, vol. 5846, pp. 1–1. Springer, Heidelberg (2009). https://doi.org/10.1007/978-3-642-04912-5_1
35. Lau, K.: A beginner's course on reasoning about imperative programs. In: Proceedings of CoLogNET/FME Symposium on TFM, pp. 1–16 (2004)
36. Lau, K.-K.: A beginner's course on reasoning about imperative programs. In: Dean, C.N., Boute, R.T. (eds.) TFM 2004. LNCS, vol. 3294, pp. 1–16. Springer, Heidelberg (2004). https://doi.org/10.1007/978-3-540-30472-2_1
37. Anderson, L.W., Krathwohl, D.R., Bloom, B.S.: A taxonomy for learning, teaching, and assessing: A revision of Bloom's taxonomy of educational objectives (2001)
38. Mandrioli, D.: Advertising formal methods and organizing their teaching: *Yes, but*. In: Dean, C.N., Boute, R.T. (eds.) TFM 2004. LNCS, vol. 3294, pp. 214–224. Springer, Heidelberg (2004). https://doi.org/10.1007/978-3-540-30472-2_14
39. Mandrioli, D., Ghezzi, C.: Theoretical Foundations of Computer Science. John Wiley & Sons, New York (1987)
40. Naumowicz, A.: Teaching how to write a proof. In: Formal Methods in Computer Science Education, p. 91 (2008)
41. Noble, J., Pearce, D.J., Groves, L.: Introducing alloy in a software modelling course. In: Formal Methods in Computer Science Education, p. 81 (2008)
42. Ölveczky, P.C.: Teaching formal methods based on rewriting logic and maude. In: Gibbons, J., Oliveira, J.N. (eds.) TFM 2009. LNCS, vol. 5846, pp. 20–38. Springer, Heidelberg (2009). https://doi.org/10.1007/978-3-642-04912-5_3
43. Paige, R.F., Ostroff, J.S.: Specification-driven design with eiffel and agents for teaching lightweight formal methods. In: Dean, C.N., Boute, R.T. (eds.) TFM 2004. LNCS, vol. 3294, pp. 107–123. Springer, Heidelberg (2004). https://doi.org/10.1007/978-3-540-30472-2_7
44. Poll, E.: Teaching program specification and verification using JML and ESC/Java2. In: Gibbons, J., Oliveira, J.N. (eds.) TFM 2009. LNCS, vol. 5846, pp. 92–104. Springer, Heidelberg (2009). https://doi.org/10.1007/978-3-642-04912-5_7
45. Reed, J.N., Sinclair, J.E.: Motivating study of formal methods in the classroom. In: Dean, C.N., Boute, R.T. (eds.) TFM 2004. LNCS, vol. 3294, pp. 32–46. Springer, Heidelberg (2004). https://doi.org/10.1007/978-3-540-30472-2_3
46. Robinson, K.: Embedding formal development in software engineering. In: Dean, C.N., Boute, R.T. (eds.) TFM 2004. LNCS, vol. 3294, pp. 203–213. Springer, Heidelberg (2004). https://doi.org/10.1007/978-3-540-30472-2_13
47. Robinson, K.: Reflecting on the future: Objectives, strategies and experiences. In: Formal Methods in Computer Science Education, p. 15 (2008)
48. da Rosa, S.: Designing algorithms in high school mathematics. In: Dean, C.N., Boute, R.T. (eds.) TFM 2004. LNCS, vol. 3294, pp. 17–31. Springer, Heidelberg (2004). https://doi.org/10.1007/978-3-540-30472-2_2
49. Schwartz, B.: The Paradox of Choice (2004)
50. Simonot, M., Homps, M., Bonnot, P.: Teaching abstraction in mathematics and computer science (2012)

51. Simonot, M., Homps, M., Bonnot, P.: Teaching abstraction in mathematics and computer science - A computer-supported approach with alloy. In: Proceedings of the 4th International Conference on Computer Supported Education, vol. 2, pp. 239–245 (2012)
52. Spichkova, M.: "Boring formal methods" or "Sherlock Holmes deduction methods"? In: Milazzo, P., Varró, D., Wimmer, M. (eds.) STAF 2016. LNCS, vol. 9946, pp. 242–252. Springer, Cham (2016). https://doi.org/10.1007/978-3-319-50230-4_18
53. Spichkova, M., Zamansky, A.: Teaching of formal methods for software engineering. In: ENASE, pp. 370–376 (2016)
54. Sznuk, T., Schubert, A.: Tool support for teaching Hoare logic. In: Giannakopoulou, D., Salaün, G. (eds.) SEFM 2014. LNCS, vol. 8702, pp. 332–346. Springer, Cham (2014). https://doi.org/10.1007/978-3-319-10431-7_27
55. Tarkan, S., Sazawal, V.: Chief chefs of Z to alloy: using a kitchen example to teach alloy with Z. In: Gibbons, J., Oliveira, J.N. (eds.) TFM 2009. LNCS, vol. 5846, pp. 72–91. Springer, Heidelberg (2009). https://doi.org/10.1007/978-3-642-04912-5_6
56. University of Torino: GreatSPN: Graphical editor and analyzer for timed and stochastic petri nets (2001). http://www.di.unito.it/greatspn/index.html
57. Department of Information Technology at Uppsala University, Sweden, the Department of Computer Science at Aalborg University in Denmark: Uppaal (2008). http://www.uppaal.org/
58. Woodcock, J., Larsen, P.G., Bicarregui, J., Fitzgerald, J.: Formal methods: Practice and experience. ACM Comput. Surv. **41**(4) (2009)
59. Zot: A bounded satisfiability checker (2012). github.com/fm-polimi/zot

A Review of the Structure of a Course on Advanced Statistics for Data Scientists

Mohammad Reza Bahrami[(✉)] [iD], Sergey Masyagin[iD], and Giancarlo Succi[iD]

Innopolis University, Innopolis 420500, Russia
mo.bahrami@innopolis.ru

Abstract. This paper presents a review of an innovative course on "Advanced Statistics" for a master program in data science. The prerequisites for this course include fundamental knowledge in Mathematics, Computer Science, and Economics. The expected learning outcome is centered on the ability to model empirical investigations in terms of hypotheses to prove via suitable statistical tests. The paper contains general goals, description of the content, description of the structure of each week, description of the evaluations, and overall outcomes from students of the course.

Keywords: Advanced statistics · Inferential statistics · Data science · Course structure

1 Introduction

Data Science, consists of techniques and theories extracted from statistics, computer science, and machine learning, is a constantly developing field. In this paper we present the innovative approach taken in teaching a course on "Advanced Statistics" to first year master students in data science. The core subject of the course is the quantitative relations of qualitatively defined socio-economic phenomena, and the laws of their relationship [1,15,34,49,50], together with a large set of connections to software engineering [10,11,14,26–30,35,36,41,43–45].

The purpose of studying this course is to form theoretical knowledge and practical skills in the field of modern statistics, as well as the formation of general cultural and professional competencies necessary for the implementation of professional tasks [5,17,23].

To this end we have focused mostly in supplying the students with a fundamental theoretical and practical knowledge in the basics of statistics, focusing on the clear understanding of the underlying phenomena and mathematical structures.

This approach is different from many proposed on the field and looking at the syllabus the striking difference is the amount of material that is being presented, much less than the usual. However, the depth of such material is well above what is commonly taught and we are convinced that a small but very fundamental and

© Springer Nature Switzerland AG 2020
J.-M. Bruel et al. (Eds.): FISEE 2019, LNCS 12271, pp. 19–27, 2020.
https://doi.org/10.1007/978-3-030-57663-9_2

deep content equips the students with all the relevant competence in Advanced Statistics that is then used inside Data Science [2,4,6,46].

This paper is organized as follows. The course starts from basic information about the subject, methods and tasks of statistics, statistical observation, grouping and summarizing statistical observations, absolute and relative values, average values and indicators of variation, sample observation, statistical study of the relationship between phenomena, statistical study of the dynamics of socio-economic phenomena, indices [7,18] (Sect. 2). Then it follows by covering commonly used statistical inference methods for numerical and categorical data. It covers the procedure of setting up and conducting hypothesis tests, inference p-values, and the results of analysis [3,19]. The syllabus of the course is developed in accordance with the requirement of higher professional education in the training of data scientists.

2   General Goals

The main purpose of this course is to present the fundamentals of inferential statistics to the future software engineers and data scientists, on one side providing the scientific fundamentals of the disciplines, and on the other anchoring the theoretical concepts on practices coming from the world of software development and engineering. The course covers the statistical analysis of data with limited assumptions on the distribution, with reference to testing hypotheses, measuring correlations, building samples, and performing regressions. In general the key concepts of the course are statistical inference, non parametric statistics, test of statistical hypotheses, and simple linear regression and correlation analysis. The course also draws its fundamental data often from software metrics, the subject of a preliminary course on this matter [9,12,13,21,24,25,38–40,48], and also referring to techniques of machine learning and computational intelligence [31,32].

2.1   Course Objectives Based on Bloom's Taxonomy

The students learning objectives are set using Bloom's Taxonomy. Bloom's Taxonomy is a powerful tool, which explains framework for categorizing educational goals: Taxonomy of Educational Objectives, consists of six major categories. This work explains the learning process including the following categories: remember, understand, and apply.

We expect that by the end of the course, the students should be able to *remember* the fundamentals of inferential statistics, the specifics and purpose of different hypothesis tests, and distinguish between parametric and non parametric tests.

By the end of the course, the students should be able to *understand* the basic concepts of inferential statistics, the fundamental laws in statistics, the concept of null and alternative hypotheses, and the hypotheses test procedure.

Finally we expect that the students should be able to *apply* statistically analysis of the problems related to data that are not distributed normally, to apply the more recent computationally-intensive techniques that can help to describe samples and to infer properties of populations in absence of normality, to identify situations when the data is on nominal scales so alternative techniques should be use, and act accordingly, and to run experiment to evaluate hypotheses for situation of scarce data, distributed non normally, on different kinds of scales.

2.2   Course Evaluation

We carry out the course evaluation in the forms of weekly quizzes (in lectures and labs), participation, midterm and final exam. The final rating is determined by the system of point-rating assessment of the work as shown in Table 1. We try to maintain an "agile" approach in our evaluations to ensure that early feedback and flexible assignments support the different learning modes of the different students [20].

Table 1. Course evaluation.

Type	Proposed points	Grade	Interpretation	Proposed range
Weekly quizzes	10	A	Excellent	95–100
Midterm	20	B	Good	75–94
Final oral exam	35	C	Satisfactory	55–74
Final written exam	30	D	Poor	0–54
Participation	5			

3   Structure of the Course

The course has three main sections (Table 2):

- Sampling Distributions Associated with the Normal Population
- Test of Statistical Hypotheses
- Simple Linear Regression and Correlation Analysis

Section 1: Sampling Distributions Associated with the Normal Population. This section starts with an introduction to inferential statistics. The process of obtaining conclusions about a certain population based on randomly extracted samples from it (in essence, in parts or subsets of it) is called Statistical inference.

Then it follows by the introduction of a few unique distributions of discrete and continuous probability with the representation of a pattern. Given the shape of a function, the probability density of a few distribution properties is also discussed.

Table 2. Course sections and subsections.

Section	Section and subsection titles	Teaching hours
1	Sampling Distributions Associated with the Normal Population	12
	Introduction to the course, toward inference	
	Student's t-distribution	
	Bernoulli and binomial distribution	
	Chi-square distribution	
	Snedecor's F-distribution	
2	Test of Statistical Hypotheses	24
	Z-test	
	Student's t-test	
	Chi-square test	
	Snedecor's F-test	
3	Simple Linear Regression and Correlation Analysis	12
	Kolmogorov-Smirnov test	
	Size of samples, Kolmogorov-Smirnov, Fisher exact	
	Logistic regression	

Section 2: Test of Statistical Hypotheses. Statistical inference theory can be used to assess the likelihood that private samples belong to a known population. The process of statistical inference begins with the formulating of the null hypothesis (H_0), consisting in the assumption that sample statistics are obtained from a certain set. The null hypothesis is maintained or rejected depending on how likely the result is. If the observed differences are large relative to the magnitude of the variability of the sample data, the researcher usually rejects the null hypothesis and concludes that the alternative hypothesis holds which means there are extremely small chances that the observed differences are due to the case: the result is statistically significant.

There exist several methods of testing hypotheses that some of them in this section are covered.

Section 3: Simple Linear Regression and Correlation Analysis. In the previous chapter, we were introduced to a statistical community consisting of one or more variable values. Sometimes the analyst is interested in studying two or more statistical traits at a time. If the two variables are examined, the correlation between them, regression and the testing of the hypotheses on the regression line parameters are discussed in this section.

Starting point of point and interval estimation or statistic tests is drawing a random sample $X_1, X_2, ..., X_n$ of size n from a known distribution. Here, to apply the theory to data analysis, one has to know the sample distribution. Usually, the analyst based on the experience and nature of subject supposes the distribution of the sample. To validate analyst's assumption (from where the sample is drawn), goodness of fit tests are conducted. Two common goodness of fit tests that frequently used are the Kolmogorov-Smirnov (KS) test and the Pearson chi-square (χ^2) test.

The last part of this section covers "Logistic regression". The main idea of logistic regression is to analyse the correlation between multiple independent variables and a categorical dependent variable, and predicts the occurrence probability of an event by fitting data to a logistic curve.

4   Description of the Structure of Each Week

Methodical instructions for students to master the discipline in preparation for classroom classes, directly during lectures, seminars, and practical classes, and in the course of individual work, students can use educational literature (according to the approved list of basic and additional literature on this discipline).

In the process of mastering the discipline "Advanced Statistics", classical forms and methods of teaching are used, primarily lectures, practical and seminar classes.

When conducting lectures, students should learn the topic and purpose of the lesson, the main theoretical provisions on the topic of the lesson, definitions of basic concepts and calculation formulas, examples given by the teacher. It should be mentioned that the lectures start with a weekly test from the topic of previous lecture.

During practical classes (labs), students are expected to learn the topic and purpose of the lesson, answer questions submitted to the lab (practical class), actively participate in the work on issues and problems, formulated by the instructor, to conduct analysis and generalization of the studied practical material (in written form and/or in open discussion). Each lab terminated by a weekly quiz from the topic of that day.

Individual work of students in the discipline "Advanced Statistics" contributes to deeper assimilation of the studied discipline, develops research skills and focuses the student on the ability to apply the theoretical knowledge in practice.

Types of independent extracurricular work of students in the discipline "Advanced Statistics" are including performing individual home tests and homework.

The results of independent works are checked by the instructors considering the deadline.

It should be mentioned that the discipline "Advanced statistics" is taught using as reference programming language Python, and, for those students not comfortable with Python, Excel.

It should be mentioned that students use Excel when require the understanding of statistical concepts and behaviour of the data, but when the data set is huge or some specialized data analysis model such as linear or regression are needed, we go for advanced tools such as Python. We also try to emphasize the role of open source tools and code to acquire, share, and then divulge their competences [8, 16, 22, 33, 37, 42, 47].

5   Assessment

A "traditional" exam and a project are used to assess the knowledge gained by the students. The selection of the form of assessment is up to the student, under the premises that everyone has a different learning approach and different "measurement" techniques can be used with the same final goal, still using the approach most suited for each individual.

The project has the goal of exposing the students to a real life situation where they should apply in a reasoned way the material learnt in class. It should terminate with a report. The report should starts with a good introduction and overview of background material and follows by the description of the problem and the formalization of the problem in terms of statistical hypotheses. Then it continues with the application of suitable statistical techniques to assess the hypotheses, and terminated by final conclusion on such hypotheses.

6   Overall Outcomes from Students

By the end of the course, we expect that students should know skills of processing and analysis of primary statistical data to conduct the information base of statistical tests, skills of statistical tests and inference of its results, the skills of applying the concept of the theory of statistics to solve problems arising in the practical activities (in industries), and the process of conducting, analyzing and applying regression.

7   Conclusions

This article aims to review the innovative course on "Advanced Statistics" for a master's program in data science. Basic knowledge of Mathematics, Computer Science, and Economics are required for this course. The course expected learning outcome focuses on the ability to model empirical research in terms of hypotheses for evidence to prove via suitable statistical tests. In this article, general goals, description of the content, description of structures of the lecture and the practical class for each week, assessment, and overall outcomes from students of the course are described.

Acknowledgments. We thank Innopolis University for generously funding this endeavour.

References

1. Amrhein, V., Trafimow, D., Greenland, S.: Inferential statistics as descriptive statistics: There is no replication crisis if we don't expect replication. Am. Stat. **73**(sup1), 262–270 (2019)
2. Aron, A., Aron, E.N.: Statistics for Psychology. Prentice-Hall, Inc. (1999)
3. Asadoorian, M.O., Kantarelis, D.: Essentials of Inferential Statistics. University Press of America (2005)
4. Bahrami, M.R., Abed, S.A.: Mechanics of robot inspector on electrical transmission lines conductors: performance analysis of dynamic vibration absorber. Vibroeng. Proc. **25**, 60–64 (2019)
5. Bahrami, M.R., Abeygunawardana, A.W.B.: Modeling and simulation of tapping mode atomic force microscope through a bond-graph. In: Evgrafov, A.N. (ed.) Advances in Mechanical Engineering. LNME, pp. 9–15. Springer, Cham (2018). https://doi.org/10.1007/978-3-319-72929-9_2
6. Bahrami, M., Ramezani, A., Osquie, K.G.: Modeling and simulation of non-contact atomic force microscope. In: ASME 2010 10th Biennial Conference on Engineering Systems Design and Analysis, pp. 565–569. American Society of Mechanical Engineers Digital Collection (2010)
7. Bowker, A.H.: Engineering statistics. Technical report (1972)
8. Clark, J., et al.: Selecting components in large cots repositories. J. Syst. Softw. **73**(2), 323–331 (2004)
9. Coman, I.D., Robillard, P.N., Sillitti, A., Succi, G.: Cooperation, collaboration and pair-programming: Field studies on backup behavior. J. Syst. Softw. **91**, 124–134 (2014)
10. Corral, L., Georgiev, A.B., Sillitti, A., Succi, G.: A method for characterizing energy consumption in Android smartphones. In: 2nd International Workshop on Green and Sustainable Software (GREENS 2013), pp. 38–45. IEEE, May 2013
11. Corral, L., Georgiev, A.B., Sillitti, A., Succi, G.: Can execution time describe accurately the energy consumption of mobile apps? An experiment in Android. In: Proceedings of the 3rd International Workshop on Green and Sustainable Software, pp. 31–37. ACM (2014)
12. Corral, L., Sillitti, A., Succi, G.: Software assurance practices for mobile applications. Computing **97**(10), 1001–1022 (2015)
13. Corral, L., Sillitti, A., Succi, G., Garibbo, A., Ramella, P.: Evolution of mobile software development from platform-specific to web-based multiplatform paradigm. In: Proceedings of the 10th SIGPLAN Symposium on New Ideas, New Paradigms, and Reflections on Programming and Software, Onward! 2011, pp. 181–183. ACM, New York, NY, USA (2011)
14. Di Bella, E., Sillitti, A., Succi, G.: A multivariate classification of open source developers. Inf. Sci. **221**, 72–83 (2013)
15. U.S.O. of Educational Research, I.C. for Education Statistics, US of Education Sciences, I.: Digest of education statistics, vol. 44. US Department of Health, Education, and Welfare, Education Division (2008)
16. Fitzgerald, B., Kesan, J.P., Russo, B., Shaikh, M., Succi, G.: Adopting Open Source Software: A Practical Guide. The MIT Press, Cambridge, MA (2011)
17. Garfield, J.: Teaching statistics using small-group cooperative learning. J. Stat. Educ. **1**(1), (1993)
18. Hastie, T., Tibshirani, R., Friedman, J.H.: The Elements of Statistical Learning, 2nd edn. ISBN: 10: 0387848576; ISBN: 13: 978–0387848570 (2008)

19. Hollander, M., Wolfe, D.: Nonparametric Statistical Methods, 2nd edn. John Wiley & Sons, New York (1999)

20. Janes, A., Succi, G.: Conclusion. Lean Software Development in Action, pp. 355–357. Springer, Heidelberg (2014). https://doi.org/10.1007/978-3-642-00503-9_12

21. Kivi, J., Haydon, D., Hayes, J., Schneider, R., Succi, G.: Extreme programming: A university team design experience. In: 2000 Canadian Conference on Electrical and Computer Engineering. Conference Proceedings. Navigating to a New Era (Cat. No.00TH8492), vol. 2, May 2000

22. Kovács, G.L., Drozdik, S., Zuliani, P., Succi, G.: Open source software for the public administration. In: Proceedings of the 6th International Workshop on Computer Science and Information Technologies, October 2004

23. Krieg, R.G., Uyar, B.: Student performance in business and economics statistics: Does exam structure matter? J. Econ. Financ. **25**(2), 229–241 (2001)

24. Marino, G., Succi, G.: Data structures for parallel execution of functional languages. In: Odijk, E., Rem, M., Syre, J.-C. (eds.) PARLE 1989. LNCS, vol. 366, pp. 346–356. Springer, Heidelberg (1989). https://doi.org/10.1007/3-540-51285-3_51

25. Maurer, F., Succi, G., Holz, H., Kötting, B., Goldmann, S., Dellen, B.: Software process support over the internet. In: Proceedings of the 21st International Conference on Software Engineering, ICSE 1999, pp. 642–645, May 1999

26. Moser, R., Pedrycz, W., Succi, G.: A comparative analysis of the efficiency of change metrics and static code attributes for defect prediction. In: Proceedings of the 30th International Conference on Software Engineering, ICSE 2008, pp. 181–190. ACM (2008)

27. Moser, R., Pedrycz, W., Succi, G.: Analysis of the reliability of a subset of change metrics for defect prediction. In: Proceedings of the Second ACM-IEEE International Symposium on Empirical Software Engineering and Measurement, ESEM 2008, pp. 309–311. ACM (2008)

28. Musílek, P., Pedrycz, W., Sun, N., Succi, G.: On the sensitivity of COCOMO II software cost estimation model. In: Proceedings of the 8th International Symposium on Software Metrics. METRICS 2002, pp. 13–20. IEEE Computer Society, June 2002

29. Paulson, J.W., Succi, G., Eberlein, A.: An empirical study of open-source and closed-source software products. IEEE Trans. Softw. Eng. **30**(4), 246–256 (2004)

30. Pedrycz, W., Russo, B., Succi, G.: A model of job satisfaction for collaborative development processes. J. Syst. Softw. **84**(5), 739–752 (2011)

31. Pedrycz, W., Russo, B., Succi, G.: Knowledge transfer in system modeling and its realization through an optimal allocation of information granularity. Appl. Soft Comput. **12**(8), 1985–1995 (2012)

32. Pedrycz, W., Succi, G.: Genetic granular classifiers in modeling software quality. J. Syst. Softw. **76**(3), 277–285 (2005)

33. Petrinja, E., Sillitti, A., Succi, G.: Comparing OpenBRR, QSOS, and OMM assessment models. In: Ågerfalk, P., Boldyreff, C., González-Barahona, J.M., Madey, G.R., Noll, J. (eds.) OSS 2010. IAICT, vol. 319, pp. 224–238. Springer, Heidelberg (2010). https://doi.org/10.1007/978-3-642-13244-5_18

34. Randles, R.H., Wolfe, D.A.: Introduction to the theory of nonparametric statistics, Technical report. John Wiley (1979)

35. Ronchetti, M., Succi, G., Pedrycz, W., Russo, B.: Early estimation of software size in object-oriented environments a case study in a CMM level 3 software firm. Inf. Sci. **176**(5), 475–489 (2006)

36. Rossi, B., Russo, B., Succi, G.: Modelling failures occurrences of open source software with reliability growth. In: Ågerfalk, P., Boldyreff, C., González-Barahona, J.M., Madey, G.R., Noll, J. (eds.) OSS 2010. IAICT, vol. 319, pp. 268–280. Springer, Heidelberg (2010). https://doi.org/10.1007/978-3-642-13244-5_21

37. Rossi, B., Russo, B., Succi, G.: Adoption of free/libre open source software in public organizations: Factors of impact. Inf. Technol. People **25**(2), 156–187 (2012)

38. Scotto, M., Sillitti, A., Succi, G., Vernazza, T.: A Relational approach to software metrics. In: Proceedings of the 2004 ACM Symposium on Applied Computing, SAC 2004, pp. 1536–1540. ACM (2004)

39. Scotto, M., Sillitti, A., Succi, G., Vernazza, T.: A non-invasive approach to product metrics collection. J. Syst. Architect. **52**(11), 668–675 (2006)

40. Sillitti, A., Janes, A., Succi, G., Vernazza, T.: Measures for mobile users: An architecture. J. Syst. Architect. **50**(7), 393–405 (2004)

41. Sillitti, A., Succi, G., Vlasenko, J.: Understanding the impact of pair programming on developers attention: A case study on a large industrial experimentation. In: Proceedings of the 34th International Conference on Software Engineering, ICSE 2012, pp. 1094–1101. IEEE Press, Piscataway, NJ, USA, June 2012

42. Sillitti, A., Vernazza, T., Succi, G.: Service oriented programming: A new paradigm of software reuse. In: Gacek, C. (ed.) ICSR 2002. LNCS, vol. 2319, pp. 269–280. Springer, Heidelberg (2002). https://doi.org/10.1007/3-540-46020-9_19

43. Succi, G., Benedicenti, L., Vernazza, T.: Analysis of the effects of software reuse on customer satisfaction in an RPG environment. IEEE Trans. Softw. Eng. **27**(5), 473–479 (2001)

44. Succi, G., Paulson, J., Eberlein, A.: Preliminary results from an empirical study on the growth of open source and commercial software products. In: EDSER-3 Workshop, pp. 14–15 (2001)

45. Succi, G., Pedrycz, W., Marchesi, M., Williams, L.: Preliminary analysis of the effects of pair programming on job satisfaction. In: Proceedings of the 3rd International Conference on Extreme Programming (XP), pp. 212–215, May 2002

46. Townsend, M.A., Moore, D.W., Tuck, B.F., Wilton, K.M.: Self-concept and anxiety in university students studying social science statistics within a co-operative learning structure. Educ. Psychol. **18**(1), 41–54 (1998)

47. Valerio, A., Succi, G., Fenaroli, M.: Domain analysis and framework-based software development. SIGAPP Appl. Comput. Rev. **5**(2), 4–15 (1997)

48. Vernazza, T., Granatella, G., Succi, G., Benedicenti, L., Mintchev, M.: Defining metrics for software components. In: Proceedings of the World Multiconference on Systemics, Cybernetics and Informatics, vol. XI, pp. 16–23, July 2000

49. Wasserman, L.: All of Nonparametric Statistics. Springer Science & Business Media, New York (2006)

50. Wilson, S.G.: The flipped class: A method to address the challenges of an undergraduate statistics course. Teach. Psychol. **40**(3), 193–199 (2013)

Reflections on Teaching Formal Methods for Software Development in Higher Education

Mansur Khazeev[1], Hamna Aslam[1,2(✉)], Daniel de Carvalho[1],
Manuel Mazzara[1], Jean-Michel Bruel[2], and Joseph Alexander Brown[1]

[1] Innopolis University, 420500 Innopolis, Russian Federation
h.aslam@innopolis.ru
[2] Université de Toulouse, IRIT-CNRS, 31000 Toulouse, France

Abstract. Despite the increasing attention to formal verification techniques by industry and academia, the programs of Higher Education to this regard still lie behind, and these concepts are not presented to the majority of Computer Science students trained to be future IT specialists. The primary reason is the presumed complexity of the concepts, tools, and formal processes together with a believed moderate interest of employers, which tends to demotivate students. The starting point of any process of change is typically higher education, which should introduce a thoughtful plan of teaching and practice for the students to get acquainted with these techniques. To do so, it is necessary to preliminary identify the obstacles. The user study described in this paper is examining AutoProof tool to identify the complexities attributed to formal methods. We worked with a cohort of master students in Software Engineering at an Information Technology University and monitored and analyzed their performance and feedback on a pedagogical experience. The work presented in this paper extends our previous research on formal methods education by confirming the findings and adding qualitative considerations to quantitative ones.

Keywords: Formal methods · Pedagogy · Software verification tools · Essay-based investigation

1 Introduction

In the past decades, researchers and practitioners deployed a significant effort to develop and improve formal verification tools and the related methodologies [14]. It soon became clear that the benefits of static analysis and formal verification play a determinant role in the deployment of safety-critical and mission-critical systems but, at the same time, can support quality assurance for off-the-shelf software. In order to exploit the positive effects of these solutions, it is necessary to spread this understanding and educate specialists and engineers. The starting point of any process of change is typically higher education. Despite increasing

J.-M. Bruel et al. (Eds.): FISEE 2019, LNCS 12271, pp. 28–41, 2020.
https://doi.org/10.1007/978-3-030-57663-9_3

attention to this research field in the research departments of big software companies and the academic world, the teaching of formal techniques is still limited to some advanced courses, and academic education does not sufficiently work towards an improvement in this situation.

It naturally emerges the question of what should be done within educational systems to change the trend slowly. In this article, we are discussing a teaching experience conducted at an Information Technology (IT) University during the academic year 2018/2019. A class of about 28 Master students attended the course of *Analysis of Software Artifacts*. During the delivery of the course, the *Eiffel programming language* [8] was introduced and explained together with the *Design-by-Contract (DbC)* methodology [20] and the *Autoproof* verification tool [11]. The course had a very formal backbone and approached the activities of requirements elicitation and software specification from a rigorous point of view. It was indeed a good laboratory to analyze the reaction of Master students when using DbC and a static verifier.

In this paper, we present quantitative and qualitative results of the study conducted with this cohort of students:

– The quantitative results are based on the performance of students in solving tasks about formal software specification. The students have been monitored in these activities to unambiguously determine if they could apply the techniques they were introduced to.
– The qualitative results complement the quantitative study. Students have been asked to submit essays and comments describing their experience while solving the tasks and studying the topic. The essays were analyzed one by one, summarizing the pros and cons that students have identified. This provides means for understanding the subjective perceptions of the individuals: both those who succeeded and those who failed.

The work presented in this paper extends the previous research [17] by confirming the findings on a new cohort of students and adding qualitative considerations to quantitative ones. Here we are addressing a more general set of research questions than in the previous work, and we are answering with a synergy of objectives but also subjective elements:

1. To what extent are our students ready to apply formal techniques, and why or why not?
2. What kinds of prerequisites are necessary to face the challenges?
3. To what extent our results can be generalized to any cohort of Computer Science students in other technical educational institutions?

The paper is organized as follows: Sect. 2 describes Autoproof, the verification tools targeted by this study; Sects. 3 and 4 focus on the qualitative and quantitative parts of the analysis; Sect. 5 provides our reflection on the results of the analysis and Sect. 6 presents similar investigations conducted in the field of verification and education. Section 7 analyses some possible factors limiting the study. Finally, Sect. 8 summarizes our findings and our understanding of them.

2 The Tool

The research conducted in this study is based on a specific course using a specific methodology and a tool to specify and verify software formally. We try to generalize the findings to formal methods. However, the qualitative analysis of the collected data suggests that different techniques may result in different levels of effectiveness of learning. A broader generalization may require further research. We reflect on this in Sect. 5.

The tool used in this study was *AutoProof* [27], a static analyzer for contracted code written in the *Eiffel programming language*. The core idea behind Eiffel is related to "contracts" inside the source code. The software correctness methodology is called Design By Contract (DbC) [20]. It uses invariants to document program state properties, and preconditions and postconditions to document the change in the state. Some aspects of the usability of AutoProof have been already studied before [11].

We have been using AutoProof and Eiffel for two principal reasons:

1. Eiffel is purely object-oriented. Modularity and scalability offered by object-orientation are of paramount importance in the development of large software systems and widely used in modern software engineering [23]. Eiffel is the kind of programming language that Master graduates can practice to develop skills required by industry.
2. Design By Contract (DbC) [20] is a methodology introduced about thirty years ago, and it did not stay confined within the Eiffel programming language. Instead, it has been gradually adopted by other popular programming languages: Java with JML [4], C# (Spec#) [1], C++ (*expects* and *ensures* clauses), and Kotlin (preconditions), to mention some. We are confident that the methodology implemented in AutoProof is transferable to any other Object Oriented programming language, which means that the findings of this work can be generalized at least to the Object-oriented paradigm (further generalization may be less evident).

2.1 Basic Notions on DbC

To understand the results of the study, it is not necessary to have complete mastery of the methodology used by the students. Above, we have just described tools and approaches in general terms, with pointers to the literature that could help interested readers to understand more details. However, we still report here some basic notions of DbC to make the rest of the paper smoother to read.

DbC and Dynamic Check. In programming languages based on the notion of *class* (*object-oriented* programming languages), *design-by-contract* is a methodology defining "rights" and "obligations" of a class (or a developer) and its clients (hence the metaphor of *contract*). Contracts are the assertions: preconditions - properties that the developer takes for granted and the client is "obliged" to fulfill; postconditions and invariants - "obligations" for the developer and properties that the clients might reckon on. During the *execution* of the program these assertions can be checked and an exception raised in case of violation. This is a way to find bugs in the program for then resolving them.

Assertions in AutoProof. Code contracts are defined using assertions of the following types:

- *Precondition* and *postcondition* of a method/feature/function: The caller of a method/feature/function has an obligation to satisfy its preconditions, while the callee is obliged to guarantee its postconditions to hold at the end of its execution.
- *Class invariant*: Class invariants define properties of the state of an object that should be preserved during the execution of the program.
- *Loop invariant*: It is an assertion that should be maintained at each iteration of the loop.
- *Framing assertion*: Framing assertions express which objects can have their state modified.

Furthermore, a *loop variant* is a measure that must decrease strictly at each iteration of the loop to ensure that the loop eventually terminates [9].

Static Analysis. Instead of checking *dynamically* (that is, *during* the execution of the program), it is possible to check *statically* (that is, analysing source code of the program *without* executing it) the enforcement of contracts. In other words, to *prove* that, for *any* execution of the program, none of the assertions specifying the rights and obligations might be violated, but without running the program. AutoProof statically checks the assertions described above and informs the user about the outcome of the analysis.

3 Quantitative Analysis

In this section, we describe the setup of the experiment. We explain the study design, the data collection process, and the conclusions we draw out of this experience.

3.1 Study Design

The essay was conducted as a supplementary home assignment in the "Analysis of Software Artifacts" course at an IT University. Preliminarly, the students have received a lecture on Model Checking and Formal Verification as a part of the course. The main goal of the assignment was to demonstrate the advantages and challenges of formal verification. Furthermore, to allow getting practical experience with the tool demonstrated during the lecture, check the students' understanding of the topic and skills to specify requirements formally. In this paper, with the word *approach*, we intend teaching DbC, Autoproof, the way of delivering this material and how we assessed understanding.

Rationale for Choosing the Exercises. The assignment was based on the material of the tutorial of AutoProof. It contains a set of exercises of different complexity and provides an online version of the tool. The material was chosen for the simplicity of the set-up phase. Not only did this help to avoid a complicated installation and configuration phase of the verification tool, allowing students to concentrate on specification and verification immediately, but this also allowed us to examine the usability of the tool by non-expert users.

Profile of Participants. The study has been conducted on 28 participants of the Master Program in Software Engineering. All participants had a background education in Information Technology from different universities all over Russia and other countries such as India, Sri Lanka, Bolivia, Ghana, Jordan, and Kazakhstan.

Prior to the assignment, the students had a course on formal specification and verification where they have studied required theory starting with very foundations: formal systems, set theory, predicate and temporal logic; and experienced variety tools of different purpose and level of automation - from model checkers to proof assistants - LTSA, Z, Isabelle and Coq. Concepts relevant for AutoProof tool - such as Hoare logic were also discussed.

Assignment Description. The participants were given a home assignment consisting of three parts. In the **first part**, students had to do two exercises available within the tutorial, simultaneously logging their progress. In the **second part**, they had to write a short essay about their assessment of the previous encounter with formal methods, to describe what they found easy or hard, what obstacles they encountered, the relation to their experience as a software developer and student. Finally, the **third part** was to fill in a form where they had to describe their industrial experience. The assignment was submitted *via* Moodle.[1]

Helping Material Provided. Before the assignment, the students had one lecture on formal verification in general where the essential concepts and principals for AutoProof tool were presented, as well as the proof process on particular examples, was demonstrated and discussed. The lecture took 1.5 hours and refreshed knowledge on Hoare logic, DbC, that was covered in another course one semester earlier. The lecture introduced AutoProof tools and discussed its application to specific examples.

After all of these concepts were studied and the tool was introduced, the students were left on their own as the assignment assumed as an individual effort. However, they had access to the online document[2] explaining the concepts and examples. As the students were not acquainted with Eiffel syntax, they were also provided with the link[3] to the basic language constructs presented on the same website.

---

[1] https://moodle.org/.

[2] http://se.inf.ethz.ch/research/autoproof/tutorial/downloads/tutorial.pdf.

[3] http://se.inf.ethz.ch/research/autoproof/manual/.

Exercises Description. The tutorial covers two examples (BANK_ACCOUNT and MAX_IN_ARRAY) and several exercises: on verification of *Basic Properties* (a **CLOCK** exercise), *Algorithmic Problems* (several searching and sorting algorithms) and *Object Consistency* (exercises on data structures). The students were allowed to pick any two exercises of nine in total. All exercises varied in complexity, incorporating different verification challenges.

As a sample, the exercise **CLOCK** is partially depicted in Fig. 1. This code snipped omits all features except featuring *increase_minutes* and invariant of the class. Each exercise comprised of several tasks. Here, on lines 9 and 17, Task 5 is to specify *require* (precondition) and *ensure* (post-condition) clauses for the feature; on line 20 Task 2 - to provide the *invariant* of the class.

```
class CLOCK
    . . . -- Some features were omitted
feature
increase_seconds
    -- Increase 'minutes' by one.
  note
    explicit: wrapping
  require
    -- TASK 5: Specify procedure.
  do
    if seconds = 59 then
      set_seconds (0)
      increase_minutes
    else set_seconds (seconds + 1)
    end
  ensure
    -- TASK 5: Specify procedure.
  end
invariant
    -- TASK 2: Add class invariant.
end
```

Fig. 1. Extract of **CLOCK** exercise

In order to succeed in verification, the students had to specify valid values for attributes *hours*, *minutes* and *seconds*. Moreover, as part of Task 5, they had to define a frame condition denoting the attributes allowed to be modified. Here, *seconds* as well as *minutes* and *hours*, since increasing by one when *seconds* equal to 59 should update *minutes*, and similarly *hours* should be updated when *minutes* is 59. Lastly, the student had to add post-conditions describing how these three attributes should be modified. In the same manner, all other features of the exercise had to be specified.

Similarly, Algorithmic Problems included tasks on the specification of pre- and post-conditions, and in addition, to provide loop invariants and variants.

3.2 Collection of Data

The students have tackled exercises from all categories, but the majority tried and could complete only the exercises about verification of *Basic Properties* and the *Algorithmic Problems*. As it was mentioned above, students were asked to record their verification process in a free format. A key aspect of this part of the assignment was to write down the encountered difficulties and track the time spent to overcome them. Many participants have created a very detailed log. Some of them even provided screenshots. Several reports were brief and less informative; however, they managed to capture the main blockers and total time spent.

Table 1. Number of students doing **CLOCK** and **LINEAR_SEARCH** exercises

	Succeeded	Failed	Total
CLOCK	10	16	26
LINEAR_SEARCH	1	24	25

Two exercises that were attempted by the majority of the students are **CLOCK** and **LINEAR_SEARCH**. The data regarding the number of students doing these exercises is depicted in Table 1. Furthermore, the data on time spent, trying to specify and verify these exercises, is depicted in Table 2. Compared to the results presented in [17], these results appear to be weaker in terms of the ratio of succeeding and failing attempts. However, from Table 2, it is clear that the students were less persistent and have put less effort into completing the exercises.

Table 2. Time spent on exercises (in minutes)

		Succeeded	Failed	Total
CLOCK	Min	24	37	24
	Max	240	315	315
	Mean	111	105	107
LINEAR_SEARCH	Min	137	30	30
	Max	137	287	287
	Mean	137	95	96.5

4 Analysis of Essays

This section complements the analysis of the data collected with information acquired from the students' essays. For that, detailed essays of 28 students were analyzed by the authors. Despite different experiences, opinion, and writing styles, some aspects appear as common, and that we try to summarize in this section. On the negative and limiting side, the students said that:

General Comments (negative)

- Lack of documentation (can be generalized, not only AutoProof)
- Concrete use limited to safety-critical systems
- Costs of training specialists
- The job market is small for verification specialists

Specific to AutoProof (negative)

- AutoProof is too specific to Eiffel language. LTSA, OCL seem more flexible and preferable
- Feedback given by the tool is unclear

Some positive comments were given on the usefulness of the approach:

General Comments (positive)

- Formal verification is useful in some market niche, but they never worked there
- The verification process is fun

Specific to AutoProof (positive)

- AutoProof works nicely since the model, and the code is in the same place (this is different, for example, for Model Checking).
- Tutorial, as a specific part of the documentation, is useful.

5   Reflections

Students' feedback, the analysis of their performance and detailed logs demonstrated that formal techniques at the moment are hard to be acquired even by future IT specialists. As educators, we need to facilitate the learning process, being this a way to support more widespread use. The verification process, when applying specific techniques, should be more firmly supported, and possibly more details about the internal implementation of the tools should be given. This might allow future engineers to appreciate the ingenuity of the solutions and the value of theory.

In general terms, the results of this study are confirming the ones that have been presented with a previous cohort of students [17]. This way, we can generalize the conclusions and answer broader research questions as defined in Sect. 1. One notable difference that can be identified concerning the previous study is that, on average, the time spent on the exercise was 1:50 hours instead of 3 hours. This can be explained by the fact that in the previous study, the task was a prerequisite for the project, such as necessary to complete for the continuation of the course, while this time, it was just the part of supplementary material not of the core content.

The students' feedback and the teacher's experience while teaching the course indicate certain areas for concentration. Figure 2 summarizes these areas. A significant aspect of learning is being able to perceive the importance of topics being taught. We identified that the students were not enthusiastic about learning formal methods as they presumed these solutions to be invaluable for their future careers. The students' had a perception that:

1. Learning AutoProof would only benefit Eiffel users.
2. Formal methods are required for software that is designed for safety and mission-critical applications.
3. There is no job market for those specialized in formal methods.

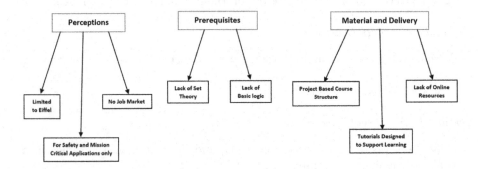

Fig. 2. Identified potential areas of improvement to support teaching of formal methods and verification tools

The perception of students does not appear completely accurate. Let us discuss the points above one by one:

1. Although AutoProof is and Eiffel-based tool, the idea of Design-by-Contract has been implemented natively in languages such as Kotlin and Scala, plus libraries, preprocessors, and other tools have been developed for a large number of programming languages without native support, among all Java and C.
2. Formal methods and their applications, some heavy-load methodologies are indeed justified mostly in the case of safety- and mission-critical applications. However, Design-by-contract is not one of them, and its applicability is lightweight and does not require a significant effort or a steep learning curve to be applied. Design by contract does not replace testing, but it complements it to ensure quality code.
3. The market for verification specialists is indeed tiny. However, acquaintances with some lightweight formal techniques such as Design-by-contract, especially when integrated with testing, leads to an improved profile for any software developer interested in quality.

These perceptions can be addressed by stating the application areas as well as the usefulness of formal methods for developing everyday systems.

The other significant observation was the need for *prerequisites* covered before teaching formal methods. Courses such as set theory and logic contribute to the understanding of formal methods. Furthermore, in the teaching directions, the structure of the course is of great significance. The results of the case study suggest that a project-based course would contribute to the systematic course design that would give students the experience of working with formal methods.

Considering course material, students pointed out the *lack of online resources*. Students are habitual of consulting online resources. As stated in feedback, they could not find much help online about AutoProof. In this regard, teachers can refer to solid material available online.

The points stated above are based upon the feedback and teacher's experience of teaching formal methods. These areas can be addressed with a systematic course design as well as taking into account students' perceptions about the subject. We believe, after addressing the points identified, teachers would be able to make the learning process desirable. Students' perceptions about the subject introduced unnecessary hurdles in learning as they deemed it to be insignificant for themselves in terms of prospects. Therefore, it is crucial to educate students of the usefulness and the applications of formal methods.

6   Related Work

In the investigating papers on education, we found several related reports (the following groups of references are not exhaustive):

Mathieu and Théo [16] emphasize on the need for teaching formal methods at an undergraduate level. A suggestion is to incorporate FoCaLiZe as a teaching tool at an undergraduate level. Liu et al. [18] also elaborates on the significance of teaching formal methods in the context of software engineering. They suggest having a project-based course along with a systematic curriculum. Their findings are aligned with our research conclusions. These suggestions are not recent and have been discussed since years, such as Gibson and Méry [12] have presented the same arguments two decades ago. They recognize the need for interactive teaching between the instructor and their students. A strong emphasis is made on using the tools to support the teaching of formal methods. Active learning is recognised to provide benefits to grades and outcomes in STEM [10].

Miller [21] provides details on aspects of teaching and how learning can be enhanced. As an example, Miller states that the meaning of productivity is different for a learner of formal methods and a professional using them. While incorporating tools as part of teaching, we should be careful about the outcomes we want to get. Sotiriadou and Kefalas [25] demonstrates through a case study, the significance of teaching formal methods at an undergraduate level. They present their course structure and teaching material. The use of the Z specification language has provided positive outcomes from the students' learning aspect. The study results indicate that a structured course with appropriate teaching tools enhances learning and understanding of formal methods. Sobel et al. [24] identifies that formal methods teaching needs to address the issue of students rushing to the implementation phase without reasoning about the correctness of the system.

Furthermore, making students aware of the application areas might also increase their interest in learning and applying these concepts in a wide range of projects. Néstor Cataño [5] provides reflections from their experience of teaching *Models of Software Systems* course. The use of proof assistants in the class has been recommended, e.g., the author has used EventB2Java during lectures. Students have demonstrated a thorough understanding by working on modelling tools.

Ishikawa et al. [15] provides an overview of the ten years of the software engineering program. The report discusses the experience of teaching formal methods. The emphasis is on the need to bridge the gap between academia and industrial needs. Along with a representation of a well-structured program, the key findings are: having lecturers from industry also as well as covering non-technical aspects such as planning and reporting. Tretmans et al. [26] discusses the seven myths about formal methods in relation to the successfully completed project, a control system for a movable dam. The seven myths as stated by Tretmans et al. [26] are:

1. formal methods can guarantee that software is perfect;
2. formal methods are all about program proving;
3. formal methods are only useful for safety-critical systems;
4. formal methods require highly-trained mathematicians;
5. formal methods increase the cost of development;
6. formal methods are unacceptable to users;
7. formal methods are not used on real, large-scale software.

The project results are sometimes in agreement with the myths and sometimes not. However, these myths are the most common challenges we face as educators. Our research team has also been active in the field of education, both for what concerns teaching formal specification [7] and verification [17] and in the design and delivery of courses related to DevOps [2,3,19], in academic and industrial environments.

The findings of our research are aligned with the reports we have mentioned. In addition to this, we have identified the prerequisites for the course of formal methods. The absence of these prerequisites was a hurdle in the learning process. For the future, we plan to propose this model of teaching to the education administration for a systematic teaching program.

7   Threats to Validity

One of the limitations that we have identified during the study and that could have interfered is the fact that the lecturer mentioned the average duration of the time needed in a previous study, and possibly some of the participants may have limited themselves, as visible form some comments written in the logs. This may have influenced the study, although not in a dramatic way. For future study, it will be necessary to avoid such a mention.

Another limiting factor is the nature of the sample of participants, that it is limited to students of one university, although international and heterogeneous and with coding proactive. The study should be extended to currently employed professionals.

Areas of improvements depicted in Fig. 2 are derived mostly from the feedback of students, and can also be confirmed by lecturers. However, some bias may have influenced the outcome: for example, students with prior knowledge, the lecturer's ability, or the enthusiasm put in the delivery.

We should also consider another aspect that could limit a broader validity of the conclusions of the study. The subject under consideration, methodology, and tool, was covered in a very short time-span and challenged the class with a single assignment. The concepts are non-trivial. Different results may have been possibly obtained, providing multiple examples with a more varied complexity in a more extended time.

8   Conclusions

After analyzing quantitative and qualitative aspects, there are individual lessons that we have learnt on how the pedagogical process could be improved at the university and we are confident that these lessons could be generalized.

- Teaching DbC [7] seems to be a useful choice, together with other solutions such as OCL [13], Z [22] and Model-checking [6]. These are different techniques that could offer different flavours. For example, some students found more general the use of OCL that AutoProof, still being based on similar underlying concepts. The fact that OCL is applicable to UML, therefore to any software development process allows newcomers to appreciate it better. At the same time, the concept deployed for one formalism also simplifies the understanding of the other.
- More exposure to formal techniques can certainly support the pedagogical process. *Predicate Logic* and *Set Theory* appeared to be a prerequisite of paramount importance for being able to approach formal techniques.
- The knowledge of the target programming language may make the difference. Students in their essays declared that a significant portion of time was spent in learning and understanding the syntax of Eiffel.

References

1. Barnett, M., Leino, K.R.M., Schulte, W.: The Spec# programming system: an overview. In: Barthe, G., Burdy, L., Huisman, M., Lanet, J.-L., Muntean, T. (eds.) CASSIS 2004. LNCS, vol. 3362, pp. 49–69. Springer, Heidelberg (2005). https://doi.org/10.1007/978-3-540-30569-9_3

2. Bobrov, E., Bucchiarone, A., Capozucca, A., Guelfi, N., Mazzara, M., Masyagin, S.: Teaching DevOps in academia and industry: reflections and vision. In: Bruel, J.-M., Mazzara, M., Meyer, B. (eds.) DEVOPS 2019. LNCS, vol. 12055, pp. 1–14. Springer, Cham (2020). https://doi.org/10.1007/978-3-030-39306-9_1

3. Bobrov, E., et al.: DevOps and its philosophy: education matters!. Microservices, pp. 349–361. Springer, Cham (2020). https://doi.org/10.1007/978-3-030-31646-4_14

4. Burdy, L., et al.: An overview of JML tools and applications. Int. J. Soft. Tools Technol. Transf. **7**(3), 212–232 (2004). https://doi.org/10.1007/s10009-004-0167-4

5. Cataño, N.: An empirical study on teaching formal methods to millennials. In: Proceedings of the 1st International Workshop on Software Engineering Curricula for Millennials, SECM '17, Buenos Aires, Argentina, pp. 3–8. IEEE Press (2017)

6. Clarke Jr., E.M., Grumberg, O., Peled, D.A.: Model Checking. MIT Press, Cambridge (1999)

7. de Carvalho, D.: Teaching programming and design-by-contract. In: Auer, M.E., Tsiatsos, T. (eds.) ICL 2018. AISC, vol. 916, pp. 68–76. Springer, Cham (2020). https://doi.org/10.1007/978-3-030-11932-4_7

8. ES: The Eiffel Method and Language. https://www.eiffel.org/doc/eiffel/Eiffel

9. Floyd, R.W.: Assigning meanings to programs. In: Proceedings of the Symposium on Applied Math, vol. 19, pp. 19–32. American Mathematical Society (1967)

10. Freeman, S., et al.: Active learning increases student performance in science, engineering, and mathematics. Proc. Natl. Acad. Sci. **111**(23), 8410–8415 (2014)

11. Furia, C.A., Poskitt, C.M., Tschannen, J.: The autoproof verifier: usability by non-experts and on standard code. In: Proceedings of Formal Integrated Development Environment, F-IDE 2015 (2015). Electron. Proc. Theor. Comput. Sci. **187**, 42–55 (2015)

12. Gibson, P., Méry, D.: Teaching formal methods: lessons to learn. In: Proceedings of the 2nd Irish Conference on Formal Methods, IW-FM'98, Swindon, GBR, pp. 56–68. BCS Learning & Development Ltd. (1998)

13. Object Management Group: Object constraint language. https://www.omg.org/spec/OCL/About-OCL/

14. Hoare, C.A.R., Misra, J., Leavens, G.T., Shankar, N.: The verified software initiative: a manifesto. ACM Comput. Surv. **41**(4), 22:1–22:8 (2009)

15. Ishikawa, F., Yoshioka, N., Tanabe, Y.: Keys and roles of formal methods education for industry: 10 year experience with top SE program. In: Bollin, A., Margaria, T., Perseil, I. (eds.) Proceedings of the First Workshop on Formal Methods in Software Engineering Education and Training, FMSEE&T 2015, co-located with 20th International Symposium on Formal Methods (FM 2015), Oslo, Norway, 23 June 2015. CEUR-WS.org (2015). CEUR Workshop Proc. **1385**, 35–42 (2015)

16. Jaume, M., Laurent, T.: Teaching formal methods and discrete mathematics. In: Dubois, C., Giannakopoulou, D., Méry, D. (eds.) Proceedings 1st Workshop on Formal Integrated Development Environment, Grenoble, France, 6 April 2014. Open Publishing Association (2014). Electron. Proc. Theor. Comput. Sci. **149**, 30–43 (2014)

17. Khazeev, M., Mazzara, M., Aslam, H., de Carvalho, D.: Towards a broader acceptance of formal verification tools. In: Auer, M.E., Hortsch, H., Sethakul, P. (eds.) ICL 2019. AISC, vol. 1135, pp. 188–200. Springer, Cham (2020). https://doi.org/10.1007/978-3-030-40271-6_20

18. Liu, S., Takahashi, K., Hayashi, T., Nakayama, T.: Teaching formal methods in the context of software engineering. ACM SIGCSE Bull. **41**(2), 17–23 (2009)

19. Mazzara, M., Naumchev, A., Safina, L., Sillitti, A., Urysov, K.: Teaching DevOps in corporate environments. In: Bruel, J.-M., Mazzara, M., Meyer, B. (eds.) DEVOPS 2018. LNCS, vol. 11350, pp. 100–111. Springer, Cham (2019). https://doi.org/10.1007/978-3-030-06019-0_8

20. Meyer, B.: Applying "design by contract". Computer **25**(10), 40–51 (1992)

21. Miller, J.F.: Teaching and learning formal methods, improving productivity. In: Butterfield, A., Haegele, K. (eds.) 3rd Irish Workshop on Formal Methods, Galway, Ireland, July 1999. Workshops in Computing. BCS (1999)

22. O'Regan, G.: Z formal specification language. Concise Guide to Formal Methods. UTCS, pp. 151–166. Springer, Cham (2017). https://doi.org/10.1007/978-3-319-64021-1_8

23. Pressman, R.S.: Software Engineering: A Practitioner's Approach, 7th edn. McGraw-Hill Higher Education, New York (2010). OCLC: ocn271105592

24. Sobel, A.E.K., Saiedian, H., Stavely, A., Henderson, P.: Teaching formal methods early in the software engineering curriculum. In: Proceedings of the 13th Conference on Software Engineering Education & Training, CSEET '00, p. 55. IEEE Computer Society (2000)

25. Sotiriadou, A., Kefalas, P.: Teaching formal methods in computer science undergraduates. In: International Conference on Applied and Theoretical Mathematics (2000)

26. Tretmans, J., Wijbrans, K., Chaudron, M.: Software engineering with formal methods: the development of a storm surge barrier control system revisiting seven myths of formal methods. Formal Meth. Syst. Des. **19**(2), 195–215 (2001)

27. Tschannen, J., Furia, C.A., Nordio, M., Polikarpova, N.: AutoProof: auto-active functional verification of object-oriented programs. In: Baier, C., Tinelli, C. (eds.) TACAS 2015. LNCS, vol. 9035, pp. 566–580. Springer, Heidelberg (2015). https://doi.org/10.1007/978-3-662-46681-0_53

Experience of Mixed Learning Strategies in Teaching Lean Software Development to Third Year Undergraduate Students

Ilya Khomyakov[✉], Sergey Masyagin[✉], and Giancarlo Succi[✉]

Innopolis University, Innopolis, Russia
{i.khomyakov,s.masyagin,g.succi}@innopolis.ru
http://university.innopolis.ru

Abstract. Teaching is always a challenging task, especially in the current fast-paced and changing world. Universities curricula and instructional practices should take into account growing and changing demands of both industry and students themselves. Given all these factors, a Lean Software Development course for third year BS has been developed and continues to evolve at Innopolis University, Russia. In the course, lean methods are used both for teaching lean software development skill, and for teaching Lean via other, not directly related to programming, collaborative tasks, i.e. writing a research paper. Besides, lean methodology is used by the course development team for course design. As a result, this approach helps not only to develop the theoretical and practical skills that students can apply in various spheres of life but also to engage the students and to maintain their attention throughout the course without any overload.

Keywords: Lean Software Development · Teaching · GQM · Experience Factory · Non-invasive Measurement

1 Introduction

Introducing students to new concepts can be difficult. In this article, we discuss how we address this challenge of knowledge transfer to students during the training for Lean Software Development. We describe the ways of developing students' theoretical knowledge and practical skills related to Lean Software Development by using non-programming assignments and Lean techniques during Lean training.

Recently, the Lean becomes very popular, even in education But authors mostly describes how to teach Lean Software Development using the concept of Software Projects and programming tasks [8, 19, 22, 24, 46] Our approach in the opposite is focused on developing meta-knowledge of Lean Software Development by applying non-programming assignments in the course, which are described in the article. Additionally, compared to other works [8, 19, 22], the approach includes course evolution and renovation.

© Springer Nature Switzerland AG 2020
J.-M. Bruel et al. (Eds.): FISEE 2019, LNCS 12271, pp. 42–59, 2020.
https://doi.org/10.1007/978-3-030-57663-9_4

This paper is organized as follows: Sect. 2 provides details about the Lean software development course taught to 3rd year undergraduate students, as well as the course motivation and goals. Sect. 3 covers the background behind the course main concepts such as Lean and Lean in Software development. Sect. 4 to 6 describe the course structure and all specific for the course general activities, such as Goal-Question-Metric approach (GQM) in teaching activities.

2   About the Course

The course exposes the student to the core concepts behind Lean Development in Software Engineering, beyond myths and legends, emphasizing how it relates to the general principles of Lean Development. It discusses different possible software processes, and how they can be tailored, enacted, and measured. In addition, a significant part of the course is centered around the application of Lean in software development to knowledge-intensive areas not necessarily connected to the software. The overall goal of the course is that students should learn the fundamental principles behind Lean Management, identify the key role of measurement in Lean Management. Moreover, we consider it particularly important that students are able to relate various approaches of Agile Methods to the overall principles of Lean Management in order for them to be able to define a suitable process for a new organization, including an approach to measure the outcome of such process introduction and institutionalization. Besides, throughout the course, we try to create a "lean environment" itself, that should help students to understand in practice what we mean by the lean organization.

3   Background

The term Lean was proposed [64] for production approach developed and applied by Toyota Motor Company [58], which was not only successfully used by the creators but served as a powerful revolutionary impetus in the management and creation of the production process in the automotive industry from the second half of the twentieth century. However many authors, for example, such as Stone [54], demonstrate that "lean" is no longer unique for automobile industry and it has found application in many different and naturally distant from each other industries and sectors.

Lean production was conceptualized as a way to reduce waste, upskill workers, improve quality and provide more variety in products than it was possible with mass production [64]. Gradually, the method spread to every field of human activity, from offices and government organizations to hospitals, universities, and software production. Despite the differences between, for example, medicine and automotive industry, many of Lean principles and concepts are applicable with great benefit to organizations, employees, customers. Lean manufacturing is also used in non-industrial fields, such as education [8,19]. Also, a framework was developed to apply lean to the learning process - The Lean Teaching and

Learning (LTL) model was firstly presented by Dinis-Carvalho and Fernandes [18].

The demand for cost savings in recent years has forced the software industry to look at lean methods with the ambition of applying them to "software production" [39]. Obviously, Lean cannot be applied to software production without adaptation, since the production of a software product is more creative than a typical pipelining. In this regard, at the moment there are various rethinking, adapting lean approach to creating software, for example [40] or LSD [23]. Lean development can be summarized by seven principles, very close in concept to lean manufacturing principles [39]:

1. Eliminate waste
2. Amplify learning
3. Decide as late as possible
4. Deliver as fast as possible
5. Empower the team
6. Build integrity in
7. Optimize the whole

In our corse we focus on these principles and also use proposed Lean pillars [23] as learning material and, moreover, as a toolset for course teaching process itself, building on previous experiences [26]. According to [23], the main lean software development pillars are the Goal Question Metric (GQM), the Experience Factory, and the Non-invasive Measurement. The listed pillars are briefly described in the following section. When developing and conducting the course, we tried to use only proven techniques, methods and tools, such as GQM [4], PDSA [18], Simulation Games [60] etc., which we discuss in more detail in the following sections.

3.1 GQM

Regular measurements in software development are important for a variety of outcomes: for understanding, controlling, improving the development process, also for creating and assessing the quality of the product itself. Throughout the years there have been published sequences of papers evidencing empirically such importance [11,14,29,31–35,43,44,47,51,52,55–57,61,63]. But not all metrics should and could be collected and measured. It is critical to understand why and how they should be measured during a particular software development process step and the reasoning behind that, otherwise, the effort would be just a waste. Any measurement should draw upon particular goals. For this reason, the Goal Question Metric (GQM) model proposed by Basili and Weiss is so important [4]. The GQM describes the process of establishing a data collection framework, helps to answer the questions - what data and why should be collected and how it should be interpreted afterword. The framework is defined in three levels [12,13,15]:

1. *Conceptual* – It defines goals, according to different points of view on the selected object of study and current environment.

2. *Operational* – It establishes questions. Questions are measurable entities that establish a link between the object of study and its goals, and they define what parts of the object of study should be considered and what the signs of achievement of the related goal are.
3. *Quantitative* – It deduces metrics. Metrics in our case are software measurements needed to answer the questions in a quantitative way.

3.2 Experience Factory

The experience is defined as "valuable, stored, specific knowledge that was acquired in the previous problem-solving situations" [42]. Lean cannot be introduced without respect for the existing knowledge and experience of a company stuff. This consideration is most applicable and important for software companies. Therefore, the question arises of how to create an environment in which such knowledge and experience are created, stored and ready for quick and high-quality use, even by new employees, in new projects, etc. The solution introduced by Basili [3,62] addresses this requirement, presenting Experience Factory. The Experience Factory is an approach to collect and reuse past experiences, based on the Plan-Do-Study-Act paradigm (PDSA) [62]. The purpose of the PDSA [16] is to create a flow of constant quality improvement based on the following steps:

1. **plan** the activities we need to perform so that we achieve the desired improvement and their expected outcome;
2. **do** execute the plan;
3. **study** the outcome, measure it, and compare it with the expected outcome; understand the reasons for the difference between reality and expectations;
4. **act** according to the results, that is, institutionalize the planned activities or adjust them.

The Experience Factory uses the Plan-Do-Study-Act approach, adapted to the software development domain, called the Quality Improvement Paradigm (QIP) [1]. The QIP—as the PDSA approach—is a process model. It prescribes a set of activities that have to be executed in the prescribed order to achieve the expected results. It is an iterative model, i.e., it is based on the idea that a set of steps is executed repeatedly until all the work is done. The steps are organized using two cycles: the first is for long-term learning, and the second is executed during the project phase and provides early feedback while the project is carried out.

The main cycle consists of the following six steps [2]:

1. Characterize and understand
2. Set goals
3. Choose processes, methods, techniques, and tools
4. Execute, which includes Process execution, Result Analysis, and Feedback, in cycles
5. Analyze results
6. Package and store experience.

3.3 Non-invasive Measurement

Measurement in software development is essential for understanding, controlling, and improving the development process. Software is invisible; therefore, we need a way to make it visible [23]. The term "non-invasiveness" comes from the medical field, in which it means that the diagnosis does not require to actually look into the body [10]. In software measurement, we mean the use of methods to collect data about the software development process, about the product, and about the employed resources that do not require the personal involvement of the participants of the process [49,50]. It is highly important to have non-invasive instead of pervasive measurement at least for two reasons 1) we don't need to spend employees time, for example, developers on collecting the data and 2) we want to have clear non-touched data, because of inaccuracy and incompleteness of data that could be achieved using pervasive measurement [23].

In the next sections, we describe how we use such principles in teaching Lean Software Development.

4   The Course

4.1   Course Goals

For deeper understanding of the course and underlying motivation behind activities, we are showing course goals in the following section. The goal of the course is to make students understand the core aspects of software development, that is, the creative nature of software production as an act of creation performed by human mind, the substantial differences between tame and wicked problems, the core concepts of measurement in software engineering, the fundamentals of Taylorist/Fordist approaches to (software) production, the basis of lean and agile software development, and the importance of knowledge and knowledge sharing in producing software. This translates into the ability of students to determine when a problem is "easy to solve" provided enough effort is put into such solution, and when it is not, why it is important and how we can define and perform measurements in software engineering, especially in lean and agile development environments, how to organize the development process to collect metrics non invasively, the difference between pulling and pushing in (software) development, and the fundamental principle of agility [30,48].

Moreover, the objective is to equip students with the ability to compute the fundamental software metrics to track the evolution of a project, to organize the aims of a (software) development organization in terms of Goals, Questions, and Metrics, to create a tailored (lean and agile) development process for an organization producing software, to define a path to insert and manage such (lean and agile) development process into an organization producing software, to structure the experience of gathering data while inside an organization and as a result it the future to be able to make strategic decision in such organization, and, especially, to relate various approaches of Agile Methods to the overall principles of Lean Management.

To summarize, the main purpose of the course is to expose students to the principles of lean software development via non-coding tasks and help them to develop lean mindset, transferable skill of lean operational practice, including lean application in software development, and also to teach students meta-knowledge, which could be applicable in each life sector.

4.2 Course Structure

The course has a variety of approaches to designing learning experiences for two main reasons:

1. to maximize the learning outcome: a particular teaching technique will be most appropriate for the specific learning objective of the instructional purpose, and
2. to make students aware of and prepared to handle different teaching approaches used in academia and industry.

The course is organized in 15 weeks with every week 2 academics hours of lectures and 4 academic hours of labs. Significant amount of course time is dedicated for self-study: 6 h/week on reading, homework, and preparation for each class (this time will contribute to the project assignment as well) 6 h/week specifically on project/report assignments.

A balanced mixture of "standard" frontal classes, "standard" labs, class discussions and presentations by experts (will be described later on) is used in the course. The style of teaching is highly informal and experiential. Students are required to participate intensively, give their presentations, and also, sometimes, take a leading role in the discussion. The data we collected as a result of surveys demonstrate that students learn more by applying the ideas and explaining them to others than by listening to a frontal explanation. The surveys showed that more than 70% of students prefer application and explanation to others rather than traditional teacher-to-student frontal explanation.

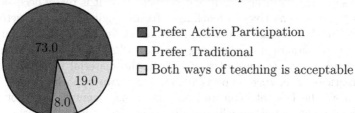

As it was mentioned earlier, in the course we use the concept of Experience Factory, i.e. students have the opportunity not only to listen or read about, but also to experience the concept, by, for example, creating and improving lectures notes, thus linking conceptual knowledge to real life.

The course currently requires various activities from students, including standard ones, such as reading or watching materials related to software development as a homework, to reason on the content of the course, where tasks will involve Higher Order Thinking skills, e.g. analyse, criticize, suggest a solution/an improvement.

Moreover, there is a batch of non-standard activities used in the course. For example, a report of Lean application in different areas of life, such as sports. This task allows students to empirically focus on the application of lean approaches to the non-traditional organizational context in the "joint educational work," in which students are assigned to write a book by first, independently studying a selected new topic and writing their chapters, and then by joining those chapter in a book.

Another example of such non-standard collaborative task is when, students are required to study and to present a chapter of a book on poetics, linking it with what has already been explained in the class and with the general theory of software development. All kinds of specific for the course activities are described in the following sections.

Additionally, class collaborative participation is a part of the course assessment scheme, as the course is mainly informed by social constructivism approach and Lean principle of shared knowledge. Hence discussions are the essential part of instructional practice. To contribute to students' engagement in class discussions, active participation is also promoted with grades to enrich class discussions with student knowledge, relevant experience, critical questions, and material analysis. Another example when students are promoted for participation is when they are evaluated for their participation in presentations by invited speakers. Each student should write a question, which can subsequently be asked to the speaker, if after a students voting it will appear in top 10. Moreover, students are involved in team projects followed by reports and presentations in order to understand one of the main Lean principles in the practice, non-invasive measurement in a poor environment.

Given current dynamic status of Computer Science as discipline, it is difficult to formalize all the knowledge that is required for a future Software Engineer, so we expose students to state-of-the-art knowledge along with the experiences from successful software engineers. As it is described in [7] it is really necessary to engage industry representatives in teaching software engineering. Instructors and guest contributors, who are practicing software engineers, are often much better placed to teach practical software engineering skills than pure academics, and naturally, lend a greater sense of relevance to the material being taught. Drawing on practical experience, experts demonstrate two opposite topics: 1) best practices from the field of Lean and project management 2) how not to lead projects, why projects fail, on which concepts students should concentrate more in the future in order to avoid the same mistakes. That is why during the course we periodically have very experienced people from the industry. As we use the concept of Experience Factory, all guest presentations are recorded and published, so each student could access them whenever they want.

5   Course Design (Teaching Approaches and Process)

During the teaching process we are focusing on the use of the Lean Teaching and Learning model and applying previously mentioned LSD pillars such as GQM and Experience Factory, and PDSA as part of it. Since high applicability of PDSA during teaching has been proven [18], we actively use this approach in this course. Goals and metrics obtained with GQM allow us to control the course program, its relevance and at the same time comply with state education standards. Lean lists two types of process improvements: *kaikaku* (radical improvement) and *kaizen* (continuous, incremental improvement). One of the main tools used in the model for continuous improvement is the so-called *PDSA* – *P*lan, *D*o, *S*tudy, *A*ct. This approach has been proven and tested by various researchers, for example, in [19]. PDSA is used in the course design for ongoing and timely course update and delivery. Each class is planned (Plan) according to the existing government and university standards and then executed (Do) according to the plan. At the end of each activity of the course (lecture,lab etc.), feedback from students is collected and analyzed (Study). Based on the feedback analysis, the course material is updated and can be changed if necessary (Act).

We are interested in continuous course improvement and we use GQM and PDSA cycle to improve the course. We regularly use students' feedback, as its effectiveness has been proved in e.g. [28], and we follow the procedure described in this source. Figure shows an example of questionnaire.

Based on GQM and PDSA techniques we chose to use the following metrics for continuous assessment of the course quality:

1. Student Satisfaction Rating
2. Course Clarity Assessment
3. Lecture Quality Assessment
4. Assessment of the quality of laboratory studies
5. Students' interest in further, in-depth study of the lean topics

Data for metrics 1–4 are collected from the questionnaire in Fig. 1. Metric 5 is measured by collecting statistics on students employment, industry feedback, and students publications.

In the last 3 issues of the course, students rated it with an average score of 4.5 on a 5-point scale every year. Moreover, several students who were attending this course have successfully developed their theses in the Lean Software Development field, with about 10% of the course participants having published on Lean related topics in Scopus indexed international conferences. Finally, several former students were hired by companies that use flexible methods and they continued their practice as well as training in Lean methodologies area. A significant number of students were hired for flexible positions in software companies, some were even hired as so-called Masters in various forms of dexterity.

We are also using other Lean techniques for teaching the course. For example, teamwork is an integral part of each class as well as the majority of out-of class assignments (those will described in more details in the next section). Also,

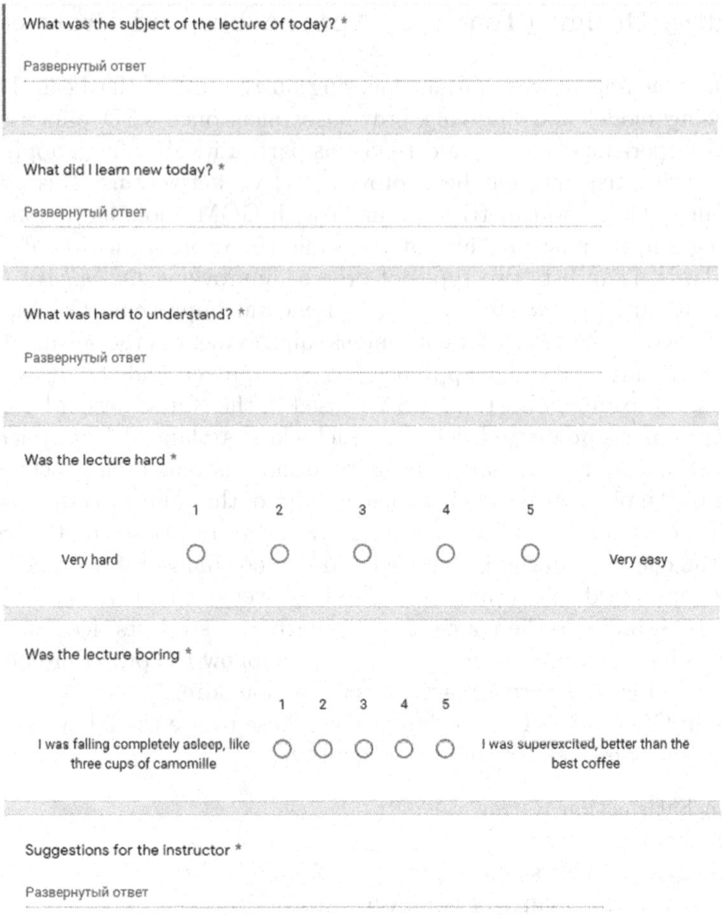

What was the subject of the lecture of today? *

Развернутый ответ

What did I learn new today? *

Развернутый ответ

What was hard to understand? *

Развернутый ответ

Was the lecture hard *

	1	2	3	4	5	
Very hard	○	○	○	○	○	Very easy

Was the lecture boring *

	1	2	3	4	5	
I was falling completely asleep, like three cups of camomille	○	○	○	○	○	I was superexcited, better than the best coffee

Suggestions for the instructor *

Развернутый ответ

Fig. 1. Questionnaire example

the concept of the focus on the client is applied via periodic student representative meetings and feedback from students which together allow us to better understand students' needs. As a last point, during the course we encourage the use of open source tools and methods, to promote the diffusion of knowledge [17,20,27,38,45]. Moreover, to build models we also use techniques from machine learning and computational intelligence [36,37].

6 Course Activities

Our task is not only to teach theoretical foundations, but also to create conditions for expanding and deepening our horizon, as well as developing practical skills, moreover, skills that a person cannot use thoughtlessly, but soberly and clearly understanding the need and importance of each of necessary actions and their timeliness, taking advantage from previous experiences [9,53]. We believe that the use of non-programmatic methods can no less effectively solve the educational task. First, we aim to teach Lean framework itself, so it can be taught on any appropriate content. Second, the curriculum is built so that students enrolled in this core course are simultaneously involved in two programming projects in other courses and they can transfer lean technology tools on those projects. So, for example, we assign writing collective works, books, creating group projects that not only acquaint participants in the course with basic concepts but through accurate and constant mentoring lead to the formation of skills for adapting lean approaches not only for software development. In this section, we list and describe all the main activities that were used during the Lean Software Development course.

6.1   Reports

On of the examples of the course activities is reports. Reports are very typical in the industry, therefore these tasks constitute a very important component in the preparation of future software engineers. Reports assignments imply reading and presenting work related to lean software development, with also a particular interest in measurements in order to broaden the understanding of the subject. These are small group assignments covering several areas of creative production, for example: lean in art, lean in cooking, lean in sport, lean in volunteering, lean in games, etc. Students voluntarily choose a topic from such list, one topic per each small group. Particular emphasis is placed on empirical research, which is also one of the key tenets of lean, and on historical work that shows the roots of existing technologies, explaining how they came into existence and the reasons for specific constraints on them.

In the reports students purpose is to determine: goals of the chosen report topic, material from the lectures, labs, articles which covers the topic right way, identification of what "lean" would mean for the chosen topic, description of the techniques related to (lean) software development, checking presented articles on the selected topic and taking examples to their reports from the articles, identification of what:

- the reader's topic under study could learn from (lean) software development,
- (lean) software development could learn from the industry under study.

Each report is undertaken by a group of at most 10 students. Reports require a review of the existing material (books, scientific papers, articles, ...), with all such material duly collected, analyzed, cited. The reports are organized in homogeneous chapters, where each student is required to be responsible for at least one chapter (that is, a report needs to have at least as many chapters as students), which requires serious and thorough group work. Typical chapters explore the different aspects of the topic, like, if dealing with sport, for instance, basketball, football, volleyball, etc. The report task is given in the first lecture and continues thought the course. At the end of the course, students should present the work. During the presentations, they should carefully listen not only to their teammates but also to other groups team members, because students are asked to grade each other's materials and presentations. Also, the grade should be supported by valuable feedback. While they are listening to each other, they learn new lean applications and can compare with their findings. Each activity is performed under careful supervisor control, to highlight problems, correct students answers and lead the discussion. The example of reports content could be found in Fig. 2.

5 Lean in Snooker **18**
5.1 Rules of Snooker 18
5.2 Create knowledge in Snooker 18
5.3 Deliver fast in Snooker 19
5.4 Respect people in Snooker 19
5.5 Optimize the whole in Snooker 19
5.6 GQM of Snooker 19

6 Lean in Basketball **21**
6.1 Rules of Basketball 21
6.2 Eliminating Waste in Basketball 21
6.2.1 Physical waste 21
6.2.2 Managerial waste 22
6.3 Autonomation in Basketball 22
6.4 Knowledge creation in Basketball 22
6.4.1 Agile NBA framework 22

Fig. 2. Reports content example

6.2 Projects

As mentioned earlier, non-invasive measurement is one of the LSD pillars. Even qualitative and subjective measures are more effective than no measures. For instance, in our life we live with qualitative measures. Consider how we select restaurants, or even how we hire people. In these processes there are indeed quantities components, but the core of the measure is qualitative and subjective. To introduce the concept of non-invasive measurement we use Innometrics [6], that helps students improve their performance by comparing their current metrics with the previous ones. The project assignment aims at supporting the most motivated students, mitigating what Leans defines the waste of unused talent, and it is focused on providing students with real-life problems. The project goal is to contribute to the overall support system for the key foundation of Lean software development: non-invasive measurements. It consists of creating a plug-in for a tool for non-invasively retrieving the actions that the user performs. The project consists of the components, which are expected to be implemented jointly and synergistically, including setting goals, developing a solution, confidently implementing the solution, and thoroughly reviewing the solution. The participants needed not only to provide a working solution but also to perform competent planning, in accordance with lean technologies, the use of lean software methods, for example, building quality. As Lean requires short cycles and regular feedback, the projects are evaluated weekly. Each project includes a review of existing material (books, scientific articles, press articles, websites, news, ...), with all similar materials properly collected, analyzed, cited. In addition, if necessary, an empirical study of the problem should be carried out, including also interviews with key experts in this field. Since the project is designed for practical aspects, it is necessary to develop a suitable set of code and tests in a programming language that depends on the problem that needs to be encountered and must be agreed with the instructor.

6.3 Chapters

As mentioned earlier, the creation and storage of past experience is one of the most important tasks for Lean practitioners. Chapters assignment is one of the mechanisms for implementing this concept in the course. Chapters are intended to systematize the knowledge of the subject. This assignment implies listening in the class, with further reading and presenting the material that students have learned for other people, to enhance the subject understanding. Each next semester contributes to the work that has been in progress in the previous Lean Software Development semesters, spanning this undergraduate class, and also the graduate classes of Metrics and Empirical Methods, and of Advanced Statistics. The book of such chapters is being written in LaTeX, using Overleaf which allows for comfortable writing collaboration. The typical structure of a chapter consists of the motivation of the content of the material in the chapter; presentation of a problem to solve; explanation of the theory underneath, with the justification of every part, using all the required mathematical infrastructure; solution of the originally posed problem; proposition and solution of other similar problems (at least 2). As the course evolves over time, students are welcome to find any inconsistency or extend the material including examples and solutions by themselves. The Chapters found wide application in the student community, as they are not only a repository of established paradigms and theories, but also practical knowledge and skills that are constantly improving, and are in accordance with the current demands of both industry and students. The Chapters are a part of the realization Experience Factory in the course, which is a crucial element of lean environment.

6.4 Simulation Games

The concept of using simulations games for teaching Lean basis becomes popular nowadays popular nowadays, and the literature describing such cases is rich, e.g. [25,41,59]. A variety of simulation games have proved to be efficient, e.g. [60], so we decided to apply Paper Planes simulation in the course. Paper Planes [21] is a collaborative hands-on learning experience used to introduce lean software development main concepts. It requires to engage in production of paper planes within time-boxed intervals and iterations, using different ways of process management, from craft way of production till the lean process establishment. The main focus of the simulation is on the iterative, incremental delivery model within changing requirements environment and tight time frames, which look like real-life situations. A professor or a TA who performs as a facilitator, simulates the role of a customer, providing requirements on each iteration, or even changing them during one iteration. The facilitator at the start of each iteration describes the rules and watches time. The simulation usually includes no more than three iterations and lasts around two hours. At the start of each iteration, teams have a planning stage, and then on completion of production - a reflection stage, when, guided by the facilitator, students identify production problems, discuss possible solutions, make decisions how those problems will be resolved, and implement those solutions in the next iteration. The simulation, while putting participants in real-life product creation conditions, allows us to introduce the students with the concepts and show the reasoning behind main lean principles in a short two hours time frame. The workshop helps students make the connection between the new concepts and previous learning experiences, build on their previous knowledge and see successful examples of new concepts implementation. Besides, it helps to reaffirm their confidence by practicing their newly acquired knowledge in their own production project. This instructional approach helps bridge the gap between what the students are learning and what they will experience in the real world. Hence, it is likely to better prepare the students for assisting companies to improve the profitability of manufacturing companies, thus help advance the manufacturing industry.

6.5   GQM

The GQM approach was introduced by Basili and Weiss [5], around 1984. From this point on, it becomes one of the most recognizable and widely used methodologies. We use GQM in the course in several perspectives. The way it is used from the course designers perspective is described in Chapter 5. Course Design, of the current paper. For students - GQM allows to control the process of achieving their goals while studying one of the Lean software development pillars. There are two types of GQM assignments that should be performed and continuously updated by the students - Global or Overall, and Weekly. Both GQMs should consist of Goals, Questions, and Metrics, as it is proposed by the methodology designers. In the Overall GQM, students list all their goals, present corresponding goals refining questions, and goal achievement metrics for the whole semester when the course is taught. Since clear articulation of feasible goals and the control of the process a big Overall goal achievement is a challenging task, each week students break down their global goals, set metrics and measures for a week to control the process of achieving the goals within a small timeframe - the activity is called Weekly GQM. By Weekly GQM students can constantly improve their goals statements, refine questions, accept or reject selected metrics while checking achieved results. Moreover, they find out whether metrics are really aligned with their goals, and if their goals really represent their wishes. Goal achievement progress is evaluated through weekly grading and feedback from a course instructor. Since each Weekly GQM has to be completed before each lab session, students get their grading and feedback during the lab session, which allows for their continuous improvement. There is an ongoing tradition of presenting GQM during student lab sessions. Presentations are made to elicit feedback from students' teammates and get a different perspective on their work. During such presentations, students discuss the applicability of the selected indicators and their suitability, give their suggestions and share knowledge and experience. In this assignment, it is not the content of a goal or a metric that is evaluated, but rather students' ability to follow the GQM framework for goals setting, refining and designing appropriate achievement metrics.

For example, if some student states as a goal to "improve his English", but the only metric they suggest is "the number of pages of an English book I have read today", the course instructor will request to refine the goal and will guide such student through the Goal-Question-Metric refinement process. Metrics should be highly related to the Goals and should show the progress of achieving the Goals. In this particular case, the refined Goal was worded like "to extend English vocabulary", and the metric became - "the number of new words, the translation of which I don't know yet, per page". The most rewarding outcome of the course for us as practitioners, is that students point out the high value of using GQM for everyday life and continue using it after the course.

7   Conclusion

The article describes an approach of using non-programming methods to teach lean software development, a course, that having been taught for three years, regularly receives an average of more than 4.5 out of 5 points from students evaluations. Despite the fact that the basic structure remains unchanged, it is constantly evolving, from course to course, from student to student, making content more friendly for students, replacing the old obsolete with a new one in demand. We showed our experience, and we hope that it will inspire practitioners to use such approach in their instructional practice for the benefit of their students.

Acknowledgments. We thank Innopolis University for generously sponsoring these studies.

References

1. Basili, V.R.: Quantitative evaluation of software methodology. Technical report, TR-1519, Department of Computer Science, University of Maryland, College Park (1985)
2. Basili, V.R.: The experience factory and its relationship to other improvement paradigms. In: Sommerville, I., Paul, M. (eds.) ESEC 1993. LNCS, vol. 717, pp. 68–83. Springer, Heidelberg (1993). https://doi.org/10.1007/3-540-57209-0_6
3. Basili, V.R., Caldiera, G., Rombach, H.D., Marciniak, J.J.: Encyclopedia of Software Engineering, vol. 1. Wiley, New York (1994)
4. Basili, V.R., Caldiera, G., Rombach, D.H.: The Goal Question Metric Approach. Wiley, Hoboken (1994)
5. Basili, V., Weiss, D.: A methodology for collecting valid software engineering data. IEEE Trans. Softw. Eng. SE. **10**(6), 728–738 (1984)

6. Bykov, A., et al.: A new architecture and implementation strategy for non-invasive software measurement systems. In: Proceedings of the 33rd Annual ACM Symposium on Applied Computing, SAC 2018, pp. 1832–1839. Association for Computing Machinery, New York (2018)
7. Chatley, R., Field, T.: Lean learning - applying lean techniques to improve software engineering education. In: 2017 IEEE/ACM 39th International Conference on Software Engineering: Software Engineering Education and Training Track (ICSE-SEET), pp. 117–126 (2017)
8. Chatley, R., Field, T.: Lean learning: applying lean techniques to improve software engineering education. In: Proceedings of the 39th International Conference on Software Engineering: Software Engineering and Education Track, ICSE-SEET 2017, pp. 117–126. IEEE Press (2017)
9. Clark, J., et al.: Selecting components in large COTS repositories. J. Syst. Softw. **73**(2), 323–331 (2004)
10. Collins, C.: English Dictionary – Complete & Unabridged, 10th edn. HarperCollins (2009). (December 2013)
11. Coman, I.D., Robillard, P.N., Sillitti, A., Succi, G.: Cooperation, collaboration and pair-programming: field studies on backup behavior. J. Syst. Softw. **91**, 124–134 (2014)
12. Corral, L., Georgiev, A.B., Sillitti, A., Succi, G.: A method for characterizing energy consumption in Android smartphones. In: 2nd International Workshop on Green and Sustainable Software (GREENS 2013), pp. 38–45. IEEE, May 2013
13. Corral, L., Georgiev, A.B., Sillitti, A., Succi, G.: Can execution time describe accurately the energy consumption of mobile apps? An experiment in Android. In: Proceedings of the 3rd International Workshop on Green and Sustainable Software, pp. 31–37. ACM (2014)
14. Corral, L., Sillitti, A., Succi, G.: Software assurance practices for mobile applications. Computing **97**(10), 1001–1022 (2015)
15. Corral, L., Sillitti, A., Succi, G., Garibbo, A., Ramella, P.: Evolution of mobile software development from platform-specific to web-based multiplatform paradigm. In: Proceedings of the 10th SIGPLAN Symposium on New Ideas, New Paradigms, and Reflections on Programming and Software, Onward! 2011, pp. 181–183. ACM, New York (2011)
16. Deming, W.E.Q.: Productivity, and competitive position. Massachusetts Institute of Technology, Centre for Advanced Engineering Study (MIT-CAES), Cambridge (1982)
17. Di Bella, E., Sillitti, A., Succi, G.: A multivariate classification of open source developers. Inf. Sci. **221**, 72–83 (2013)
18. Dinis-Carvalho, J., Fernandes, S.: Students role in the implementation of a lean teaching and learning models. In: Proceedings of the PAEE/ALE 2016, 8th International Symposium on Project Approaches in Engineering, Guimaraes, July, pp. 6–8, 284–293 (2016)
19. Dinis-Carvalho, J., Fernandes, S.R., Filho, J.: Combining lean teaching and learning with eduScrum. Int. J. Six Sigma Competitive Adv. **10**, 221 (2017)
20. Fitzgerald, B., Kesan, J.P., Russo, B., Shaikh, M., Succi, G.: Adopting Open Source Software: A Practical Guide. The MIT Press, Cambridge (2011)
21. Heintz, J.: Agile Airplane Game, Gist Labs (2016). Accessed 9 May 2018
22. Hoda, R.: Using agile games to invigorate agile and lean software development learning in classrooms. In: Parsons, D., MacCallum, K. (eds.) Agile and Lean Concepts for Teaching and Learning, pp. 391–414. Springer, Singapore (2019). https://doi.org/10.1007/978-981-13-2751-3_18

23. Janes, A., Succi, G.: Lean Software Development in Action. Springer, Heidelberg (2014). https://doi.org/10.1007/978-3-642-00503-9

24. Järvi, A., Taajamaa, V., Hyrynsalmi, S.: Lean software startup – an experience report from an entrepreneurial software business course. In: Fernandes, J.M., Machado, R.J., Wnuk, K. (eds.) ICSOB 2015. LNBIP, vol. 210, pp. 230–244. Springer, Cham (2015). https://doi.org/10.1007/978-3-319-19593-3_21

25. Johnson, T., Fesler, J.: Teaching Lean Manufacturing Principles in a Capstone Course with a Simulation Workshop Paper presented at Annual Conference, Nashville, Tennessee, June 2003

26. Kivi, J., Haydon, D., Hayes, J., Schneider, R., Succi, G.: Extreme programming: a university team design experience. In: 2000 Canadian Conference on Electrical and Computer Engineering. Conference Proceedings. Navigating to a New Era (Cat. No.00TH8492), vol. 2, pp. 816–820, May 2000

27. Kovács, G.L., Drozdik, S., Zuliani, P., Succi, G.: Open source software for the public administration. In: Proceedings of the 6th International Workshop on Computer Science and Information Technologies, October 2004

28. Kregel, I.: Kaizen in university teaching: continuous course improvement. Int. J. Lean Six Sigma **10**(4), 975–991 (2019). https://doi.org/10.1108/IJLSS-08-2018-0090

29. Marino, G., Succi, G.: Data structures for parallel execution of functional languages. In: Odijk, E., Rem, M., Syre, J.-C. (eds.) PARLE 1989. LNCS, vol. 366, pp. 346–356. Springer, Heidelberg (1989). https://doi.org/10.1007/3-540-51285-3_51

30. Maurer, F., Succi, G., Holz, H., Kötting, B., Goldmann, S., Dellen, B.: Software process support over the internet. In: Proceedings of the 21st International Conference on Software Engineering, ICSE 1999. ACM, May 1999

31. Moser, R., Pedrycz, W., Succi, G.: A comparative analysis of the efficiency of change metrics and static code attributes for defect prediction. In: Proceedings of the 30th International Conference on Software Engineering, ICSE 2008, pp. 181–190. ACM (2008)

32. Moser, R., Pedrycz, W., Succi, G.: Analysis of the reliability of a subset of change metrics for defect prediction. In: Proceedings of the Second ACM-IEEE International Symposium on Empirical Software Engineering and Measurement, ESEM 2008, pp. 309–311. ACM (2008)

33. Musílek, P., Pedrycz, W., Sun, N., Succi, G.: On the sensitivity of COCOMO II software cost estimation model. In: Proceedings of the 8th International Symposium on Software Metrics, METRICS 2002, pp. 13–20. IEEE Computer Society, June 2002

34. Paulson, J.W., Succi, G., Eberlein, A.: An empirical study of open-source and closed-source software products. IEEE Trans. Softw. Eng. **30**(4), 246–256 (2004)

35. Pedrycz, W., Russo, B., Succi, G.: A model of job satisfaction for collaborative development processes. J. Syst. Softw. **84**(5), 739–752 (2011)

36. Pedrycz, W., Russo, B., Succi, G.: Knowledge transfer in system modeling and its realization through an optimal allocation of information Granularity. Appl. Soft Comput. **12**(8), 1985–1995 (2012)

37. Pedrycz, W., Succi, G.: Genetic granular classifiers in modeling software quality. J. Syst. Softw. **76**(3), 277–285 (2005)

38. Petrinja, E., Sillitti, A., Succi, G.: Comparing OpenBRR, QSOS, and OMM assessment models. In: Ågerfalk, P., Boldyreff, C., González-Barahona, J.M., Madey, G.R., Noll, J. (eds.) OSS 2010. IAICT, vol. 319, pp. 224–238. Springer, Heidelberg (2010). https://doi.org/10.1007/978-3-642-13244-5_18

39. Poppendieck, M., Poppendieck, T.: Lean software development: an agile toolkit. Addison-Wesley Prof. **13**, 321–15078 (2003)
40. Poppendieck, M., Poppendieck, T.: Implementing Lean Software Development: From Concept to Cash. The Addison-Wesley Signature Series. Addison-Wesley Professional (2006)
41. Hoda, R.: Using agile games to invigorate agile and lean software development learning in classrooms. In: Parsons, D., MacCallum, K. (eds.) Agile and Lean Concepts for Teaching and Learning, pp. 391–414. Springer, Singapore (2019). https://doi.org/10.1007/978-981-13-2751-3_18
42. Ralph, B.: Experience Management: Foundations, Development Methodology, and Internet-Based Applications, vol. 2432. Springer, Heidelberg (2002). https://doi.org/10.1007/3-540-45759-3
43. Ronchetti, M., Succi, G., Pedrycz, W., Russo, B.: Early estimation of software size in object-oriented environments a case study in a CMM level 3 software firm. Inf. Sci. **176**(5), 475–489 (2006)
44. Rossi, B., Russo, B., Succi, G.: Modelling failures occurrences of open source software with reliability growth. In: Ågerfalk, P., Boldyreff, C., González-Barahona, J.M., Madey, G.R., Noll, J. (eds.) OSS 2010. IAICT, vol. 319, pp. 268–280. Springer, Heidelberg (2010). https://doi.org/10.1007/978-3-642-13244-5_21
45. Rossi, B., Russo, B., Succi, G.: Adoption of free/libre open source software in public organizations: factors of impact. Inf. Technol. People **25**(2), 156–187 (2012)
46. Sawhney, R., et al.: Teaching sustainable lean: the next step towards inculcating a critical problem-solving mindset. In: Alves, A.C., Kahlen, F.-J., Flumerfelt, S., Siriban-Manalang, A.B. (eds.) Lean Engineering for Global Development, pp. 61–94. Springer, Cham (2019). https://doi.org/10.1007/978-3-030-13515-7_3
47. Scotto, M., Sillitti, A., Succi, G., Vernazza, T.: A relational approach to software metrics. In: Proceedings of the 2004 ACM Symposium on Applied Computing, SAC 2004, pp. 1536–1540. ACM (2004)
48. Scotto, M., Sillitti, A., Succi, G., Vernazza, T.: A non-invasive approach to product metrics collection. J. Syst. Architect. **52**(11), 668–675 (2006)
49. Sillitti, A., Janes, A., Succi, G., Vernazza, T.: Measures for mobile users. In: Al-Ani, B., Arabnia, H.R., Mun, Y. (eds.) Proceedings of the International Conference on Software Engineering Research and Practice (SERP), vol. 1. CSREA Press, Las Vegas (2003)
50. Sillitti, A., Janes, A., Succi, G., Vernazza, T.: Non-invasive measurement of the software development process. In: Orso, A., Porter, A. (ed.) Proceedings of the International Workshop on Remote Analysis and Measurement of Software Systems (RAMSS). IEEE, Portland (2003)
51. Sillitti, A., Janes, A., Succi, G., Vernazza, T.: Measures for mobile users: an architecture. J. Syst. Archit. **50**(7), 393–405 (2004)
52. Sillitti, A., Succi, G., Vlasenko, J.: Understanding the impact of pair programming on developers attention: a case study on a large industrial experimentation. In: Proceedings of the 34th International Conference on Software Engineering, ICSE 2012, pp. 1094–1101. IEEE Press, Piscataway, June 2012
53. Sillitti, A., Vernazza, T., Succi, G.: Service oriented programming: a new paradigm of software reuse. In: Gacek, C. (ed.) ICSR 2002. LNCS, vol. 2319, pp. 269–280. Springer, Heidelberg (2002). https://doi.org/10.1007/3-540-46020-9_19
54. Stone, K.: Four decades of lean: a systematic literature review. Int. J. Lean Six Sigma **3**(2), 112–132 (2012)

55. Succi, G., Benedicenti, L., Vernazza, T.: Analysis of the effects of software reuse on customer satisfaction in an RPG environment. IEEE Trans. Softw. Eng. **27**(5), 473–479 (2001)
56. Succi, G., Paulson, J., Eberlein, A.: Preliminary results from an empirical study on the growth of open source and commercial software products. In: EDSER-3 Workshop, pp. 14–15 (2001)
57. Succi, G., Pedrycz, W., Marchesi, M., Williams, L.: Preliminary analysis of the effects of pair programming on job satisfaction. In: Proceedings of the 3rd International Conference on Extreme Programming (XP), pp. 212–215, May 2002
58. Sugimori, Y., Kusunoki, K., Cho, F., Uchikawa, S.: Toyota production system and Kanban system: materialisation of just-in-time and respect-for-human system. Int. J. Prod. Res. **15**(6), 553–564 (1977)
59. Terelak-Tymczyna, A., Biniek, A., Nowak, M.: The use of simulation games in teaching lean manufacturing. In: Hamrol, A., Kujawińska, A., Barraza, M.F.S. (eds.) MANUFACTURING 2019. LNME, pp. 358–369. Springer, Cham (2019). https://doi.org/10.1007/978-3-030-18789-7_30
60. Burch, V., Reuben, F., Smith, B.: Using simulation to teach lean methodologies and the benefits for Millennials. Total Qual. Manag. Bus. Excellence **30**(3–4), 320–334 (2019)
61. Valerio, A., Succi, G., Fenaroli, M.: Domain analysis and framework-based software development. SIGAPP Appl. Comput. Rev. **5**(2), 4–15 (1997)
62. Basili, V., Caldiera, G., McGarry, F., Pajerski, R., Page, G., Waligora, S.: The software engineering laboratory - an operational software experience factory, pp. 370–381 (1992)
63. Vernazza, T., Granatella, G., Succi, G., Benedicenti, L., Mintchev, M.: Defining metrics for software components. In: Proceedings of the World Multiconference on Systemics, Cybernetics and Informatics, vol. XI, pp. 16–23, July 2000
64. Womack, J., Jones, D., Roos, D.: The Machine that Changed the World. Free Press, New York (1990)

Teaching Theoretical Computer Science at Innopolis University

Manuel Mazzara[✉]

Innopolis University, Innopolis, Russian Federation
m.mazzara@innopolis.ru

Abstract. Innopolis is a new IT city incorporating a technopark and a university, aiming at prioritizing the development of IT and software engineering in Tatarstan and in the Russian Federation. Innopolis University (IU) is a young university pioneering several research and pedagogical projects and experiments with innovative teaching methods and curricula. This paper describes the experience of teaching a Theoretical Computer Science course at the bachelor level in a practice-oriented institution.

1 Introduction

Innopolis University (IU) [1] is a young and ambitious university in Tartarstan in the Russian Federation, which has a strong focus on education, and scientific research in the field of IT and robotics [13]. It is located in the newly created Innopolis City (near the capital city Kazan) which also comprises ICT companies and the Innopolis Special Economic Zone. Innopolis aims to be the major Russian IT hub. In its development the University was trying to follow the main trends of IT education borrowed from the world's leading higher education institutions.

Innopolis University was founded in year 2012 and started his pilot bachelor program in 2014. A brief history of the university and its internationalization trajectory cand be found in [12]. The initial curriculum was based on a limited number of core courses complemented by electives. While core courses were mostly thought by full staff faculty, electives were mostly run by visiting professors. As a first full time faculty member of the university I was in charge of the course of Theoretical Computer Science as part of the basic curriculum. The university is a practice-oriented university meant to produce highly qualified specialists mostly for the local market. The only apparent contradiction between the focus of the university and the name of the course have been solved via specific design decisions and refined over the years thanks to students and colleagues' feedback.

The Lecturer
As a founding faculty I had the privilege and duty to choose and being assigned to design and teach *Theoretical Computer Science*. As part of the start-up period

J.-M. Bruel et al. (Eds.): FISEE 2019, LNCS 12271, pp. 60–70, 2020.
https://doi.org/10.1007/978-3-030-57663-9_5

of Innopolis I have also spent two months at ETH Zurich [4] in order to collect material, study and prepare three courses, including this one. My profile was particularly suitable for this subject given my research experience in formal methods and concurrency theory [16], formal specification and service modelling and reconfiguration [5,10,14,15,17,18].

Course Objectives

A good software developer ignorant of how the mechanics of a compiler works is not better than a good pilot when it comes to fix the engine and he will definitively not be able to provide more than average solutions to the problems he is employed to solve. Like automotive engineering teach us, races can only be won by the right synergy of a good driving style and mechanics. Most importantly, limits of computation cannot be ignored in the same way we precisely know how accelerations, forces and frictions prevent us from racing at an unlimited speed. The course investigates the prerequisites to understand compilers functioning. Although the act of compilation appears deceptively simple to most of the modern developers, great minds and results are behind the major achievements that made this possible. All starts with the Epimenides paradox (about 600 BC), which emphasizes a problem of self-reference in logic and brings us to the short time window between WWI and WW2 when, in 1936, Alan Turing proved that a general procedure to identify algorithm termination simply does not exist. Another major milestone has been reached by Noam Chomsky in 1956 with his description of a hierarchy of grammars. In this long historical timeframe we can put most of the bricks with which we build modern compilers. The course will be an historical tour through the lives of some of the greatest minds who ever lived on this planet.

Mathematics and Beauty

The first lecture is an opening on mathematics, nature and art. We introduce students to the importance of mathematics starting from geometry and sacred architecture using as an example the golden ratio and how it has been used in innumerable contexts in history, for example like in Fig. 1, the Bramante Staircase of the Vatican Museum.

The opening has been designed with the idea to be unconventional on one hand, and on the line of science popularization on the other hand. It has the ability to attract attention since the early minutes of the first lecture.

Outline

In this article, we discuss the design of the course, its delivery and successive refinements. After this introduction the paper is structured as follows: Sect. 2 describes the basic design ideas behind the course; Sect. 3 defines the material that it is presented and how; Sect. 4 provides information about yearly feedback

Fig. 1. The Opening - a jump into beauty and mathematics

and to what changes this led; Sect. 5 discusses the idea of Guest Lectures and why they are important; Sect. 6 describes the way we assess students while Sect. 7 offers a view on the future potential developments of the course.

2   Solving the Apparent Paradox

Innopolis University had since the beginning a strong orientation to practice. During the original curriculum design, for which I was responsible with some colleagues, the attention was on how important is fundamental knowledge. Bachelor students may not appreciate it at the early stages of their careers, but strong foundations will eventually bring advantages also in terms of employment. There was agreement that "Theoretical Computer Science" had to be part of the core bachelor curriculum since 2014.

After the decision at the curriculum committee level, the details were moved to the instructor level for the syllabus design, in this specific case myself. The challenge was to design a course from an engineering point of view emphasizing practical application. There are three major software artifacts that are paradigmatic examples of how theory and mathematics are applied in practice in computer science:

- Operating Systems (OS)
- Database Management Systems (DBMS)
- Compilers

If we want to be more specific, we can add to this list theorem provers, and perhaps type checkers, although they may be included as part of compilers.

We will not here discuss Operating Systems, algorithms and DBMS, but only compilers, that originally were however intended as integral part of Operating Systems. Compilers are a perfect example of how theory is fundamental to create artifacts that simplify people's life, here in particular developers' life.

Furthermore, this course also offers the possibility for students to practice rigorous formalization of ideas and principles that is fundamental, for example, in requirements engineering where they will need to be the communication channel between humans, maybe specialists of different disciplines, and machines.

The course is very much practice-based with programming assignments and tries to limit the use of heavy mathematical notation whenever possible, and always introducing concepts via intuition and examples, as detailed later in this paper.

3   Content and Delivery

The course since the beginning has been organized in three parts:

- Automata and Models of Computation
- Formal Grammars and Chomsky's Hierarchy
- Computability

The material does not follow specifically any textbook being a digest of the lecturer of various sources. This on one hand gives an advantage to students that could follow the course slides and find the major highlights and pointers; on the other hand students not attending non-mandatory classes may have problems in retrieving studying material, and often there have been questions about how to find specific concepts in some textbook. Although there is no textbook covering the material in the same way, clearly the course content is somehow the one commonly thought in similar courses and in good recommended textbooks such are [11] and [8].

Course Organization
The course has been organized initially as lectures only (4 h/week), then lectures and labs (2 + 2 h/week) and finally as lectures, tutorials and labs (2 + 2 + 2 h/week). Lectures introduce new concepts, tutorials show at the whiteboard, after lectures, exercises solved by the teacher, labs involve students in smaller groups (maximum 30) to engage solving the exercises. The duration of a semester is 15 weeks, followed by 3 weeks of exams sessions.

Team
The teaching team is generally composed by a Principal Instructor, a Tutorials Instructor and a number of Teaching Assistants (TAs), which depends on the enrollment of that specific year. Typically an enrollment is of about 150 students

organized in 6 different groups, since by regulation a group cannot be larger than 30 students. Contractually TAs have to teach a number of groups, and typically they teach 2 groups in the same course. A teaching team has therefore an average of 3 TAs.

Approach to Delivery

Here we will show how the topics are typically introduced. Each aspect is always presented following the scheme refined over the years:

– Intuition
– Example
– Formalization

The power of mathematical notation is synthesis; however, if intuition and examples are missing the notation may become hard to understand and may completely lose the simplifying power. As an example we show here a simple, but potentially cumbersome, topic as Finite State Automata (FSA) is presented in the course. Figure 2 is a slide introducing the idea using the game Pac-Man and explaining as how the behavior of the ghosts in the game can be modelled with an FSA. Figure 3 present some FSA in their diagrammatic notation. This notation is also a formal notation, but somehow more digestible that the formalization presented in Fig. 4 where we start presenting the formalization of the concepts in a synthetic manner.

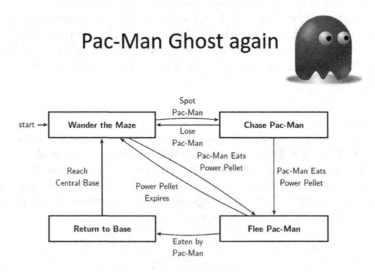

Fig. 2. Intuition

Simple examples
T
On
Off
T
What are these two FSAs modelling?
S
R
R
On
Off
S

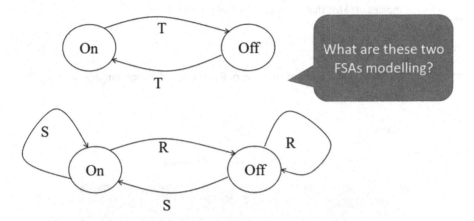

Fig. 3. Example

Course Conclusion

The last lecture of the course covers the major impossibility results of Computability and Computer Science, i.e. *Rice Theorem*, following the same approach formal vs informal (see Fig. 5 and Fig. 6).

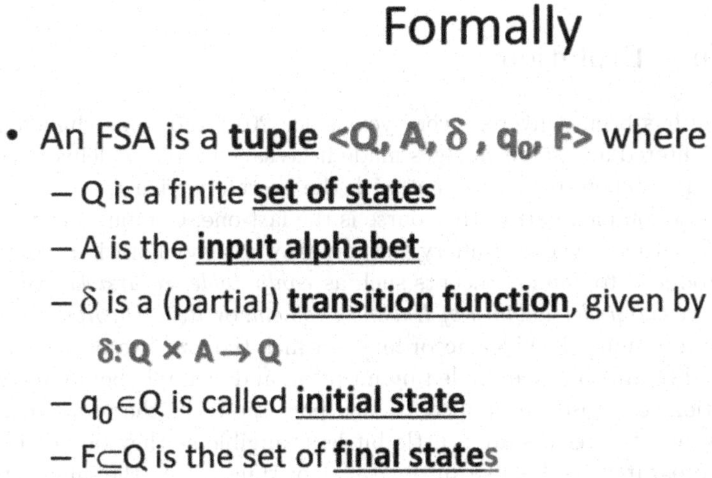

Formally
• An FSA is a tuple <Q, A, δ, q0, F> where
– Q is a finite set of states
– A is the input alphabet
– δ is a (partial) transition function, given by
δ: Q × A → Q
– q0∈Q is called initial state
– F⊆Q is the set of final states

Fig. 4. Formalization

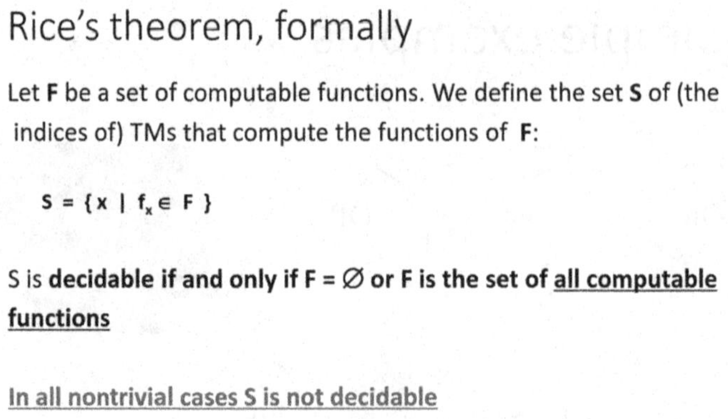

Rice's theorem, formally

Let **F** be a set of computable functions. We define the set **S** of (the indices of) TMs that compute the functions of **F**:

$$S = \{ x \mid f_x \in F \}$$

S is **decidable if and only if F = $\emptyset$ or F is the set of <u>all computable functions</u>**

<u>In all nontrivial cases S is not decidable</u>

Fig. 5. Rice Theorem - Formal

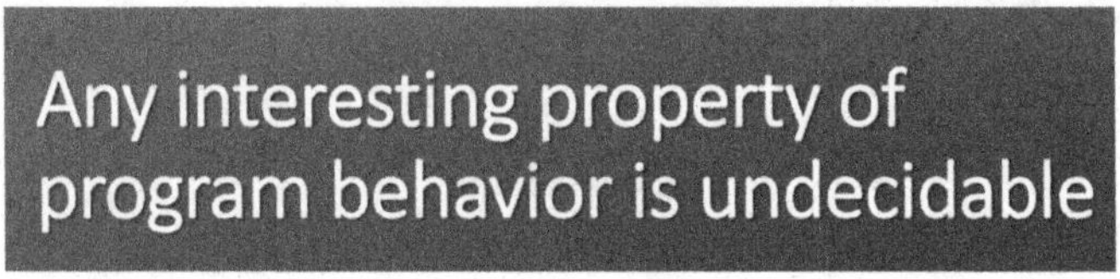

Any interesting property of program behavior is undecidable

Fig. 6. Rice Theorem - Informal

Rice theorem is presented as the key impossibility result around which Software Verification has to work presenting approximate solutions, i.e. with false positive and false negatives, to problems that cannot have a precise solution.

4   Course Evolution

The course has been delivered every year since 2014 and some challenges have been encountered and some changes made necessary to better deliver the material and better integrate the content with the overall curricula.

The most complex part of the course is the last one, Computability. There is a complex mathematical machinery and somehow a heavy notation that requires to be introduced to define concepts such as *computable, recursively enumerable* and to prove the *undecidability of Halting Problem*, or *Rice Theorem* by a *diagonalization* technique. The idea according to which the first two parts (Automata Theory and Grammars) can be led by intuition and example before introducing any notation, can also be applied to this part, however the ideas behind the definitions and the results are a little bit less tangible as they do not belong to everyday programmers' life like automata, algorithms and to the same extent formal grammars (think of, for example, regular expressions). This section requires to slowly introduce a mathematical machinery supported by intuition, but also requires students to pay attention and be sufficiently patient to figure out how these ideas really apply into practice. The course leads a student to understand

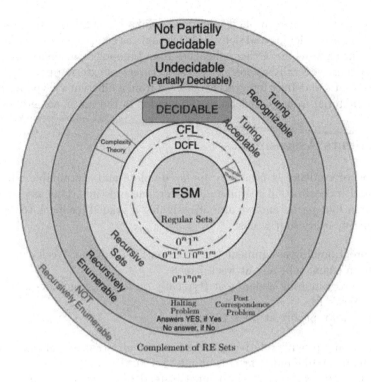

Fig. 7. Overview of the course

languages inclusion and relationship with formal Chomsky Hierarchy and models of computation as shown in Fig. 7.

The most significant change we have introduced over the year is going from essays and presentations-based assignment to programming assignments. We understood that, even in a theoretical course, it is better to keep alive the coding practice. This approach has received more interest from students than the previous one were we were asking to write an essay on a theoretical topic and present it. Programming assignments are connected to theoretical topics, such as writing an FSA simulator, and help students in familiarising with concepts through a form of gamification. Another refinement of the course based on gamification has been the introduction of weekly quizzed based on *Kahoot!* were students can play and compete and receive extra points at the end of the semester.

5 Guest Lectures

One of the common traits that characterized the course since the beginning is hosting one or two classes from an external lecturer. Often this lecturer has been Bertrand Meyer [3] who has a great experience of compilers construction, formal methods and Software Engineering. At times other lecturers delivered additional content, for example Daniel de Carvalho [2] who has extensive experience in Lambda-calculus and delivered this topic as complementary equivalent model to Turing Machine. Other colleagues from Innopolis University also intervened. Students generally appreciate guest lecturers as external participants to the course that can deliver integrative material from a different viewpoint. Sometimes the material from guest lectures is included in the exam, sometimes not.

6   Students Assessment

Evaluation of students is necessary for a complete and sustainable education process and its realization requires also attention and time. Our assessment is organized in four parts, and we aim at assigning a graded feedback to students approximately every four weeks:

- First programming assignment (typically on FSA): due at Week 4
- Mid-term exam: typically at week 7 or 8
- Second programming assignment (typically on formal grammars or regexp): due at Week 12
- Final exam: typically at week 16 or 17

We generally provide relative grading via normalization. Usually the passing level is about 90/100 and A level is about 85/100.

The first two editions of the course instead of programming assignments had essays on topical Computer Science paper with related public presentation. This was a valuable activity, but at some point we preferred to integrate the acquisition of theoretical concepts with the development of programming skills. This move was generally well taken by both student and teaching team.

7   Towards the Future

Innopolis University is now in its seventh year and reached a students population of about 800 with 300 employees of which about 30 faculty members and teaching and research stuff up to 80 people. On top of this there is a unit for commercial Research and Development with about 120 employees. The city of Innopolis itself has about 6000 inhabitants. The numbers of development in the first seven years are impressive.

Innopolis has an extensively developed network of international institutions collaborating under different forms: students exchange, Erasmus+, visiting professors, joint PhD supervision and joint projects. One of the collaborative projects sees as partners CERN and Newcastle university [6, 7] and collaborative PhD supervisions involve several universities including Toulouse, University of Souther Denmark and University of Messina. All these activities dramatically supported the development of the university and, in turn, of the city itself.

What are the further refinements and changes that should be applied to this course and, in general to the university curriculum? Despite the fact the

Theoretical Computer Science is now a well-designed and polished course that received positive feedback from students and colleagues, it is not exempt from the need of further steps of refinement:

- On top of the programming assignments we would like to introduce the use of some tool that can help appreciating mathematical modelling (for example Microsoft Z3 [9]).
- Better alignment with successive course on Compilers Construction.
- Better alignment with prerequisite course on Logic and possibly with Discrete Math.
- An idea for the future is to write a textbook or booklet including the material of lectures, tutorials and labs.

Acknowledgment. It is fundamental here to thank TAs and instructors that helped delivering this course since 2014: Daniel de Carvalho, Mohamed Elwakil, Leonard Johard, Mansur Khazeev, Munir Makhmutov, Ruslan Mustafin, Swati Megha, Alexander Naumchev, Mariya Naumcheva, Larisa Safina, Alexander Tchitchigin and Victor Rivera.

References

1. About IU. https://university.innopolis.ru/en/about/. Accessed 26 Aug 2018
2. Bertrand Meyer on Wikipedia. https://en.wikipedia.org/wiki/Bertrand_Meyer. Accessed 10 Feb 2020
3. de Carvalho, D.: https://scholar.google.com/citations?user=AFRx_0kAAAAJ&hl=fr. Accessed 10 Feb 2020
4. ETH Zurich. https://ethz.ch/en.html. Accessed 12 Feb 2020
5. Abouzaid, F., Mazzara, M., Mullins, J., Qamar, N.: Towards a formal analysis of dynamic reconfiguration in WS-BPEL. Int. Dec. Tech. **7**(3), 213–224 (2013)
6. Bauer, R., et al.: The BioDynaMo project: experience report. In: Advanced Research on Biologically Inspired Cognitive Architectures, pp. 117–125. IGI Global (2017)
7. Breitwieser, L., et al.: The BioDynaMo project: creating a platform for large-scale reproducible biological simulations. In: 4th Workshop on Sustainable Software for Science: Practice and Experiences (WSSSPE4) (2016)
8. Davis, M.D., Sigal, R., Weyuker, E.J.: Computability, Complexity, and Languages. Fundamentals of Theoretical Computer Science, 2nd edn. Academic Press Professional Inc. (1994)
9. de Moura, L., Bjørner, N.: Z3: an efficient SMT solver. In: Ramakrishnan, C.R., Rehof, J. (eds.) TACAS 2008. LNCS, vol. 4963, pp. 337–340. Springer, Heidelberg (2008). https://doi.org/10.1007/978-3-540-78800-3_24
10. Dragoni, N., Mazzara, M.: A formal semantics for the WS-BPEL recovery framework. In: Laneve, C., Su, J. (eds.) WS-FM 2009. LNCS, vol. 6194, pp. 92–109. Springer, Heidelberg (2010). https://doi.org/10.1007/978-3-642-14458-5_6
11. Hopcroft, J., Ullman, J.: Introduction to Automata Theory, Languages, and Computation. Addison-Wesley, Boston (1979)
12. Karapetyan, S., Dolgoborodov, A., Masyagin, S., Mazzara, M., Messina, A., Protsko, E.: Innopolis going global. In: Ciancarini, P., Mazzara, M., Messina, A., Sillitti, A., Succi, G. (eds.) SEDA 2018. AISC, vol. 925, pp. 138–145. Springer, Cham (2020). https://doi.org/10.1007/978-3-030-14687-0_12

13. Kondratyev, D., Tormasov, A., Stanko, T., Jones, R.C., Taran, G.: Innopolis university-a new it resource for Russia. In: 2013 International Conference on Interactive Collaborative Learning (ICL), pp. 841–848, September 2013
14. Mazzara, M., Abouzaid, F., Dragoni, N., Bhattacharyya, A.: Toward design, modelling and analysis of dynamic workflow reconfigurations. In: Carbone, M., Petit, J.-M. (eds.) WS-FM 2011. LNCS, vol. 7176, pp. 64–78. Springer, Heidelberg (2012). https://doi.org/10.1007/978-3-642-29834-9_6
15. Mazzara, M.: Timing issues in web services composition. In: Bravetti, M., Kloul, L., Zavattaro, G. (eds.) EPEW/WS-FM -2005. LNCS, vol. 3670, pp. 287–302. Springer, Heidelberg (2005). https://doi.org/10.1007/11549970_21
16. Mazzara, M.: Towards abstractions for web services composition. Ph.D. thesis, University of Bologna (2006)
17. Mazzara, M., Abouzaid, F., Dragoni, N., Bhattacharyya, A.: Design, modelling and analysis of a workflow reconfiguration. In: International Workshop on Petri Nets and Software Engineering, pp. 10–24 (2011)
18. Salikhov, D., Khanda, K., Gusmanov, K., Mazzara, M., Mavridis, N.: Jolie good buildings: internet of things for smart building infrastructure supporting concurrent apps utilizing distributed microservices. In: CCIT, pp. 48–53 (2016)

Lessons Learnt

Teaching Software Testing to Industrial Practitioners Using Distance and Web-Based Learning

Eduard Paul Enoiu[✉]

Mälardalen University, Västerås, Sweden
eduard.paul.enoiu@mdh.se

Abstract. Software testing is a business-critical process used by private and public organizations and an important source of market competitiveness. Employees of these organizations are facing tough competition and are required to be able to maintain and develop their skills and knowledge in software testing. In the education market, many commercial courses and certifications are available for industrial engineers who wish to improve their skills in software development. Nevertheless, there is a lack of access to world-leading research within the software testing field in these commercial courses that supports the companies' innovation in software testing. As an alternative, universities are approaching this challenge by developing academic courses on software testing that can suit professionals who need to be able to combine work and studies. This study highlights several good approaches and challenges in developing and teaching three distance web-based software testing courses targeting test practitioners. The proposed approaches for enhancing teaching of software testing in an online setting for industrial practitioners are: active participation at the student's pace, inclusion of software testing artifacts from the student's organization as part of assignments, continuous access to online materials, the use of short video materials on testing theory, and setting clear expectations for performing online test design assignments. Finally, several challenges have been identified: poor feedback on assignments, distances between students and teachers, the use of non-realistic assignments and the difficulty for industrial practitioners to complete academic assignments each week. Future work is needed to explore these results in practice, for example on how to shorten distances between students and teachers, as well as how to enhance the inclusion of real-world testing artifacts in course assignments.

Keywords: Software testing education · Web-based learning · Online education · Industrial practitioners · Software engineering education

1 Introduction

Software plays a vital role in our daily lives and can be found in a number of domains, ranging from mobile applications to medical systems. The emergence and wide spread usage of large complex software products has profoundly

© Springer Nature Switzerland AG 2020
J.-M. Bruel et al. (Eds.): FISEE 2019, LNCS 12271, pp. 73–87, 2020.
https://doi.org/10.1007/978-3-030-57663-9_6

influenced the traditional way of testing software. Nowadays, organizations need skilled engineers that should maintain their software testing knowledge throughout their careers. Even if many online courses on software engineering[1] and testing[2] are available from both private and public sectors, there is a lack of evidence on how to design and teach such courses, what particular challenges teachers are facing and how these courses can be improved and tailored to industrial practitioners [11]. Specifically, software testing education [2] is an important aspect of a thorough software engineering education. In these courses, students learn to apply specific test design techniques and technologies for a given software under test.

In this paper we present the results of a longitudinal study on three online software testing academic courses targeting industrial practitioners[3]. We identified several challenges that should be taken into account when designing online courses on software testing: poor feedback on assignments, distances between students and teachers, poorly supported assignments and some industrial practitioner specific challenges. In addition, we identified several good approaches for enhancing the development of online courses in software testing: active participation at the student's convenience and pace, inclusion of software testing artifacts from industrial practice and creation of short video lectures of software testing theory. These results can be used to improve online courses in software testing that can suit industrial practitioners who need to be able to combine work and studies.

2 Software Testing Education

Software testing education is an important aspect of learning software engineering. Education in software testing should ensure the supply of software testing knowledge. Testing is widely considered to be an under-prioritized activity in software and systems development. Courses in testing are providing an understanding of the fundamental problems, as well as practical methods and tools for a systematic state-of-the-art approach to software testing. Books such as the one written by Ammann and Offutt [1] are used in teaching as a pedagogical approach to software testing instruction method in many university courses.

Garousi et al. [8] performed a literature review to map the topic of software-testing education. There are many pedagogical approaches and specific tools used in testing education. For example, Hynninen et al. [13] performed a survey to find out the current state of industry in software testing education. According to their results, some key learning objectives in software testing disciplines can be used to identify the knowledge expectations from university graduates and

---

[1] For example Edx and Coursera offer MOOC-based software engineering courses.

[2] Udemy is one of the providers that offer software testing MOOC courses.

[3] The courses are given within the frameworks of PROMPT (https://www.prompt edu.se/) and FUTURE (https://www.mdh.se/en/malardalen-university/research/research-projects/futuree), cooperation projects between academia and industry with the aim of strengthening competitiveness in Swedish companies.

to align with the industry requirements. Garousi et al. [8] has also identified the ways how to overcome some of these challenges in testing education, including the alignment with industry needs. Nevertheless, there is a lack of distance and online education course offerings for industrial practitioners. In this paper we aim to cover this subject and identify the challenges and good approaches in teaching software testing to industrial practitioners.

3 Moving to Distance and Web-Based Learning for Industrial Practitioners

In the last five years, we have started digitizing campus courses and developing new online courses to be exclusively given to industrial professionals. Working in this new setting involves a close interaction with students using digital tools. Nowadays, teaching has evolved and teachers are adopting blended learning techniques throughout the whole process of giving a course. Similarly to the results outlined in the study of Garrison et al. [9], we acknowledge that exploring and assessing the impact of blended learning is important in bringing more relevant learning experiences in these online courses. In the following sections, we outline three online courses on software testing given at Mälardalen University.

3.1 A Course Module on Advanced Topics in Software Testing

This course developed at Mälardalen University provides an understanding of the fundamental problems, as well as practical methods and tools for a systematic state-of-the-art approach to software testing[4]. After the course, the participants are expected to have an overview knowledge in more advanced testing methods (such as model-based testing, mutation testing and search-based testing), and in the state-of-the-art in software testing research. As shown in Fig. 1, the course is given in a flexible format where the theoretical content, covered in video lectures, is interleaved with practical exercises. The course is divided into five 1.5-credit modules: Introduction to software testing and test design, unit testing, test design and automation, testing at integration and system level, static and dynamic analysis and advanced test design (the course module under investigation).

3.2 Model-Based Testing Course

This online course deals with model-based testing[5], a class of technologies used to assess the quality and correctness of large software systems in a more efficient and effective way than traditional testing methods. Throughout the course the participants learn how to design and use model-based testing tools, how to

---

[4] https://www.promptedu.se/quality-assurance-the-applied-science-of-software-testing.

[5] https://www.promptedu.se/quality-assurance-model-based-testing-in-practice/.

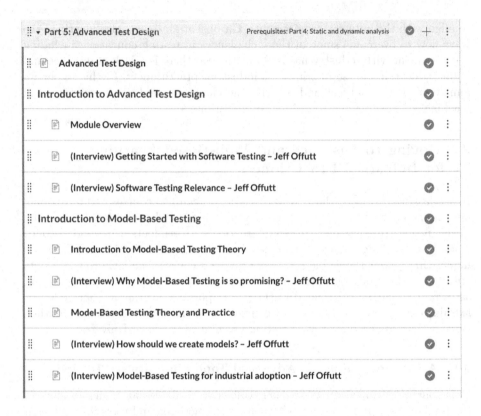

Fig. 1. An overview of the course material as part of the advanced test design module containing video lecturers and interviews with experts.

create realistic models and how to use these models to automate the testing process in their organisation. We developed online material (including recorded videos of certain lectures as shown in Fig. 2) on basic model-based testing terminology, creating models from industrial code, executing model-based tests and how to use model-based testing in practice. After completing the course, the students are expected to have acquired knowledge about models and understand model-based testing, develop practical skills and abilities on applying model-based testing in industrial practice, to test software using model-based testing in structured, organised ways. The students are admitted based on both specific entry requirements for credits in computer science and industrial experience. The students can apply for the course and get their eligibility evaluated based on knowledge acquired in other ways, such as work experience, and other studies.

3.3 Automated Test Generation Course

The automated test generation course is focusing on how to generate tests automatically in the sense that test creation satisfying a given test goal or given

Fig. 2. A video lecture on model-based testing recorded using a campus course set-up.

requirement is performed automatically[6]. This course provides an understanding of automating software testing using program analysis with the goal of intelligently and algorithmically creating tests. The course covers search-based test generation, combinatorial and random testing while highlighting the challenges associated with the use of automatic test generation. The student is learning about how to automatically generate test cases with assertions and to have a working knowledge and experience in static and dynamic generation of tests. The course is using a learning management system based on a discussion forum (as shown in Fig. 3) in which students and teachers collaborate with each other throughout the course.

4   A Longitudinal Study of Developing and Teaching Three Online Courses in Software Testing

We present our experiences from developing and running three online courses (described in Sect. 3) during the last five years. The courses were offered as individual courses focused on flexible learning especially suited for working professionals with a large part of the teaching being web-based.

4.1   Case Study Methodology

Little longitudinal research has examined online teaching in software engineering or software testing. This study helps fill this gap. The approach uses a case

---

[6] https://www.mdh.se/utbildning/fortbildning/ai-och-mjukvaruutveckling/futuree-automated-test-generation.

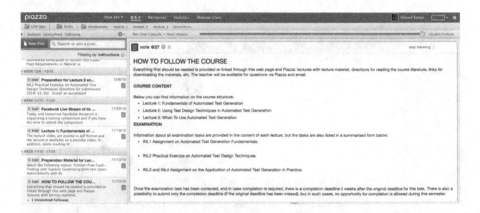

Fig. 3. A view of the forum learning platform used in the automated test generation course.

study design methodology informed by a number of methods from ethnography[7], including the use of repeated surveys, anchored in discussions of artefacts created by the course responsible. We followed the qualitative approach recommended by Calderhead [6] in the form of a case study for gaining insights into teaching through a variety of data collection methods over time. This study was conducted as a multiple case study comprising three individual case studies, each focusing on one of the courses described in Sect. 3. The research questions are: (1) What challenges are affecting online teaching of software testing for industrial practitioners? (2) What good approaches for improving distance and web based learning of software testing are found when teaching industrial practitioners?

This study takes a qualitative approach, focusing on the experiences of the course responsible and incorporating the knowledge of the context and its insights and perceptions, while attempting to better understand online teaching of software testing. The research was undertaken longitudinally to identify and interpret the commonalities in each course instance from spring semester 2015 until spring 2020. Data was collected through analysis of study materials at the end of each course by focusing on learning objectives, learning activities and assessment tasks. No personal data was collected during this process. Data analysis was conducted to generate hypotheses and broader concepts [3] that can be used by both researchers in investigating online teaching as well as by teachers that can include these results in their own courses.

Methodological Approach for Data Collection. As ethnography aims to explore a particular social phenomenon through research methods such as observations, we used this approach for data collection. This allowed the researcher to gather data within the course environment (the context of the study).

---

[7] Ethnography is a research method for gathering data by active participation in the studied phenomenon [14].

We captured and interpreted the experiences of the students. The researcher observed the activities in these course settings, taking handwritten notes. These activities included interactions between the teachers and the learners as well as the development of each course.

Data Analysis. We employed a process of thematic analysis to identify themes emerging from the data set (i.e, researcher's observations and personal reflections). This data was coded manually by grouping data (i.e., in segments of text) under individual codes. These codes were organized into two categories: good approaches and challenges. In addition, from the ensuing categories two other overarching themes emerged: teaching and learning software testing with digital tools and asynchronous communication between students.

4.2   On Teaching and Learning with Digital Tools

In practice, in the three courses under study, we are delivering online content outside of the virtual classroom and students can watch online lectures in advance, have online discussions at home while learning new concepts in the virtual classroom with teacher guidance through step-wise progression. This is achieved by tackling content complexities with digital assignments that support progressive learning [12]. During this longitudinal study we have learned how to use a variety of pedagogical techniques, including the use of visual aids (e.g., dynamic diagrams, interactive slides, videos and audio recordings), virtual group-work, student presentations and use case discussions. In addition, the use of learning platforms such as Piazza[8], Scalable Learning[9] and Canvas[10] is important in using the teaching aids in an efficient and effective manner. We have developed material for online courses, including:

- Course Marketing Material. (e.g., Automated Test Generation[11], Software Testing in the Video Game Industry[12], Software Testing Course[13])
- Audio Podcast. In 2017 we have started a podcast called Testing Habits[14] in which we have conversations with researchers, scientists and technologists about technology transfer, software testing and software engineering research. We have used this audio material in all ongoing courses.
- Video Recordings of Lectures. We have developed video recordings of regular lectures to be used in the flipped classroom method (e.g, Model-Based Software Testing Lecture[15]).

---

[8] https://piazza.com/.
[9] https://www.scalable-learning.com/.
[10] https://www.instructure.com/canvas/higher-education/platform.
[11] https://play.mdh.se/media/0_f1243mpq.
[12] https://www.youtube.com/watch?v=CBIhu_9OolY.
[13] https://www.youtube.com/watch?v=OR63w8Iod9I.
[14] https://podcasts.apple.com/us/podcast/testing-habits/id1255653631.
[15] https://www.youtube.com/watch?v=4fXBrZnj2JU.

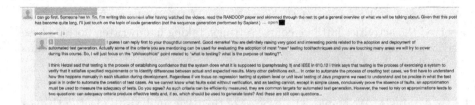

Fig. 4. An example of a synopsis and evaluation conversation during a reading assignment.

– Interviews with Experts. We have developed video interviews with relevant academics to be used during lectures[16]. Voice over Slides Material. Some of the videos we developed are in the form of voice over slides (e.g., Lecture on Requirement based Testing[17]).

   During the last five years we observed that continuous teaching in online courses is a source for the teacher's digital learning evolution. The learning evolves especially when students ask direct questions and through the correction of online assignments. This is part of continuously improving the video lectures and assignments by directly reflecting on how students are able to solve them in an innovative way.

4.3   Asynchronous Communication and Course Assignments

For all three online courses most of the class is taught asynchronously and assignments leverage online educational opportunities to virtually merge students. All groups in these case studies are using the same learning platform, watch the same lectures, and read and discuss testing subjects. One example of such a specific activity is an assignment in which students are summarizing, evaluating and critiquing a certain scientific paper on software testing. In this chosen assignment, one student examines and critiques certain software testing papers while others have the opportunity to critique the original synopsis. A snapshot of a part of such a synopsis is shown in Fig. 4. For the set of papers, each student must submit a simple evaluation. The evaluation should be about a page long and must be posted on the learning platform. Several people will be assigned to write and post a synopsis evaluation for each paper. The synopses should: (1) describe the testing problem, (2) describe the goals of the paper, (3) describe and analyze the testing technique presented or the experimental setup, (4) discuss the results and (5) analyze the industrial applicability. Two students are designated as "skeptics" for each paper and are required to disagree with the posted synopsis and provide reasonable arguments. All students can join in the discussion for each paper throughout this assignment. All postings, including

---

[16] https://www.youtube.com/watch?v=jbrhbnmkyAI.
[17] https://www.youtube.com/watch?v=1pnqEom-xOw.

the reviews are done using the learning platform and all students can join the discussion and read these comments.

Since this assignment is supposed to provide a collaborative learning opportunity and the discussions are asynchronous, the aim is to focus on the learner and not the teacher, implying a more reliable understanding of the content [4]. In this way we aim to directly improve learning by focusing on the outcomes students are meant to deliver during the assignment. This focus opens up different perspectives on how knowledge and learning is transformative in these strict conditions of time and space. One perspective on learning achieved during several assignments during the last five years is related to the theory of collective activities to produce scientific knowledge [16]. Roth and Lee argue that knowledge and learning from scientific articles as a collective praxis process achieve more advanced forms of knowledge than individual could produce. This implies that an assignment that tries to create opportunities for literacy that emerges from a collective activity can be used to develop communities of praxis inside a course. Another highly-related perspective of knowledge and learning relates to Dewey's pragmatism [15]. This is where knowledge takes action form and theories (i.e., papers and reports read by students) become a tool and the application of such a tool (i.e., critique work during the assignment) is producing and reorganizing the experience needed for obtaining more understanding. In addition, we observed during multiple course instances that the chosen assignment relies on the problem-solving abilities of the students involved in this process.

These two perspectives of pragmatism and praxis on this kind of assignments can be used to focus on different aspects of quality in learning and teaching. Since online courses attract larger cohorts, the emerging community contained in some cases unengaged students and lack of interactivity between them. Assignments from this perspective can result in ineffective assessment and relatively limited feedback. To counteract this, some researchers [7] have proposed new engagement strategies for community learning by using more interactive digital content and gamification. Given the environment and online platform used, there are ways in which the pragmatic perspective can support learning and development for this particular assignment. The issue here is that our own experiences in using these assignments are not profound given that the assignment under study has been tested in practice in couple of instances of the course. There is a scant opportunity for improving it, but there is some evidence [18] that more analysis of these experiences together with constructs of pragmatic interactions can be used for a proper analysis. This is especially needed when taking into account that the technology used can influence the context of pragmatic learning.

Our experience is that when designing software testing assignments the teacher interaction and reflection is important when providing learning opportunities for feedback and critical review. We discovered that ceding control of learning and knowledge acquisition to the learner can be formative and encourage community reflection. In the end, our scope is to develop a small community in an online setting which is a challenging proposition in itself since learning is a social process made up of connections between the concepts learned and the other learners in the community. This assignment is constructively aligned with the rest of the course since the other assignments are built on stepwise analysis and reflection by the students. The peer review assignment was used as a method for this particular learning activity and the course is all about learning how to be a tester. The link between the other assignments and this one is strong given that only a successful engagement in the activities and completion of the assessment task can make a student achieve the subsequent individual learning outcomes related to peer review and experimentation.

In addition, the peer review activities used in all three courses can be redesigned and improved using the behaviorist theory of teaching [5]. The idea would be to use both positive and negative reinforcement to shape the online behavior of students by focusing on blended learning. The objective of the redesign should focus on creating a more dynamic community where active participation and teacher reinforcement can be implemented by using awards and gamification aspects through competitions. In these sessions, the community members can realize that they are not alone in experiencing the reinforcements and lead to a sense of trust in the group and their achievements.

4.4   Challenges and Good Approaches

In this section we outline the identified challenges affecting online teaching of software testing for industrial practitioners. In addition, we present several good approaches for improving distance and web based learning of software testing. We collected these results based on our experiences from teaching several instances of these courses in the last five years using an ethnography-based case study and thematic analysis.

The identified challenges are outlined in Table 1. For all three courses we experienced that poor feedback on assignments can influence the progression of the student throughout the course. One recommendation is to define a clear success criteria and how you as a teacher are going to measure it in an online setting. Getting the students to keep going throughout the course, means that the teacher needs to ask for feedback early and give feedback early and often. To address this challenge we used audio and video assignments feedback instead of a traditional source code and tests solution. In this way, the student could rather quickly gather evidence needed to modify the assignment for passing the stated learning outcome.

Another challenge relates to the geographical, social, cultural, and temporal distances that can have an impact on online teaching. These distances are not well studied in the teaching of software testing literature. We experienced concerns from students that factors related to these distances are making communication between teacher and student more difficult. For example, we observed that spoken language in videos affects the communication of different testing theory subjects. In our experience, a way of overcoming this type of distances is to use different tools and techniques such as filming a practical test session in the test environment while performing a certain assignment. However, the use of testing and programming tools can negatively impact learning efficiency.

Table 1. Overview of challenges and recommendations for teachers.

Challenge	Recommendations
1. Poor feedback on assignments	Speed up feedback loops by providing audio or video feedback
2. Distances between students and teachers	Short distances improve online teaching of software testing. Some distances can be mitigated with certain tools
3. Testing topics are not sufficiently explored in certain assignments	Use realistic testing assignments that includes uncontrolled variables which creates the complexity necessary to fully understand the practical testing challenges involved in a certain topic
4. Poorly supported assignments by other teaching means	Assignments need to be clearly connected to the testing-related lecture material, but also to the reading instructions
5. Difficulty for industrial practitioners to complete academic assignments each week	Assignments need to be relevant for the company and the student
6. For industrial practitioners completing the course is not as desirable as it is for regular students	Learning effects are more important and students need to be engaged for visible results throughout the course

The challenge is that these tools may have compatibility distances and may not always work well given that some are used in ways they are not designed for.

Just as in empirical and experimental software research, the use of controlled experiments as assignments where we are able to control all independent variables in order to measure the dependent variables seems needed. The challenge we have faced (Challenge 3 in Table 1) relates to cutting away all that which is not relevant in an assignment, and hence the solution was easier to comprehend. For some classes of testing assignments (e.g., test design techniques theory) we found that this is not a problem, whereas for other more hands-on assignments we found that developing realistic scenarios is a challenge. Our recommendation is to include assignments that contain uncontrolled variables in which the actual complexity is needed to fully understand the practical challenges involved in a testing topic. For example, software testing courses are often taught with a focus on test design techniques and test execution, whereas the real challenges arises from software testing "at large" such as in the case of model-based testing and automated test generation, where intelligent and automated methods need to be used when thousands of new code changes happen per week and ambiguously specified test specifications are used. Clearly, the latter situation calls for different pedagogy methods and more realistic assignments to be created.

Another challenge relates to assignments that are loosely connected to the lectures and the course book. Some students were not able to directly identify the

Table 2. Overview of good approaches and their implications for teachers.

Approach	Recommendations
1. Active participation in teaching at the student's convenience and pace (although within a specified time frame)	Encourage collaboration given that learners are strongly motivated to acquire new testing skills and make professional progress. The learning activities need to be flexible in time, place and form to cater for different learning styles and circumstances among the involved testing practitioners and their companies
2. Inclusion of software and testing artifacts from the student's organization as part of the course assignments	Testing education for professionals with employment in software companies needs context-specific learning elements by choosing situated learning
3. Continuous access to key concepts and online course materials	Motivate your students by providing mandatory and optional materials. Make sure to link all the related material explicitly and throughout the course
4. Video segments on testing theory should be restricted to a few minutes	Human attention span is short and hence your recorded video segments should be restricted to a few minutes (at most 15–30 min)
5. Provide clear expectations together with the needed tools and frameworks needed for performing assignments	Use suitable tools and make sure they can be used by all students given that you communicate clear expectations

material that is required to understand what an assignment is about and how to conduct it. In an online setting, a practitioner has a limited time to perform an assignment. A recommendation for addressing this challenge is to design online assignments that are clearly connected to both the lecture material and also to the reading instructions.

In all three courses we observed that it is more difficult to motivate industry practitioners to continuously perform an academic assignment. As a recommendation, a teacher in software testing needs to design assignments that are relevant for the company and the student. In addition, the assignment needs to contain precise instructions throughout the entire assignment. Another identified challenge relates to industrial practitioners' lack of desire to obtain credits and completing all parts of a course. In our online courses, we observed that obtaining credits and completing the course were not important reasons for performing certain assignments. Some students did not complete a certain assignment on time and drop out of the course. As a recommendation, teachers might not want to maintain strict deadlines during the course.

In addition, we identified several good approaches for online teaching of software testing (shown also in Table 2). A first approach is to encourage active participation by following the actual pace of the student. A second good approach relates to the inclusion of software artifacts from the student's context in the course assignments. This is important, since different learning goals require different ways of teaching and learning. Testing examples and exercises should connect to the students' companies and application domains. A third good approach is focusing on providing, throughout the course, all the material including concept maps as inventories for all course modules. These are powerful tools for outlining and relating key testing concepts. In addition, we included stories since these tend to be remembered better than facts or abstract principles. Given that these courses were separated in modules, we spaced out the study material since, in our experience, this leads to better long-term learning than providing everything in a single module. A fourth good approach identified in several course instances is to make sure that students can actually follow lectures. One should record video segments on software testing theory that are not longer than a few minutes. It is more important to give an easily accessible overview of the testing topic that can continue with an in-depth exercise. In addition, a fifth good approach is to provide clear expectations on each assignment and use tools that can be used easily by all students. It is important that each module has a workload breakdown structure for all expectations per week, including how communication should take place (e.g., in discussion groups).

5   Discussions and Limitations

Overall, the results from this study are obtained using the experiences in teaching software testing in an online setting targeting industrial practitioners in three separate courses. Even if these results are directly related to online education in software testing, some of the listed challenges and good approaches are generic enough and can target any online course. We recommend evaluating these challenges and good approaches in teaching of more software engineering topics. Nevertheless, when developing online courses in software testing one should try to address the challenges of understanding the objectives and details of the testing topics explored in each assignment and how these testing assignments are supported by all the needed instructions and details. Some of the mitigations to the described challenges are already known to other domains [10,17]. This is an indication that these results could be relevant to other software engineering practices, both for an academic and an industrial perspective. For research, the experiences provided in this paper are useful as they bring knowledge from teaching industrial practitioners in an online setting into academia. By understanding that teaching practitioners is not a trivial approach, further research is made possible. We invite other researchers to revisit in other contexts the experienced challenges and good approaches.

Our main aim with this paper is to highlight the themes, challenges and approaches that arose from the development and running of online courses in software testing targeting industrial practitioners. This qualitative approach has produced an understanding of the challenges and good approaches in online teaching of software testing in the industrial context. This approach has its limitations regarding the small sample size of courses used in this analysis and the uni-dimensional collection of observations; therefore, no attempt to generalize the results of this study is made. We hope the findings of this study will stimulate further research on teaching software testing to industrial practitioners in an online setting.

6   Conclusions

This study has illustrated how advanced topics in software testing practice and research can be taught to industrial practitioners. We report several good approaches and challenges in developing and teaching distance web-based courses in three software testing topics: software testing theory of advanced test design, automated test generation and model-based testing. We identified several challenges in online teaching of software testing: poor feedback on practical assignments, distances between students and teachers, poorly supported assignments, and also some industrial practitioner-specific challenges. In addition, we identified several good approaches for improving online courses in software testing: active participation at the student's convenience and pace, inclusion of software artifacts from industrial practice and creation of short video lectures among others. Finally, our results show that more research on online teaching of software testing is needed and that teachers and researchers need to take the aspects of teaching industrial practitioners more clearly into account.

Acknowledgment. This research was supported by the Knowledge Foundation (KKS) through the FuturE and PROMPT projects as well as the ECSEL Joint Undertaking under grant agreement No. 737494 and the Swedish Innovation Agency, Vinnova (MegaM@Rt2 and XIVT projects).

References

1. Ammann, P., Offutt, J.: Introduction to Software Testing. Cambridge University Press, Cambridge (2016)
2. Astigarraga, T., Dow, E.M., Lara, C., Prewitt, R., Ward, M.R.: The emerging role of software testing in curricula. In: 2010 IEEE Transforming Engineering Education: Creating Interdisciplinary Skills for Complex Global Environments, pp. 1–26. IEEE (2010)
3. Bazeley, P.: The contribution of computer software to integrating qualitative and quantitative data and analyses. Res. Sch. **13**(1), 64–74 (2006)
4. Biggs, J.B.: Teaching for Quality Learning at University: What the Student Does. McGraw-Hill Education, New York (2011)
5. Boghossian, P.: Behaviorism, constructivism, and socratic pedagogy. Educ. Philos. Theory **38**(6), 713–722 (2006)
6. Calderhead, J.: Teachers: Beliefs and Knowledge (1996)

7. De Freitas, S.I., Morgan, J., Gibson, D.: Will MOOCs transform learning and teaching in higher education? Engagement and course retention in online learning provision. Br. J. Educ. Technol. **46**(3), 455–471 (2015)
8. Garousi, V., Rainer, A., Lauvås Jr., P., Arcuri, A.: Software-testing education: a systematic literature mapping. J. Syst. Softw. 110570 (2020)
9. Garrison, D.R., Kanuka, H.: Blended learning: uncovering its transformative potential in higher education. Internet High. Educ. **7**(2), 95–105 (2004)
10. Ghezzi, C., Mandrioli, D.: The challenges of software engineering education. In: Inverardi, P., Jazayeri, M. (eds.) ICSE 2005. LNCS, vol. 4309, pp. 115–127. Springer, Heidelberg (2006). https://doi.org/10.1007/11949374_8
11. Hadjerrouit, S.: Learner-centered web-based instruction in software engineering. IEEE Trans. Educ. **48**(1), 99–104 (2005)
12. Hrastinski, S.: Nätbaserad utbildning: en introduktion. Studentlitteratur (2009)
13. Hynninen, T., Kasurinen, J., Knutas, A., Taipale, O.: Guidelines for software testing education objectives from industry practices with a constructive alignment approach. In: Proceedings of the 23rd Annual ACM Conference on Innovation and Technology in Computer Science Education, pp. 278–283 (2018)
14. Karn, J., Cowling, A.J.: Using ethnographic methods to carry out human factors research in software engineering. Behav. Res. Methods **38**(3), 495–503 (2006)
15. Miller, F.G., Fins, J.J., Bacchetta, M.D.: Clinical pragmatism: John Dewey and clinical ethics. J. Contemp. Health L. & Pol'y **13**, 27 (1996)
16. Roth, W.M., Lee, S.: Scientific literacy as collective praxis. Public understanding of Science (2016)
17. Stuchlikova, L., Kosa, A.: Massive open online courses-challenges and solutions in engineering education. In: International Conference on Emerging eLearning Technologies and Applications), pp. 359–364. IEEE (2013)
18. Taguchi, N.: "Contextually" speaking: a survey of pragmatic learning abroad, in class, and online. System **48**, 3–20 (2015)

Towards Code Review Guideline in a Classroom

Victor Rivera[1(✉)], Hamna Aslam[2], Alexandr Naumchev[2], Daniel de Carvalho[2], Mansur Khazeev[2], and Manuel Mazzara[2]

[1] Australian National University, Canberra, Australia
victor.rivera@anu.edu.au
[2] Innopolis University, Innopolis, Russia
{h.aslam,a.naumchev,d.carvalho,m.khazeev,m.mazzara}@innopolis.ru

Abstract. Software companies generally adopt code review to identify errors and suggest improvements to code, and share knowledge in the team. Companies assume a pre-knowledge on their engineers to undertake the activity. This could be difficult for freshly graduated students as in an academic environment code review is not often exercised: it is not an individual activity and requires substantial interaction among students, educators, deliverance, and acceptance of feedback, timely actions upon feedback as well as the ability to agree on a solution in the wake of diverse viewpoints. This paper proposes a guideline to code reviewing in a classroom. We report on the lessons learnt after applying the proposed guidelines to a large course in Computer Science. Students' feedback suggests that the process has been well received with some points to be improved.

1 Introduction

Professional Software Engineers and developers regularly implement code review, i.e. they review each other's code to identify errors, suggest improvements, and share knowledge in the team. Code reviews are useful and common in the industrial environment, e.g. they are part of the software development at Google where it is applied by more than 25K developers making more than 20K source code changes each workday [1]; however, code reviews are not always applied as they should in academia, neither for what concerns research and development nor regarding pedagogical approaches. We consider code reviews a best practice to be applied in the academic environment.

Tools to support code reviews are abundant (see some of these in Sect. 2); in this paper, we are not introducing another tool of this kind, but proposing a process on how to perform a code review session in the university classroom, in particular in large size courses. This paper also reports on experience from applying the process on a first year, large course in Computer Science (CS). Our work follows the convergent practices across several code review processes and contexts identified in [2]: it is a lightweight and flexible process; reviews happen

© Springer Nature Switzerland AG 2020
J.-M. Bruel et al. (Eds.): FISEE 2019, LNCS 12271, pp. 88–105, 2020.
https://doi.org/10.1007/978-3-030-57663-9_7

early (before a change is committed) and quickly; code sizes are small; few people are involved; and it is a group problem solving activity. We describe how this process can help in the development of the course and how it helps students to understand colleagues' mistakes and learn coding best practices. In particular, students can reflect on **Documentation**: Is the code properly documented and commented? Where should the documentation be better?; **Error handling**: Does the code handle errors properly? Where should the error-handling be better?; **Suggestions**: Provide two suggestions for the author on how to improve the code.

In this work, we try to understand:

Q1: *What are the benefits and pitfalls for a course performing code reviews?* educators need to achieve specific learning outcomes for a course in a specific time frame. We want to explore how code review sessions can help lecturers in the process. We are also interested in exploring the consequences of performing code review as part of the course.

Q2: *What are the benefits and pitfalls for students participating in code reviews?* We want to get a hint on whether code reviews help or hinder the learning process in students. This is important as it is directly related to students' motivation. The more motivated students are the more engaged they are in the course [3]. There is also a need to understand what the pitfalls of the activity are so lecturers can focus on those elements.

The following high-level objectives motivate these questions. *Keep the syllabus of the course realistic:* the course may not cover topics that should be covered. It may also loosely cover some of its topics, or cover some topics too extensively. We believe that conducting communication-intensive activities such as code review sessions may help uncover these problems; *Ensure good enough learning quality:* we may not deliver some topics of the course well enough. The course consists of both lectures and lab sessions. While the lectures may cover up-to-date theory, the labs may insufficiently or inadequately practice that theory. Some teaching assistants may practice the topics that they appreciate more. They also may have different backgrounds; this will likely affect their perception and delivery of the material; *Ensure adequacy of the exercise itself:* the setting of the code reviews may require adaptation. It was the first time we applied code reviews for teaching first-year bachelor's. We designed the exercise based on how a code review would look like in a software company. The participants of code reviews in such companies understand very well the importance of code reviews. They also understand what aspects of the artifacts under review they should especially focus on. First-year bachelors most likely do not have that level of awareness. By studying their behaviour during code review sessions, we may learn how to adjust the setting of the exercise.

2 Related Work

Code inspection consists of a manual review of the code by other developers than its authors to identify its defects. Already thirty-five years ago, it was recognised as a good engineering practice, which was successfully applied in several programming projects improving productivity and product quality [4]. At that time, it was done with in-person meetings: such code inspections can be called *traditional* in contrast with practices that have been more recently introduced. In particular, [5] defines *Modern Code Reviews* as informal, tool-based and regular peer code reviews. Kemerer and Paulk [6] analyse the impact of designing and performing code reviews in assignments of a Personal Software Process course written in C or C++: they empirically verify that allowing sufficient preparation time for reviews and inspections can produce better performance; this probably explains why doing such research in a teaching environment is easier than in an industrial one, which tends to try to decrease the short-term costs. Nevertheless, such research in an industrial environment exists: as an example, Sadowski *et al.* [7] studies the practice of Modern code reviews at Google and its impact. Interestingly, they do not only study the impact on the codes themselves but also on knowledge transfer due to code review; indeed, at Google, knowledge transfer is part of the educational motivation for code review. This educational capability of reviews was already emphasised in [8]. Rigby and Bird [2] attempt to measure such spread knowledge across the development team through review. As recalled above, modern code reviews in industry are tool-based. Some example of these tools are: Github [9], where code review is built up in pull requests; CodeFlow [10] used by Microsoft; Gerrit [11] used by Google; ReviewBoard [12] used by LinkedIn and Mozilla; Phabricator [13] used by Facebook.

There are peculiarities of academic teaching that make the context different from the industrial one. This does not allow to fully implement a commercial code review processes so that students can get all the constructive comments about their code in the same way they would get in industry [14]. The size of assignments could be smaller, for example, and the timing of delivery can be different (sometime shorter or longer). Furthermore, team composition in terms of experience and motivation can be biased, and also the incentive system is very different. The team dynamics is also not the same most of the time, and the openness of team members may be influenced by the way in which the teacher has conducted the operations. It is clear that the academic environment is a simulation of *real life*. Still, it can be informative. Code review in education has also been experimented in the context of secondary school [15], where students perceived code review activities positively, and such activities helped in achieving good results in programming projects.

University lecturers who at the same time work in software production understand well the importance of code reviews, and realise the difficulties of teaching and implementing them in a class environment. Lecturers might not have a prior experience in presenting the topic, how to asses it, and even less how to coordinate the action over large groups. In this paper, we try to answer some of these questions. Some techniques applied in a university environment are informally described by D. Wind in [16]. Wind discusses their approach and conclude that students actually learn from reviewing code and can assess quality, but also that generally, and understandably, do not like to grade the work of their peers. Hundhausen *et al.* presents a list of best practices for implementing code reviews in an academic setting [17], the list is derived from empirical studies. Our work follows most of the practices: *establishing ground rules* and *modelling the activity* are part of the activities in phases (1) and (2) in Fig. 1. We did not, however, perform "mock" reviews beforehand; *requiring both independent and team reviews* is part of step (2) in Phase (3) (Fig. 1); *avoiding redundancy in reviewing* is achieved by the nature of our work as we suggest to code review in a more realistic scenario, students need to perform this activity before committing their code to a repository; we did not *use trained moderators*. Moderators were trained, but they were students of the same course, we did not take into consideration their experience.

3 Code Review Process

Code review is a process in which a piece of code is manually inspected by developers other than the authors. The primary purpose of the code review is to improve the quality of software projects. Code reviews are frequent in the industry (e.g., [7]) where code is inspected before committing the changes in centralised repositories. Reviews ensure that quality code adheres to the company's best practices. The review process in the industry happens seamlessly as part of the software development; however, freshly graduated students are not prepared to perform the review (they instead learn the process on the fly). This section describes the process of performing a code review in an academic environment. This section only describes the process; we let educators choose the different tools that can be used. For instance, Phase 3 in Fig. 1 can be performed using pull requests in GitHub.

The code review process defined in this paper assumes a project-based course that has at least six undergraduate students, so at least one review session is performed. The process can handle large size courses; for instance, we applied it to a group of 129 students of a first year undergraduate course, a total of 22 reviews were performed (see Sect. 4). Figure 1 depicts the whole process. The process has two main components: the upper part of the figure shows the process that educators performing the review need to follow. Detailed in Sect. 3.2; the lower part of the figure shows the process of the actual code review that students need to follow. Detailed in Sect. 3.3.

3.1 Components of the Code Review

Artifacts. An artifact is one of many tangible products produced during the development of software. It can be any documentation of the software, e.g. UML diagrams, Internal/External documentation; an agile artifact from an Agile methodology, such as User Stories, acceptance criteria; or a piece of code such as a class (or a small number of closely related classes). The artifact in the code review has an owner and is the element reviewers comment on.

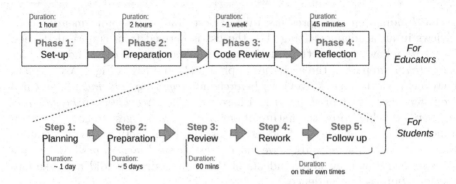

Fig. 1. Code review process for the Classroom.

The artifact should not be extensive, as this would impact (negatively) the effectiveness of the review. It should be around 10 pages of text, for artifacts of software documentation, or around 250 LOC for artifacts of software code (otherwise, the effectiveness of the review is affected [18]). The process described in the present paper assumes an artifact of software code.

Roles. There are three leading roles in a code review (roles are mutually exclusive, e.g., an *owner* cannot be at the same time a *reviewer* or a *moderator*). *(i)* *Owners*: they are the owners of the artifact. Their role is to provide the artifact of the review, along with an explanation. *Owners* receive comments from *reviewers* about the artifact. Each comment needs to be addressed. *Owners* can defend their code and reject the comment, or accept the comment and work on it. *(ii)* *Reviewers*: the set of people reviewing the artifact. Their role is to carefully read the artifact provided by *owners* and make comments on it based on the review scope (see below). If a comment needs further explanation, *reviewers* are required to provide it. *(iii)* *Moderators*: they keep *reviewers* focussed on the process and the discussion on track. They also organise the review meeting and moderate it. After the review is done, *moderators* need to ensure that the follow-up step happens and prepare a final report. This is important to keep the effectiveness of the process. During the review, *moderators* need to have good skills of facilitation: not just moderating the review but also correcting inappropriate behaviour; they should be impartial.

Review Scope. The review of the artifact has a scope to keep participants focussed. Bertrand Meyer [19] defines the following review scope sections to be discussed, from high-level to more implementation-oriented:

1. *Design decisions*: the high-level design of the artifact, e.g. Is a certain class really justified? Should it have its functionalities merged with another class?;
2. *API design*: the usability of software elements by others, in particular to reuse, e.g. Do any derived classes have common members that should be in the base class?;

3. *Architecture*: the architecture of the artifact, e.g. Should a class really inherit from another or instead be a client?;
4. *Implementation techniques*: the choices of data structures and algorithms, e.g. Can better data structures or more efficient algorithms be used?;
5. *Exceptions handling – Contracts*: how the artifact handles unexpected behaviours or about the use of code contracts, e.g. Have all array indexes been prevented from going out-of-bounds?;
6. *Programming style, names*: the conventions of the code style and conformance to standards and specifications, e.g. Are descriptive variable and constant names used in accord with naming conventions?;
7. *Comments and documentation*: Is documentation complete, including Design By Contract or Error checking specs as appropriate? are error messages comprehensive and provide guidance as to how to correct the problem?

Reviewers' comments will belong to one of these seven sections. Each comment will be tagged by *owners* with one of the following tag categories: [CLOSED], when there was a clarification about the comment and the *owner* (with the *reviewer*'s consent) decides to close the comment. This comment does not need any follow up; [TO BE IMPLEMENTED], when the *owner* agrees with the comment and decides to take action on it. These comments need to be implemented only after the review meeting; and [TO BE DISCUSSED], when, after a short discussion about the comment, the *owner* and *reviewer* reach an impasse. Comments with this tag are the ones being discussed during the actual code review meeting.

3.2 Code Review (for Educators)

This section describes the process that educators need to follow to apply a code review session. The process contains four phases: Set-up, Preparation, Code Review and Reflection (upper part of Fig. 1). Phases 1 and 2 could be shortened after the first time the process is done. In a project-based course, the code review can be done several times. After the first time around, there is no need to spend time setting up or preparing the group. Although it is advised to revisit those phases.

Phase 1: Set-Up. In Phase 1, educators instruct students on the process. The level of motivation and engagement of students highly depends on this phase, as a consequence the success of the code review activity. This phase also comprises the explanation of the process. Starting with the explanation of the different roles, what an artifact is and the review scope. Finally, an explanation on the process to follow (as explained in Sect. 3.3).

After the corresponding explanation, review groups are formed. Groups will have between five to seven participants: the *owner* of the artifact, the *moderator* of the process, and between three to five *reviewers*. It is essential to have at least three *reviewers*, so the feedback about the artifact is meaningful, and less than five so the review is kept within limits (the length of the sessions increases per participant). Phase 1 might take around one hour.

Phase 2: Preparation. Three meetings take place in Phase 2: one meeting per role. Participants in the specific role must attend their role meeting. Although they can attend all three meetings. Each meeting starts by explaining the specific role. Part of this explanation was already given (Phase 1); the difference is that the audience is more focussed. Several examples of code reviews are shown so they get an initial idea of how they should perform theirs. At the end of the meeting, there is a QA session. Each meeting has some specific discussions. *(1)* The meeting with *owners*: educators should mention how feedback should be received. Some of the students might not be comfortable receiving negative feedback. It is important to remind them that this activity is for their benefit and that no one is trying to do harm. Educators should also mention that *owners* need to be responsive (answering to comments on a regular basis) as this affects the effectiveness of the review. Finally, *owners* should be open-minded about the comments of their peers. *(2)* The meeting with *reviewers*: educators should mention how feedback should be given. This might be the first time for some students to give feedback. Feedback should be descriptive and not evaluative. The more specific, the better. If a reviewer finds a problem in the code, they should say where exactly and how it can be reproduced. They can also suggest how to solve the problem; take into consideration the needs of the artifact (do not show off how much better/smarter you are); be balanced. It is important to acknowledge *owner*'s effort as well; be sensitive to *owners*: instead of "you didn't initialise this variable" you could write "I didn't see where this variable was initialised". *(3)* The meeting with *moderators*: educators should mention the relevance of moderating a session. They should also explain some of the techniques for facilitating a session and resolving conflicts. It is also important to tell them that a *moderator* should be impartial and should not impose their judgement. Each meeting in phase 2 takes around 40 min.

Phase 3: Code Review. Steps of phase 3 are explained in detail in Sect. 3.3.

Phase 4: Reflection. Once the review meeting (Step 3 in phase 3) takes place, there is a Reflection (Phase 4) session. The reflection session is performed to help students organise their thoughts around the activity. All participants (in all roles) are asked to reflect upon the review process activity. This session follows the Focused Conversational Model [20]. The model enables a conversation to flow surface to depth. It follows the Objective-Reflective-Interpretative-Decisional (ORID) method for asking questions. This model is being practised in various domains to examine an individual's perception of the process they are involved in and their corresponding affordances, primarily investigations on design interactions [21]. In the method, the purpose of *Objective* questions is for participants to think about the facts of the activity. There is no interpretation or feeling involved at this stage. Participants should recall all steps of the activity, e.g. could anyone recall the steps of the review process? The purpose of the *Reflective* questions is to evoke immediate personal reactions, emotions, feelings, or associations, e.g. What do you feel when the *owner* marked a comment as

[CLOSED], but you thought it was not? The purpose of the _Interpretative_ questions is to draw out meaning, significance, or implications about those reactions, e.g. What new insight did you, as *moderator*, get from the activity? Finally, the purpose of the _Decisional_ questions is to bring the conversation to a close, eliciting resolution and enabling participants to make a decision, e.g. What have you learned from this activity? Phase 4 might take around 30 min.

3.3 Code Review (for Students)

This section describes the process that participants need to follow, the actual code review process. The process contains five steps: Planning, Preparation, Review, Rework and Follow-up (as depicted in the bottom of Fig. 1).

Step 1: Planning. The *owner* decides on an artifact and freezes it in the repository. The artifact cannot be modified during the review process. It needs to be ready for comments at least five days before the actual meeting. *Moderators* determine the objectives of the review session and share it with participants. Objectives of the review in a classroom need to be aligned with the objectives of the course. This process is highly influenced by the educator of the course. *Moderators* also create a shared Google document in which *owners* write a short overview of the artifact, along with some useful information for its understanding. The description should not be a full description of the project, rather a brief overview of the artifact. The Google document should also have a link to the artifact's repository. *Moderators* grant write permissions of the document to all *reviewers* and to the educator of the course and distribute the link among them[1].

Step 2: Preparation. *Reviewers* should read the artifact and start commenting on the Google doc based on the review scope. This is an initial interaction between them and the *owner*. This activity lasts for five days, one day before the actual review meeting is held. *Reviewers* are not supposed to run the code. Their comments should be solely based on the artifact in isolation. Meanwhile, *owners* reply to their comments. The purpose is to reduce the number of topics to be discussed during the actual meeting. Some of the comments can be cosmetic; some others need no discussion as an agreement can be found. For this, the *owner* will try to clarify the comments and will tag each comment in the Google doc with one of the following categories [CLOSED], [TO BE IMPLEMENTED], [TO BE DISCUSSED][2].

Step 3: Review. The actual review meeting is held. *Reviewers*, *owner* and *moderator* sit together for around 60 min (it could be as long as 90 min). The

---

[1] An excerpt of the shared Google document can be found in here.
[2] Examples of different tags: [CLOSED] here, [TO BE IMPLEMENTED] here and [TO BE DISCUSSED] here.

meeting starts with an introduction of all participants (so everyone knows their role), then a statement of objectives (so everyone is on the same page). During the meeting, *owner* and *reviewers* discuss those comments in the Google doc that require attention, those tagged as [TO BE DISCUSSED]. The *moderator* facilitates the meeting, making sure all comments are addressed, all *reviewers* participate, and no one monopolises the review.

Step 4: Rework and Step 5: Follow Up. These steps of the process are offline. In the rework step, *owners* should investigate the issues in the Google document tagged as [TO BE IMPLEMENTED] and implement them, or at least report them as issues in a tracking system. This is important not just because the *owner* fully takes advantage of the code review, but also because *reviewers* can see the progress on the comments they had spent time on. In the follow up step, *owners* should report on the Google document the results of the code review. Participants can access the doc to confirm that fixes have been implemented. *Moderators* collect data such as the number of defects, number of participants, number of fixes, and saved as issues, and total time spend reviewing. This is used to improve any upcoming review process.

4   The Process at Work

This section reports on the code review process performed in a large size course of a Computer Science program.

4.1   Course Structure

The *Introduction to Programming II* course at Innopolis University is a 6 ETCS course delivered to freshmen in the second semester. This course is a continuation from *Introduction to Programming I*, a course that focuses on Object-Oriented Programming and the notion of Software Contract using the metaphor of business contract [22,23]. *Introduction to Programming II* is a project-based course. After successfully taking this course, students will master the fundamental data structures and algorithms, modular programming, exception handling, and programming language mechanisms, as well as the fundamental rules of producing high-quality software. The teaching team is composed of a Principal Instructor (PI) in charge of delivering lessons and Teaching Assistants (TA) in charge of delivering lab sessions. Around 90% of the first-year students are between 17 and 19 years old (the rest are no older than 31), due to the specific structure of the Russian scholastic itinerary and around 80% of the students are Russians.

The course's project was the classical Library Management System (LMS). LMSs are used in libraries to track the different items of the library. The system also keeps track of people allowed to check out those items and people in charge of the management of the library. The project was divided into four deliveries, and students were free to use any programming language, paradigm, or framework, the only restriction was that they had to host the source code in a subversion repository (for monitoring purposes). The course size was 193 students.

4.2   Code Review Phases

Phase 1: Set-Up. Students were instructed on the different elements of the review, the artifacts, the roles, the review scope, along with the tags for comments and the code review process. They formed teams of five to seven participants and were asked to assigned roles. They were advised to form different groups for the review than the groups of the project. This phase was performed in 1.5 h.

Phase 2: Preparation. Three different meetings were scheduled. These meetings happened outside the lecture time. Meetings were open to all participants. During these meetings, the PI explained in more detail the process of the review and each role. Examples of code reviews were shown so participants could get an idea of the process. Each meeting lasted for about 30 min. The longest one was with *moderators* as this role is less natural for students: they had not moderated a meeting before.

Phase 3: Code Review. As the size of the course was large, the actual code reviews were done in parallel with the help of Teaching Assistants (TA). They were instructed to spend the first ten minutes of the session to remind students about the activity: logistics, how the meeting was to be conducted, the duration (60 min) and a quick reminder about roles. Then, students were split among their review teams and placed them around the classroom. The classroom should be big enough to allow at most three different teams to discuss without affecting each team. The review starts: the *moderator* starts facilitating. During the review, TAs cannot influence or participate in the discussions. Although, TAs should be alert in case there is a misconduct. In such a case, TAs can intervene just to guide them to reach consensus rather than impose an opinion. TAs notify students when there were ten minutes left to finalise the review. More details about the review are shown in Sect. 4.3 below.

Phase 4: Reflection. TAs were instructed on how to conduct the reflection session. After the review meeting was over, TAs gathered all students and reminded *owners* to take care of the Follow-up part of the exercise. As well as to update the document once they take care of issues. The reflection session is for students to think and reflect upon the activity that they were exposed. TAs conduct this activity using the ORID method. TAs were also instructed to make students participate in the activity, e.g., by asking direct questions. This activity lasted for 30 min.

4.3   Code Review Steps

Step 1: Planning. Owners were instructed to freeze the artifacts and to produce a description of them. *Moderators* were instructed to determine a set of objectives for the review. The PI influenced this process as the objectives should be aligned with those of the course. The objectives of the review were set to answer the following questions: *(i)* Does the artifact make use of the appropriated data structures? Is the code scalable?; *(ii)* What is the level of quality of the artifact presented? Is the owner using Design by Contract mechanisms? are unexpected behaviours being handled (Exceptions)?; *(iii)* Does the artifact follow a defined architecture?; and *(iv)* Is the artifact maintainable?

Moderators were also instructed to create a Google document and share it (with write permissions) to all *reviewers* and the PI (for monitoring). The document contained *owner*'s description of the artifact and the link to the artifact.

Step 2: Preparation. During five days, *reviewers* reviewed the artifact and made comments on the Google document. *Owners* continuously answered those comments adding the respective tag. During this time, *moderators* made sure that the process was in place and that all participants were working on it. As the PI has permission to the shared documents, the PI continuously monitored the progress of this step. PI should intervene in this process only if no one is working or to give feedback on how to write comments (to reduce ambiguity).

Step 3: Review. The actual meeting happened. As explained before, this was a large size course, so the reviews were monitored by the PI and TAs. They were supposed to intervene only in case something went out of control. Nothing damaging happened during the sessions. Some groups had more discussions than others, but overall respect governed the process. All shared documents are available in [24] (*Code Reviews* folder). Names were changed to protect the identity of students, and links to their code were removed. The reader can used these review documents to show students before performing a code review session in their courses.

Step 4 and 5: Rework and Follow Up. *Moderators* were instructed to monitor the progress of the work after the review meeting. They had to check whether *owners* were updating the shared document. If *owners* did not update the document, *moderators* could send a reminder to them. The PI checked all shared documents at the end of the course, and all comments were tagged as [CLOSED]; some of those comments were reported as tickets to be taken care of in the future. *Moderators* also collected data about the activity.

4.4   Data/Observations

There were a total of 129 students who participated in the activity. There were 22 groups for code review: 19 groups had 4 *reviewers* and the rest had 3 *reviewers*. The artifacts contained, on average, 200 Lines of Code. After the review process, *moderators* reported that *owners* found a total of 122 bugs off-line (before the review meeting) and 19 bugs during the review. There were a total of 656 interactions on the Google documents between *owners* and *reviewers*. All Google docs can be accessed in [24] (*Code Reviews* folder). Table 1 shows the different categories on the Google docs and the number of comments per tag. The bottom row and rightmost column show the totals. Around 41% of the comments were tagged as [CLOSED]: *owners* explained the issues offline and decided to take no action; around 52% of the comments were tagged as [TO BE IMPLEMENTED]: *owners* decided to implement *reviewers*' comments after the review process is finished; and only 21 comments (around 7%) [TO BE DISCUSSED]. The review meeting focuses only on these comments, so the meeting is very concrete, making it more effective. We have found out that there are fewer comments about the high-level aspect of the artifact (categories (1) to (3)) than about the implementation-oriented aspects (categories (4) to (7)). The reason is that it is more difficult to focus on high-level aspects by looking only at a piece of code. Around 30% of the comments were about the high-level aspect of the artifact and 70% about the implementation-oriented aspects.

Table 1. Code review categories and number of comments per tag.

Category	CLOSED	TO BE IMPLEMENTED	TO BE DISCUSSED	
(1) Design Decisions	19	20	5	44
(2) API Design	10	7	2	19
(3) Architecture	10	12	3	25
(4) Impl. Techniques	24	27	2	53
(5) Exception Handling	16	23	3	42
(6) Programming Style	22	47	3	72
(7) Comments and Doc.	21	22	3	46
	122	158	21	

Table 1 also shows that the most common comments were on `Programming Style`. This was expected as *reviewers* only have access to the artifact and could not run the code. Most of the comments, around 65%, are to be implemented. This is followed by comments on `Implementation techniques` and `Comments and Documentation`. The behaviour was expected and went in the direction of the code review practices at Google [7]. Categories with the least comments were `API Design` and `Architecture`. It is challenging to comment on these two categories having only the artifact. Typically, artifacts are not large so *reviewers* cannot see the big picture. Although, in these two categories, around 42% of the comments were tagged to be implemented. Meaning, even though these categories are difficult to comment on, those few comments were necessary.

After the code review activity, *reviewers* were asked to fill up a questionnaire about the reviewed code. 98 of the *reviewers* participated in the survey. The survey contained four *Likert* questions (linear scale from 1 to 5 – from `Strongly Disagree` to `Strongly Agree`): *(1)* Is the reviewed code modular? *(2)* Does the reviewed code implement a proper logging mechanism? *(3)* Is the reviewed code understandable? *(4)* Does the reviewed code handle exceptions?

Figure 2 shows the results of the questionnaire (full responses can be accessed from [24], in *QuestionnaireResponses* folder). This questionnaire and the results for the code review (Table 1) can be used to check how students are performing in the course. Around 45% of the comments for `Design Decisions`, `API Design` and `Architecture` are tagged as [CLOSED], as shown in Table 1, and from Fig. 2(a), 61% agree that the reviewed code is modular. These two readings suggest that in general, one of the objectives of the course was achieved, Modular Programming. On the other hand, we can observe from Table 1 that around 55% of the comments for `Exception handling` are tagged as [TO BE IMPLEMENTED], and from Fig. 2(d), 35% disagree that the reviewed code properly handle exceptions. These two readings suggest that more work needs to be done to achieve one of the objectives of the course, Exception Handling, impacting another objective on High-quality Software. Figure 2(b) did not let us make clear conclusions regarding the coverage of logging mechanisms in the course. The even "agree" vs. "disagree" distribution of the responses (41% vs. 40%) suggests two possible explanations: students either have no clear knowledge of how a proper logging mechanism looks like, or they have such knowledge but do not apply it. To cover both of the possibilities, we will need to simultaneously increase the amount of theory in the lectures and introduce more practical exercises to the lab sessions.

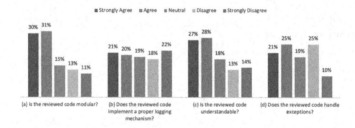

Fig. 2. Postmortem questionnaire's results on the code review activity.

5   Lessons Learnt and Discussion

We report on the lessons learnt after implementing the code review in a classroom mentioned in previous sections. These lessons are supported by feedback provided by students via a questionnaire (that can be found in [24]). Lessons cover aspects related to the technicalities of the code review process, and some suggestions are in regards to improving the work atmosphere to avoid unnecessary difficulties and achieve productive outcomes.

Discipline. Students need explicit guidelines to maintain the positivism of the work environment. Some of the participants (being young) did not know how to take the suggestions as feedback and not as criticisms. They emphasise that developers must try to accommodate reviewers' comments as much as possible. Therefore, the argument of *respect* was brought onto the surface as students stated that respect among team members should be maintained at all times.

Reference Material. Students need elaborated reference material. The reference material must include a code review document. The instructions regarding the activity must be precise and supported with examples.

Reviewers' Related Guidelines. The number of reviewers should be between three to five. Less than three reviewers might end up in useless or contradicting comments, e.g., one reviewer says A, and the other says *no A*. More than five reviewers will make the review session (the actual meeting) too long, affecting the outcome of the process negatively; *reviewers* must have clarity that their task is to identify problems and provide suggestions for improvement, not solving it for the developers; quantifiable goals should be set prior the activity, and the number of lines of code should be between 200 and 300. Some students reported that 200 LOC is not enough; however, having more LOC will make the review session (the actual meeting) too long, affecting the outcome of the process negatively.

Motivation to Work. To maintain a certain level of motivation (among all participants) during the code review process, the provision of review statistics can be useful. At the end of each review session, the *moderator* can check and report whether all issues were resolved, i.e. are all "TO_BE_IMPLEMENTED" tags addressed? They could also report on the achieved goals of the activity. Students recommended instructors' involvement to address the issues that are beyond the control of the teams such as, participants not responding on time.

Feedback Structure. It is essential to emphasise the need to have balanced feedback. It is not just about pointing out mistakes in the code, but also acknowledging those good and smart implementations (e.g. from the activity in Sect. 4: "Smart choice to use implemented DS in MySQL database for data queries").

Clarity upon Grading Schema of the Code Review. The code review activity should be part of the course grading schema, clear to students and fairly distribute (the risk of unfair grades' distribution, if not managed, may harm the students' motivation). This will not just play well in students' motivation, but also the code review could be used to determine any correlation between the number of bugs found in a student's code and their final grades.

Code reviews should not be placed close to major milestones of the course, for instance, close to a project delivery or final exam. Some students reported (quoted): *"It would be better to do this activity in the time when we don't have to prepare for our finals so that we could dedicate more time on this activity."* and "Don't organize it at the end of the semester before finals".

Activity Technicalities. Educators should give feedback on the spectrum of goals to ensure that they are doable in the available time frame. Educators should also read and give feedback on students' comments to reduce ambiguity.

Discussion. We now summarise the results of the code review activity against the questions stated in Sect. 1. The summary relies on the following key sources of information: students' evaluations of each other's code (Fig. 2); students' responses to a postmortem reflection questionnaire that we handed out to them after the code review activity. We received 78 responses in total, which is slightly more than half of the students (all responses can be found in [24]); and our gained experience.

Q1: What are the benefits and pitfalls for a course performing code reviews?

Aligning both the code review and course goals can be used to boost the quality of teaching: the activity can be used to: *(i)* assess students. Code review activities can be part of the grading criteria of the course. Scores can be calculated by the engagement of the student during the activity, e.g. the number of comments reported, the number of answers given. Or it could be used in a student peer assessment, in which students assess the work of their peers against set assessment criteria (defined by the educator). When students act as the assessor, they gain an opportunity to better understand assessment criteria potentially increasing their motivation and engagement [25]; *(ii)* keep track of the course objectives development. Code reviews can be used as a formative assessment if done repeatedly during the course. Educators can track the course objectives and act according to the findings, improving the learning outcomes of the course. For instance, the code review session described previously helped us spot well-developed and underdeveloped topics of the course. The course

– does not cover exception handling well enough (Fig. 2(d)),
– does cover modular programming in depth (Fig. 2(a)),
– trains students to write understandable code (Fig. 2(c));

track students' learning. Students need to constantly commit their development to a repository. Educators can check their progress and take action if needed. Educators can also check the comments of the code review session. The latter will help educators track the learning process of the group involved rather than individuals.

Code review is an *active learning* activity. It involves students in the learning process by doing things (phase (3) in Fig. 1) and making them think about what they are doing (phase (4) in Fig. 1). Students use their own efforts to construct their knowledge, guided by educators. This makes code review an effective tool in making classrooms more inclusive, students more engaged, improving their critical thinking, in general, increasing students' performance in the course [26].

Code reviews can fall into different pitfalls that require an immediate action from educators. Code review is a multistep process that requires considerable time and effort during both the preparation and execution phases. Overlooking possible problems during these phases will result in cascading problems during the execution phase. The likelihood increases with large size courses. An example of possible problems is not having *moderators* well prepared. This will affect the outcome of the activity as students will not be well guided.

Motivating students is a key factor in the code review process. Failing to do so might reflect on students' final grade of the course. Students should have a clear understanding of the activity and educators need to make them engage in every step.

Q2: What are the benefits and pitfalls for students participating in code reviews?

Code reviews help students developing both hard and soft skills. Students reported that the activity helped them learn to read and understand other people's code; take an external look at their code and thus improve it; practise organising their thoughts clearly; practise working under tight deadlines; and how *not* to write code. They have understood that writing code is for the benefit of humans reading the code (machines do not read source code but low-level code). Some of the soft skills exercised were collaborative and teamwork, give and receive appropriate feedback (how to deal with criticism), and how to resolve conflicts. Code reviews also prepare students to an industrial environment that widely uses reviews as part of their software development process.

Some students do not know how to deal with criticism, though, influencing negatively their motivation. Industrial practitioners of code reviews understand the benefits of the activity from a tremendous experience. But, first-year bachelor students practising it for the first time instinctively take the outcome as a personal criticism. Educators need to be vigilant to this situation and take immediate action to mitigate the problem, not just because it may reflect on the outcome of the activity, but also because it may affect students' personal success. Some responses to the postmortem questionnaire support this conclusion. As a possible remedy, the participation of higher-grade students, TAs or educators can be used to make their verdicts in possible conflicts.

Owners of the code may fall prey to the *reviewers'* low discipline. Motivation plays a key role once again. A motivated *reviewer* might give a substantial feedback to the *owner*, unlike a unmotivated one. One of the answers we received on this regards reads: *"It would be much better if reviewers have not started two hours before the deadline"*.

There is a risk of one student damaging the grade of another one during the code review activity. Especially, if *student peer assessment* is exercised. This should be carefully managed as it may impact both students' final grades and motivation.

6   Conclusions

Code reviews are widely used in industry. However, freshly graduated students are not prepared to undertake them. This paper describes a process to perform code reviews in an academic environment that seeks, inter alia, prepare students for the future. The process defines two sub-processes to be carried out: one by the educator of the course and the other one by students. The process for educators is composed of four phases, namely *Set-up*, *Preparation*, *Code Review* and *Reflection*. We found out that the *Reflection* phase is of paramount importance in an academic environment as great part of students' learning about the process happens here. The process for students is composed of five steps, namely *Planning, Preparation, Review, Rework* and *Follow-up*. While these steps are not closely followed in industry, e.g. reviews in industry do not take 5 days, the steps help students to grasp the main idea behind Code Review. We applied the process to a first year, large size course in Computer Science. We also presented the findings of the activity and described the lessons learnt after the activity. This paper can be used as a guide to implement code reviews in a classroom (examples of code reviews and material can be found in [24]).

We plan to repeat the activity in a similar scenario (we invite educators reading this paper to do so as well). We plan to apply the process several times throughout the semester. In each iteration, we will gradually reduce the time of the Code Review activity. Thus, students will eventually exercise a more realistic situation. Performing the activity several times in a semester gives us also the opportunity to let students experience different roles.

References

1. Potvin, R., Levenberg, J.: Why Google stores billions of lines of code in a single repository. Commun. ACM **59**(7), 78–87 (2016). https://doi.org/10.1145/2854146
2. Rigby, P.C., Bird, C.: Convergent contemporary software peer review practices. In: Proceedings of the 2013 9th Joint Meeting on Foundations of Software Engineering, ser. ESEC/FSE 2013, pp. 202–212. ACM, New York (2013). https://doi.org/10.1145/2491411.2491444
3. Saeed, S., Zyngier, D.: How motivation influences student engagement: a qualitative case study. J. Educ. Learn. **1**(2), 252–267 (2012)
4. Fagan, M.E.: Design and code inspections to reduce errors in program development. IBM Syst. J. **15**(3), 182–211 (1976). http://domino.research.ibm.com/tchjr/journalindex.nsf/495f80c9d0f539778525681e00724804/91d9f4f02fea9d9085256bfa00685ad3?OpenDocument
5. Bird, C., Bacchelli, A.: Expectations, outcomes, and challenges of modern code review. In: Proceedings of the International Conference on Software Engineering. IEEE, May 2013. https://www.microsoft.com/en-us/research/publication/expectations-outcomes-and-challenges-of-modern-code-review/
6. Kemerer, C.F., Paulk, M.C.: The impact of design and code reviews on software quality: an empirical study based on PSP data. IEEE Trans. Softw. Eng. **35**(4), 534–550 (2009)
7. Sadowski, C., Söderberg, E., Church, L., Sipko, M., Bacchelli, A.: Modern code review: a case study at Google. In: International Conference on Software Engineering, Software Engineering in Practice Track (2018)
8. Johnson, P.M.: Reengineering inspection. Commun. ACM **41**(2), 49–52 (1998). https://doi.org/10.1145/269012.269020
9. Github Inc.: Write better code (2020). https://github.com/features/code-review/. Accessed June 2020
10. Czerwonka, J., Greiler, M., Bird, C., Panjer, L., Coatta, T.: CodeFlow: improving the code review process at Microsoft. Queue **16**(5), 81–100 (2018). https://doi.org/10.1145/3291276.3292420

11. Gerrit: Gerrit Code Review, June 2020. https://www.gerritcodereview.com/. Accessed Apr 2020
12. Rawat, S.: Getting Started with Review Board. Packt Publishing (2014)
13. Phacility Inc.: Discuss. Plan. Code. Review. Test. (2020). https://www.phacility.com/phabricator/. Accessed Apr 2020
14. Tatarchenko, E.: Analysis of performing code review in the classroom. Master's thesis (2012). http://up.csail.mit.edu/other-pubs/elena-thesis.pdf
15. Kubincová, Z., Csicsolová, I.: Code review in high school programming. In: 2018 17th International Conference on Information Technology Based Higher Education and Training (ITHET), pp. 1–4 (2018)
16. Wind, D.K.: Teaching code review to university students, August 2017. https://towardsdatascience.com/teaching-code-review-in-university-courses-using-peer-feedback-5625fe039f2a. Accessed May 2020
17. Hundhausen, C.D., Agrawal, A., Agarwal, P.: Talking about code: integrating pedagogical code reviews into early computing courses. ACM Trans. Comput. Educ. 13(3), 1–28 (2013). https://doi.org/10.1145/2499947.2499951
18. Cohen, J.: White paper: 11 proven practices for more effective, efficient peer code review. IBM, Technical report, January 2011. https://www.ibm.com/developerworks/rational/library/11-proven-practices-for-peer-review/index.html
19. Meyer, B.: Design and code reviews in the age of the internet. Commun. ACM 51(9), 66–71 (2008). https://doi.org/10.1145/1378727.1378744
20. Stanfield, B.: The Art of Focused Conversation: 100 Ways to Access Group Wisdom in the Workplace. New Society Publishers, Gabriola Island, B.C (2000)
21. Aslam, H., Brown, J.A.: Affordance theory in game design: a guide toward understanding players. Synth. Lect. Games Comput. Intell. 4(1), 1–111 (2020)
22. de Carvalho, D., et al.: Teaching programming and design-by-contract. In: Auer, M.E., Tsiatsos, T. (eds.) ICL 2018. AISC, vol. 916, pp. 68–76. Springer, Cham (2020). https://doi.org/10.1007/978-3-030-11932-4_7
23. Meyer, B.: Object-Oriented Software Construction, 2nd edn. Prentice-Hall Inc., Upper Saddle River (1997)
24. Rivera, V.: Code Review in the classroom, Data (2020). https://github.com/varivera/CodeReview. Accessed Apr 2020
25. Ng, V., Fai, C.M.: Engaging student learning through peer assessments. In: Proceedings of International Conference on E-Education, E-Business and E-Technology, ser. ICEBT 2017, pp. 30–35. ACM, New York (2017). https://doi.org/10.1145/3141151.3141165
26. Freeman, S., et al.: Active learning increases student performance in science, engineering, and mathematics. Proc. Natl. Acad. Sci. 111(23), 8410–8415 (2014). https://www.pnas.org/content/111/23/8410

IT Education in St. Petersburg State University

Terekhov Andrey[✉] and Mariia Platonova

Department of Software Engineering, St. Petersburg State University,
Saint-Petersburg, Russian Federation
a.terekhov@spbu.ru, platonova.maria@outlook.com

Abstract. For many years, the world IT industry seems to have insatiable needs for qualified IT specialists. Russian higher education produces a large number of IT graduates each year, and the global market values them highly, recruiting both remotely and onsite.

In this article we explore three success factors of the Russian IT education: thorough grounding in fundamental mathematics, adherence to international educational standards and close connections with IT industry.

Since the early 1990s, Saint Petersburg State University (SPbU) accumulated an immense experience in collaboration with IT companies on education. Moreover, SPbU has developed a set of tools for IT education purposes, providing significantly better control of student user errors, both static and dynamic. This helps controlling the quality and progress of students in the real-life tasks of IT, alongside with their academic progress.

In this article we compare the efficiency of preparing new IT specialists via joint educational programs of universities with IT companies, with the alternative of the traditional recruitment followed by additional training in the workplace.

Keywords: Education · IT industry · Algorithmic languages · Educational tools

1 Introduction

IT industry success and growth as a whole depends largely on a few basic principles. Perhaps one of the most important of them is education. Educating qualified specialists in the IT industry is an ongoing issue, and Russia is no exception, because the market is large – the software exports market from Russia is approaching 8 billion dollars annually and also the domestic market grows rapidly, although not as fast as we would like.

Unlike oil and gas, software is a renewable resource. The main condition for increasing software export is the rapid growth of qualified IT resources of various profiles – such as software architects, developers, QA, graphic designers,

J.-M. Bruel et al. (Eds.): FISEE 2019, LNCS 12271, pp. 106–114, 2020.
https://doi.org/10.1007/978-3-030-57663-9_8

marketers and HR. IT specialists are typically well-paid, they pay taxes and expand the middle class - a welcome growth in any country. Russian Federation appreciates the importance of its IT industry as a driving force of economic development, and therefore grants budget to the IT industry, for example increasing the quotas of budget-funded education in IT in Russian universities.

State sponsorship helps fast growth of IT education in Russia: increasingly the universities open new directions and expand the existing teaching programs, regularly hosting large conferences on IT education. Student software development teams prepared in several Russian universities took ACM ICPC competition world championship 13 times since 2000, coming second and third even more times. It is remarkable that the award-winning teams often come from smaller Russian cities. Most of the students participants in ACM ICPC champions later continue to outstanding career as high-profile developers. For example a member of the first Russian champion team (2000 and 2001) Nikolay Durov became the key author of the most popular Russian social network – Vkontakte, and after that the Telegram messenger. However, champions are and will remain exceptions. The task is to teach hundreds and hundreds of students well, so that a few of them reach star status, while all graduates make very good candidates to be hired by any IT company.

In the global division of software labour, Russia historically took the niche of producing software that requires deep mathematical proficiency. It is appropriate to note that Google, Kaspersky and a number of world brands in complex software have graduates of Russian education system in the background. Also many large Western companies continue with their R&D centers in Russia (e.g. Dell, EMC, T-Systems, Nokia).

These successes are partially rooted in the historical merging of Russian software industry with Russian universities. Teaching software engineering requires material and licensing that have not been readily available via the education budgets, so joining forces with the existing SW companies was a natural choice for many.

The challenges are still great. Russian labour market needs many more fresh graduates in IT and SW disciplines than the institutions are preparing now. It is also necessary to increase their education achievements and keep programs up to date in the fast changing world of IT technologies. Last but not least the competition in the international software market is growing: India and China are large players, and more countries such as Mexico, Philippines, Israel, Eastern Europe are active and growing, too.

2   IT Education Standards

In 2005 the largest professional international associations ACM and IEEE issued a common standard for computing [1], which includes 5 disciplines: computer science, information systems, software engineering, computer engineering, information technology. These education standards for Computer Science and Software Engineering were immediately translated into Russian, and Russian education standards adapted to them (the authors have participated in this process at the time). After that many Russian universities have tailored their education programs to these standards.

The standards contain not only the specifications of programs and standards to achieve, but open the subject on a deeper philosophical level, with numerous essays, for example, on what is common between software and traditional engineering and how they differ, what role the mathematics plays, and so on.

It was not an easy task to combine the international educational standards with Russian ones: on the one hand, many of the disciplines that were mentioned in the standards have never earlier been taught either in the USSR or in Russia, for example, the economics of the IT industry, the organization of teamwork, and the sociological aspects of the profession. We had to create and run these courses to adhere to international standards and serve the emerging Russian SW industry.

On the other hand, we have traditionally taught much higher content of math subjects to the future SW engineers. For example, the first year students of the Faculty of Mathematics and Mechanics of SPbU take 8 h per week of calculus, 6 h per week of algebra and 4 h per week of geometry, which is roughly double the content of comparable international programs. This is all based on the strong foundation of the Saint Petersburg school of mathematics, which has been developing for 300 years since the great mathematician Leonard Euler, who lived in Saint Petersburg for many years and was buried here. Over the past 30 years, the level of IT education at the Faculty of Mathematics and Mechanics has been significantly improving by structural, organizational and personnel decisions under the guidance of the long-standing dean (until 2018), mathematician Gennadiy Leonov. He is one of the most cited mathematician in the world (more than 14000 citation).

Several branches of mathematics have direct relation to information technology – studies in continuity, discreteness and finiteness. Some other branches, such as mathematical statistics, have applied value for programming, for example the Big Data processing. Still other mathematical methods of theoretical and applied cybernetics guide the construction of effective algorithms and study of operations.

The immersive study of the more abstract fundamental branches of mathematics, such as algebra, functional analysis or topology, has intrinsic value for the students. They form practical skills of working with complex formal constructions. The ability to efficiently work with complex concepts at a high level of abstraction distinguishes specialists and architects who have received a fundamental mathematical education from their more "practically oriented" colleagues.

To conclude, the development and implementation of algorithms for solving the problems formulated as mathematical models is one of the main goals of SW engineering training in SPbU. A mighty scion of deep mathematical education in SW sciences was for example Svyatoslav Lavrov, who was the head of the Department of Computer Software of the Faculty of Mathematics and Mechanics of SPbU. He influenced deeply the teaching of mathematical disciplines in SW engineering training programs. Svyatoslav Lavrov is not as well-known abroad as his achievement warrants (for the reasons of the USSR isolation from the rest of the world), but his contribution as the head of external ballistic laboratory in Korolev Institute, responsible for Sputnik 1 and Gagarin's trajectories and the first USSR Algol 60 compiler (1964), is highly recognized in Russia.

3   IT Companies' Support of Education

Over the past 15 years, it has been known the understanding of the fundamental problems associated with the training of specialists in the field of the modern IT industry, that there is a fundamental gap between the profile of academic education of university graduates and the profile of the needs of IT companies [2,3]. Two main factors are distinguished of the existence of such a gap.

Firstly, the high dynamics of changes of the IT industry. Every year, new technologies, tools, software and hardware platforms appear, and this process conducts to a rapid change of the industrial environment in which graduates of IT specialties have to work after graduation. It is practically impossible to keep up with all the latest changes in products and technologies within the framework of the academic environment and the traditional educational process, and as a result, students have in fact to retrain when they come to work, and companies have to spend additional funds on training and specialization of students.

Secondly, the difference between "the rules of the game" that taken by IT companies and the stereotypes that students encounter during their studies at the university. Usually educational tasks are clearly defined self-sufficient tasks, the main criterion for them is to obtain the correct result. In production projects, on the contrary, often the tasks are not clearly defined, they require communication with other project participants to clarify the details, and the conditions may change during the work on the task. The measure for the task is not only getting the right result, but also how this result was achieved, including the quality and style of the code, complying with the various agreements took in the project, documenting the solution, etc. Moreover, for successful work in the IT industry, a graduate is required, in addition to the actual education, to possess a number of soft skills, such as business communication skills, teamwork, the ability to present the results of their work, etc. It is very difficult to train these skills for a student in the framework of the academic process - to acquire them, immersion in a real production environment is required.

The ways to solve the problem lie up in formation relations between the university departments preparing IT specialists and large IT companies working in the Russian and world markets. It is possible to organize the process of immersing students in an industrial environment close to reality, while remaining within the framework of the university educational process.

The specific forms of organizing such cooperation can be different - both the traditional mechanism for organizing university departments and joint laboratories, and the organization of joint education courses and intensive student practices with IT companies, conducted with the active participation of developers, managers and other specialists.

The Software Engineering Curricula 2004 standard is quite complete and constructive, it pays a lot of attention to production practice, work on projects, and the importance and advantages of teamwork on a graduation project are also emphasized. However it is almost impossible to teach in the classroom weekly reporting, software configuration management, QA, teamwork, etc., so the following system of additional production education in student projects was created.

Different IT companies have adopted different methods of planning and organizing a team of developers, as well as different programming technologies. As a result, even the most successful university graduates have to spend 1 to 3 months after starting work in a company for additional education before they become useful in the workplace. Moreover, they will require existing staff's valuable time for answering questions and advice.

Therefore, more than 15 years ago, we began to implement a different approach. We invite local IT companies to select at least two tutors among their employees for managing student projects (since one tutor may fall sick or go on a business trip). The subject of the project should be interesting to the company, but at the same time, it should be scientifically intensive to be accepted as a topic of course work or diploma. University strictly cuts off attempts to use students as a free workforce, but almost every IT company has an interest in assaying new technologies, some research that seems not worth to spend time and money, and a student project allows them to assay new ideas and technologies at the lowest cost.

In addition, there is another issue - retention. It is no secret that IT industry has very high staff turnover percentage. A few years ago, A. Terekhov took part in a large project to study staff turnover and retention in large Russian (Lanit-Tercom) and Finnish (Nokia) companies. It turned out that employees who came to the company by HR worked in the company for 2–3 years, and those who came through student projects - 6–7 years. If we recall that the "from the street" employees need about 1–3 month to become a part of the team, we can compare this with those, who took part at a student project while were educating at the university, are ready to work immediately, so the economic benefit becomes even more obvious [4].

When we started student projects organization process, we heard objections from different sides: industry members said that they did not want to pay money (salaries to tutors) for educating, they said that this is the task of the country or the student himself, and in addition, the university does not want to allow people without appropriate education to teach students for.

It is easier to answer the second objection: our graduates are often working as tutors from IT companies. They know all our orders and traditions, moreover, students usually trust them more due to the connection of the university generations.

The first objection usually sounds like this: "We will invest the money and the efforts of our tutors, but students may decide to work for other companies." Firstly, according to Russian laws, anyone can apply for dismissal and be fired in two weeks. Secondly, many years of statistics show that if a student was educated in a student project at IT company, he knows its subjects, working conditions, salary, he is familiar with the team, it is highly probably that he will come there to work after graduation and will remain there for many years.

The most important argument in favor of our education is the quality of the resulting specialists. Classical university education with additional professional education gives our graduates enormous advantages in the labor market. We can clearly see this on the example of our employees.

Nowadays in St. Petersburg, as in many other cities of Russia, many IT companies have taken up this practice, and each company chooses a university which is close to it subjects.

4 Programming Learning Tools

One of the most important parts of IT education for student are quality programming tools. On the one hand, the main goal of professional programmers is the efficiency of their programs, but on the other hand, beginners especially need clearness of the error messages, strict reference to the error place and the maximum possibility of controlling of the dynamic errors. Moreover, professional programmers know how to localize the error place, how a compiler can respond to an error situation and how to respond to warnings. For beginners, the tasks of working with errors are highly difficult, therefore, the implementation of special tools for teaching programming is necessary.

In the field of creating critical software and hardware systems a paradoxical situation arises: firstly, programmers write programs in languages that do not provide sufficient control for user errors, then they or specially educated specialists work hard to find and fix these errors. Many years ago scientists and industry experts understood this problem and invented programming languages and systems aimed at creating programs with the control of errors both while compilation time and runtime. For example, we can mention the languages Oberon by Niklaus Wirth [5] and Eifel by Bertrand Meyer [6], however, like many other languages created for the same purpose, these have not become widespread. Unfortunately, this often happens in programming, and the reasons must be sought in the fields of engineering psychology and economics. The most famous not accepted by the society programming language is Algol 68 - the first high-level language in the world with a well-defined syntax and semantic, which remains problematic for many present-day languages. Many features that firstly appeared in Algol 68, for example, full control of the compilation time, consecutive sentences and conditional expressions, operators with assignment of type +:=, recursive types, etc, were then successfully applied in Pascal, C, Ada and other languages that appeared later.

We decided to choose another way for our project to develop. We did not invent a new language, but took C, changing it in order to increase protection against user errors, and carried out our own implementation, not only of the compiler, but also of a full-fledged IDE. This project is called RuC.

Initially, the project arose from the needs of school teachers of robotics circles. For a long time they have been using our graphics technology - TRIK-studio, it is especially well suited for primary and secondary school students, but at the same time it is desired for students' ability to read the programs that are automatically generated from graphic diagrams. Nowadays in many countries the approach of programming which is based on graphical models with automatic code generation in the target language is very popular. Traditionally, the C language is used [7], but we must not forget that primary and secondary school students practically do not know English, so it's hard to learn programming language like this. Therefore, the idea arose to develop a C compiler into the codes of a virtual machine that we invented with additional Russian messages, keywords and identifiers, and an interpreter for this machine. The virtual machine provides easy portability to any platform. Although it works a little bit slower due to codes decrypting, good architecture makes this problem insignificant.

Both the compiler and the language interpreter are implemented in C standard, so they can easily be ported to all platforms, in particular, the interpreter is transferred to the TRIK robot designer [8], which is developed by employees and students of the Departments of Software Engineering and Theoretical Cybernetics of St. Petersburg State University.

Gradually, the scope of the RuC project was expanded: firstly, it turned out that using the example of this project can help to conduct compiler techniques classes with students. Then the military and other customers became interested in this project, for whom the reliability of the created software systems is important, that was supported by the renouncement of address arithmetic, obligatory control of indices in arrays and detailed information of user errors.

In fact, the introduction of restrictions on the input of a language during the implementation of the compiler is a bad matter, it is the evidence of the authors' low qualifications, so we looked with some thrill at the options for C language restrictions in order to increase the protection users from their own errors. However, it turned out that we are far from being the first ones on this path. Many authors tried to "improve" C, for example, languages D [9], Cyclone [10]. Compared to our aims, these languages and programming systems have a different goal - to prevent the penetration of malware into programs written in C. We pursue a much more modest task - to prevent the programmer from making many typical mistakes and to facilitate the localization and correction of those mistakes that he still managed to make.

It is interesting that these two goals do not conflict with each other, since generally malware penetrates the applications through the places where the authors relied on the compiler with no reason, and so did not find the error on time. However, these mistakes, even without malware, can result in many troubles!

Let us consider in detail the differences between RuC and the classical C.

1. We abandoned "union" in structures. Firstly, this is a rarely used C language feature. Secondly, the level of security is decreasing with this feature usage.

2. RuC does not contain pointer arithmetic. User can describe pointer variable, create a pointer using the & operation, assign a pointer to a variable of a suitable type, but at the same time user cannot, for example, add a constant to the pointer and write or read anything for the received address. All operations of dynamic memory allocation have as an operand the type of value for which memory is allocated. Thus, any pointer knows the type of value to which it refers.

3. The dereferencing of a pointer at the moment when its NULL is one of the most frequent and difficult errors, on the other hand, inserting a check for NULL with each call to the pointer sharply affects the efficiency of the code. A few years ago it was thought up how to get around this difficulty. In addition to the usual pointer type (for example, int *), another pointer type (for example, int @) is introduced. The second type is called Never Null Pointer, that is, a pointer that never takes a NULL value. Variables of this type should always be initialized, with a value other than NULL. The use of such pointers does not require a NULL check; if you assign a variable of this type to a regular pointer, the compiler will automatically insert a NULL check. As a result, for example, chain lists will be implemented using ordinary pointers, but there and so NULL checking is necessary to determine the end of the list, and, for example, files after opening will have a second pointer type, therefore, in bulk operations like scanf or printf files can use safely and without checking for NULL.

4. An array in RuC is a normal language object, although it does not exist in the base C language. It can be described, including with dynamically calculated boundaries (in C, borders are only static), slice out an element from it, for example, a[i][j], or even a[i] for a multidimensional array, assign it to another array, enter or print. The number of array elements is stored in front of the first element of an array, which makes it possible to dynamically check if the index is out of the array. Usually translators neglect this check, and this is one of the most difficult user errors to be detected. In the process of analyzing the literature on the problems of error protection, we stumbled upon the publication of a Russian author, who recommended not to use indexing arrays, but to use only pointer arithmetic, he said that it is more efficient. In our opinion, this advice is very dangerous, and the same indexing efficiency can be provided with fairly simple optimizations.

5. Language C provides a large amount of ways to describe the formal parameters of functions. We have chosen, in our opinion, the most expressive one, and tightened the checking on the compliance of the actual parameters with the formal ones.

6. A lot of efforts have been spent to provide a detailed and understandable error reporting system with reference to the place where the error occurred.

5   Conclusion

In this paper the methodology of IT education in Russia was presented with the example of SPbU experience. Our methodology based on three rules: fundamental mathematics basement, following international education standards, including nontraditional courses for Russia, and the connection with IT industry. Success of such approach can be demonstrated by graduated students who are effectively working in Russian and western companies, such as Google, Microsoft, Oracle etc.

References

1. Computing Curricula 2005. Book ACM and IEEE (2005)
2. Leonov, G.A., Kiyaev, V.I., Kuznetsov, N.V., Onosovsky, V.V., Seledzhi, S.M.: Computers and software engineering: developing new models for educating mathematicians. In: Book Computers in Education, vol. 2, pp. 157–169. Nova Science Publishers (2012)
3. Abramovich, S., Kuznetsov, N.V., Kuznetsov, S.V., Leonov, G.A., Onosovsky, V.V., Seledzhi, S.M.: Learning to develop and use software products: some common aspects of educational preparation of mathematicians and schoolteachers. In: 3rd World Conference on Information Technology, vol. 3, pp. 44–52 (2013)
4. Terekhov, A., Terekhova, K.: The economics of hiring and staff retention for an IT company in Russia. In: Nordio, M., Joseph, M., Meyer, B., Terekhov, A. (eds.) SEAFOOD 2010. LNBIP, vol. 54, pp. 54–63. Springer, Heidelberg (2010). https://doi.org/10.1007/978-3-642-13784-6_6
5. Wirth, N., Gutknecht, J.: Project Oberon the Design of an Operating System and Compiler. Addison-Wesley Publishing Co., Boston (1992)
6. Meyer, B.: Touch of Class, Learning to Program Well with Objects and Contracts. Springer, Heidelberg (2009). https://doi.org/10.1007/978-3-540-92145-5
7. Kernighan, B.W., Ritchie, D.M.: The C Programming Language. Prentice Hall, Englewood Cliffs (1988)
8. Terekhov, A., Luchin, R., Filippov, S.: Educational Cybernetical Construction Set for Schools and Universities. Advances in Control Education (2012)
9. Alexandrescu, A.: The D Programming Language. Adison-Wesley, Boston (2010)
10. Grossman, D., Hicks, M., Trevor, J., Morrisett, G.: Cyclone: a type-safe dialect of C. C/C++ Users J. **23**, 112–139 (2005)

Ten Unsafe Assumptions When Teaching Topics in Software Engineering

David Vernon(✉)

Carnegie Mellon University Africa, Kigali, Rwanda
vernon@cmu.edu
http://www.vernon.eu

Abstract. Software engineering is a branch of systems engineering and, to be successful, software engineering students must work in a systems-focussed manner. Instructors, including the author, routinely assume that students have the requisite skills for this or can learn them quickly. This article identifies ten common assumptions that are unsafe to make and, if made, impact negatively on the ability of a student to acquire the essential foundation on which to build their understanding of the technical aspects of software engineering. The ten unsafe assumptions are that students understand how to decompose problems, that they know that systems have to be specified at different levels of abstraction, that they know how to bridge different levels of abstraction, that they understand how software and hardware reflect these different levels, that they can follow instructions and pay attention to detail, that they can easily follow oral or written explanations, that they are able to stress test their own software, that they understand the relevance of professional practice, that they are adept at self-criticism, and they understand the relevance of examples. In each case, we identify the implications for teaching practice of not making these assumptions.

Keywords: Teaching practices · Unsafe assumptions · Foundational skills · Effective learning

1 Introduction

Software engineering is a branch of systems engineering and, as such, it is concerned with analysing, modelling, designing, implementing, and delivering large-scale complex software systems. Consequently, there are multiple dimensions to software engineering. One dimension embraces the tools, techniques, methods, and processes required to develop software. A second embraces the management techniques required to organize software projects successfully, to monitor the effectiveness of the development, and to improve the development process. A third addresses the way in which the non-functional attributes of the software being developed are achieved. Non-functional attributes refer not to what the software does (its function) but instead to the manner in which it does

© Springer Nature Switzerland AG 2020
J.-M. Bruel et al. (Eds.): FISEE 2019, LNCS 12271, pp. 115–130, 2020.
https://doi.org/10.1007/978-3-030-57663-9_9

it (its dependability, security, composability, portability, interoperability, sometimes referred to as the "-ilities" [18]).

Software engineering degrees comprise courses that cover all of these topics. However, the instructors who teach these courses, including the author of this essay, often assume that students are well equipped with the requisite foundational skills to learn the technical material in these courses. In the following, I suggest that such assumptions are not always safe[1] and that making them can have a significantly adverse impact on the students' learning experience and the effectiveness of the instructor's teaching practice. On the contrary, I suggest the changes that are required to compensate for not making these assumptions might possibly contribute to more effective teaching practice in general.

While much of what follows might seem trivial and the suggestions almost self-evident, that does not diminish the impact of taking them on board and putting them into practice. As we will see, they are consistent with pedagogical principles, both in computer science and software engineering [11] and in education generally [1]. Most of the suggestions focus on first and second year students. Others, especially the last three which are concerned with professional practice and soft-skills, will benefit students at all levels as they become increasingly accomplished.

The contribution this essay makes to a volume devoted to exploring the frontiers in software engineering education is less about advocating some specific approach such as component-based software engineering, much less about introducing a revolutionary new pedagogy, but rather about adjusting teaching practices to address some of the foundational systems-oriented skills that underpin a student's ability to engage successfully with software engineering education.

2   Unsafe Assumptions

2.1   Students Understand How to Decompose Problems

Software engineering is concerned with solving problems and building reliable software systems that meet the needs of users. When setting software engineering assignments, it is common practice to state the problems in the form of functional requirements. In contrast to the requirements which are elicited when working with an industrial or commercial client, these requirements are usually complete and unambiguous and, hence, rather atypical. The job of a student

---

[1] When teaching software-focussed courses to students from eighteen countries in Africa I encountered several difficulties in delivering material in a style that had apparently worked well in other parts of the world, including Europe, the Middle East, and Russia. I say "apparently" because, when forced to address these difficulties by adopting a more student-centric stance and questioning what I was assuming about students' foundational skills, it became clear that other students might benefit from the changes to teaching practice that arose from not making these evidently unsafe assumptions.

is to deploy her or his knowledge and know-how to transform these requirements into to a software system. One of the principal difficulties is that mapping from requirements—even complete unambiguous requirements—to finished system requires the student to formulate a feasible way of attacking the problem. There are several aspects to this plan of attack, all of which are evidently very difficult for inexperienced students. They include the processes of problem decomposition, problem modelling (typically requiring the identification of a computational model of the problem), systems analysis (involving the generation of functional, data, and behavioral models, as well as the modelling of non-functional aspects), design (involving the selection of effective and efficient algorithms and data structures), implementation, and various forms of verification and validation testing. In terms of abstraction, the gap between problem statement and final operational solution is big. We will address the pivotal issue of abstraction in more detail in subsequent sections. Here we focus on the very first process: problem decomposition and the identification of a plan of attack.

Experienced practitioners, including instructors, find the process of problem decomposition and coming up with a plan of attack straightforward [16]. It is evident that inexperienced students find the very opposite: the ability to decompose problems doesn't come naturally to many students. The solution is straightforward: demonstrate how it is done.

Since demonstrations are most successful when they matter to the person observing the demonstration and they have something to gain from it, one successful approach is to fashion laboratory exercises for each assignment with detailed instructions on how to attack the problem, typically ten to twenty individual steps, each step comprising a distinct fine-grained sub-problem that is clearly-stated and amenable to direct attack. As the course progresses, assignments are accompanied by laboratory exercises comprising fewer and fewer instructions, progressively weaning the students off this form of assistance. The final assignment provides none. Employing this approach changes the class dynamic and results in significantly greater motivation on the part of the students, increased rate of learning, and, ultimately, the acquisition of reasonable skill in problem decomposition.

2.2   Students Know that All Systems Have to Be Specified at Different Levels of Abstraction

One of the most important concepts we teach in software engineering is the power of abstraction [11]. In the previous section, we noted the big gap between the high level of abstraction of a problem statement and the low level of abstraction of final operational solution. This gives rise to two key difficulties faced by students: (a) to recognize that this gap exists at all, and (b) to learn how to bridge the gap effectively.

Regarding the first, it is apparent that many students do not realize that problems, solutions, and systems in general need to be understood at different levels of abstraction and that doing so is necessary if one is to map from problem to solution. The concept of abstraction is routinely taught in courses on data

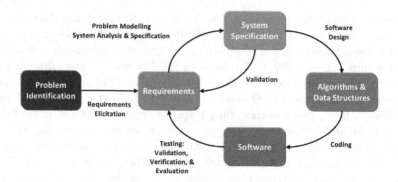

Fig. 1. One version of the software development life cycle.

structures and algorithm when introducing abstract data types (ADTs) and the associated concept of data hiding [12]. The same applies at the implementation level, manifested in programming languages that expose functionality through abstract interfaces [11]. However, here we are generalizing this beyond the design and implementation phases and we are applying it across the complete software development life cycle, from problem modelling to solution implementation (see Fig. 1). The key idea is that the level of abstraction become progressively lower as we proceed from the early problem modelling phases (which are typically understood at a high level of abstraction) through to system modelling, to design, and finally to implementation (which is specified at the lowest level of abstraction) [7]. As we progress, more and more detail is added to the description as the concepts are specified in less abstract terms. One of the most common difficulties encountered by students is that, almost always unwittingly, they suffer from level confusion where they don't realize that they are applying the wrong form of analysis in the wrong phase of the development life cycle, e.g. establishing a theoretical understanding of the solution when developing an algorithm or, most common of all, formulating an algorithm when writing the code during the implementation phase.

More generally, all systems can be viewed at different levels of abstraction, successively removing specific details at higher levels and keeping just the general essence of what is important for a useful model of the system.[2]

As part of his influential work on modelling the human visual system [8], David Marr advocated a three-level hierarchy of abstraction, often referred to at the *Levels of Understanding* framework; see Fig. 2. He argued that the framework applies to any information processing system. At the top level, there is the computational theory. Below this, there is the level of representation and algorithm. At the bottom, there is the hardware implementation. At the level of the computational theory, you need to answer questions such as "what is the goal of the computation, why is it appropriate, and what is the logic of the

---

[2] The remainder of this section on levels of abstraction follows closely the treatment in [19].

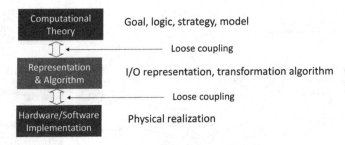

Fig. 2. The three levels at which an information processing system should be understood and modelled: the computational theory that formalizes the problem, the representational and algorithmic level that addresses the implementation of the theory, and the hardware level that physically realizes the system (after David Marr [8]). The computational theory is primary and the system should be understood and modelled first at this level of abstraction, although the representational and algorithmic level is often more intuitively accessible.

strategy by which it is carried out?" At the level of representation and algorithm, the questions are different: "how can this computational theory be applied? In particular, what is the representation for the input and output, and what is the algorithm for the transformation?". Finally, the question at the level of hardware implementation is "how can the representation and algorithm be physically realized?" In other words, how can we build the physical system? Marr emphasized that these three levels are only loosely coupled: you can—and, according to Marr, you should—think about one level without necessarily paying any attention to those below it. Thus, you begin modelling at the computational level, ideally described in some mathematical formalism, moving on to representations and algorithms once the model is complete, and finally you can decide how to implement these representations and algorithms to realize the working system. Marr's point is that, although the algorithm and representation levels are more accessible, it is the computational or theoretical level that is critically important from an information processing perspective. In essence, he states that the problem can and should first be modelled at the abstract level of the computational theory without strong reference to the lower and less abstract levels.[3]

Marr illustrated his argument succinctly by comparing the problem of understanding vision (Marr's own goal) to the problem of understanding the mechanics of flight.

"Trying to understand perception by studying only neurons is like trying to understand bird flight by studying only feathers: it just cannot be done.

---

[3] Tomaso Poggio recently proposed a revision of Marr's three-level hierarchy in which he advocates greater emphasis on the connections between the levels and an extension of the range of levels, adding *Learning and Development* on top of the computational theory level (specifically hierarchical learning), and *Evolution* on top of that [13]. Tomaso Poggio co-authored the original paper [9] on which David Marr based his more famous treatment in his 1982 book *Vision* [8].

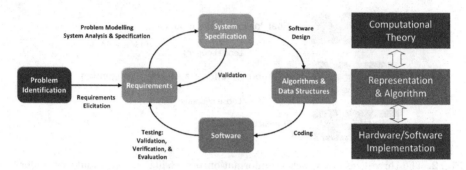

Fig. 3. The different levels of abstraction mapped to the software development life cycle.

> In order to understand bird flight, we have to understand aerodynamics; only then do the structure of feathers and the different shapes of birds' wings make sense"

Objects with different cross-sectional profiles give rise to different pressure patterns on the object when they move through a fluid such as air (or when a fluid flows around an object). If you choose the right cross-section then there is more pressure on the bottom than on the top, resulting in a lifting force that counteracts the force of gravity and allows the object to fly. It isn't until you know this that you can begin to understand the problem in a way that will yield a solution for your specific needs.

Of course, you eventually have to decide how to realize a computational model but this comes later. The point Marr was making is that you should decouple the different levels of abstraction and begin your analysis at the highest level, avoiding consideration of implementation issues until the computational or theoretical model is complete. When it is, it can then subsequently drive the decisions that need to be taken at the lower level when realizing the physical system.

Marr's dissociation of the different levels of abstraction is significant because it provides an elegant way to build a complex system by addressing it in sequential stages of decreasing abstraction. It is a very general approach and can be applied successfully to modelling, designing, and building many different systems that depend on the ability to process information.

Introducing Marr's levels of understanding framework is a very effective way of exposing students to the need to treat problems at different levels of abstraction at different phases of the software development life cycle (thereby addressing the first difficulty identified at the start of this section) and it also provides a way of mapping it to the software development life cycle itself; see Fig. 3.

2.3 Students Know How to Bridge Different Levels of Abstraction

Knowing that any complex system can be modelled and understood at several levels of abstraction is essential in being able to engineer effective, efficient, and appropriate software. However, there still remains the problem of knowing how to map from one level of abstraction to another. This isn't trivial [7]. As we saw above, this mapping happens when one goes from the computational model to the design and from the design to the implementation. When teaching software engineering, we often use the mapping from computational theory to design as the archetypal example of this process, pointing out how a given model and the associated solution strategy often has many possible algorithms and data structures. We call these *design choices*. For example, a digital filter can be modelled as a spectral process using the Fourier transform but there are several Fourier transform algorithms that can yield the required transformation from temporal or spatial data to frequency spectral data, e.g. the discrete Fourier transform (DFT), the fast Fourier transform (FFT) [4], and different implementations, e.g. the fastest Fourier transform in the west (FFTW) [5]. Sorting a list can be characterized as the identification of the permutation of the elements of the list that satisfies an ordering constraint, with many different sorting algorithms to choose from, and with the choice depending on the required computational complexity, space complexity, and need for stability or not.

However, the level-of-abstraction mapping problem occurs at the transition of every phase of the development life cycle and the goal is to help students understand that there are choices to be made at each transition and that the only way to do the mapping effectively is to enumerate the choices and identify the selection criteria. By continually making these choices explicit, the message is absorbed by the interested student.

There exists yet another situation in which this level-of-abstraction mapping problem arises: when developing solution strategies. Typically, these are initially expressed in high-level abstract strategies and the difficulty is to translate this conceptual understanding into detailed low-level unpacked tactics [16].

The key to overcoming these difficulties is through the copious use of examples. People learn by induction: by inferring general principles from multiple instances of particular cases. The second key to overcoming these difficulties is though practice: repeated engagement with the process so the inductive insight is revealed quicker with experience.

The general approach, then, is to expose students to the practice of *progressive deepening*: covering the same material multiple times at different levels of abstraction or detail.

Some readers may be uncomfortable at this point with an approach based on establishing an intuitive appreciation for the process and an understanding that it requires as much skill and experience as it does knowledge. These readers might justify these concerns on the basis that we are dealing here with science and engineering, and that, as such, the problem would be finessed if we simply followed established engineering practices or methodologies. Model-driven software engineering [3,14] or formal methods [2,10,15] would, to some extent, alleviate these concerns. However, it should be remembered that we are speaking here of both understanding the process and using an effective methodology to bridge the gap in abstraction between requirements and implementation in several steps. Even if in possession of tools to help automate this process, it is essential that the student understand what the tool is helping to automate.

2.4   Students Understand How Software and Hardware Reflect the Different Levels of Abstraction

As we have said, software engineering rightly emphasizes the importance of abstraction [7,11]. As we noted in Sect. 2.2, it contributes to clarity and transparency in all phases of the software development life cycle, including computational modelling, design, and implementation. Abstraction hides the unnecessary details of the levels below. However, there are times when these details matter and they can matter at every level of abstraction and at every phase of the life cycle [7]. In Marr's levels of understanding framework, the levels are loosely-coupled, not entirely decoupled. This is where an in-depth understanding of all layers in the realization of a software system—from application to the hardware architecture—can help with developing effective, efficient software. Developers with this knowledge are often referred to as *full-stack* engineers or developers.[4] Regrettably, many students are exposed only to high-level abstract knowledge and this has two negative effects.

First, it means that the instructor is not able to revert to low-level implementation details, typically at the level of middleware, operating systems, and computer architecture, to explain key topics.

For example, when teaching pointers, it is often helpful to explain to students that they are effectively memory addresses and that referencing and dereferencing involves the manipulation of addresses of data and access to the data at given addresses. The purely abstract concept of referencing and dereferencing, while valid, involves more sophisticated semantics than the semantics of location and content and often takes students longer to grasp. Furthermore, understanding that pointers are memory addresses helps students understand why dereferencing an uninitialized pointer is dangerous and potentially harmful without some form of memory protection. It also helps when explaining the meaning of segmentation errors, i.e. attempts the access memory via pointers that lie outside the user's memory space.

When teaching the semantics of the CAR, CDR, and CONS function in Common Lisp [6], understanding that lists are implemented as linked lists with two fields, both of which are pointers (and that CAR and CDR derive from reference to an address register), helps greatly in getting the semantics of these functions across to students. Without that implementation level understanding,

---

[4] In the past few years, the concept of a full-stack developer has changed in a significant way, referring not to a developer with knowledge of all levels of the implementation of a system, including the underlying middleware, operating system, and computer architecture, but instead to a developer who is conversant with both front-end and back-end development in client-server architectures. This alternative meaning loses the emphasis on mastery of the many levels of abstraction, substituting instead a mastery of user-interface programming and information processing.

the different forms of equality operator, e.g. EQ, EQL, EQUAL, and EQUALP are very difficult to grasp.

When explaining the semantics of recursion and the role of the implicit stack, it helps to refer to the implementation of this stack in the operating system, specifically the use of the process stack for dynamic memory allocation and the associated time and space cost of pushing and popping the function state when calling functions recursively and returning from recursive calls. Given the importance of recursive algorithms and their dependence on the persistence of local variables during recursion, this low-level understanding, well-below the level of abstraction necessary to explain the semantics of recursion, helps student understanding.

Similarly, when explaining dynamic memory allocation by a client programmer, knowledge of the operating system heap is helpful (and is essential if one is to make any sense of "stack overruns heap" fatal error messages). It also helps understand why buffer overruns can be difficult to trace and why memory leakage is such an important problem.

Knowledge of computer architecture too, even the basic von Neuman architecture, can help students understand key concepts such as caching and the relevance of cache memory. Arguably, it is essential to understand why caching may not be of any value when accessing dynamic data structures that have physical addresses which are not all be present in the current memory cache.

These are just some examples to make the point that full-stack knowledge can aid both in instruction and in building a more complete picture for the student of the trade-offs required when designing efficient software.

We mentioned above that there are two negative effects from being exposed only to high-level abstract knowledge. The second is to do with how learning works. As Ambrose et al. point out, [1], p. 49, experts and novices organize knowledge in different ways. Specifically, experts have a much higher density of connections between concepts, facts, and skills. Exposing these connections and highlighting cross-linkage among topics helps novices transition to expert-level understanding. Exploiting full-stack knowledge is an effective way of demonstrating this and, in the process, helping the student build a deeper understanding of software engineering. Professionals—experts—typically see the software in the context of the full stack, always working at the correct level of abstraction but always being aware of the network of connections to the other levels.

2.5   Students Can Follow Instructions and Pay Attention to Detail

Students are human beings and human beings have limited working memory and a natural capacity for pattern recognition. Consequently, students often tend to look at things— problem statements, algorithms, and code—from a global holistic perspective first and then infer the details. This causes many problems because, while this may well help in forming an intuitive understanding of the issue, it is very problematic when it comes to bridging the gap to the necessary detailed description of the issue at hand.

One striking example of this is the inclination of students to look at a code segment or a pseudo-code representation of an algorithm and then try to understand what is happening by looking for a pattern in the description as a whole. Unfortunately, the meaning of the whole, at least in software, emerges from an understanding on the individual statements and their relationship to each other: meaning emerges from the detail and an understanding of that meaning requires students to inhibit their predisposition to look at the code and infer what it means. Consequently, it turns out that the key to success in this is to get the students to adopt a letter-box view of code, seeing only one statement at a time, inhibiting the natural tendency to link it to all the other parts of which you are aware, and build the understanding of the process, step by step. As we will see in Sect. 2.6, fine-grained diagrams help greatly with this.

The same issue arises when students attempt to assimilate written material. There is a prevalent tendency to try to get the gist of the material by skimming through it. While this is of itself fine, the problem arises with the belief that complete understanding follows multiple skims through the material. This becomes particularly problematic when following detailed written instructions, e.g. detailed software installation instructions or lengthy on-line tutorials [17]. Students very often don't have the patience or discipline to follow each instruction exactly, one step at a time. Either they skip steps in the instructions or they guess what is meant without digesting fully what is meant. The idea that instructions mean exactly what the say and only what they say is often hard for students to grasp. The problem is exacerbated by providing fewer richer instructions because these individual instructions then become subject to the same skimming process to establish the gist and guess the meaning as larger tracts of material. Paradoxically, the solution is to provide very fine grained highly-explicit detailed instructions that minimize the tendency to skim and to demonstrate that following them exactly does lead to success.

Of course, students also need to learn to follow coarse-grained instructions. To facilitate this, the instructions for laboratory exercises that support assignments (see Sect. 2.1) might take the form advocated above, i.e. many fine-grained detailed explicit instructions, but reducing their number and making them progressively more coarse-grained over the course of a semester.

2.6   Students Can Easily Follow Oral or Written Explanations

We depend on spoken and written language as the main medium of instruction when teaching. As with all forms of effective communication, one needs to keep the vocabulary focussed and not use language that is unnecessarily complex. The exception, of course, is where one is introducing new technical vocabulary and the semantics of new concepts. However, this, in itself, is not enough. Something more is needed: graphic depiction of material. Diagrammatic illustration matters, far more than one might expect. This becomes particularly evident when performing structured walkthroughs of software code. The need to understand both the syntax and the semantics of the code is often difficult for many students. This is compounded when you factor in the temporal nature of code execution. Unwinding iterative constructs by describing in words what is happening is inadequate, even if it's common practice. Unwinding recursion is even worse. However, when supported by diagrams that show each step graphically—each change of state that results from each statement in the software—using a very fine-grained approach, the computational processes become much clearer to the students. In essence, diagrams matter when describing structure and they matter even more when describing processes. Processes need to be illustrated at a fine level of temporal detail. Depending on language-based explanation alone doesn't work well. Conversely, using diagrams to unwind temporal processes and visualize key concepts makes a significant difference to the student's learning experience.

2.7 Students Are Able to Stress Test Their Own Software

Every software engineering course has at least a few classes devoted to testing. We distinguish between verification (of functionality against specifications), validation (of functionality and non-functional characteristics against requirements), and benchmarking (against the performance of other solutions or systems). We explain the important of static testing, dynamic testing, black box testing, white box testing, grey box testing, stress testing, unit tests, integration tests, system tests, acceptance tests, and regression tests. And we assume that students can learn and apply the testing techniques effectively and efficiently. This assumption may not be safe, especially when it comes to stress testing.

Despite being made aware of Dijkstra's warning that testing can only be used to demonstrate the presence of errors in software, not their absence, students often see testing as demonstration that their software "works". Reversing the logic and seeing testing as an exercise in trying to break the software is not something that comes naturally to students, particularly when testing their own code. This is a natural consequence that they have a vested interest in their code—their creation—and they are psychologically ill-equipped to intentionally damage it by subjecting it to data that undermines its functionality, i.e. to be aggressive in developing test strategies and to identify particularly difficult unforeseen boundary test scenarios.

The resolution of this problem turns out to be quite straightforward. By adopting a policy of providing sample test cases when issuing an assignment but of always assigning marks on the basis of performance against a large set of blind test cases, students quickly learn to be more aggressive in testing. It may take three or four assignments to grasp the message, but eventually, as marks are consistently deducted for failures on boundary cases, students come to understand that showing the program works on typical data is far from sufficient to get a good grade. That requires a more aggressive approach and, as a result, the stress tests become more thorough.

In all of this, however, it is equally important to emphasize the truism of software engineering that you can't test quality into a program: it must be designed in.

2.8   Students Understand the Importance of Professional Practice

Students are often required to engage with companies, either individually or in teams, as part of their program of education in order to prepare them for the realities of working in a commercial or industrial environment after they graduate. Often, these exercises involve the development and delivery of some form of software systems. Typically, the industry client has some problem that needs to be solved or some new capability they would like and they expect the students to solve it or provide the required system. More often than not, they only have vague notions of exactly what they want delivered at the end of the project but they are very adept at recognizing what they do not want.

Students, when charged with liaising with clients are invariably shocked to discover that the client doesn't have a clear set of requirements and, worse, that they are often too busy to engage in a lengthy requirements elicitation process with the students. This is because, while the difficulty of the requirements elicitation process is always taught in class, the reality is that students are usually given assignments couched in terms of a clear requirements document and with clear acceptance tests in the form of a grading rubric. Students rarely have to concern themselves with what is unknown about the project they have to complete and, over time, this lulls them into a false sense of security that the requirements elicitation process is straightforward. Nothing, of course, could be further from the truth.

Having to confront these difficulties provides one of the most valuable lessons a student of software engineering can learn. They begin to appreciate the importance of dealing with uncertainty and ambiguity, striving to understand what the client needs, rather than what the client says they need. In the process, they also learn some of the most important soft skills that underpin success in the commercial world of software engineering, specifically how to manage the client—with politeness, respect, and patience—in order to maximize the value of the limited time the client is willing to invest when meeting with the students. This requires two adjustments in teaching practice: (a) don't always provide complete specifications and let the students grapple with that uncertainty (this point appears in a different guise in the section on testing), and (b) be prepared to tutor students as much in professional practice, e.g. the soft skills of client liaison, meeting etiquette, writing minutes, timely delivery of documents being tabled for discussion, as you do in the technical aspects of software engineering.

2.9   Students Are Adept at Self-criticism

Just as we teach students that one of the main goals of software engineering is continuous process improvement, including quantitative and qualitative quality assessment, we often assume that students understand that they are part of the process and, consequently, the same goals apply to them and the manner in which they conduct themselves as aspiring professionals. However, it is evident that often students do not make the connection with the attendant need to continually question everything they say and everything they do. In other words, students don't automatically see the need for self-referential (or reflexive) quality assurance. Moreover, even when they are made aware of this, they don't typically have a ready disposition to engage with it.

Teaching quality assurance in software engineering—something that should not be relegated to a single course or even a part of a course—offers another opportunity to help students learn the importance of professional practice and soft skills. Since a software engineer is an intrinsic part of the software engineering process, the two issues—quality assurance in software engineering and quality assurance in professional practice—are just two sides of the same coin.

The magnitude of the task of inculcating a disposition to engage in the practice of self-referential quality assurance is more considerable than one might imagine. People are generally not self-critical. We met a similar trait in Sect. 2.7 on stress testing your own code. There are many ways one can approach it. For example, by imposing exacting standards for the manner in which students frame questions in class (and elsewhere): saying exactly what they mean and meaning exactly what they say. Often, students will have a vague notion of what they don't understand and, when asking a question, it's not uncommon for them to begin to speak while not yet having a clear idea of what it is they want to establish in the answer they expect. Very often, they expect the instructor to interpret their poorly- and partially-framed question and infer their intent and meaning. And very often, we do. However, in doing so, we do them no favors because we then reinforce this poor style of questioning and, implicitly, teach them poor professional practice. It can be painful and slow, but working with a student to have them re-frame their question and re-frame it again and again until they are finally asking exactly what the need to know. It comes down to precision of expression, something that should permeate the professional life of a software engineer. The same approach can be applied to written reports, to software documentation, to algorithm design, and to computational modelling: to every aspect of the software development life cycle.

Finally, as instructors in software engineering, it is imperative that we, in turn, embrace this almost obsessive-compulsive attachment to precision in all our dealings with students so that they learn by example. This is not as easy as it sounds. It means we must adopt a teaching practice that is founded on leading by example and by being transparently self-critical in everything we do. The transparency is important. We must correct ourselves in class when we identify a weakness or flaw in what we've said. When writing reports or papers, we routinely make multiple passes at editing the text, applying red ink copiously and without restraint in an effort to polish our writing in search of precision (as well as brevity, simplicity, and clarity). It can be a helpful device to keep these multiple edits on hand to show students that we apply to ourselves the same standards that we expect of them. This leads to the tenth and final unsafe assumption.

2.10   Students Understand the Relevance of Examples

Examples provide essential illustration. However, examples can expose far more than just the meaning of the principle, practice, or technique currently being examined. Important though that is, examples also provide an opportunity to leverage several of the evidence-based principles of how learning works, as expounded by Ambrose *et al.* [1]. These principles can be exploited in many other ways, of course, but here we will take the opportunity to show how examples provide a concrete way to leverage them to achieve more effective educational practice.

One of the principles is that "to develop mastery, students must acquire component skills, practice integrating them, and know when to apply what they have learned" [1], p. 95. When coupled with Meyer's observation that "to learn a technique or a trade it is best to start by looking at the example of excellent work produced by professionals, and taking advantage of it by (in order) using that work, understanding its internal construction, extending it, improving it – and starting to build your own" [11], the power of a well-presented example is clear.

Examples demonstrate the process of application. Furthermore, if the examples relate to one another, they provide another opportunity to demonstrate the difference between the way an expert organizes knowledge and the way a novice organizes knowledge, as we noted already, with the former having a much higher density of connections among concept, facts, and skills. Exposing these connections and highlighting cross-linkage among topics can be accomplished by stating them but demonstrating them through examples is even more effective.

The other aspect of examples is that they provide an opportunity for practice through well-designed assignments, especially ones that reflect authentic, real-world tasks: these are the types of example that feed student motivation. The importance of assignments is well understood but it is worth re-emphasizing: "Students must learn to assess the demands of the task, evaluate their own knowledge and skills, plan their approach, monitor their projects, and adjust their strategies as needed" [1], p. 191, reflecting another of the principles that goal-directed practice coupled with targeted feedback are critical to learning [1], p. 125. It is even better if scaffolding can be built into assignments, later assignments leveraging what has been learned in earlier assignments. This demonstrates the importance of reuse in a very practical manner while also speaking to the core importance of systems thinking in software engineering.

3   Conclusion

In this essay, I have tried to convince that questioning assumptions about the degree to which students possess foundational skills serves to reveal ways in which teaching practice might be improved. It is important to emphasize that this makes no value judgement about the aptitude or ability of the student but rather targets the idiosyncrasies of how people learn to master the *skills* that underpin software engineering. The contention is that recognizing these idiosyncrasies can help improve educational practice and contribute to more effective teaching. It rebalances a possibly unbalanced approach that might favor a focus on content over the object of teaching, i.e. the student. This more balanced approach is captured succinctly by the exhortation to "Teach students, not content" [1].

Acknowledgements. Many thanks go to the reviewers of an earlier version of this paper for their helpful and constructive comments.

References

1. Ambrose, S.A., Bridges, M.W., DiPietro, M., Lovett, M.C., Norman, M.K., Mayer, R.E.: How Learning Works: Seven Research-Based Principles for Smart Teaching. Wiley, Hoboken (2010)
2. Bjørner, D., Havelund, K.: 40 years of formal methods. In: Jones, C., Pihlajasaari, P., Sun, J. (eds.) FM 2014. LNCS, vol. 8442, pp. 42–61. Springer, Cham (2014). https://doi.org/10.1007/978-3-319-06410-9_4
3. Bruyninckx, H., Klotzbücher, M., Hochgeschwender, N., Kraetzschmar, G., Gherardi, L., Brugali, D.: The BRICS component model: a model-based development paradigm for complex robotics software systems. In: Proceedings of the 28th Annual ACM Symposium on Applied Computing, SAC 2013, pp. 1758–1764. ACM, New York (2013)
4. Cooley, J.W., Tukey, J.W.: An algorithm for the machine calculation of complex fourier series. Math. Comput. **19**(90), 297–301 (1965)
5. Frigo, M., Johnson, S.G.: The design and implementation of FFTW3. Proc. IEEE **93**(2), 216–231 (2005)
6. Graham, P.: ANSI Common Lisp. Prentice Hall (1996)
7. Kramer, J., Hazzan, O.: The role of abstraction in software engineering. In: Proceedings of International Conference on Software Engineering (ICSE 2006), vol. 31, pp. 1017–1018. ACM SIGSOFT Software Engineering Notes, Shanghai (2006)
8. Marr, D.: Vision. Freeman, San Francisco (1982)
9. Marr, D., Poggio, T.: From understanding computation to understanding neural circuitry. In: Poppel, E., Held, R., Dowling, J.E. (eds.) Neuronal Mechanisms in Visual Perception, Neurosciences Research Program Bulletin, vol. 15, pp. 470–488 (1977)
10. Why don't people use formal methods? https://www.hillelwayne.com/post/why-dont-people-use-formalmethods/
11. Meyer, B.: Touch of Class - Learning to Program Well with Objects and Contracts. Springer, Heidelberg (2013). https://doi.org/10.1007/978-3-540-92145-5
12. Parnas, D.L.: On the criteria to be used in decomposing systems into modules. Commun. ACM **15**(12), 1053–1058 (1972)
13. Poggio, T.: The levels of understanding framework, revised. Perception **41**, 1017–1023 (2012)
14. Schlegel, C., Steck, A., Lotz, A.: Model-driven software development in robotics: communication patterns as key for a robotics component model. In: Introduction to Modern Robotics. iConcept Press (2011)
15. Schumann, J.M.: Formal methods in software engineering. In: Schumann, J.M. (ed.) Automated Theorem Proving in Software Engineering, pp. 11–22. Springer, Heidelberg (2001). https://doi.org/10.1007/978-3-662-22646-9_2

16. Skiena, S.: The Algorithm Design Manual, 2nd edn. Springer, Heidelberg (2010). https://doi.org/10.1007/978-1-84800-070-4
17. CRAM simple mobile manipulation plan. http://cramsystem.org/tutorials/intermediate/simple_mobile_manipulation_plan
18. Vanthienen, D., Klotzbücher, M., Bruyninckx, H.: The 5C-based architectural composition pattern: lessons learned from re-developing the iTaSC framework for constraint-based robot programming. J. Softw. Eng. Robot. 5(1), 17–35 (2014)
19. Vernon, D.: Artificial Cognitive Systems – A Primer. MIT Press, Cambridge (2014)

Curriculum and Course Design

Analysing the SWECOM Standard for Designing a DevOps Education Programme

Alfredo Capozucca(✉) and Nicolas Guelfi

Department of Computer Science, Faculty of Science, Technology and Medicine,
University of Luxembourg, Maison du Nombre,
6, Avenue de la Fonte, 4364 Esch-sur-Alzette, Luxembourg
alfredo.capozucca@uni.lu

Abstract. Developing academic education programmes for software engineers is a difficult task mainly due to three main factors: (1) ever-changing information and communication technologies produced by the industry and meant for citizens living in digital disruptions age, (2) lack of official or de-facto standards for the software engineering domain, (3) slow pace of the standardisation bodies and of the academia for deploying standard competence frameworks or education programmes. This applies more especially to DevOps which regroups a set of skills being the most demanded today by the job market. This paper is a first attempt to introduce a standard based development process to derive a DevOps education programme for graduate education. It is introduced as a generic process mainly based on the SWECOM standard. This process is applied to generate a proposal for a significant DevOps graduate academic programme definition in a comprehensive and, most importantly, in a skill oriented manner.

1 Introduction

Software engineers initial education is mainly provided by universities or higher education schools. Education is these types of institutions are organised in programmes that are often aligned in two types of degrees: a bachelor degree (undergraduate) which lasts for 3 years, followed by a master degree (graduate) of 2 years. Thus, higher education of software engineers is done into the context of these degrees.

The design of an education program for software engineers has been a difficult task since the creation of software engineering as a discipline in the NATO meeting of 1968 [26]. A first significant effort has been released by the ACM and IEEE standardisation organisations in the provision of the SE2004 - Curriculum Guidelines for Undergraduate Degree Programs in Software Engineering. This effort has been complemented with the provision of a software engineering body of knowledge in 2005 [19].

The software engineering domain as well as all domains directly related to the digital world is rapidly evolving. Unfortunately the time scale of standardisation

© Springer Nature Switzerland AG 2020
J.-M. Bruel et al. (Eds.): FISEE 2019, LNCS 12271, pp. 133–150, 2020.
https://doi.org/10.1007/978-3-030-57663-9_10

bodies and academia is far slower than the one of the digital economy sector. In addition to this fact, their is a huge gap between the software engineering methods and tools effectively used by the economical sector and the ones covered in standards of education programmes. This applies especially to the two main software engineering development processes that are largely adopted by industry: Agile [5] and DevOps [12,23].

Despite the fact that SE2004 and SWEBOK have been updated in 2014 ([1, 20]), it must be noticed that the academia failed to deploy programs in software engineering that are complete, consistent and satisfactory for industry, as partly shown in these studies of the SWEBOK coverage in education [18,18,20,20].

Concerning DevOps, the problem is critical since it is, along with agile methods, one of the first competence domain required by the job market as shown by this study of nearly 100 000 job offers [17].

As of today, in the scientific community, there is no common agreement (standard, competence framework,...) about the definition of DevOps [21,25] nor acknowledged standard that can be used as fundamental building block for clarifying what it means and covers [31]. Concerning education, there neither exist a recognised content for a DevOps course and even less for a DevOps graduate education programme.

Despite of this lack of common agreement in the community, it is already possible to glimpse with an important level of confidence that main concerns addressed by DevOps belong to the domain of software engineering (e.g. methods and tool to architect software systems targeting continuous delivery, dependability while increasing delivery performance, etc.).

Thus, one of the current challenges for academic researches in education is to contribute to deliver a new generation of software engineers being trained to acquire the necessary initial knowledge and experience on DevOps principles and practices.

Such a program should satisfy the following high level requirements: (1) be based on the best available standard knowledge domain or competence framework directly related to DevOps, (2) be complete and sound from a scientific and technical point of view, (3) be coherent with the required initial competencies expressed by the job market, (4) adapted to a graduate education level assuming a common knowledge set acquired on software engineering and computer science at undergraduate level, and, most importantly, (5) be skill oriented by defining operational capabilities rather than static knowledge on DevOps notions.

This paper, describes a process and its application for deriving a DevOps education programme that satisfies those requirements. It is structured in the following way: presentation of the background on the standards used in the process, definition of the generic DevOps programme design process, application of the generic process and derivation of a DevOps graduate education programme, discussion about the proposals and results, presentation and analysis of related work and conclusion.

2   Background

This section presents the concepts on which this work relies on. These concepts are presented to make the paper self-contained, and in consequence, to ease its understanding.

2.1   The Cognitive Process and Its Categories

As part of the process that leads to the specification of a DevOps programme, it is required to collect and classify learning objectives. These learning objectives are expected to be presented in a skill oriented manner, describing what a person is expected to be able do about certain subject. What the person is able to do is described using a verb, whereas the subject describes the knowledge area on which the verb applies.

A skill is a capability applied on a knowledge area (e.g. use a versioning system).

In order to identify the main categories of abilities (i.e. groups of verbs), it is used the taxonomy proposed by Anderson et al. [3], which is a revision of the seminal work made by Bloom [6] and known as the *Bloom's taxonomy* of educational objectives.

At difference with Bloom's taxonomy, this revised work proposes a two-dimensional taxonomy: the cognitive process, and knowledge. The cognitive process dimension captures the cognitive complexity of associated to each capability. This revised work also proposes abilities (19) and categories (6) to group these abilities. It also proposes an complexity order among these categories.

Table 1 summarises information provided in the book of Anderson et al. ([3], pp. 67–68) about the cognitive process, the categories of cognitive complexity brought by this process, and how such as categories are ordered in terms of increasing complexity.

Table 1. Categories within the cognitive process

Category level	Category name	Category description
L1	Remember	Retrieve relevant knowledge from long-term memory
L2	Understand	Construct meaning from instructional messages, including oral, written and graphic communication
L3	Apply	Carry out or use a procedure in a given situation
L4	Analyse	Break material into constituent parts and determine how parts related to one another and to an overall structure or purpose
L5	Evaluate	Make judgements based on criteria and standards
L6	Create	Put elements together to form a coherent whole; reorganise into a new pattern or structure

This work relies on these categories and the complexity order established among them to classify the abilities that should acquired.

For what concerns the knowledge areas (i.e. the subjects), this papers focuses on DevOps. Thus it is necessary to define all the knowledge areas related to DevOps and useful to define the skills to be acquired by a person once he/she completes the programme: i.e. what the person should be able to do as a DevOps professional.

2.2   SWECOM

In order to define the DevOps knowledge area, this work proposes a standard based approach. The process proposed is standard agnostic since the selection of the standard to be used for driving the design of the programme is one of the steps of such a process. However, as already stated, the paper is aimed at being self-contained. Thus, very high level information on the standard that was selected when executing the design process (described in Sect. 3) is presented in this section. This information should ease understanding the rationale behind the results obtained on each step of the process (described in Sect. 4).

The selected standard chosen to illustrate our approach (for the reasons described in Sect. 4.1) is SWECOM [29] whose name stands for "Software Engineering Competency Model". It is a standard branded by the IEEE Computer Society[1], and it was first released in 2014. This standard presents a competency model for "software engineers who participate in developing and modifying software-intensive systems".

The abilities needed for the targeted software engineers to perform successfully their job are organised according to a specific structure which relies on the terms: activity, skill and skill area. The term "activity" is used to refer to a self-contained unit of work to be performed. A group of logically related activities is referred to as "a skill" and the term "skill area" is used to refer to a group of skills.

Using this structure, the standards presents 13 skill areas related to software engineering: Requirements, Design, Construction, Testing, Sustainment, Process and Life Cycle, Systems Engineering, Systems Engineering, Quality, Security, Safety, Configuration Management , Measurement and, lastly, Human-Computer Interaction.

Despite the fact these skill areas are presented in a flatten manner, they are implicitly grouped in 2 categories: "life cycle" and "crosscutting". A skill area belonging to the life cycle category contains skills need to fulfil some activities covered within a phase of the software development process (e.g. requirements engineering, design), regardless the chosen methodology to perform such a process. On the other hand, a crosscutting skill area is one that applies across all life cycle skill areas (e.g. safety, security). There are 5 life cycle skill areas and 8 crosscutting skill areas.

---

[1] https://www.computer.org/about.

3   DevOps Programme Design Process

3.1   Requirements

The programme to be defined is meant for a graduate level. This means that each participant in the programme is supposed to have a background in informatics: i.e he/she has completed an undergraduate programme in computer science /information technology, or has enough working experience on the field to let him/her accredit the required minimal knowledge.

The program is structured in 4 ordered levels of learning. These learning levels are organised according to the cognitive efforts participants should make to acquire the expected knowledge and skills. Obviously, lower levels require less efforts than higher levels.

It is worth mentioning that these 4 levels fit the standard organisation of graduate programmes organised by higher education institutions. Thus, the programme presented in this paper represents a good reference for curricula designers and quality officers of such as institutions.

3.2   Scope

The programme to be designed is aimed at specifying the core learning outcomes to be acquired once the student has successfully completed the programme. A core learning outcome is defined as a capability (or skill) related to a DevOps concept. For example, at the end of the programme, the student is expected to *use the appropriate DevOps terminology*, or *select appropriate languages and tools for the construction of a delivery ecosystem*.

The so-called soft skills (e.g. communication and team management capabilities) are not covered in the resulting specification of having applied the process described in this section. However, it must be said that such soft-skills are considered in the extended version of the programme specification. This extended version also has to contain details about the activities that would allow students to meet the core learning outcomes, pedagogical approaches applied in the delivery of those activities, as well as the the grouping of the activities into blocks (i.e. courses).

This work only focuses on describing the process that leads towards the specification of the core learning outcomes.

3.3   Process

Selection of the Standard. The first step of the process corresponds with the selection of the standard to be used as driver of the knowledge and capabilities to be covered by the programme under design. The criterion to select the standard is defined by the following attributes:

- **Reputation of the organisation:** the organisation that either leads the work to create it, or supports the task force in charge of its creation is a well-known organisation with a long history in creating standards. In may also be the case that the organisation is very new, but the task force behind the creation of the standard is composed of people recognised by the community where the standard is supposed to be used.

- **Software Engineering oriented:** the standard must be focused on Software Engineering (SE) as there is not any standard specific to DevOps; and it is considered that DevOps is logically included in the Software Engineering domain.
- **Skill oriented:** the content of the standard should provide insights about what a person should be able to do (i.e. person's skills) rather than what the person knows. This means that the chosen standard must be skill oriented, rather knowledge oriented.
- **Job role oriented:** Academic education has for aim to contribute to prepare the learner to the job market. To this aim, the standard content is analysed for its aim of defining job roles.
- **Academic education oriented:** since the target is the design of a academic education programme, it is important to determine if the standard is intended to be used for defining education programmes at academic level.

It is worth mentioning that due to the lack of DevOps-specific standard, it is of outmost importance that at least the standard to be considered focuses on Software Engineering. Thus, the *Software Engineering oriented* attribute has a higher priority with respect to the other inspected attributes.

Standards that capability-oriented are also more relevant than organise information in terms of knowledge coverage. In this work, it is central the idea of expressing learning outcomes in terms of the capabilities acquired by a person (i.e. rather than what the person hows, what he/she is able to do). Thus, standards that are skill-oriented are also of higher priority than other.

The notion of priority is materialised by weighting the attributes. An attribute with a higher priority is considered to weight twice as a non-high priority attribute. This policy then leads to the following distribution of weights (over a scale of 100%):

- Reputation of the organisation: 14,29%
- Software Engineering oriented: 28,57%
- Skill oriented: 28,57%
- Job role oriented: 14,29%
- Academic education oriented 14,29%

These weights are used to find out which one of the assessed standards scores the best.

Data Extraction. Once the standard has been selected, the next step is to extract the skills prescribed into such a standard. This extraction has to be made such that every single skill is collected while respecting the organisational structure and semantics proposed by the standard. Therefore, the expected outcome of this step is a data set containing skills, which are organised respecting the same grouping principle as defined in the standard.

Data Analysis. The skills collected in the previous step have to be analysed according to the following properties of interest:

1. **Knowledge suitability:** a statement describing a skill should contain one verb and (at least) one noun. The verb refers to the kind of cognitive capability needed (e.g. remember, understand, apply, analyse, evaluate and create) regarding the capability subjects (i.e. the nouns). This stage of the process is aimed at assessing whether the knowledge described in the studied standard describes a skill that is indeed relevant from perspective of the DevOps program under development.
2. **Cognitive complexity:** each relevant skill has to be analysed to determine its complexity in terms of the efforts required to be made by the person to acquire such competency (considering an initial knowledge status to be defined). Each skill has to be associated to a level representing the cognitive complexity of acquiring such a skill. It has been decided to use the categories within the cognitive process proposed by Anderson et al. [3] as levels to categorise each collected skill (see Sect. 2 for details about this work).

Programme Specification. The last step of the process consists in writing the specification of the programme. It consists in:

1. Defining the program structure exploiting:
   - the *Cognitive Complexity Levels*
   - a thematic hierarchical structure made of *Topics, Sub-Topics, and Skills*.
   - a *Programme level* as an integer representing a strictly ordered set of modules to represent a program decomposition in consistent sub-programme increments.
2. Mapping all the skills extracted from the standard to the program structure
3. If necessary, rewriting all the skill definitions to get a uniform and systematic skill definitions. This happens especially when the standard, being not DevOps tailored, provides too abstract skill definitions for skills of interest.
4. If necessary, add skills that are not covered by the standard but are known, from experience, to be necessary to include in the program.
5. Mapping of timing information (durations, periods, . . .) to the thematic structure components to ease the organisation of the delivery of such as activities on a particular time frame and devoted hours.

4   Results

4.1   Selection of the Standard

The first step of the process leads to the selection of a standard such that it fits (as best as possible) the selection criterion. In the context of this work, as an attempt to reduce the threats to validity on the results to be produced, the organisations to be considered are the IEEE[2] and the ACM[3]. These two organisations have a long history and very well reputation on the creation of standards related to education. Since there is no standard explicitly focusing on DevOps, the best option is to rely on SE-oriented standards coming from those institutions.

Table 2. Comparison of standards

Attributes	Standards			
	CS2013 [10]	SE2014 [11]	SWEBOK [30]	SWECOM [29]
Organisation's reputation (14,29%)	Y	Y	Y	Y
SE-oriented (28,57%)	N	Y	Y	Y
Skill-oriented (28,57%)	Y	N	N	Y
Job-role-oriented (14,29%)	N	N	N	N
Academic Education-oriented (14,29%)	Y	Y	N	N
Score	57,14%	57,14%	42,86%	71,43%

The assessed standards are: CS2013, SE2014, SWEBOK, and SWECOM. Only CS2023 is branded by the ACM, the others belong to the IEEE. It is worth mentioning that CS2013 and SE2014 are standards which were initially conceived for educational purposes (i.e curricula design), whereas SWEBOK and SWECOM were meant for providing guidelines to the SE community in terms of knowledge (SWEBOK) and capabilities (SWECOM) coverage.

Table 2 sums up the assessment results based on selected criteria which shows that the standard that best fits the selection criterion is SWECOM.

4.2 Data Extraction

This step refers to retrieving the relevant information conveyed by SWECOM such that it can tractable for further analysis. Table 3 shows a subset of the extracted data from SWECOM. This table presents the kind of information being collected and how it is structured. This structure corresponds to the same provided by the standard (and described in Sect. 2). Thus, the data is grouped in skills areas, skills, and activity description. The table presents the part corresponding to the "Software Requirements" skill area. This area contains 11 skill oriented activities, grouped in 5 skill sets.

In total, this extraction step resulted in collecting 244 skill oriented activities, grouped in 13 skill areas, and 59 skill sets. The data set that contains the complete extracted information from the standard can be found at https://messir.uni.lu/downloads/devops-programme/. Notice that any other data set produced as result of having executed this process is also available in the same address.

---

[2] https://www.ieee.org/.
[3] https://www.acm.org//.

Table 3. SWECOM data extraction - software requirements skill area

Skill area name	Skill set name	Activity description
Soft. Requirements	Elicitation	Identify stakeholders for elicitation of requirements
		Engage stakeholders in elicitation of requirements
		Use appropriate methods to capture requirements
		Negotiate conflicts among stakeholders during elicitation
	Analysis	Use appropriate domain analysis techniques
		Perform analysis of requirements for feasibility and emergent properties
	Specification	Use appropriate notations for describing requirements
	Verification and Validation	Check requirements for accuracy, lack of ambiguity, completeness, consistency, traceability, and other desired attributes
		Construct and analyse prototypes
		Negotiate conflicts among stakeholders during verification
	Process and Product Management	Use appropriate methods for management of requirements, including configuration management

These data sets are released as .csv files, as the intention is to make them available in a tool agnostic manner.

It must be noticed that SWECOM also includes the description of activities grouped by competency level (based on seniority). As this work relies on a different competency level categorisation, such kind of activity descriptions were not taken into account during the data extraction.

4.3   Data Analysis

The analysis of the data collected in the previous step is done using two dimensions: (1) the cognitive categories (and their complexity order) as presented by Anderson et al. [3][4], (2) earlier teaching experiences on SE and DevOps [7–9,24] and (3) the DevOps study market analysis [17]. While the first dimension is used to categorise each collected activity, the second and third ones are used to

---

[4] Duly introduced in Sect. 2.

determine whether an activity is relevant (or not) for then programme under specification.

Despite of mapping an activity to a cognitive category is a subjective process, it was done using the 19 cognitive processes that further clarify each of the cognitive categories provided in [3]. This means that the (main) verb used in the activity description was compared with the 19 cognitive processes to determine to which it is closest (in terms of semantic meaning), and then find out the most suitable cognitive category for such a activity.

For example, in the originally stated activity "Uses appropriate methods to capture requirements" the main verb is "to use"; when comparing this verb with the 19 specific cognitive processes, it is concluded that the closest one (among the 19) is "implementing" (as in [3] "using" is considered as part of this cognitive process). Finally, it only remains to look to which category "implementing" belongs to: the answer is "'Apply', which is notated as L3. This explains how the activity "Uses appropriate methods to capture requirements" is categorised as cognitive complexity level L3.

The process to determine whether an activity is (or not) relevant for DevOps is mainly based on: (1) if it is NOT expected to be already acquired by the learner, (2) if it applies to the software development phases covered by developers and/or operators, and (3) if it is relevant when engineering a delivery ecosystem (known also as DevOps environment -DevOpsEnv). As a consequence, (some) activities related to requirements elicitation, or human-computer interaction were left out.

Table 4 provides a subset of the outcome produced in this step. This table shows the results of having analysed the "Software Requirements" skill area. From this analysis, it has been concluded that 2 (out of 11) activities are not going to be considered in the next steps of the process[5]. However, these 2 activities, as any other else have been categorised according to the cognitive complexity levels.

4.4 Programme Specification

The final step is aimed at producing the programme specification according to the established structure. The obtained programme specification after having executed this step consists of 211 skills, grouped in 13 topics, and 47 sub-topics.

The 13 topics are:

1. DevOps Fundamentals
2. DevOps Process
3. DevOps Requirements
4. DevOpsEnv Design
5. DevOpsEnv Construction
6. Testing Management
7. DevOpsEnv Sustainment
8. DevOpsEnv Engineering
9. DevOpsEnv Quality
10. DevOpsEnv Security
11. Configuration Management
12. Metrics
13. DevOpsEnv Platform

---

[5] These activities are expected to be already acquired by the learner.

Table 4. SWECOM data analysis - software requirements skill area

Cognitive complexity level	Skill name	Activity description	Relevance for DevOps
L1	Software Requirements Elicitation	Identify stakeholders for elicitation of requirements	N
L3		Engage stakeholders in elicitation of requirements	N
L3		Use appropriate methods to capture requirements	Y
L5		Negotiate conflicts among stakeholders during elicitation	Y
L3	Software Requirements Analysis	Use appropriate domain analysis techniques	Y
L4		Perform analysis of requirements for feasibility and emergent properties	Y
L3	Software Requirements Specification	Use appropriate notations for describing requirements	Y
L5	Software Requirements Verification and Validation	Check requirements for accuracy, lack of ambiguity, completeness, consistency, traceability, and other desired attributes	Y
L6		Construct and analyse prototypes	Y
L5		Negotiate conflicts among stakeholders during verification	Y
L3	Software Requirements Process and Product Management	Use appropriate methods for management of requirements, including configuration management	Y

Most of the resulting skills are refinement of those proposed in the standard, except for the skills enclosed in the unique newly proposed topic named "DevOpsEnv Platform". This new topic covers the skills required to deal with virtualisation and networking. The full list of skills cover by this topic, as well as any other topic can be found at https://messir.uni.lu/downloads/devops-programme/.

However, to make the paper self-contained, a small sub-part of the programme specification is shown in Table 5. This table contains the skills that have been obtained after refining the activities shown in Table 4. This refinement has led to the definition of skills grouped in two different topics ("DevOps Fundamentals" and "DevOps Requirements"). Moreover, it must be noticed that the skills grouped into "DevOps Requirements" are split between program levels 1 and 2 of the programme, whereas those in "DevOps Fundamentals", are all into programme level 1. However, the cognitive complexity level remains the same as those assigned during the analysis step.

Table 5. Programme specification - Topics: "DevOps Fundamentals" and "DevOps Requirements"

Programme level	Sub-topic	Skill description	Cognitive complexity level
Topic: DevOps Fundamentals			
1	Requirements Elicitation	Use appropriate methods for retrieval of DevOps requirements	L3
1		Collect requirements for DevOps environment (aka DevOpsEnv)	L4
1	Requirements Analysis	Use appropriate domain analysis techniques	L3
1		Perform analysis of DevOps requirements for feasibility and emergent properties	L4
1	Requirements Specification	Use appropriate notations for describing DevOpsEnv requirements	L3
Topic: DevOps Requirements			
1	DevOps Requirements Verification and Validation	Construct and analyse prototypes for components of the DevOpsEnv	L4
1	DevOps Requirements Process and Product Management	Use appropriate methods for management of requirements, including configuration management	L3
2	DevOps Requirements Verification and Validation	Check requirements for accuracy, lack of ambiguity, completeness, consistency, traceability, and other desired attributes	L4
2		Negotiate conflicts among Devs and Ops during verification	L5

5   Discussion

In this work, the selected standard is SWECOM as it scores the best (among the assessed) using the proposed selection criterion. SWECOM is a relatively new standard (2014), based on other primary SE references like [14,28,30,32]. Thus, it is not surprising that it has a large coverage in terms of SE knowledge. However, what it makes it the best, it is the proposed SE capability model which is skills-oriented. For a vocational domain like DevOps, it is much more insightful to present the expected abilities a person should have rather what he/she should know.

However, it is worth noticing that the proposed programme design process is standard independent. That means that in case a newer standard appears (let Std_2 be this new standard), it can be evaluated using the given criterion to determine how it scores among any the other already assessed standards.

In case this new standard scores better than the standard used in the first run (let Std_1 be this standard), then it makes perfect sense to re-run process using the new standard (i.e. Std_2).

The new run of the process will eventually result in a DevOps programme specification based on Std_2 (let $DevOps_{Prog}^{Std_2}$ be this resulting programme specification). The question that arises now is: *what to do with* $DevOps_{Prog}^{Std_1}$ *?* There is no precise answer to this question as such a situation has not yet been experimented. However, based on earlier experiences on updating course syllabuses, the advise will be to "merge" $DevOps_{Prog}^{Std_1}$ and $DevOps_{Prog}^{Std_2}$ into one (i.e. $DevOps_{Prog}^{Std_1,Std_2}$). Merging means (1) to identify the differences between both programmes, (2) to determine what it has to be kept on each of them, and (3) combine the kept elements into one programme.

The number of differences between $DevOps_{Prog}^{Std_1}$ and $DevOps_{Prog}^{Std_2}$ can be used as metric to assess the quality of former programme with respect to the new one. A small number of differences would mean $DevOps_{Prog}^{Std_1}$ is still of good quality despite of being based on no the best available standard. For example, it could be assumed that the DevOps programme based on SWECOM is of good quality if the number of new skills brought by the a programme based on a standard scoring better than SWECOM is less than 40 (i.e. 80% of the SWECOM based programme[6] is still valid).

Up to now, it has been discussed the qualities that make SWECOM the best choice among the selected standards, and how to proceed in case a better standard appears. The proposed design process has also been discussed in terms of suitability in case a new standard wants to be used. However, when talking bout the suitability of the process, it has also to be discussed the possibility of changing the proposed assessment criterion (by adding a new property or weighting the proposed properties). In this case any selected standard has to be re-assessed. Unless the standard to be selected using this new criterion is not "skill oriented", the proposed process remains valid.

This means that the next steps of the process have to be executed as prescribed since they are independent from the selected standard: i.e. extract the skills (or whatsoever they are referred to - abilities, capabilities, know-how, etc.), and then categorise them using the cognitive categories provided in [3]. The use of a standard competency level which is independent from the selected standard makes the design process generic. For example, SWECOM defines its own competency levels (Technician, Entry Level Practitioner, Practitioner, Technical Leader, and Senior Software Engineer) to refine the specification of the activities. However, activities described using these competency these levels were not considered. Conversely, the level-independent activity description versions were considered during the data extraction step.

Therefore, a priory, it can be concluded that the proposed design process is quite general. However, it is acknowledged that this work only reports an initial experience. This means that more experiments have to be executed to get empirical evidence supporting the claim of a generic process.

---

[6] This programme covers 211 skills.

6   Related Work

This section focuses on already existent works that are related to the use of standards for the design of a DevOps curriculum driven by know-hows.

First of all, among all the sources found, there exist no work that exploits or even cite the SWECOM Standard. It has been understood that, even though SWECOM is around since 2014, studies that design education programmes are not using standards that are know-hows driven. They prefer to use standards that focus on knowledge first and are already well spread in education. This includes mainly CS2013 [2] and SE2014 [1]. A second reason is that SWECOM is less known in the academic community than SWEBOK [15] which is knowledge based and is not DevOps specific.

Another important finding is that no study has been found which exploits the standard job profiles which are by definition know-hows driven and that cover DevOps. More specifically the DDaT - Digital, Data and Technology Profession Capability Framework used as a standard by the UK government. [16], and the DASA - DevOps Competence Model [4]. The DDaT is the most advanced job profile standard definition covering DevOps and introduces 6 roles precisely defined: Apprentice DevOps engineer, Junior DevOps engineer, DevOps engineer, Senior DevOps engineer, Lead DevOps engineer and Principal DevOps engineer.

Despite those preliminary remarks, it can be found nonetheless three studies that contain interesting findings or proposals related to the work addressed in this paper.

- The PhD thesis of Candy Siu Tung Pang [27] entitled "Grounded Theory for DevOps Education" confirms that there is no existing DevOps standard or "true authority" that provides a reference for what is DevOps. It shows that there exist very few academic courses on DevOps and mostly non standard based. An analysis of the computer science curricula of the top 50 institutions listed in the 2017 QS World University Rankings by Subject - Engineering and Technology is described. The DevOps coverage of the study programmes is made according to the following five domains: Continuous Integration, Testing, Build, Repository and Version Control, Deployment. Among all the 50 programmes, none is addressing the 5 dimensions and only 3 are addressing partly 4 dimensions. None contains a module (set of courses) aiming at covering DevOps principles and practices.
- In "A Proposal for Integrating DevOps into Software Engineering Curricula" [22], Christopher Jones provides an approach for a integrating DevOps into software engineering curricula. He advocates a large DevOps programme rather than a single course. The programme proposed is more software engineering oriented and covers 9 topics (Agile Development Frameworks, Architecting for DevOps, Infrastructure and Automation, Configuration Management, IT Operations, IT Security, Organizational Transformation, Software Delivery Automation, Software Economics, Software Testing). This programme is designed according to a study of standards focusing mainly on

maturity models including CMMI variants, InfoQ Continuous Delivery maturity model, and IBM DevOps maturity model. The ACM 2014 Curricula Recommendations for Software Engineering is analysed and 180 instruction hours are extracted and associated to the DevOps topics proposed.

- In "Teaching DevOps and Cloud based Software Engineering in University Curricula" [13], the authors present an interesting work that aims at introducing a standard body of knowledge for DevOps and use it for designing a DevOps course. It is noticed the lack of academic or professional standard for DevOps. A list of Knowledge Units grouped in 12 Knowledge Areas is proposed in order to define a DevOps Software Engineering Body of Knowledge (DevOpsSE BoK). The Knowledge Areas are: DevOps fundamentals, Organisational impact of DevOps, Agile software development, DevOps Tools and Processes, DevOps Practices and Platforms, Cloud Computing Architectures, Cloud powered software development, Cloud monitoring tools, Cloud Automation Overview, Cloud automation tools, Cloud Security Architecture, DevSecOps. This body of knowledge table of content is very lightly defined and loosely related to SWEBOK, CS-BoK, DS-BoK and CS2013. Nonetheless, this study shares many concerns that are addressed in this paper.

7   Conclusion

This paper presents a standard based process to derive a DevOps graduate education programme. The derived programme, based on the SWECOM standard as a result of the selection phase, is presented in a comprehensive manner such that it can be used for curricula designers as reference when designing their own programmes according to the constraints imposed by their educational institutions. However, the aim of these DevOps based programmes, regardless the institution where they are delivered, is the same: to form the next generation of software engineers with DevOps abilities. This will help to catch up the today's job market needs.

The standard based programme design process presented in this paper is at its early stages, and it has been barely validated. The same, to certain extend, applies to the skill oriented DevOps programme obtained after having enacted the process. Nevertheless, it is worth concluding that the initial results reported in this paper are grounded on solid bases (well referred standards and first-hand experience of the paper's authors on the fields of software engineering, and in particular DevOps).

The results presented in the paper, despite of being very preliminary, are also very promising. However, both the process and the programme will required the efforts of the community (i.e. software educators, quality officers, curricula designers, etc) to validate and improve them. Therefore, by making both the process and the programme publicly available to the community, it is expected not only to contribute to make the task of designing of software engineering education programmes easier, but also to reinforce their validation.

Last, but not least important, it is worth mentioning that some actions aimed at enhancing the validation of the contributions brought by this paper related are already planned. A second iteration of the process is being considered to be done including the Digital, Data and Technology Profession Capability Framework (DDaT) [16] as a new standard to be assessed during the execution of the process. This is a promising standard since it is also skill oriented as SWECOM and dedicates a section specifically to DevOps. Therefore, regardless how this standard scores the given criterion, the process will be continued using it to drive the next phases. The purpose of doing so is twofold: first to assess the process by doing a new iteration but with a different standard, and secondly to obtained a second DevOps programme which could be used to judge the one proposed in this paper, and then proceed according to the approach presented in Sect. 5.

References

1. ACM/IEEE: Software Engineering 2014 - Curriculum Guidelines for Undergraduate Degree Programs in Software Engineering. ACM, New York (2015). https://www.acm.org/education/SE2014-20150223_draft.pdf
2. ACM/IEEE-CS Joint Task Force on Computing Curricula: Computer science curricula 2013 (2013). https://doi.org/10.1145/2534860
3. Anderson, L., Krathwohl, D., Bloom, B.: A taxonomy for learning, teaching, and assessing: a revision of Bloom's taxonomy of educational objectives. Longman (2001). https://books.google.lu/books?id=EMQlAQAAIAAJ
4. DDAS Association: Dasa - competence and maturity models. https://www.devopsagileskills.org/dasa-competence-model/. Accessed Mar 2020
5. Beck, K., et al.: The agile manifesto (2001)
6. Bloom, B.: Taxonomy of Educational Objectives: The Classification of Educational Goals. Mackay (1956)
7. Bobrov, E., Bucchiarone, A., Capozucca, A., Guelfi, N., Mazzara, M., Masyagin, S.: Teaching DevOps in academia and industry: reflections and vision. In: Bruel, J.-M., Mazzara, M., Meyer, B. (eds.) DEVOPS 2019. LNCS, vol. 12055, pp. 1–14. Springer, Cham (2020). https://doi.org/10.1007/978-3-030-39306-9_1
8. Bobrov, E., et al.: DevOps and its philosophy: education matters!. Microservices, pp. 349–361. Springer, Cham (2020). https://doi.org/10.1007/978-3-030-31646-4_14
9. Capozucca, Alfredo, Guelfi, Nicolas, Ries, Benoît: Design of a (yet another?) DevOps course. In: Bruel, Jean-Michel, Mazzara, Manuel, Meyer, Bertrand (eds.) DEVOPS 2018. LNCS, vol. 11350, pp. 1–18. Springer, Cham (2019). https://doi.org/10.1007/978-3-030-06019-0_1
10. AfCMA Joint Task Force on Computing Curricula, IC Society: Computer Science Curricula 2013: Curriculum Guidelines for Undergraduate Degree Programs in Computer Science, vol. 999133. ACM, New York (2013)
11. TJTF on Computing Curricula: Curriculum guidelines for undergraduate degree programs in software engineering. Technical report, New York, NY, USA (2015)
12. Debois, P.: DevOps days Ghent. DevOps Days (2009). https://devopsdays.org/about/
13. Demchenko, Y., et al.: Teaching DevOps and cloud based software engineering in university curricula. In: 2019 15th International Conference on eScience (eScience), pp. 548–552 (2019)

14. Diaz-Herrara, J., Hilburn, T.B.: Software engineering 2004: Curriculum Guidelines for Undergraduate Degree Programs in Software Engineering. IEEE Computing Society(IEEE-CS), Association of Computing Machinery (ACM) (2004)
15. Fairley, R.E., Bourque, P., Keppler, J.: The impact of SWEBOK version 3 on software engineering education and training. In: CSEE&T, pp. 192–200 (2014)
16. UK Government Digital Service: DDaT - digital, data and technology profession capability framework. https://www.gov.uk/guidance/development-operations-devops-engineer. Accessed March 2020
17. Guelfi, N.: Preventing the AI crisis: the AISE Academy proposal for Luxembourg. Farvest Group, ITOne Luxembourg (2019). http://www.itone.lu/pdf/AISE-academy.pdf. Accessed 03 Apr 2014
18. Guelfi, N., Capozucca, A., Ries, B.: Measuring the SWEBOK coverage: an approach and a tool. In: SWEBOK Evolution - Virtual Town Hall Meeting. IEEE (2016). Virtual presentation of accepted peer reviewed paper
19. ISO/IEC: Software Engineering - Guide to the Software Engineering Body of Knowledge (SWEBOK). International Organization for Standardization, iSO-IEC TR 19759–2005 (2005)
20. ISO/IEC: Software Engineering - Guide to the Software Engineering Body of Knowledge (SWEBOK). International Organization for Standardization, iSO-IEC TR 19759–2014 (2014)
21. Jabbari, R., bin Ali, N., Petersen, K., Tanveer, B.: What is DevOps?: A systematic mapping study on definitions and practices. In: Proceedings of the Scientific Workshop Proceedings of XP 2016, pp. 12:1–12:11. ACM, New York (2016). https://doi.org/10.1145/2962695.2962707. https://doi.acm.org/10.1145/2962695.2962707
22. Jones, Christopher: A proposal for integrating DevOps into software engineering curricula. In: Bruel, Jean-Michel, Mazzara, Manuel, Meyer, Bertrand (eds.) DEVOPS 2018. LNCS, vol. 11350, pp. 33–47. Springer, Cham (2019). https://doi.org/10.1007/978-3-030-06019-0_3
23. Kim, G., Debois, P., Willis, J., Humble, J., Allspaw, J.: The DevOps Handbook: How to Create World-Class Agility, Reliability, and Security in Technology Organizations. ITpro Collection, IT Revolution Press (2016). https://books.google.dk/books?id=ui8hDgAAQBAJ
24. Konchenko, S.: Quality assessment of DevOps practices and tools. Master's thesis, Faculté des Sciences, de la Technologie et de la Communication, University of Luxembourg (2018)
25. Leite, L., Rocha, C., Kon, F., Milojicic, D., Meirelles, P.: A survey of DevOps concepts and challenges. ACM Comput. Surv. 52(6) (2019). https://doi.org/10.1145/3359981
26. Naur, P., Randell, B.: Software engineering report of a conference sponsored by the Nato science committee Garmisch Germany 7th–11th October 1968 (1969). http://homepages.cs.ncl.ac.uk/brian.randell/NATO/nato1968.PDF
27. Pang, C.: Grounded theory for DevOps education (2019). https://era.library.ualberta.ca/items/c1c2ac64-c553-4be0-9bde-85148d2a6def
28. Pyster, A., et al.: Graduate software engineering 2009 (gswe2009) curriculum guidelines for graduate degree programs in software engineering. Stevens Institute of Technology (2009)
29. IC Society: Software engineering competency model version 1.0. SWECOM 2014 Software Engineering Competency Model (2014)
30. IC Society, Bourque, P., Fairley, R.E.: Guide to the Software Engineering Body of Knowledge (SWEBOK(R)): Version 3.0, 3rd edn. IEEE Computer Society Press, Los Alamitos (2014)

31. Standard, N.I.: DevOps - standard for building reliable and secure systems including application build, package and deployment (2016). https://standards.ieee.org/develop/project/2675.html
32. Trustees of the Stevens Institute of Technology: GRCSE V1.1. In: Pyster, A., et al. (eds.) Graduate Reference Curriculum for Systems Engineering. Hoboken, NJ, USA (2015). www.bkcase.org/grcse/

Teaching Logic, from a Conceptual Viewpoint

Daniel de Carvalho$^{(\boxtimes)}$ and Nikolai Kudasov

Innopolis University, 1, Universitetskaya Str., Innopolis 420500, Russia
{d.carvalho,n.kudasov}@innopolis.ru

Abstract. Logic is not only of foundational importance in mathematics, it is also playing a big role in software engineering and formal verification. Its different roles influence its teaching, which has to take into consideration the recent developments in category theory and proof theory. We show that teaching set theory from a categorical viewpoint, in contrast with Zermelo-Fraenkel axioms, helps develop proper skills that are essential in mathematics and software engineering. The use of a proof assistant provides students with another perspective on both subjects: basic category theory and proof theory.

> "Since the most fundamental social purpose of philosophy is to guide education and since mathematics is one of the pillars of education, accordingly philosophers often speculate about mathematics. But a less speculative philosophy based on the actual practice of mathematical theorizing should ultimately become one of the important guides to mathematics education."
>
> F. William Lawvere, [30]

In his famous proposal for reforming the teaching of mathematics [10], Jean Dieudonné notices: "In order to provide what they think is a satisfactory course in mathematics, university professors consider that a first-year student should (...) already be fairly well trained in the use of logical deduction and have some idea of the axiomatic method." The purpose for such a proposal was the striking revolution in mathematics with the dramatic increase of abstraction since around 1880. As Dieudonné says, "there is no turning back in science, and one cannot even contemplate renouncing the new methods and new results; this would be the very negation of what is the essential mission of higher education".

This proposal was held sixty years ago and had a strong influence in the wave of New Math in the secondary education in the 1970's (even if Dieudonné himself felt this reform betrayed it—see [42, Chapter 10] for an account of this influence). Since then new methods and new results continued to appear; would any of them justify new proposals to prepare better first-year students in order to avoid renouncing them and thus negating "the essential mission of higher education"? On the other hand, industrial software engineering has emerged and the

© Springer Nature Switzerland AG 2020
J.-M. Bruel et al. (Eds.): FISEE 2019, LNCS 12271, pp. 151–177, 2020.
https://doi.org/10.1007/978-3-030-57663-9_11

importance of formal verification has increased; how could we take into account these new needs in our proposals? The aim of the current paper is to contribute to answer these two questions for teaching logic, taking into consideration:

- the tremendous developments in category theory and proof theory;
- the move in software engineering from programming computers with machine codes to high-level programming languages and building complex information systems and the formal verification techniques, which require good reasoning and abstraction skills.

Other proposals taking into account such developments in category theory and proof theory to renew the way to teach logic exist; let us mention in particular:

- the series of papers [14], which relates how Dan Ghica experimented with teaching seven-and eight-year-olds about monoidal categories;
- the recent talk by Emily Riehl [52], which argued that ∞-categories should be taught to undergraduate students taking into account the discovery of homotopy type theory [57]; our proposal is probably less radical than hers and perhaps a course based on our principles could be seen as an introduction to a course based on her principles.

Sections 1 and 2 consider some of the main achievements in category theory and proof theory respectively that can have a direct impact in teaching logic: axiomatizing sets and mappings with category theory, use of natural deduction in formalizing proofs and its implementation in proof assistants. Nevertheless, the reader should be aware that the two fields have not the same status here: while an introductory course in logic can have as a primary objective to introduce proof theory, we do not evoke how to teach category theory (for instance, even the word "functor" could/should be avoided in such an entire course), but we show how developments in category theory inspire a way to teach set theory providing an axiomatization of the category of sets that helps develop proper skills that are essential in mathematics and software engineering. Finally, Sect. 3 discusses relevant trends in software engineering and formal verification, reinforcing the motivation from the perspective of IT industry for the approach discussed in the preceding sections.

1   From a Categorical Viewpoint

1.1   Two Guiding Principles

According to Dieudonné, the teaching of mathematics should follow two fundamental guiding principles.

"The first (...) is that a mathematical theory can only be developed axiomatically in a fruitful way when the student has already acquired some familiarity with the corresponding material—a familiarity gained by working long enough with it on a kind of experimental, or semi-experimental basis, *i.e.*, with *constant appeal to intuition.*"

Indeed, mathematics is not only an ἐπιστήμη , it is also a τέχνη ; now, according to Immanuel Kant [24], the geometer "gelangt auf solche Weise durch eine Kette von Schlüssen, immer von der Anschauung geleitet, zur völlig einleuchtenden und zugleich allgemeinen Auflösung der Frage."[1]

We illustrate this principle with the concept of *isomorphism of sets* (Subsect. 1.3) and the concept of *equalizer* (Subsect. 1.4).

"The other principle (...) is that when logical inference is introduced in some mathematical question, it should always be presented with absolute honesty—that is, without trying to hide gasps or flaws in the argument; any other way, in my opinion, is worse than giving no proof at all." An axiomatic approach allows such an *absolute honesty* and we could identify *absolute honesty* with *precision.* As an example, one can consider the book [11] whose principal contribution "is an axiomatic approach to the part of algebraic topology called homology theory"— what we want to emphasize here is the fact that the origin of this axiomatization, which was an outcome of the most advanced research in this abstract field of mathematics, "was an effort, on the part of the authors, to write a textbook" (thus the axiomatization of the homology theory had *pedagogical* motivations, like it has been the case of Elementary Theory of Category of Sets on the part of Lawvere, as we show it in Subsect. 1.2). Its authors wrote: "In spite of this confusion, a picture has gradually evolved of what is and should be a homology theory. Heretofore this has been an imprecise picture which the expert could use in his thinking but not in his exposition. A precise picture is needed. It is at just this stage in the development of other fields of mathematics that an axiomatic treatment appeared and cleared the air" [11]. Ralf Krömer [27] commentates:

What is interesting here is how they use the term "precise". They think apparently that precision has the task to render communication possible, in particular in cases where the expert (who has at his disposal a "picture" serving his purposes) wants to impart something to the non-expert (that is for example the student). They seem to think further that precision is to be attained in particular by an axiomatic treatment. Hence, for Eilenberg and Steenrod precision is not a property related to the adequateness of an explication! (but to the adequateness of a means of communication.) And this precision, it seems undebatable, is to be attained by a formal presentation: the receiver is able to decode the message following a scheme agreed on beforehand. The formal creates intersubjectivity: all participants of the discourse have a kind of standard key. But this is insufficient to grasp the intention. (...) In the continuity of this distinction, one can distinguish between the communication function and the denotation of an expression–and focus on both or only on the denotation. Now, Eilenberg and Steenrod consider precisely the axiomatic treatment as establishing the possibility of a communication while the "initiated" (who has at his

---

[1] "In such a way, through a chain of inferences that is always guided by intuition, he arrives at a fully illuminating and at the same time general solution of the question." [25].

disposal an unexplicated common sense) has access to the concept in a different way.

As a consequence of this second principle, if we want to teach some theory to beginners (for instance, set theory), we need a formalization of this theory. Several formalizations of set theory exist; in particular,

- Zermelo-Fraenkel (ZF) axioms, which axiomatize a *material* set theory;
- Elementary Theory of Category of Sets (ETCS), which axiomatizes a *structural* set theory and are an outcome of category theory.

The latter formalization reflects more faithfully Cantor's viewpoint since a set in a model of ETCS is not supposed to be endowed with a membership relationship that relates its elements between them—compare how cardinal numbers are defined in [6], p. 282:

> "Mächtigkeit" oder "Cardinalzahl" von M nennen wit den Allgemeinbegriff, welcher mit Hülfe unseres activen Denkvermögens dadurch aus der Menge M hervorgeht, daß von der Beschaffenheit ihrer verschiedenen Elemente m und von der Ordnung ihres Gegebenseins abstrahirt wird[2]

from one hand and in ZF from the other hand, where cardinals are specific ordinals, which are *transitive* sets; this extra structure on sets of ZF can be seen as a useless *gauge* (at least as long as we do not do research into models of ZF), as explained in [44]. In the next subsections, we argue why structural set theory is more profitable to students (at least to those who do not intend to become specialists of models of ZF).

1.2   Elementary Theory of the Category of Sets

In 1963, after having completed his PhD in which he set out, among other important ideas in category theory, a new categorical viewpoint on universal algebra, William Lawvere as a new assistant professor was supposed to teach calculus to first-year students. In some interview [8], Lawvere relates:

> At Reed I was instructed that the first year of calculus should concentrate on foundations, formulas there being taught in the second year. Therefore (...) I spent several preparatory weeks trying to devise a calculus course based on Zermelo-Fraenkel set theory. However, a sober assessment showed that there are far too many layers of definitions, concealing differentiation and integration from the cumulative hierarchy, to be able to get through those layers in a year. The category structure of Cantor's structureless sets seemed both simpler and closer. Thus, the Elementary Theory of the

---

[2] "We will call by the name "power" or "cardinal number" of M the general concept which, by means of our active faculty of thought, arises from the aggregate M when we make abstraction of the nature of its various elements m and of the order in which they are given. [5], p. 86".

Category of Sets arose from a purely practical educational need, in a sort of experience that Saunders also noted: the need to explain daily for students is often the source of new mathematical discoveries.

Colin McLarty [43] notes: Lawvere "found the membership theoretic foundation for set theory pedagogically awkward and not to the point so he worked out a categorical axiomatization of the category of sets. In other words he gave a version of set theory based on functions and composition of functions-set theory without a set membership relation." This new axiomatization of set theory has been published in [28]. In its republishing [33] forty years later, Lawvere commentates:

This elementary theory of the category of sets arose from a purely practical educational need. When I began teaching at Reed College in 1963, I was instructed that first-year analysis should emphasize foundations, with the usual formulas and applications of calculus being filled out in the second year. Since part of the difficulty in learning calculus stems from the rigid refusal of most textbooks to supply clear, explicit, statements of concepts and principles, I was very happy with the opportunity to oppose that unfortunate trend. Part of the summer of 1963 was devoted to designing a course based on the axiomatics of Zermelo-Fraenkel set theory (even though I had already before concluded that the category of categories is the best setting for "advanced" mathematics). But I soon realized that even an entire semester would not be adequate for explaining all the (for a beginner bizarre) membership-theoretic definitions and results, then translating them into operations usable in algebra and analysis, then using that framework to construct a basis for the material I planned to present in the second semester on metric spaces. However I found a way out of the ZF impasse and the able Reed students could indeed be led to take advantage of the second semester that I had planned. The way was to present in a couple of months an explicit axiomatic theory of the mathematical operations and concepts (composition, functionals, etc.) as actually needed in the development of the mathematics.

Interestingly Michael Barr came to the same conclusion:

I was more-or-less familiar with Lawvere's thoughts on the subject, I had never thought too much about them until some years ago, more than 5, less than 10, when I found myself teaching a course in set theory. For the first time, I came to realize what a complex horror set membership really is. In every other type of mathematics I had ever studied, the objects were some kind of sets with some kind of structure and the arrows were the functions (or at worst equivalence classes of such) that preserved them. Mostly, the structure was given by operations, or at least partial operations (...)
But of course, Sets are an exception. Here are sets defined in terms of these elaborate epsilon trees and this structure is invariably ignored. It seemed to me intuitively, confirmed by Makkai, that the ONLY arrows between

sets that actually preserved all that structure were inclusions of subsets. (...) But of course the truth is that that epsilon structure is invariably ignored. So why is it taken as the basis of mathematics. Much better to simply define sets as the objects of a category and then an element is just a global section, or rather an equivalence class thereof.

My whole experience with category theory convinces me that membership (...) is an intrinsically obscure notion. Or rather, not that it itself is obscure, but it obscures anything it touches. (...) [3]

The concepts of sets and mappings arise not only in calculus but everywhere in mathematics. Thus mathematicians need a formalization of these concepts and teachers of mathematics need to find a way to introduce them to students: "Historically, the notion of mapping arises as an idealization of the notion of rule. And this is also how we introduce it in mathematics education." [37] Its formalization in the Zermelo-Fraenkel theory (ZF) and in Lawvere's Elementary Theory of the Category of Sets (ETCS) are radically different: in ZF the concept of mapping is *reduced* to the concept of *set*, while in ETCS, this concept is *axiomatized*. It is a first difference and in Subsect. 1.3 we exemplify how Hume's principle can be reformulated without the membership relationship but only with mappings.

At the time Lawvere introduced ETCS, this theory had a limited success. Probably one of the reasons for that is that at that time the notion of *elementary topos* was not yet introduced. Nowadays, on the opposite, ETCS can be better understood in the framework of topos theory. The notion of *topos* has been developed in three steps:

1. In the Tôhoku paper [18] Grothendieck considered (pre)sheaves on topological spaces. A presheaf on a topological space X is a contravariant functor with domain the category whose objects are the open sets of X and whose morphisms are the inclusions. In particular this way to see a topological space as a category allows to see the intersection of two open sets as a Cartesian product (in the categorical sense) in that category (thus avoiding relying on the elements of the two sets); it has eventually led to the introduction of the notions of *site* and *topos* as first introduced by Grothendieck as follows: "On appelle U-topos, ou simplement topos si aucune confusion n'est à craindre, une catégorie E telle qu'il existe un site $C \in U$ tel que E soit équivalente à la catégorie $C^\sim$ des U-faisceaux d'ensembles sur C."[3] [1] A *site* is given by a (Grothendieck) topology on a category; it is a considerable abstraction from the notion of topological space—if $\mathcal{O}$ is a topology on some set and $\mathcal{C}$ is the category obtained from this topology as described above and J associates with each object U of $\mathcal{C}$ the set of all jointly-surjective families of open inclusions $(U_i \subseteq U)_{i \in I}$, then $(\mathcal{C}, J)$ is a site.

---

[3] "We define a U-topos, or simply topos if no confusion can occur, to be a category E such that there exists a site $C \in U$ such that E is equivalent to the category $C^\sim$ of U-sheaves of sets on C.".

2. Now, for a given topos $\mathcal{E}$ there may be given many different *sites of definition for $\mathcal{E}$* (that is, sites $(\mathcal{C}, J)$ such that $\mathcal{E}$ is equivalent to the category of sheaves on $(\mathcal{C}, J)$). Since "les notions de topos et de morphisme de topos semblent être le fil conducteur indispensable, et il convient de leur donner la place centrale, la notion de site devenant une notion technique auxiliaire"[4] [1], a site of definition for a topos $\mathcal{E}$ can be seen as a presentation of $\mathcal{E}$ and it becomes desirable to be able to define the notion of topos independently of any site. It is what Giraud has done, providing an intrinsic characterization of Grothendieck toposes (intrinsic in that it does not refer to a site).

3. Finally Lawvere and Tierney, in order to provide an *elementary* (*i.e.* first-order) axiomatic approach to sheaves, define toposes as categories which have finite limits and finite colimits, are Cartesian closed and have a subobject classifier[5] [29]; (Lawvere-Tierney) topologies on such categories are endomorphisms on the subobject classifier satisfying some axioms. Every Grothendieck topos is an elementary topos and every Grothendieck topology on a small category $\mathcal{C}$ determines a Lawvere-Tierney topology on the presheaf topos $\mathbf{Set}^{\mathcal{C}^{op}}$ (see, for instance [39]). Nevertheless, some elementary toposes are not Grothendieck toposes as exemplified by Hyland's effective topos [22], a topos of great importance in computer science. These new axioms for a topos "can be understood as axioms for set theory formulated not in terms of membership, but in terms of functions and their composition" [38]. From this viewpoint the subobject classifier can be thought of as an object of truth-values, which has a structure of Heyting algebra.

ETCS can be then presented in its natural framework: a model of ETCS is an elementary topos satisfying some extra axioms.

We thus have two concurrent first-order set theories: ZF theory and ETCS. In [34] Tom Leinster addresses the following question: "What kind of set theory should we teach?" As an answer he writes: The big advantage is that a course based on ETCS "is of far wider benefit than one using the traditional axioms. It directly addresses a difficulty experienced by many students: the concept of function (and worse, function space). It also introduces in an elementary setting the idea of universal property. This is probably the hardest aspect of the axioms for a learner, but since universal properties are important in so many branches of advanced mathematics, the benefits are potentially far-reaching."

In Subsect. 1.4 we investigate some instances of this idea of universal property, which allows to substitute *reductionism* by *axiomatization* in many important cases. In our view, more generally, providing an intrinsic account of concepts rather than being satisfied with a formal reductionism is a strong trend in mathematics. Some other important examples include:

---

[4] "The notions of topos and of morphism of toposes seem to be the indispensable thread, and it is convenient to give them the central place, whereas the notion of site becomes an auxiliary technical notion".

[5] This definition has been slightly simplified later on.

- the transition from the definition by Descartes [9] of affine algebraic sets over the field of real numbers by arbitrary sets of polynomials to the ideals of polynomials that vanish on them;
- Giraud's characterization of Grothendieck toposes, which avoids presenting toposes with sites: we recalled how the notion of Grothendieck topos, "*via* the Giraud characterization theorems, led to the development of elementary topoi by Lawvere and Tierney and the consequent geometrization of logic" [17];
- the introduction of Lawvere theories providing an *objective* account[6] of algebraic theories.

An introductory course in logic has not as an objective the presentation of the general concept of universal property as a general theory with the essential concept of adjointness [23]—in our opinion it is too advanced for beginners—even if it is probably the most important concept in category theory:

> But here lies what may seem to be a mystery: why do almost all fundamental constructions performed in different fields of mathematics turn out to be adjoints? Is this an *epistemological* phenomenon, a fact of our way of thinking? Is it an *ontological* phenomenon, a fact about the way mathematical objects are? (...) We might marvel at it and try to find how this can be so. But it is simply a fact. What is wonderful is that the language of category theory allowed for the definition of adjoints, that within the categorical framework, one could find the appropriate level of abstraction. Once adjoints have been defined, once their usefulness has been recognized, once their ubiquitous character has been acknowledged, then it becomes natural to use them whenever appropriate, to look for them whenever they might show up and to exploit them as much as possible. In other words, the way one *does* and *thinks* about mathematics has changed in an irreversible manner [41].

An introductory course in logic should convey the idea of universal property only *via* some instances of this concept; we provide such instances in Subsect. 1.4. As an example, even if the categorical viewpoint reveals us that the universal property of Cartesian products of sets is more important than any of its ZF definitions, it is perfectly possible to teach it without introducing any categorical notion at all. Still, introducing ETCS requires some very basic category theory. The purposes of the book written by Lawvere and Schanuel [32], were precisely "to provide a skeleton key to mathematics for the general reader or beginning student; and to furnish an introduction to categories for computer scientists, logicians, physicists, linguists, etc. who want to gain some familiarity with the

---

[6] "Presentations of algebraic structures for the purpose of calculation are always needed, but it is a serious mistake to confuse the arbitrary formulations of such presentations with the objective structure itself or to arbitrarily enshrine one choice of presentation as the notion of logical theory, thereby obscuring even the existence of the invariant mathematical content. In the long run it is best to try to bring the form of the subjective presentation paradigm as much as possible into harmony with the objective content of the objects to be presented;" [31].

categorical method. (...) Preliminary versions of this book have been used by high school and university classes, graduate seminars, and individual professionals in several countries." This book is a great support for the student and the inspiration of the teacher; by the way its title inspired the title of our paper.

Finally, another contrast between ZF theory and ETCS is that in the former theory the membership relation is *global* while the latter one is *local* and this opposition can be seen as an opposition between *untyped* mathematics and *typed* mathematics; we argue that typed mathematics corresponds more closely to the everyday practice of mathematicians (and teachers of mathematics) than untyped mathematics in Subsect. 1.5.

1.3 Hume's Principle

Learning to count is a child's very first step into mathematics. Counting the number of elements of finite sets allows to address the following basic fundamental problem: given two *finite* sets, do they have the same number of elements? Students are familiar with this problem and thus they find it very natural to address the more general problem: given two sets, do they have the same number of elements?

A generalization of the concept of cardinality from finite sets to infinite sets would allow to solve this problem, but such a generalization is not trivial at all. In absence of the notion of cardinality for infinite sets, we can analyze the equipotency relation in light of Hume's principle: "When two numbers are so combin'd, as that the one has always an unite answering to every unite of the other, we pronounce them equal" [21].

A usual way to formalize this concept is to define the notions of *injection*, *surjection* and *bijection* as follows:

Definition 1. *Let A and B two sets and let f be a mapping from A to be B.*

We say that f is an injection *from A to B if, for any elements a_1 and a_2 of A such that $f(a_1) = f(a_2)$, we have $a_1 = a_2$.*

We say that f is a surjection *from A onto B if, for any element b of B, there exists an element a of A such that $f(a) = b$.*

We say that f is a bijection *from A onto B if it is an injection from A to B and a surjection from A onto B.*

and then to say that two sets A and B are *equipotent* if there exists a bijection from A onto B.

Now, something noteworthy is that these concepts of injection, surjection and bijection can be rephrased without relying to any set membership relation. A way to reach such a rephrasing is first to notice that, given any set 1 with exactly one element $*$, for any set A, we have a bijection from the set $\mathbf{Set}(1, A)$ onto the set A that associates with every mapping x from 1 to A the element $x(*)$ of A, where, for any sets X and Y, we denote by $\mathbf{Set}(X, Y)$ the set of mappings from X to Y. As a consequence, we get: Given any singleton 1, for any sets A and B, for any mappings f_1 and f_2 from A to B, we have $f_1 = f_2$ if and only if, for any mapping x from 1 to A, we have $f_1 \circ x = f_2 \circ x$: we say that the set 1 is a *separator* in the category of sets and mappings. Then a mapping f from A to B is an injection if and only if, for any mappings x_1 and x_2 from 1 to A such that $f \circ x_1 = f \circ x_2$, we have $x_1 = x_2$. In order to understand better what we got, it is worth introducing some terminology:

Definition 2. *Let S be some set. Let A and B two sets and let f be a mapping from A to B. We say that f is an S-injection from A to B if, for any mappings x_1 and x_2 from S to A such that $f \circ x_1 = f \circ x_2$, we have $x_1 = x_2$.*

Therefore all the injections from a set A to a set B are exactly the 1-injections from A to B, where 1 is *any* set with exactly one element.

This analysis of the concept of injection allowed us to obtain the three following consequences:

1. We have a generalization of the concept of *injection* since, now, we can consider S-injections for any set S. This generalization seems very boring and uninteresting at first glance since actually it is easy to show that:
   - if S is empty, then any mapping f from A to B is an S-injection;
   - and, if S is inhabited, then all the S-injections are exactly the injections. Nevertheless, this generalization is very important because it can be extended to toposes in which there are objects that are not initial and not separator either and extended to other concepts than injections also: such generalization interprets the internal language of the topos in the *sets* of morphisms with domain S—this interpretation is *local* and *classical* in contrast with the *global* and *intuitionistic* interpretation of the internal language in the topos. The local and classical interpretation gives opportunities to see how to manipulate first-order predicate calculus with many given structures (each object of each topos gives such a structure). The interplay between the local and the global interpretations is described by the Kripke-Joyal semantics [48] and already the notion of S-injection provides nice examples of how subtly the implication connector behaves in the Kripke semantics.
2. All the singletons play the same role—any singleton 1 can be considered and its element does not play any role: we are naturally working up to isomorphism.
3. And, finally, the notion of S-injection does not rely on the notion of any set membership relation.

While interpreting first-order predicate calculus *in general*, reflecting with the Kripke-Joyal semantics *in general*, reasoning up to isomorphism *in general* or demonstrating a property without relying on the notion of any set membership relation *in general* could scare the beginner, we can naturally introduce these ways of thinking in particular cases addressing the basic (but fundamental) problem that consists in comparing sets in their numbers of elements.

1.4   Finite Limits

Cartesian Products. Cartesian products of sets, and more generally Cartesian products, arise everywhere in mathematics and in computer science. We claim that learning the set-theoretical encoding of ordered pairs is not the best way to understand them, arguing against the reduction of ordered pairs to sets in a similar way as Paul Benacerraf argued against the reduction of natural numbers to sets [4]. There are different possible definitions of ordered pairs in the Zermelo-Fraenkel theory; for instance:

- Wiener's definition: $(a, b) = \{\{\{a\}, \emptyset\}, \{\{b\}\}\}$
- Kuratowski's definition: $(a, b) = \{\{a\}, \{a, b\}\}$

What is interesting with such definitions is that ordered sets *could* be defined as sets. But the way mathematicians use ordered pairs does not rely on these definitions: The two definitions are completely different and Wiener's definition has some properties not shared by Kuratowski's definition (and conversely). For instance taking Wiener's definition, we have $\emptyset \in \bigcup (a, b)$ whatever a and b are, which is not necessarily the case with Kuratowski's definition, while with Kuratowski's definition, we have $a \in \bigcup (a, b)$ whatever a and b are, which is not necessarily the case with Wiener's definition. Taking Kuratowski's definition, let us consider the following statement:

$$(\forall a, b) a \in \bigcup (a, b) \ (*)$$

This statement is provable: it is a theorem and we could thus use it to show other statements. Nevertheless we are embarrassed. Indeed, taking Wiener's definition this statement is not provable any more. Since ordered pairs arise everywhere in mathematics, it means that many different properties can be shown on objects according to the definition we take for ordered pairs. The experienced mathematician has the intuition that such a statement is not "legitimate". We feel as unsatisfactory to rely only on experience, intuition, on the notion of "legitimate" statement without trying to define it, especially because here intuition and experience contradict formalism; indeed formally nothing distinguishes the statement $(*)$ and the "legitimate" one:

$$(\forall a, b, a', b')((a, b) = (a', b') \Rightarrow (a = a' \wedge b = b')) \ (**)$$

Both $(*)$ and $(**)$ are theorems—the experienced mathematician knows that we should "discard" the statement $(*)$, while the statement $(**)$ is very important. And it is unsatisfactory to *teach* ordered pairs by giving such definitions to students who do not have the intuition of the teacher to distinguish between the legitimacy of these two statements, especially because such definitions do not help convey intuition.

We could tentatively define *legitimate statements* as statements that do not depend on the definition we take for ordered pairs as soon this definition is "sensible". But then we are led to define *sensible definitions*: Why are Wiener's and Kuratowski's definitions "sensible" and how to distinguish between sensible definitions and non-sensible definitions? Addressing such a question assumes to not identify the concept of ordered pair with one of its possible definitions in Zermelo-Fraenkel theory.

In Zermelo-Fraenkel theory the Cartesian product of two sets A and B is defined as the set of all ordered pairs (a, b) with $a \in A$ and $b \in B$. In category theory a Cartesian product of two sets is defined as a solution of a *universal problem*: it is a set $A \times B$ with a mapping $\pi^1_{A,B} : A \times B \to A$ and a mapping $\pi^2_{A,B} : A \times B \to B$ such that, for any set C, for any mappings $f_1 : C \to A$ and $f_2 : C \to B$, there exists a unique mapping $h : C \to A \times B$ such that the following diagram commutes:

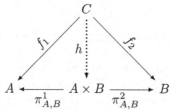

Taking for $A \times B$ the set of Wiener ordered pairs (a, b) with $a \in A$ and $b \in B$ and for $\pi^1_{A,B}$ (resp. $\pi^2_{A,B}$) the mapping that associates with every Wiener pair (a, b) the element a of A (resp. the element b of B), we obtain that the set $A \times B$ with the mappings $\pi^1_{A,B}$ and $\pi^2_{A,B}$ satisfy the property expressed by the diagram above. It is the case also if, instead, we take for $A \times B$ the set of Kuratowski ordered pairs (a, b) with $a \in A$ and $b \in B$. We could see the diagram expressing the universal property as a *specification* and the Wiener and the Kuratowski definitions as some possible *implementations* of this specification. The mathematician uses universal properties like the software engineer uses information hiding [49]: he can use once an implementation of the universal property to show its existence, but once the existence has been proved, he should not need to know how it has been proved and he does not need to rely to any specific implementation but only to the universal property—not only he should not need to use a specific implementation, but he should not use it at the risk of proving *evil* statements. What matters are the properties that axiomatize the object we consider, not how it could be (subjectively and arbitrarily) codified and reduced. Thus definitions in ZF "leak" some details that are not essential to what a mathematician is trying to formalize, allowing "bad" statements about defined objects and requiring a mathematician (or student) to understand which statements are legitimate; on the other hand a definition in ETCS allows to capture the essence of the defined object precisely: this situation is analogous to a programmer working directly with private fields of an object as compared to a programmer working with an interface that hides the specifics of implementation.

Notice a further great benefit for the student who has been taught the universal property of the Cartesian products of sets: it will help him understand the other instances of Cartesian products when he will encounter them: Cartesian products of topologies, Cartesian products of groups, Cartesian products of types... since the universal property is always the same one—while reductionist implementations of such instances can be very different.

Equalizers. Another kind of finite limit is the notion of *equalizer*. Again it is defined by a universal property: an equalizer of two parallel morphisms $f, g : A \to B$ in some category is a morphism $e : E \to A$ for some object E such that $f \circ e = g \circ e$ and, for any object E', for any morphism $e' : E' \to A$ satisfying $f \circ e' = g \circ e'$, there exists a unique morphism $h : E' \to E$ such that $e' = e \circ h$:

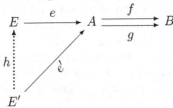

Is it enough to give such definitions to teach them? Of course not! We need to convey some *intuition*. How can it be done? A possible way is to show that Cartesian products and equalizers are an abstraction of Descartes's work in its algebraization of geometry: Before Descartes, a parabola was defined as being the locus of a point that is equidistant from a given line (the *directrix*) and a given point (the *focus*), which does not lie on that line, in that plane. With Descartes it is an equalizer of the polynomial functions $f, g : \mathbb{R}^2 \to \mathbb{R}$ with $f(x, y) = y^2 - 4cx$ and $g(x, y) = 0$, where the focus has coordinate $(c, 0)$ and the line D is represented by the equation $x = -c$ (see Fig. 1).

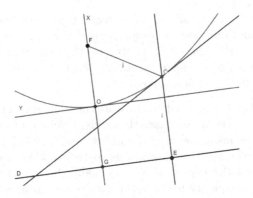

Fig. 1. Parabolas are equalizers

It is how the geometrical intuition can help get new intuition about categorical finite limits.

1.5   Sets as Types

Elementary toposes are (classical) models of a first-order theory but, at the same time, they are intuitionistic models of *local* set theories, a higher-order type theory. With the Curry-Howard isomorphism in mind, the fact that toposes can be seen as models of higher-order type theory is not surprising: we know that toposes are Cartesian closed categories and that Cartesian closed categories are models of a higher-order type theory that corresponds to the simply-typed lambda-calculus; thus toposes are a way to do mathematics in a *higher-order typed* programming way. While the fact that physics is typed is commonly accepted (there are units in physics), types in mathematics are not as well acknowledged: a common *discourse* asserts that mathematics are done in ZF; we claim that the way to do mathematics in toposes with types actually corresponds more closely to the usual *practice* of mathematics than how they are formalized in ZF. The idea to formalize mathematics within some type theory is not new, it dates back at least to 1903:

> Every propositional function $\varphi(x)$ – so it is contended – has, in addition to its range of truth, a range of significance, *i.e.* a range within which x must lie if $\varphi(x)$ is to be a proposition at all [54]

It was then an attempt to solve contradictions that arise within untyped unrestricted set theories.

Let us illustrate this difference between *global* and *local* set theories:

– In global set theory, given any two sets A and B, we can always formulate the proposition $A \subseteq B$, which bears some truth-value, and consider the set $A \cap B$, whatever A and B are.
– In local set theory, a set has always a unique type of the form PC for some set C and we can formulate the proposition $A \subseteq B$ and we can consider the set $A \cap B$ (of type PC) *only* if A and B have the same type PC; the *range of significance* of the propositional function $\varphi(x, y) = x \subseteq y$ is a type $PC \times PC$ (interpreted as an object of a topos).

Even if a teacher of mathematics does not work consciously in a typed framework, in practice he does: there are mistakes that consist (let say) to write an equality between two expressions denoting real numbers and a calculation error led the student from one of these two expressions to the another one; and there are mistakes that consist (let say) to write an equality between two expressions of different "kinds" (an equality between a function and an integer, for instance); in a global set theory, this latter equality is legitimate (it is just that it is false, like the former one), while actually the mistake is much worse—it is a not a calculation error, *it does not even make sense at all*. The fact that *it does not even make sense at all* could be formalized by saying that the two expressions have different types.

Local set theory is thus a way to make explicit the frequent implicit use of types. In Subsect. 3.3 we see that in software engineering types are used not only in an explicit way but also in an implicit way, especially with programming languages that have weakly expressive types. For instance, one can compare languages that have explicit sum types (like OCaml and Haskell) and languages (like C) that do not have such explicit types for defining records with variants; in the latter case it is matter of the discipline of the users that the fields are well initialized and inconsistencies may lead to run-time errors that are subtle to track and correct, while in the former case the discipline is enforced at compile-time by the type-checker. In the same way higher-order types in mathematics help ensure consistency and readability.

Interestingly, even explicitly *untyped* calculi like the untyped lambda-calculus can be better understood with the notion of type. Indeed, a major breakthrough in computer science has been the discovery that models of the untyped lambda-calculus are provided by reflexive objects in Cartesian closed categories and since the latter ones are models of the simply typed lambda-calculus, we get that the untyped lambda-calculus is a typed lambda-calculus with one universal type!

2   Proof Theory

In his third attempt to define what ἐπιστήμη is, Theaetetus suggests that knowledge is true judgement with a justification ("μετὰ λόγου ἀληθῆ δόξαν ἐπιστήμην εἶναι ", [50], 201c–201d). Proof theory is this branch of logic initiated by David Hilbert that make mathematical objects studied *per se* out of these justifications. Several formalisms have been introduced for defining such objects: Hilbert systems, sequent calculus, natural deduction... Unlike with a specialized and advanced course in proof theory, a general and introductory course in logic has to focus on only one formalism; we advocate for natural deduction [51] for the following reasons:

- In contrast to Hilbert systems, natural deduction is *natural* in that, like what mathematicians usually do in order to prove statements, it allows to introduce assumptions that can be applied during the proof. So, natural deduction is much closer to usual practice of mathematicians than Hilbert systems. It is a strong argument in favour of using natural deduction as a pedagogical tool to teach how to write usual proofs in English.
- In contrast to sequent calculus, natural deduction proofs enjoy nice properties, while in sequent calculus different cut-free proofs must be identified and we have no perfect correspondence between cut-free proofs and simply-typed lambda-terms: the syntactic objects of the natural deduction proofs correspond better to their *objective content* than the syntactic objects of the sequent calculus proofs.

Our colleagues of the University Grenoble 1 made this decision [47], choosing natural deduction to teach reasoning to undergraduate students. After several years of experimentation, they concluded that the experience was successful and advocated that it "is the good way to introduce logic to beginners, at least for students in computer science"; and even more: "In particular, proof-trees are simple to understand and funny. They require no mathematical background. We think that they could be introduced at the highschool, at least for propositional logic, thus helping scholars in their scientific activities."

A further argument in favour of introducing natural deduction for teaching logic is that proof-assistants like Coq, Agda, Lean, Isabelle are based on natural deduction. This gives a benefit of double perspective on the topic – from the point of view of using a proof assistant, and from proof theory – which helps improving understanding of the topic.

2.1 Toposes in the Teaching of Proof Theory

A very common confusion is to consider many proofs that are not proofs by contradiction as proofs by contradiction. It is thus often said that the usual proofs of the Pumping lemma for regular languages or the irrationality of $\sqrt{2}$ are by contradiction while it is not the case. It is an essential objective of a proof theory course to clarify what proofs by contradiction are and a syntactic viewpoint is enough to distinguish between proofs that are by contradiction and those that are not by contradiction. Nevertheless, a semantic viewpoint allows to prove that a statement cannot be proved without proving it by contradiction by exhibiting a topos that does not satisfy this statement.

Let us consider, as an example, the two following statements that are usually taught to first-year students in mathematics:

1. Cantor's theorem: For any set X, there is no surjection from X to the set $\mathcal{P}(X)$ of subsets of X.
2. For any (finite) set X, the set $\mathcal{P}(X)$ is finite and its cardinality $|\mathcal{P}(X)|$ is $2^{|X|}$, where $|X|$ is the cardinality of X.[7]

The two statements are related in that the second statement implies the first one (at least if we have the same assumptions on X) but they should not be confused and they are independent of each other in that:

- One can prove the first one by a proof that is not a proof by contradiction, while the second one can be proved only by contradiction.
- There are universes in which the first one holds and not the other one.

By *universes* we mean here: *toposes*. It is easy to exhibit toposes in which Cantor's theorem holds (Cantor's theorem holds in any non-degenerate topos) and not the second statement; it is a striking way to get the independence of these two statements and how the second one can be denied by *showing* some universe in which this happens, and it is where toposes can be useful—*Seeing* it is a way to get some intuition about the distinction between the two kinds of proofs. One of the most easiest toposes to describe in which such phenomenon appears is probably the Sierpinski topos: we have three different truth-values and thus $|\mathcal{P}(X)| = 3^{|X|}$ for any object X—this topos can be described in an informal

---

[7] This statement can be strengthened by removing the assumption that X is finite, but it requires to introduce the notion of cardinality for infinite sets, which is often always done only in more advanced courses.

way by sets that evolve along the time (we have two stages: earlier/later) and doing mathematics in this topos is very instructive in that it allows to distinguish between concepts that are often confused in assuming that we have only two truth-values.

2.2 Coq Proof Assistant

Coq is a proof assistant and provides, among other things, interactive proof methods, decision and semi-decision algorithms, and a tactic language for letting the user define its own proof methods. It has many applications, from formalization of mathematics [16,58] and certification of properties of programming languages [35,61], to formal verification of algorithms [12] and even extracting certified, correct implementations from specifications [7,36], which is a direct application of the Curry-Howard isomorphism for software engineering.

A general course in logic aiming to enhance the ability of students to work with proofs can benefit from the aid of a proof-assistant like Coq, at the very least to serve as proof-checks: if a student can convert a proof written in English into a proof that Coq accepts, then the proof is probably correct. On the other hand, interactive capabilities of the Coq IDE can give insights even when a student does not have a complete proof.

In this section we describe how we integrated Coq in a logic course addressed to the first year bachelor students of Innopolis University, Russia. Note that a similar approach can be used with some other proof assistants that have similar type-theoretic foundation, such as Agda, Isabelle or Lean. For example, [2] has been used to teach propositional and classical logic with Lean. Perhaps introducing a proof assistant might complicate the course delivery for some students that are not oriented at software engineering, as they are required to learn a new tool. Nevertheless, from our experience, many students gain a much better understanding of the material after having worked with a proof assistant, which is a strong argument in favour of using a proof assistant as an alternative method of working through the proofs without strong requirement for all students to be proficient with the tool (it can be introduced in one or two classes to students).

Subset of Coq for Teaching. Coq has many features, which is nice for the Coq users, but this good point has two drawbacks: It requires much time to learn all of them and it helps too much the student for "trivial" proofs (trivial enough for Coq being able to provide efficient automatic tools). In order to avoid these two drawbacks, we can limit the use of Coq to a small subset of its features, specifically only allowing the following tactics in proofs:

- `intros` for function arguments, premises of implication and `forall`;
- `destruct` for conjunction and `exists` in premises;
- `unfold`;
- `split` for splitting conjuction in conclusion into two separate goals;
- `exists` for construction of a proof of existential proposition;
- `apply` to apply a lemma or theorem to the goal;

- **exact** to provide exact expression for the goal;
- **rewrite** for substitution using equality;
- **reflexivity** for trivial proofs of form x = x;
- **assumption** for using one of the assumptions as proof.

It is quite easy to go back and forth between formal proofs in Coq using these few tactics and informal written proofs for the reason we already highlighted that Coq is based on natural deduction and that natural deduction is a formalism that is "natural" in that it is quite closed to the usual way for mathematicians to prove theorems.

The Exercise Axiom. For the convenience of students, we can provide a placeholder axiom for unsolved exercises. This axiom prevents Coq from failing on unsolved exercises, allowing students to skip any intermediate exercise and focus on the one they want to solve first. Removing the axiom from the code allows to immediately see what exercises have not been solved yet.

```
(* ATTENTION: remove this axiom to step through exercises. *)
Axiom exercise : forall (Anything : Type), Anything.
```

Exercises on Sets and Mappings in Coq. It would be tempting to provide exercises about sets and mappings in Coq immediately, without explicit axiomatization of set theory. Unfortunately, working with native Sets in Coq can often become considerably more tedious than it is on paper.

One of the biggest problems is working with subsets. For instance, while it is easy to define on paper the subset $[n] = \{i \in \mathbb{N} \mid i < n\}$ of $\mathbb{N}$ and the inclusion from $[n]$ to $[n + 1]$ for each natural number n, in Coq, on the contrary, even if the "set" nat is available, it is not so easy to define the "sets" $[n]$ as "subsets" of $[n + 1]$ and nat at the same time.

Another problem is dealing with existential quantifiers that arise as consequences of the Principle of Unique choice. An example of an application of this principle is to prove that bijections have inverses. In usual mathematics (on paper), we implicitly use this principle, while it does not hold in Coq's type theory; instead, this principle has to be introduced as an axiom and dealt with explicitly.

Category Theory in Coq. Working with an explicit axiomatization of sets and mappings based on category theory as described in Sect. 1 removes these issues. The notion of category is easily modelled in Coq and allows for nice formal proofs. A possible way that is easy to use is shown on Fig. 2.

Proofs in English and in Coq. To emphasize similarity between formal proofs in Coq and in English, we suggest the following examples.

Exercise 1. Let $\mathcal{C}$ be a category. Let A be an object in $\mathcal{C}$. Show that the identity morphism $id_A : A \to A$ is an isomorphism.

```
Record category : Type := Category {
    obj : Type;                    (* what are objects *)
    mor : obj -> obj -> Type; (* what are morphisms *)
    (* identity and composition *)
    mor_id      : forall {X}, mor X X;
    mor_comp    : forall {X Y Z}, mor X Y -> mor Y Z -> mor X Z;
    (* axioms *)
    mor_idL   : forall X Y (f : mor X Y), mor_comp f mor_id = f;
    mor_idR   : forall X Y (f : mor X Y), mor_comp mor_id f = f;
    mor_assoc : forall X Y Z W
      (f : mor X Y) (g : mor Y Z) (h : mor Z W),
        mor_comp f (mor_comp g h) = mor_comp (mor_comp f g) h
}.
```

Fig. 2. Formalising the notion of category in Coq

Proof. It is enough to find $g : A \to A$ such that $id_A \circ g = id_A$ and $g \circ id_A = id_A$. We set $g = id_A$. Then both equations are satisfied with such a morphism g.

A formalization of this proof in Coq is given in Fig. 3. We note that some proofs will require students to be more explicit in the formal proof in Coq, although sometimes, proofs in Coq may be more succinct. The latter is often the case when `apply` tactic can be used directly without specifying any additional arguments for the lemma. Still, Coq allows and often even demands from the user to be explicit about the steps in a proof, which is instrumental in developing a good intuition about the structure of proofs.

```
Example mor_id_is_iso (C : category) (A : obj C)
   : is_iso C A A (@mor_id C A).
Proof.
    unfold is_iso.        (* Unfold the definition of isomorphism. *)
    exists (mor_id C).    (* Let identity morphism be the inverse. *)
    split.                (* Prove the two equations separately. *)
    - apply mor_idL.      (* Use left identity axiom. *)
    - apply mor_idR.      (* Similarly for the second equation. *)
Defined.
```

Fig. 3. Exercise 1 in Coq

Exercise 2. Let X and Y be two objects in some category $\mathcal{C}$. Let $s : X \to Y$ and $r : Y \to X$ be two morphisms in $\mathcal{C}$ such that $r \circ s = id_X$. Show that s is a monomorphism.

Proof. Let S be an object in $\mathcal{C}$. Let x and x' be two morphisms $S \to X$ such that $s \circ x = s \circ x'$. Then, by postcomposing with r on both sides we have $r \circ s \circ x = r \circ s \circ x'$. Since $r \circ s = id_X$, we have $id_X \circ x = id_X \circ x'$. By identity

```
(* A lemma for constructing equalities using postcomposition *)
Lemma postcomp_eq (C : category) (X Y Z : obj C)
       (f f' : Y ~> Z) (g : X ~> Y): f = f' -> f o g = f' o g.
Proof.
   intros H. rewrite H. reflexivity.
Defined.

Theorem section_is_mono (C : category) (X Y : obj C)
        (s : X ~> Y) (r : Y ~> X)
        (rs_eq_id : r o s = mor_id C): is_monomorphism C X Y s.
Proof.
   unfold is_monomorphism. intros S.
   unfold S_injection. intros x x' sx_eq_sx'.
   (* Apply postcomposition lemma to one of the assumptions *)
   apply (postcomp_eq _ _ _ _ _ r) in sx_eq_sx'.
   (* Reassociate parentheses *)
   rewrite <- mor_assoc, <- mor_assoc in sx_eq_sx'.
   (* Replace (r o s) with identity *)
   rewrite rs_eq_id in sx_eq_sx'.
   (* Eliminate identities *)
   rewrite mor_idL, mor_idL in sx_eq_sx'.
   (* We have rewritten assumption to satisfy the goal *)
   assumption.
Defined.
```

Fig. 4. Exercise 2 in Coq

axiom we have $x = x'$. We have shown that for any object S in $\mathcal{C}$ and any morphisms $x, x' : S \to X$ such that $s \circ x = s \circ x'$, we have $x = x'$. This means that s is an S-injection for any object S and thus is a monomorphism.

A formalization of this proof in Coq is given in Fig. 4. Note that we used a lemma for postcomposing on both sides of an equation; although this is a minor inconvenience, it makes the step explicit and is very easy to formalize.

3   Logic in Software Engineering

It is generally accepted that logic is important not only in mathematics, but also in software engineering, as it is necessary to be able to reason about the program's behaviour. For instance, programmers are expected to be familiar with and be able to reason about pre- and post-conditions and invariants [19]. However, even though applied category theory reaches in many areas, including industrial software engineering, it is much less known among engineers.

In the preface to their book [13], Brendan Fong and David I. Spivak write:

We believe that [category theory] has the potential to be a major cohesive force in the world, building rigorous bridges between disparate worlds, both theoretical and practical. The motto at MIT is *mens et manus*, Latin for mind and hand. We believe that category theory and pure math in general has stayed in the realm of mind for too long; it is ripe to be brought to hand.

Unlike computer science or mathematics in general, software engineering problems often do not put a burden of proof on the engineer and instead require evidence of work. This often leads to a certain degree of trust since the code is not formally verified in many cases, as it would significantly increase the cost of development. That is why it is crucial for software engineers to employ various approaches to structure their programs in order to be able to maintain complex systems.

General ideas about program structuring are often referred to as design patterns. As it turns out, many concepts of category theory can be used to structure programs and information systems, especially but not only in functional programming languages. We argue that for future software developers and architects it is crucial to be familiar with basic concepts from category theory since they provide the basis for reasoning using (composable) abstractions.

3.1 Curry-Howard Isomorphism

We already mentioned the Curry-Howard isomorphism in two occasions:

- To explain why doing mathematics in toposes is a way of doing mathematics with higher-order types (Subsect. 1.5).
- To mention applications of proof-assistants (Subsect. 2.2).

The main idea behind the Curry-Howard isomorphism is that formulas in mathematics correspond with types in programmings, proofs of these formulas correspond with programs and cut-elimination (normalization, Gentzen's Hauptsatz) corresponds with the execution of programs. It can be formalized with natural deduction, Cartesian closed categories and typed lambda-calculus. In such a framework conjunction corresponds with Cartesian products and records, disjunction with coproducts and sum types and second order quantification of Girard's System F [15] with hyperdoctrines [55] and parametric polymorphism.

Strict applications of the Curry-Howard isomorphism consist in extracting certified correct programs in an automatic way using a proof-assistant like Coq from formal proofs in mathematics. More relax applications do not require from the user to write proofs in mathematics—the user directly writes programs specified by very expressive types, which are formulas in mathematics, and the compiler checks if the program conforms its type (Type Driven Development).

3.2 Category Theory in Functional Programming

Functional programming, stemming from lambda calculus has been borrowing ideas from category theory for many years. A famous example is the use of monads to structure programs in functional programming languages [46,60], such as Haskell [20], that require handling of input and output (or some other so called "side effects", such as state and error handling, non-determinism and more).

Many libraries in Haskell are constructed as embedded domain specific languages (eDSL), allowing for succinct, expressive sublanguage to state and solve problems in the domain. In [45] Meijer, Fokkinga and Paterson show various methods of recursive programming with F-algebras. These methods have been implemented in Haskell[8]. A pattern of creating (extensible) eDSLs using free monads has been popularized in Data types à la carte [56]. This pattern has been increasingly popular in Haskell and other languages, especially since a more efficient implementation based on Church encoding has been suggested in [59]. At the moment of writing this paper there are multiple self-contained packages that implement various ideas from category theory for practical use in Haskell ecosystem[9]. These packages are highly used in Haskell ecosystem and most of them are in transitive packages of many industrial projects.

The success of applied category theory in functional programming has led to increasing interest in category theory from software engineering industry, which provides additional motivation to teach basic category theory to students.

3.3   Implicit Types in Software Engineering

Most programming languages have some support for types and it is a common practice to use user-defined types for specific type of data one needs to work with. However, even when used in reality these types are often not precise enough and actual types programmers rely on are implicit. We give a few examples of this, specifying when the use of imprecise types is dictated by limitation of the type system or is a choice of the programmer.

Preventing Data Type Design Anti-patterns. "Stringly typed" is a slang IT term that describes the process where a software engineer uses string values excessively for variables. Stringly typed code is code in which variables are often typed as strings, and handled as strings, when there are better alternatives available to programmers. It is also a word play off of "strongly typed" code, which describes code where types are used rigidly to enforce results. Stringly typed code may be strongly typed, in that it reinforces the use of strings, but it is generally not "strongly written," as it typically does not make use of the most efficient solutions.

While "stringly typed" programming is considered an anti-pattern (see, e.g. [40]), many developers still rely on simpler default types like strings and integers to encode all sorts of data. For instance, one may use a default machine-sized

---

[8] It is available on Hackage repository at http://hackage.haskell.org/package/recursion-schemes.

[9] The list is documented in the `category-extras` metapackage in Hackage repository at http://hackage.haskell.org/package/category-extras.

integer type to represent the result of a dice roll in a game, which has a very limited set of possible values. Another example would be handling identifiers: many unique identifiers are commonly treated as integer or string values, even though they should not admit operations available for those types, such as addition or concatenation. This use of such anti-patterns motivates some research (such as [26]) aiming to recover or reinforce structured data in strings.

Sum Types. It is very common for some data to be described in terms of a disjoint union of several possible description. One example is a request response (e.g. to a database or some remote service), which can either result in a success and provide some information based on the request or it may fail, providing some error message in this case. This situation is very well modelled by so-called *sum types*, which are one more instance of the notion of finite (co)limits we already encountered in Subsect. 1.4; more precisely they are *coproducts*. For instance, here is a possible definition in Haskell programming language:

```
data Response result = Success result | Failure ErrorMessage
```

However, many languages do not have a good support (if any) to create user-defined types that enforce this disjoint union. Some well-known programming languages that properly support *sum types* are Swift, Rust, Haskell, OCaml and F#. The languages Scala, C# and some other, instead, have a limited support of sum types through the mechanism of *case classes*; the limitation in those cases is that they require the use of a `switch` statement which does not support exhaustive pattern matching in these languages, so it is up to the developer to not forget to process all possible cases.

How do programmers deal with disjointness if it is not supported by programming language? By explicit tagging and checking: a data type is created with optional fields for every possible alternative and a special *tag field* that labels which alternative needs to be considered. Note that it is common to use `switch` statement for the value of the tag which mimics pattern matching. Of course, since this relationship is not enforced by a compiler or interpreter, it may lead to illegal program states and non-exhaustive case analysis.

Data Invariants and Quotient Types. Many data structure implementations have some invariant that has to be preserved internally. For instance, when implementing a self-balancing tree one has to keep track of the balance manually. This has two important implications. One is that developers have to hide implementation of such data structures in some way to guard users from relying on its representation. However, hiding implementation sometimes entails that users do not have a (safe) way to use that data structure efficiently. Another implication is that developers need to be conscious of these invariants to avoid mistakes in the code. Since most programming languages do not have any support for keeping track of such invariants, software engineers often rely on external specification and verification tools when formally tracking these is important.

However, even when implementation is hidden some invariants may still leak to the user. For example, the result of a sorting function should produce a sorting collection, but often the type of a corresponding method will not indicate that, instead a programmer will only mention it in the documentation. On the other hand, a binary search method might assume an input array to be sorted, but again this property of input data is not (and usually cannot be) enforced by the type system.

Similar problems arise when representation used for some data structure is not unique. For instance, depending on the order in which elements are inserted into a self-balancing tree, we may get a different result, even when those different representations correspond to the same set of values. This identification of multiple possible values in a set as equal is very well modelled by quotient types, but most programming languages do not have this feature.

Both data invariants and quotient types require programming language to have some feature that enables equations about data. Only a few of programming languages with dependent type systems (e.g. Idris) and proof assistants are capable of such features.

Conclusion

Dieudonné's proposal was motivated by the increase of abstraction in mathematics. As Andrei Rodin writes [53]:

> The development of new intuitions was not wholly suppressed but it became a prerogative of a narrow circle of creative mathematicians who invented new mathematical concepts and solved with them real mathematical problems; the rest of the community received these concepts mostly in the sterilized form of formal and quasi-formal (like in Bourbaki's case) axiomatic theories. (...) However already in the second half of the twentieth century this general tendency began to change (...). Thus I claim that the tendency towards a "higher abstraction" of the twentieth century mathematics is nothing but a local effect comparable with similar tendencies taking place in other historical periods (...); it does not represent a global tendency in the historical development of mathematics.

This dialectics of abstraction and intuition is fundamental in mathematics and thus should be taken into account in teaching mathematics—teaching logic should not be an exception. Reducing teaching logic to the introduction of a dry formalism is not only useless; it reinforces wrong popular biases. Avoiding such a reduction is more ambitious and more challenging, and even more so, as noticed in [34] about ETCS, there "is at present a lack of teaching materials" (citing [31] as being the main exception); but the lack of such material just makes more important to introduce such content in courses, since it can hardly be self-taught.

Acknowledgements. We are grateful to Todd Trimble for having pointed Michael Barr's testimony to us. Also, we acknowledge an anonymous reviewer for the feedback on a previous version.

References

1. Artin, M., Grothendieck, A., Verdier, J.L.: Séminaire de géométrie algébrique du Bois-Marie - 1963–1964 - Théorie des topos et cohomologie étale des schémas (SGA 4) - Tome 1. Lecture Notes in Mathematics, vol. 269. Springer (1972)
2. Avigad, J., Lewis, R.Y., van Doorn, F.: Logic and Proof (2020). https://leanprover.github.io/logic_and_proof/. Accessed 2 July 2020
3. Barr, M.: The Category Theory Mailing List (1996). https://www.mta.ca/~cat-dist/catlist/1999/set-memb-func-comp
4. Benacerraf, P.: What numbers could not be. Philos. Rev. **74**, 47–73 (1965)
5. Cantor, G.: Contributions to the Founding of the Theory of Transfinite Numbers. Dover Books on Mathematics. Dover Publications, Mineola (1955)
6. Cantor, G.: Gesammelte abhandlungen mathematischen und philosophischen Inhalts. Springer(1932). Ernst Zermelo (ed.)
7. Chlipala, A.: Certified Programming with Dependent Types: A Pragmatic Introduction to the Coq Proof Assistant. The MIT Press, Cambridge (2013)
8. Clementino, M.M., Picado, J.: An Interview with F. William Lawvere - Part Two, Bulletin of the Centro Internacional de Matematica (2008)
9. Descartes, R.: Discours de la Méthode... plus la Dioptrique, les Météores et la Géométrie (1644)
10. Dieudonné, J.: New thinking in school mathematics, pp. 31–49. Organisation for Economic Co-operation and Development (1961)
11. Eilenberg, S., Steenrod, N.E.: Foundations of Algebraic Topology. Princeton Mathematical Series. Princeton University Press, Princeton (1952)
12. Filliâtre, J.-C., Magaud, N.: Certification of sorting algorithms in the Coq system. In: Theorem Proving in Higher Order Logics: Emerging Trends (1999)
13. Fong, B., Spivak, D.I.: An Invitation to Applied Category Theory: Seven Sketches in Compositionality. Cambridge University Press, Cambridge (2019)
14. Ghica, D.: Inventing an algebraic knot theory. Mathematics Teaching, pp. 264–268 (2018–2019)
15. Girard, J.-Y.: Une Extension De ĽInterpretation De Gödel a ĽAnalyse, Et Son Application a ĽElimination Des Coupures Dans ĽAnalyse Et La Theorie Des Types. In: Fenstad, J.E. (ed.) Proceedings of the Second Scandinavian Logic Symposium, volume 63 of Studies in Logic and the Foundations of Mathematics, pp. 63–92. Elsevier (1971)
16. Gonthier, G., Mahboubi, A., Rideau, L., Tassi, E., Théry, L.: A modular formalisation of finite group theory. In: Schneider, K., Brandt, J. (eds.) TPHOLs 2007. LNCS, vol. 4732, pp. 86–101. Springer, Heidelberg (2007). https://doi.org/10.1007/978-3-540-74591-4_8
17. Gray, J.W.: Fragments of the history of sheaf theory. In: Fourman, M., Mulvey, C., Scott, D. (eds.) Applications of Sheaves. LNM, vol. 753, pp. 1–79. Springer, Heidelberg (1979). https://doi.org/10.1007/BFb0061812
18. Grothendieck, A.: Sur quelques points d'algèbre homologique. I. Tohoku Math. J. **9**(2), 119–221 (1957)
19. Hoare, C.A.R.: An axiomatic basis for computer programming. Commun. ACM **12**(10), 576–580 (1969)
20. Hudak, P., et al.: Report on the programming language Haskell: a non-strict, purely functional language version 1.2. ACM SigPlan Notices **27**(5), 1–164 (1992)
21. Hume, D.: A Treatise of Human Nature: Being an Attempt to Introduce the Experimental Method of Reasoning into Moral, volume I (1739)

22. Hyland, J.M.E.: The Effective Topos. In: Troelstra, A.S., van Dalen, D. (eds.), The L. E. J. Brouwer Centenary Symposium, volume 110 of Studies in Logic and the Foundations of Mathematics, pp. 165–216. Elsevier (1982)
23. Kan, D.M.: Adjoint functors. Trans. Am. Math. Soc. **87**(2), 294–329 (1958)
24. Kant, I.: Kritik der reinen Venunft, volume 37a of Philosophische Bibliothek. Felix Meiner (1956)
25. Kant, I.: Critique of Pure Reason. The Cambridge Edition of the Works of Immanuel Kant. Cambridge University Press (1998). Translated and edited by Paul Guyer and Allen W. Wood
26. Kelly, D., Marron, M., Clark, D., Barr, E.T.: SafeStrings: Representing Strings as Structured Data. CoRR, abs/1904.11254 (2019)
27. Ralf, K.: Tool and Object: A History and Philosophy of Category Theory. Science Networks. Historical Studies, Birkhäuser Basel (2007)
28. Lawvere, F.W.: An elementary theory of the category of sets. Proc. Nat. Acad. Sci. **52**, 1506–1511 (1964)
29. Lawvere, F.W.: Quantifiers and sheaves. Actes Congress Int. Math. **1**, 329–334 (1971)
30. Lawvere, F.W.: Foundations and applications: axiomatization and education. Bull. Symbol. Logic **9**(2), 213–224 (2003)
31. Lawvere, F.W., Rosebrugh, R.: Sets for Mathematics. Cambridge University Press, Cambridge (2003)
32. Lawvere, F.W., Schanuel, S.H.: Conceptual Mathematics: A First Introduction to Categories, 2nd edn. Cambridge University Press, Cambridge (2009)
33. Lawvere, W., McLarty, C.: An elementary theory of the category of sets (long version) with commentary. Reprints Theory Appl. Categories **11**, 1–35 (2005)
34. Leinster, T.: Rethinking set theory. Am. Math. Mon. **121**, 403–415 (2014)
35. Leroy, X.: Formal verification of a realistic compiler. Commun. ACM **52**(7), 107–115 (2009)
36. Letouzey, P.: Extraction in Coq: an overview. In: Beckmann, A., Dimitracopoulos, C., Löwe, B. (eds.) CiE 2008. LNCS, vol. 5028, pp. 359–369. Springer, Heidelberg (2008). https://doi.org/10.1007/978-3-540-69407-6_39
37. Linnebo, Ø., Pettigrew, R.: Category theory as an autonomous foundation. Philos. Math. **19**, 227–254 (2011)
38. Mac Lane, S.: Internal logic in toposes and other categories. J. Symbol. Logic **39**, 427–429 (1974)
39. Mac Lane, S., Moerdijk, I.: Sheaves in Geometry and Logic. Springer, New York (1992)
40. Malovitsa, I.: The Most Expensive Anti-Pattern (2015). http://m1el.github.io/printf-antipattern/. Accessed 2 July 2020
41. Marquis, J.-P.: From a Geometrical Point of View: A Study of the History and Philosophy of Category Theory, Volume 14 of Logic, Epistemology, and the Unity of Science. Springer (2008). https://doi.org/10.1007/978-1-4020-9384-5
42. Maurice, M.: Bourbaki: A Secret Society of Mathematicians. American Mathematical Society, Providence (2006)
43. McLarty, C.: The uses and abuses of the history of topos theory. Br. J. Philos. Sci. **41**, 351–375 (1990)
44. McLarty, C.: The roles of set theories in mathematics. In: Landry, E. (ed.) Categories for the Working Philosopher, pp. 1–17. Oxford University Press, Oxford (2017)

45. Meijer, E., Fokkinga, M., Paterson, R.: Functional programming with bananas, lenses, envelopes and barbed wire. In: Hughes, J. (ed.) FPCA 1991. LNCS, vol. 523, pp. 124–144. Springer, Heidelberg (1991). https://doi.org/10.1007/3540543961_7
46. Moggi, E.: Notions of computation and monads. Inf. Comput. **93**(1), 55–92 (1991). Selections from 1989 IEEE Symposium on Logic in Computer Science
47. Monin, J.-F., Ene, C., Périn, M.: Gentzen-Prawitz Natural Deduction as a Teaching Tool (2009)
48. Osius, G.: A note on Kripke-Joyal semantics for the internal language of topoi. In: Lawvere, F.W., Maurer, C., Wraith, G.C. (eds.) Model Theory and Topoi. LNM, vol. 445, pp. 349–354. Springer, Heidelberg (1975). https://doi.org/10.1007/BFb0061300
49. Parnas, D.L.: Information distribution aspects of design methodology. In: IFIP Congress (1971)
50. Duke, E.A., Hicken, W.F., Nicoll, W.S.M., Robinson, D.B., Strachan, J.C.G. (eds.): Plato. Tetralogiae I-II, Volume 1 of Oxford Classical Texts: Platonis Opera. Oxford University Press (1995)
51. Prawitz, D.: Natural Deduction: A Proof-Theoretical Study. Dover Books on Mathematics. Dover Publications, Mineola (2006)
52. Riehl, E.: ∞-category for undergraduates. Berkeley Logic Colloquium, May 2020. http://www.math.jhu.edu/eriehl/berkeley-logic.mp4
53. Rodin, A.: Axiomatic Method and Category Theory, volume 364 of Synthese Library (Studies in Epistemology, Logic, Methodology, and Philosophy of Science). Springer (2014). https://doi.org/10.1007/978-3-319-00404-4
54. Bertrand, R.: The Principles of Mathematics. Cambridge University Press, Cambridge (1903)
55. Seely, R.A.G.: Categorical semantics for higher order polymorphic lambda calculus. J. Symbol. Logic **52**(4), 969–989 (1987)
56. Swierstra, W.: Data types à la carte. J. Funct. Program. **18**, 423–436 (2008)
57. The Univalent Foundations Program. Homotopy Type Theory: Univalent Foundations of Mathematics. Institute for Advanced Study (2013). https://homotopytypetheory.org/book
58. Voevodsky, V., Ahrens, B., Grayson, D., et al.: UniMath – a computer-checked library of univalent mathematics. https://github.com/UniMath/UniMath
59. Voigtländer, J.: Asymptotic improvement of computations over free monads. In: Audebaud, P., Paulin-Mohring, C. (eds.) MPC 2008. LNCS, vol. 5133, pp. 388–403. Springer, Heidelberg (2008). https://doi.org/10.1007/978-3-540-70594-9_20
60. Wadler, P.: Monads for functional programming. In: Broy, M. (ed.) Program Design Calculi, Berlin, Heidelberg, pp. 233–264. Springer, Heidelberg (1993) . https://doi.org/10.1007/978-3-662-02880-3_8
61. Xu, F., Fu, M., Feng, X., Zhang, X., Zhang, H., Li, Z.: A practical verification framework for preemptive OS kernels. In: Chaudhuri, S., Farzan, A. (eds.) CAV 2016. LNCS, vol. 9780, pp. 59–79. Springer, Cham (2016). https://doi.org/10.1007/978-3-319-41540-6_4

On the Design of a New Software Engineering Curriculum in Computer Engineering

Stefan Hallerstede$^{(\boxtimes)}$, Peter Gorm Larsen, Jalil Boudjadar,
Carl Peter Leslie Schultz, and Lukas Esterle

DIGIT, Department of Engineering, Aarhus University, Aarhus, Denmark
{sha,pgl,jalil,cschultz,lukas.esterle}@eng.au.dk

Abstract. The Department of Engineering at Aarhus University has started up a new science-based BSc degree in Computer Engineering. We report about our planning of the curriculum during the first two years in the Software Engineering area. We discuss highlights, basic concepts, selected course contents, inter and intra course progression, observations from the first two semesters taught, and our expectations concerning the learning objectives and outcomes of the curriculum as a whole.

1 Introduction

At Aarhus University (AU) the initial engineering educations originally came from the Engineering College of Aarhus, which was merged with AU in 2012. Thus, the prime focus on the original curriculum was to deliver new BSc students that directly were employable by the many local companies needing new employees with skills in the core technologies used right now. This includes programming environments such as C# and both embedded and Windows-based technologies. The courses of the curriculum we describe here are designed as independent units combining theoretical, methodological and practical aspects, emphasising their orientation towards engineering.

The perspective of local companies is brought into the curriculum design by means of an advisory board where the companies are represented. There, the proposed BSc curricula are reviewed and recommendations given. From a university perspective this curriculum strengthens the profile of the newly established faculty of technical sciences that complements the faculty of natural sciences.

When designing the curriculum we have made assumptions and decisions based on our experience at university teachers and researchers. Structure and content of the different courses is based on tried practices, and first-hand information from students in terms of direct feedback – using questionnaires and end-of-course discussions– and observing learning success – their ability to apply the acquired knowledge and reason about it. The general approach follows [1].

J.-M. Bruel et al. (Eds.): FISEE 2019, LNCS 12271, pp. 178–195, 2020.
https://doi.org/10.1007/978-3-030-57663-9_12

Overview. Section 2 describes the courses of the curriculum and their relationships, as well as, some assumptions and decisions we have made when designing the software engineering courses of the curriculum. In Sect. 3 we present an outline of selected courses to clarify the contents and level of the curriculum. Finally, in Sect. 4 we close with a discussion of some issues surrounding the Software Engineering curriculum and some insights since we have started teaching it.

2 Courses

Among the courses of the computer engineering curriculum we focus on the software engineering courses listed below. There are links to and from courses outside the software engineering scope, that are referred to, e.g., the Software Architecture course refers to the Computer Networks course in the 4th semester and Programming and Modelling refers to Classical Physics in the 1st semester. An overview of these relations is given in Fig. 1 where the software-related courses are shown in green. Although these courses are related to the Software Engineering curriculum, they are not included in the current description because their focus is not software as such. Note, however that courses like Computer Networks also uses C, a preview of which is given in the Software Architecture course. However, too much uniformity across the study would risk forcing alien concepts with a focus on software on courses where this is counterproductive.

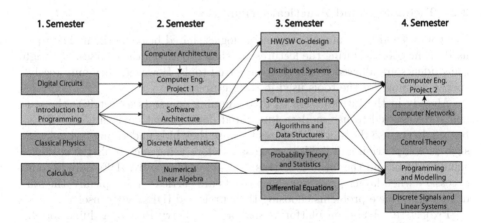

Fig. 1. The first two years of the curriculum for the Bachelor in Computer Software Engineering. Highlighted in green are courses with a focus on Software Engineering. Each column represents a single semester within the first two years of the curriculum. Arrows between the boxes indicate their main dependencies. (Color figure online)

2.1   Variation in Learning Levels

We assume that each cohort of students beginning a BSc study has a wide variety of prior knowledge and talent, and we distinguish them into three major groups (weaker, regular, stronger) for which we cater in the teaching to support the different groups according to their needs. The students are informed about the different offers at the beginning of the different courses. It should be emphasised here that although we consider the students according to the three groups, we make offers to all of them, that range from supporting students with exercises to challenge exercises and projects. The students can make informed choices depending to how they assess themselves at certain points in time. The main outcome of this approach will be a larger spread of talent in Computer Engineering providing as much support as possible to the different learning levels:

Weaker Students: Dedicated to weaker students, support with home assignments is offered in specific exercise sessions.

Regular Students: Regular students receive a large number of exercises to practice their skills, and we will also offer help with solving them, similarly to the weaker students.

Stronger Students: Dedicated to stronger students, we offer challenging voluntary projects that go beyond the course objectives. These projects bring the stronger students in direct contact with research groups.

2.2   Technology and Practical Orientation

The courses will build on software technologies shared between them. The tools used in the courses during the lectures are shared between the courses, although the students are allowed to use their preferred tools. However, they only receive specific support for the tools used in the lectures.

Already in the Introduction to Programming course (see Sect. 3.1) the students are allowed to use modern integrated development environments (IDEs) but we do not use IDEs in the lectures because they hide underlying technologies such as compilation and linking processes. Before using such tools the students should understand the basic functions that are hidden away. IDEs only become necessary when larger programming projects are carried out. Typically, the students do not have problems choosing their preferred IDEs by themselves.

Projects are based on platforms such as Raspberry Pi and Arduino for the deployment of software.

2.3   Languages and Notations

The basic programming language is C/C++ using gcc and gdb that can be installed in Linux, Windows and MacOS. The students receive help installing this software during the first programming café. At the end of the Introduction to Programming course the students receive a short introduction to Python relating it to the concepts they have encountered in C/C++. Python is used in their courses on Numerical Linear Algebra and Classical Physics (see Sect. 2). It is unrealistic to base the entire study on one programming language but we minimise the distractions caused by switching between different programming languages.

This approach permits us to focus on just one programming language to cover the Software Engineering part of the BSc programme, from the presentation of basic algorithms and application development to controller design for embedded systems. Software systems modelling uses graphical notations such as Unified Modelling Language (UML) [5], Architecture Analysis and Design Language (AADL) [3] and formal modelling language the Vienna Development Method (VDM) [4]. All of them have been standardised and a sufficient number of secondary literature is available online and in book form, permitting the students to consult additional sources as it aids their understanding.

2.4   Cross-Cutting Themes and Progression

The courses of the curriculum are connected by underlying themes that span across the two years

- problem solving (PS),
- modelling (MD),
- reasoning (RS),
- verification (VR).

In the first semester we address these connections mostly informally, and as the curriculum progresses towards the fourth semester these connections become increasingly formal. The corresponding skills that students develop are trained and refined from semester to semester. Table 1 shows on which topics and skills the different courses focus. If these were developed in isolation, they would easily end up disconnected from each other, making it difficult for the students to see the big picture of software engineering. This was a major concern when we

Table 1. The software engineering curriculum

Sem.	Lecture	ECTS	Main focus
1	Introduction to Programming	10	Problem solving, programming in C
2	Comp. Engineering Project I	5	Group work, embedded software
2	Software Architecture	5	Software qualities, principles & patterns
2	Discrete Mathematics	5	Abstraction and proof
3	Algorithms & Data Structures	5	Abstraction and efficiency
3	Software Engineering	5	Essential software technologies
3	HW/SW Co-design	5	Programming, modelling, simulation & synthesis
4	Comp. Engineering Project II	5	Planning, organising, distributed software
4	Programming and Modelling	10	Cyber-physical systems modelling, code generation

developed the first drafts of the curriculum: on one hand we have to cover quite distinct topics in a focussed way while the students attending the courses should be able to make connections themselves. We help this by giving ample indications of related courses (and how) and the intended progression during the lectures. As a consequence, the students develop a sense for their overall progression: they respond extremely well on material of this sort in the lectures.

The courses in the curriculum cover different topics of software engineering going deeper in the cross-cutting themes. Table 2 below gives an overview of the relevant themes per course. We introduce concepts for verification like pre- and post-conditions in *Introduction to Programming*, discuss these ideas in *Discrete Mathematics* more formally, consider how it is related to systematic testing in *Software Engineering* and finally combine these techniques in *Programming and Modelling*. As a result, we cover a lot of ground of what could be a course on verification without having it explicitly in the curriculum and, at the same time, provide a greater sense of coherence and continuity for the students.

Table 2. Coverage of cross-cutting themes

Sem.	Course	PS	MD	RS	VR
1	Introduction to Programming	X		X	X
2	Comp. Engineering Project I	X			
2	Software Architecture	X	X		
2	Discrete Mathematics		X	X	X
3	Algorithms & Data Structures	X	X	X	
3	Software Engineering	X			X
3	HW/SW Co-design	X	X		
4	Comp. Engineering Project II	X	X	X	
4	Programming and Modelling	X	X	X	X

The different themes are practiced until they are all used in the course Programming and Modelling in the 4th semester introducing the students to a multi-disciplinary setting around Cyber-Physical Systems [9]. This approach permits to teach advanced material at that stage in the curriculum without having explicit introductory courses on formal methods and related topics. An additional advantage is that the students see the four themes as being related to the topics of the different courses from the start. For instance, the students will learn that programming always involves some form of reasoning about why the program "works", arguing how certain functionality is implemented or why a program terminates, in particular, from the beginning of their studies. They will be aware that there are different approaches to this including informal arguments, formal proofs, testing and debugging. They will become engineers that make pragmatic choices depending on problems at hand, and we teach them a range of techniques on which they will be able to make decisions. In particular, we avoid favouring specific techniques so that the students do not get biased by our teaching.

2.5 International Collaboration

The technologies used in the courses partly are freely available, as well as locally developed and maintained. Partly they are developed at other universities and already used for teaching there. We collaborate with researchers at other universities for incorporating their technologies into our courses. At the moment these are, in particular, the following two technologies to be used in the Programming and Modelling course in the fourth semester (see Table 1 for an overview of the courses):

- The University of Bremen: We will use an automated test case generation library (FSM library at https://github.com/agbs-uni-bremen/fsmlib-cpp) that has been developed at the University of Bremen for teaching purposes. It is a scaled-down version of complex automated verification tool developed by Professor Jan Peleska and colleagues.
- Kansas State University (KSU): We will use verification tools developed at KSU [11].

We intend to extend the number of collaborations in the coming years to internationalise the study environment and ensure that the students develop a sense for the international character of the scientific and engineering communities. The collaborations themselves permit us to have access to advanced tools with a strong background in academic research, as well as, to benefit from teaching experience at those universities.

The alignment of these courses into a coherent set of interconnected topics poses a challenge. In addition to a natural progression of core skill sets such as programming, we adopt cross-cutting themes that are followed up in the different courses. As a consequence the connections between the courses go beyond mere references to related and specialised courses. This is a unique opportunity offered when designing new curricula. Adapting an already running curriculum is difficult by comparison as it means changing courses that work well. It is a continuing effort to preserve this structure.

3 Outline of Some Courses

In order to get an impression of the way the courses are taught, we outline four of them,

(1) Introduction to Programming (Semester 1)
(2) Software Architecture (Semester 2)
(3) Discrete Mathematics (Semester 2)
(4) Computer Engineering Project I (Semester 2)

where we discuss the first one in more detail to illustrate how the courses are designed. For the other three we summarise the main content and highlights.

3.1   Course: Introduction to Programming

Following the distinction of the students into three groups (weaker, regular, stronger, see Sect. 2.1), the *Introduction to Programming* course (8 h/week) uses three types of interaction with the students:

- (frontal/interactive) lectures (L),
- exercise sessions with feedback on assignments (E),
- programming cafés with active support (C).

The students receive information in the beginning of the course where we explain our approach transparently to everyone. The following is a summary of the information given in the first lecture concerning the learning environment and our rationale:

- All students should receive support
- We distinguish the learning levels of students: weak, regular, strong
- We offer a programming café every week where all students will receive help with the course material from the current week. In particular, weaker students benefit from such offers. Students get help with tools, review exercises and past exercises. Exercises for every week will have different difficulty levels with a challenge exercise for the strong students (the challenge exercise is not obligatory and open to all).
- Each week there will be a challenge exercise that students are invited to try themselves: don't do it if you are short of time (for whatever reason); don't do it if you are struggling with the regular exercises; do it otherwise and enjoy doing it!
- In week 4 of the course, a voluntary programming project will be offered to all students. We expect that this will mostly be taken on by regular and strong students. The students decide which offers they take up.

We have developed the course curriculum (Table 3) after a review of similar *Introduction to Programming* courses in many universities around the world. Each topic is introduced by first motivating it through *problem solving* in the context of programming:

- **aim** e.g. "We want to guarantee that our stack program will work as we intend it to";
- **problem with executable code examples** to concretely illustrate the problem, e.g. stepping through a series of programs that misuse the stack implementation;
- **problem formulation as a more general statement**, referring back to the problem examples, e.g. "The problem is that stack variables are exposed"
- **solution statement**, e.g. "we need to restrict access to variables that define the stack"
- **main topic**, e.g. data encapsulation and object oriented programming
- **problem revisited**, e.g. demonstrating how data encapsulation is used to solve each presented problem example.

Reasoning is first practiced *informally*, arguing for the correctness of small software artefacts, and then *formally* proving correctness of simple programs using a dedicated theorem proving environment for C programs. Topics were repeatedly revisited and referred back to throughout the course in an iterative way, to (a) emphasis the connection *between* topics and (b) give students time and opportunity to really digest and understand each topic through repetition in slightly different contexts.

Table 3. The Introduction to Programming lectures

Week	Topic	Theme	Contact Hours
1	Basics	Programming, problem solving, and reasoning	4L + 4C
2	Loops	Development and derivation of (simple) programs	4L + 4C
3	Testing	Development and analysis of correct programs	4L + 2C + 2E
4	Problem Solving	Array data structures	4L + 2C + 2E
5	Data Structures	Structured data and pointers	4L + 4C
6	Pointers to pointers	Programming with pointers	4L + 2C + 2E
7	Library modules	Programming larger software projects	4L + 2C + 2E
8	Algorithms	Designing sequences of program instructions for solving problems	4L + 2C + 2E
9	Recursion	Functions that call themselves	4L + 4C
10	Higher-order programming	Passing functions as arguments to other functions	4L + 2C + 2E
11	Problem Solving with Recursion	Verifying correctness of recursive programs	4L + 2C + 2E
12	Object-Oriented Introduction	Bundling data and their functions together	4L + 2C + 2E
13	Object-Oriented Programming Constructs	Controlling object state and access to internals	4L + 2C + 2E
14	Python & Recap	Introduction to Python	4L + 2C + 2E

We use an official course textbook [6] to provide students with further background reading and additional practice exercises outside of lectures (although the structure of our course differs significantly from the structure of the textbook). Lecture slides were developed with sufficient detail to be "self-contained" so that they also function as lecture notes, and are provided in PowerPoint and PDF format to students before the lecture; in total we produced over 1000 slides for the course, in 13 lectures (Table 3). In addition, *slidecasts* were created during the lectures and made available after the lecture until the end of the exam

Fig. 2. Live student feedback in response to the question "What were the most muddy aspects today?" collected using *mentimeter* and presented back to the students for discussion.

period i.e. recording audio from the lecture, and recording the lecturer's screen that presents the slides.

The initial size of the cohort in 2019 was 30. In Autumn 2020 this will be increased to 60. During the lecture we invite live feedback from the students (2–3 times per lecture) on their understanding of the presented topics by answering 3–4 content related questions via *mentimeter* (Fig. 2).[1] The (anonymous) answers and statistics of the responses are shown on the lecture slide and used as a focused discussion point to clarify the topic at hand.

The lectures are *interactive* in that students are able to execute code presented on the lecture slides. All code examples are made available as C programs (downloadable as a zipped folder) that can be compiled and executed, with the program file name always listed on the lecture slide. To avoid issues with differences in C compilers between operating systems, we created a Virtual Box image with all compiler and debugging tools already installed.

Assignments and Challenge Project. **Home assignments** are given weekly with sets of problems for all students and a *challenge* problem for the stronger students. The assignment sheet is made available after the lecture on a Tuesday (Fig. 3), and students are required to submit their solutions on the following Tuesday. On Thursday we run a four hour *programming café*, a friendly lab environment in which students can work on their assignment and exercises from the textbook with two teaching assistants available for discussion, input, etc. This approach permits us to give more tailored support for the three groups

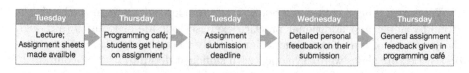

Fig. 3. Schedule for one assignment (*Introduction to Programming*).

---
[1] https://www.mentimeter.com/.

(weaker, regular, stronger) of students. One day after submission, students get a grade of either *pass* or *"more work needed"* (allowing resubmission in the subsequent weeks), with detailed personal feedback. In the following programming café one of the teaching assistants presents general feedback and common issues to the class for about 10–15 min.

In addition, a semester-long *Challenge Project* is offered to the students (intended for the stronger students but open for all). This is a programming project to be tackled by students in small self-formed groups of around 3–5 students. Each week an instructor hosts a meeting with all the challenge project students together, and discusses the project concepts, questions and progress, in a fun, friendly and informal setting. On the first iteration of the course we had 8 students (out of 28 students in the class) in two groups. This enabled us, and enthusiastic students, to get to know each other, interact and engage early on in their BSc program. The challenge project was specifically to create an interpreter for a subset of the FORTH programming language.

Assessment. The assessment at the end of the semester is by a 3 h handwritten exam without any support graded according to the Danish 7-point scale. During the semester students are required to submit and receive a "pass" grade for their weekly assignments (described above) in order to be able to go to the exam.

Learning Outcomes of the Course. The learning outcomes for this course describe *hands-on* skills related programming concepts and reasoning, the two main factors to support the course's view of *"programming as problem solving"*. At the end of the course, the participants are be able to:

- describe and discuss commands and control structures of imperative programming;
- understand the relationship between iteration and recursion;
- describe and discuss structuring mechanisms in different programming styles;
- implement their own programs using different programming styles;
- explain the concept of imperative and functional programming;
- describe assertional techniques for reasoning about programs; and
- reason informally about programs and relate this to tests.

3.2   Course: Software Architecture

The second semester course on Software Architecture is brought to the students as a continuation of the *Introduction to Programming* course. Whereas the latter course focuses on functional requirements for software, the Software Architecture course focuses on non-functional requirements. The proximity of the two courses permits to make this aspect very explicit, showing them two major concerns of programming: writing program code and organising it.

The course is taught in a standard format of two hours of lectures and two hours of exercises every week during which the students present and discuss their solutions to home assignments. A hands-on textbook is used as main text [10].

Table 4. The Software Architecture lectures

Week	Topic	Practice	Patterns	Principles	Background	Programming
1	Introduction					X
2	Language Abstraction				X	X
3	SOLID Principles			X		X
4	Design Patterns		X			X
5	Architectural Styles		X			X
6	Networking Abstraction				X	X
7	Concurrency Design Patterns		X			X
8	Network Architectural Styles		X			X
9	Software Design			X		X
10	Software Metrics			X		X
11	Software Specification			X		X
12	Software Reuse			X		
13	Application Development	X				
14	Summary and Recap					

In weeks 12 and 13 of the Introduction to Programming course the students learn basics about object-oriented programming. This is continued in the Software Architecture course emphasising programming methodology (using C++). The students learn about object-oriented concepts such as inheritance, polymorphism and genericity. However, just like in the Introduction to Programming course this is always embedded into problem solving. Each lecture relates abstract architectural concepts to concrete programming concepts that can be used to realise the abstract concepts. The software is modelled abstractly using graphical notations like UML, T-diagrams (for composing compilers and interpreters) and ad-hoc diagrams. Subsequently, appropriate implementation techniques are discussed. This makes it possible for the students to apply software architecture immediately based on their first-semester knowledge. The students grow their repertoire of problem-solving techniques to scale to larger problems (which they are told about in the first lecture).

Table 4 shows an overview of the lectures of the course.

Because the course takes place in the second semester, there are two lectures where computer engineering *background* is given: the second week discusses compilation, interpretation and languages, and the third week network technology emphasising the abstractions they provide for software development. The networking lecture is held as a guest lecture by the same lecturer who teaches the computer networks course in the fourth semester. The intention of the guest lecture is to provide a sense of continuity to the students that spans the curriculum. A collection of lectures discusses *principle* underlying architectural design, in particular, SOLID [10] and common design principles like "reduce coupling" and "program defensively". The discussion of specification and reuse go into depth with respect to the Liskov substitution principle and the idea of refinement. About a third of the course discusses *patterns* describing typical elements of software architectures. About three quarters of the course is dedicated to evolving the programming skills from the level of the Introduction to Programming course to large scale software applying the techniques taught in the course. In a final lecture called Application Development the different principles and patterns are applied to embedded, mobile and desktop software. This is complemented by a guest lecture from a local software development company.

3.3 Course: Discrete Mathematics

The second semester course on Discrete Mathematics takes the informal reasoning from the Introduction to Programming course and adds formality to it and discusses alternative strategies for arguments [2]. Discrete mathematics provides the theoretical foundation for programming. It provides mathematical models for common abstractions referred to in programming. It provides the basis on which the (theoretical) performance of programs can be judged. It permits us to make statements about properties of programs. The course will introduce first-order logic, numbers, sets, sequences, relations and graphs, their applications and techniques of proof. An overview of the course can be seen in Table 5.

Table 5. The Discrete Mathematics lectures

Week	Topic	Concepts	Proof	Programming
1–2	Introduction direct proofs and contradiction		X	
3–4:	Counterexamples and proof by contraposition		X	
5	Logic	X	X	
6	Set theory	X	X	
7	Relations	X	X	
8	Functions	X	X	
9–10	Recursion and Induction	X	X	X
11–12	Sequences and recurrence relations	X	X	
13	Graph theory	X	X	
14	Evaluation and exam preparation			

This course is designed with special principles in two separate dimensions. Firstly this course is delivered as flipped classroom where there is limited time spent on presentations of the material in the four hours of confrontation time every week (instead the students need to work with the material themselves outside class with both videos and the text book, while the remaining parts of confrontation time is spend on the lecturers assisting the students with workshops). Secondly this course is organised such that there is an oral exam where

75% of the grade is based on the students ability to present a subject in the curriculum and 25% on the students ability to critically review another student's oral presentation. Both of these principles are introduced here in order to strengthen the students abilities to work with reasoning in an independent manner and to judge where the right level of formality is.

3.4   Course: Computer Engineering Project I

The second semester course Computer Engineering Project I offers a hands-on experience with solving a comprehensive problem where students to reason, combine and apply the knowledge they learn throughout first and second semester courses. This course also offers the opportunity for students to develop new skills related to design space exploration and code optimisation. On the application side, students learn to manipulate individual technologies such as range finder sensors and light sensors to monitor an environment, Arduino boards to process collected data, Raspberry Pi platforms to actuate mechanical components. This permits the students to see the larger context in which software development typically takes place. An integration of these technologies is performed on a Turtle Bot3 Robot simulating a rescue lab where students are introduced to a set of ROS functions. The main goal is to deliver an optimal exploration plan minimising the robot effort to explore an arena and maximise the number of found "victims" to be rescued. Using their knowledge about compiling and execution, students optimise their code to improve the robot response time and reduce the memory use.

Table 6. The Computer engineering project workshops

Week	Topic	Technology	Programming
1	Lab Introduction, system architecture, subversion		X
2	Assembling Arduino and Breadboard	X	
3	Proximity sensors to Arduino	X	
6	Light sensors to Arduino	X	
7	Actuations		X
8	ROS seminar		X
9	Connecting Arduino to Raspberry Pi	X	
10–11	Robots navigation implementation		X
12–13	Optimization		X
14	Competition, demo and examination		

Regarding the design space exploration, students learn the basis of how to choose design alternatives and how to assess the different designs with respect to a set of possibly conflicting metrics. Towards the end of the semester, the students have to deliver a report documenting their implementations and justifying the design decisions taken throughout the course experience. An overview of the course can be seen in Table 6. The fourth semester project course (Computer Engineering Project II) in comparison follows the one discusses here but is more challenging with respect to group coordination and technological mastery. In particular, it will use material taught in accompanying courses on Control Theory and Networking.

3.5 Summary of the Remaining Courses

Table 7 provides an overview of the remaining courses of the curriculum. We provide only the names of the lectures as the content is mostly well-known.

The Software Engineering course has a special function in the curriculum as it collects and links material from other courses. For instance, the lecture in week 4, Software Design, discusses topics from Introduction to Programming,

Table 7. Remaining courses of the software engineering curriculum

Week	Software Engineering	Algorithms & Data Structures	HW/SW Co-design	Programming & Modelling
1	Software development processes	Basics and Introduction	Computer Engineering	Introduction
2	Requirements Elicitation and Analysis	Implementation of Sequences, Queues and Stacks	HW/SW Co-Design	Basic Technologies for Modelling, Proof and Simulationc
3	Requirements Modelling	Array Searching	Model-based Design	Logics
4	Software Design	Fixed Arrays, Dynamic Arrays, Slices and Iterators	Model-based SW Design	Programming and Proof
5	Version Control	Union Find	Model-based SW Design	Automated Reasoning about Programs
6	Software Quality	Array Sorting	SW Mini Project	Automated Reasoning about Programs
7	Formal Specification	Priority Queue	Model-based HW Design	Modelling Methodology
8	Unit Testing	Sequence and Stream Sorting and Searching	Model-based HW Design	Introduction to INTO-CPS
9	Integration Testing	Search Trees	SW-HW System Synthesis	20-sim Tutorial
10	Performance Requirements	Sets and Dictionaries	Design Space Exploration	Co-simulation & Design Space Exploration
11	Requirements Validation	Matrices	Optimisation and Validation	C Code Generation
12	Formal Verification	Graphs	Final Project	Model Validation & Fault Tolerance
13	Specification, Formal Verification and Testing	Petri Nets	Final Project	Other Approaches: JML
14	Recap	Bitsets / matrices	Summary	Recap & Summary

Software Architecture, and Algorithms & Data structures. This is done expressly in order to give more coherence to the curriculum. The topic of requirements that regularly occurs in other courses is treated systematically. This permits to argue the significance of the topic as such warranting more attention.

The Algorithms & Data structures course follows the problem solving perspective the students are already familiar with from semester one. It focuses on practical aspects using abstractions learned in Discrete Mathematics to reason about problems and algorithms that solve them. Theoretical complexity considerations are discussed and related to practical evaluation of implementation variants.

The course on HW/SW co-design permits the students to understand the specificities of hardware design and of software design, and their similarities, in particular, when done in a suitable framework, such as, System-C.

The fourth semester Programming and Modelling course requires familiarity with the four cross-cutting themes as taught throughout the curriculum. This course is directly linked to local research activities at the Department of Engineering. Whereas reasoning about programs is done informally before, it is treated formally with tool support at this stage. This is complemented by modelling of cyber-physical systems as supported by INTO-CPS [8] and continuous modelling in 20-sim [7]. The course relies particularly on the formal training the students have received in Discrete Mathematics, as well as, Differential Equations and Classical Physics that are taught along side the Software Engineering curriculum. In this respect the students will gain the important insight that software can often not be developed without considering the real world with which it interacts.

4   Discussion

In comparison to a typical curriculum in Computer Science, ours is eminently practically oriented. Although students in Computer Engineering study also more theoretical topics, this has a different focus: Computer Engineering students study necessary theoretical issues in as far as it helps for solving engineering problems, whereas Computer Science students are exposed to the theories as such. For instance, our students encounter functional programming and recursion in Introduction to Programming course indicating suitable reasoning techniques, this is pick up in Discrete Mathematics course where suitable formalised proof techniques are taught. In Computer Science the students attend a course on functional programming where they study the underlying lambda calculus and type theory. Section 4.1 discusses briefly our approach to the relationship of science and engineering in the curriculum.

In order to warrant high quality of the taught courses, we carry out regular evaluations through continual feedback from the students during the courses and collecting data about the courses. We discuss this briefly in Sect. 4.2 and give some first results from the Introduction to Programming course.

4.1 Science and Engineering

The learning objectives of the teaching are, of course, related to the contents of the different lectures. Beyond this we also introduce the students from the beginning to our research activities in engineering science. This makes it possible to offer later in their studies BSc thesis projects closer to ongoing research and strengthen the scientific orientation of their education. For the most part scientific education is treated as the background in the courses, gaining larger weight later in the curriculum. At the end of the BSc studies they have seen some scientific methodology and have applied it in their reasoning. However, through the BSc curriculum (including their BSc theses) they will be guided in that reasoning and the choice of methods. A more independent application of scientific methods is only required in their subsequent MSc studies.

4.2 Evaluation

Starting a new BSc programme is a good opportunity to evaluate effectiveness as we do not have constraints by an established course catalogue. We believe that a culture of systematic evaluation will help to create a strong programme and make a contribution to education research. In order to achieve this, we plan to collect systematically data for all the lectures. E.g., for the Introduction to Programming lecture: Numbers of students present at lectures, exercise sessions and programming cafés, number of students attempting challenge exercises, number of students attempting the programming project, number of students succeeding in the afore mentioned. In addition, we have weekly meetings where we discuss feedback from the students concerning their motivation, learning success, and workload. The aim of this is to determine whether the students get the best possible support according to their abilities. This needs to be fine-tuned permanently.

At the start of the semester, 28 students participated in the course. Of these, 23 students finished the course. The drop-outs happened early in the course. We sent out e-mail to follow up the situation from 3 week on but did not receive a response from the five students. The attendance at the lecture was at least 90% (of 23) at the lecture and a the programming café. However, we found that the café was also used by the students to work on problems from other courses. We did not stop this from happening as it turned out that the students would ask for our help with the Introduction to Programming course when they needed it. This is what had been "promised" to the students in the first lecture. The result of the written exam at the end (A: 3, B: 9, C: 9, D: 1, E: 1) confirms that the support worked well towards achieving the learning objectives.

With respect to the home assignments to be handed in by small groups we made the following observations. None of the groups attempted all challenge exercises. Seven groups attempted at least one challenge exercise, one group attempted five challenge exercises. Eight groups handed in one late assignment, one group two late assignments, and three groups three late assignments. Two groups had two resubmit 2 assignments, and 4 groups one assignment.

Eight students started on the challenge project, one group of three and one group of five. After some initial success (not solving the complete problem) the latter group disbanded. The other group continued. One of the students continues the project in the second semester following the Software Architecture lecture. It appears to be a good idea to propose the challenge project to run over two semesters in the first place because most students stopped because of short term work loads in other courses.

4.3 Concluding Remarks and Evolution

We have outlined the Software Engineering curriculum at the Department of Engineering at Aarhus University, discussed the rationale and provided some examples of concrete courses. Given that we have started teaching in the curriculum since autumn 2019 it is too early to draw any hard conclusions. We have however already learned that the students appreciate the learning environment and the material they are being taught. We believe, that asking them regularly for feedback during the lecture has two major benefits: firstly, we can make improvements while the course is running; secondly, it appears to boost the motivation of the students when they get to play an active role in the shaping of their learning environment by receiving and acting on their feedback. Of course, there are some issues that can only be solved from one instance of the course to the next, concerning, for instance, the order in which some of the material is taught where the feedback that we receive refers to the teaching that is already past.

Acknowledgements. We are grateful for the support and contributions to the preparation of teaching materials carrying our café and exercise sessions by Casper Thule, Tomas Kulik, Christian Møldrup Legaard, Benjamin Salling Hvass, Hugo Daniel Macedo, and Peter Würtz Vinther Tran-Jørgensen.

References

1. Biggs, J., Kum Tang, C.S.: Teaching for Quality Learning at University, 4th edn. McGraw Hill (2011)
2. Cusack, C.A., Santos, D.A.: An Active Introduction to Discrete Mathematics and Algorithms, Version 2.6.4 (2019)
3. Feiler, P.H., Gluch, D.P.: Model-Based Engineering with AADL - An Introduction to the SAE Architecture Analysis and Design Language. SEI Series in Software Engineering. Addison-Wesley (2012)
4. Fitzgerald, J., Larsen, P.G.: Modelling Systems - Practical Tools and Techniques in Software Development, 2nd edn. Cambridge University Press, The Edinburgh Building, Cambridge CB2 2RU, UK (2009). ISBN 0-521-62348-0
5. Fowler, M.: UML Distilled: A Brief Guide to the Standard Object Modeling Language, 3rd edn. Addison Wesley (2003)
6. Hanly, J.R., Koffman, E.B.: Problem Solving and Program Design in C. Pearson (2016)

7. Kleijn, C.: Modelling and simulation of fluid power systems with 20-sim. Int. J. Fluid Power **7**(3) (2006)
8. Larsen, P.G., et al.: Integrated tool chain for model-based design of cyber-physical systems: the INTO-CPS project. In: CPS Data Workshop, Vienna, Austria, April 2016
9. Larsen, P.G., et al.: Frontiers in software engineering education. In: Collaborative Modelling and Co-simulation in Engineering and Computing Curricula (2020)
10. Martin, R.C.: Clean Architecture A Craftsman's Guide To Software Structure And Design. Prentice Hall (2018)
11. Yi, X., Li, R., Sun, M.: Generating Chinese classical poems with RNN encoder-decoder. In: Sun, M., Wang, X., Chang, B., Xiong, D. (eds.) CCL/NLP-NABD -2017. LNCS (LNAI), vol. 10565, pp. 211–223. Springer, Cham (2017). https://doi.org/10.1007/978-3-319-69005-6_18

Collaborative Modelling and Co-simulation in Engineering and Computing Curricula

Peter Gorm Larsen[1]([envelope]), Hugo Daniel Macedo[1], Claudio Goncalves Gomes[1], Lukas Esterle[1], Casper Thule[1], John Fitzgerald[2], and Kenneth Pierce[2]

[1] DIGIT, Department of Engineering, Aarhus University, Aarhus, Denmark
{pgl,hdm,claudio.gomes,lukas.esterle}@eng.au.dk
[2] School of Computing, Newcastle University, Newcastle upon Tyne, UK
{John.Fitzgerald,Kenneth.Pierce}@ncl.ac.uk

Abstract. The successful development of Cyber-Physical Systems (CPSs) requires collaborative working across diverse engineering disciplines, notations and tools. However, classical computing curricula rarely provide opportunities for students to look beyond the confines of one set of methods. In this paper, we report approaches to raising students' awareness of the integrative role of digital technology in future systems development. Building on research in open but integrated tool chains for CPS engineering, we consider how this has been realised in two degree programmes in Denmark and the UK, and give preliminary findings. These include the need for ensuring stability of research-quality tools, and observations on how this material is presented in Computing versus Engineering curricula.

1 Introduction

Collaboration between diverse disciplines is essential to the successful development of the Cyber-Physical Systems (CPSs) that are key to future innovations [26]. However, many university curricula train professionals within long-established disciplinary silos such as mechanical, electrical, civil or software engineering, with few opportunities for interaction between them. It is therefore critical to include elements within degree programmes to prepare students for the cross-disciplinary work that will likely feature in their subsequent careers [18]. The ideal is sometimes described as a *T-shaped* professional, with deep skills in one discipline, but an awareness of and capacity to work successfully with others.

The methods and tools to facilitate cross-disciplinary collaboration in CPS design are novel, and still the product of research. Engineering disciplines have developed vocabularies, ontologies, methods, notations and tools that are sometimes very different from one another, and are certainly different from those deployed in the newer disciplines of computing and software engineering. Promoting the kinds of collaboration needed to deliver modern CPSs is therefore challenging. In our work, rather than advocate a single formalism to be used

© Springer Nature Switzerland AG 2020
J.-M. Bruel et al. (Eds.): FISEE 2019, LNCS 12271, pp. 196–213, 2020.
https://doi.org/10.1007/978-3-030-57663-9_13

across the diversity of forms of engineering in a project, we have seen some success from enabling stakeholders to use their own preferred notations and tools, but combining these in a semantically sound fashion. Our universities have been involved in joint European H2020 projects (including DESTECS [5,10] and INTO-CPS [8,17]) for over a decade, leading to the development of tools that support collaborative model-based systems engineering of CPSs, with a particular focus on co-simulation [13]. The prime goal in this work has been to enable each collaborating stakeholder to continue to use their preferred technology, coupling the different models together using co-simulation.

Given the need for T-shaped professionals in CPS engineering, but also given the relative immaturity of methods and tools to address this challenge, the question arises: how can we use research products to inform the development of cross-disciplinary skills in university curricula? Although there is a widely-felt need to deliver research-inspired teaching in universities, it faces the challenge that proof-of-concept research products such as tools are often insufficiently stable to be used by newcomers. The risk is that students have a suboptimal experience when exposed to immature prototypes, potentially colouring their future attitude to novel and advanced techniques. In this paper we describe how such new research prototypes have been used in university education by ensuring that the prototypes is sufficiently stable to be used by novices.

Boehm and Mobasser [4] identify significant differences between the 'world views' of engineers specialising in physical systems, software and human factors, ranging from the approaches to economies of scale to forms of testing, as well as the underlying technical formalisms. They describe a curriculum and courses at Masters level that aim to broaden students' skills beyond software engineering alone to embrace T-shaped characteristics. This includes opportunities for students to undertake shared activities such as: developing shared operations concepts, jointly negotiating priorities and revisions with clients, jointly setting criteria for development approaches, determining risks, and many others. They identify tools to support systems thinking in these activities. In our work, we have focussed on newly emerging tools to support cross-disciplinary model-based engineering, and specifically, we aim to give students experience of T-shaped skills including: negotiating common terms and concepts across discipline models, identifying and performing system-level tests, modifying and reassessing designs, and performing design optimisation.

In this paper we examine two approaches to the incorporation of co-simulation into university curricula as a means of introducing students to the need for cross-disciplinary design. The first, applied at Aarhus University (AU) is to approach this through overall systems engineering at Masters level. The second, applied at Newcastle University (NU), addresses this in the context of a computing (mono-disciplinary) course at Bachelors level. We give an overview of the background in Model-Based Systems Engineering (MBSE) and our open tool chain that supports the collaborative approach outlined above (Sect. 2). We then describe how collaborative modelling and co-simulation has been introduced in the engineering curriculum at AU (Sect. 3 and the undergraduate computing cur-

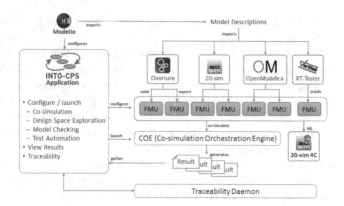

Fig. 1. Schematic of the INTO-CPS tool chain.

riculum at NU (Sect. 4). We discuss the experience so far in Sect. 5, and consider future directions in Sect. 6.

2   Background: The INTO-CPS Tool Chain

As Systems Engineering moves from document-based approaches to MBSE [30], the need arises to be able to analyse system models composed of diverse discipline-specific models, often from separate suppliers with their own intellectual property requirements. Co-modelling and co-simulation are seen as ways of meeting technical aspects of this challenge. The INTO-CPS tool chain shows how this can be realised.

The INTO-CPS Tool Chain (Fig. 1) supports an MBSE approach to CPS development that allows the Discrete-Event (DE) formalisms used to express cyber processes and Continuous-Time (CT) formalisms used for physical processes to co-exist in a common simulation framework. The act of collaboratively simulating these constituent models such that a simulation of a CPS is achieved is referred to as coupled simulation (co-simulation) [13]. A co-simulation is generally carried out by simulating the individual models while exchanging data and managing the progress of time between them.

Co-simulation requires the orchestration of a range of discipline-specific simulation tools [3,9]. The Functional Mock-up Interface (FMI) [22] is an approach to generalising the simulation interface of models that are to participate in a co-simulation. FMI provides and describes a C-interface and the structure of a model description file. A model implementing this C-interface and providing a model description file is referred to as a Functional Mock-up Unit (FMU) and it can contain its own solver. The INTO-CPS Toolchain is based on FMI 2.0 for its simulation capabilities.

The main user interface to the INTO-CPS tool chain is the INTO-CPS Application [20] which has been developed on the Electron platform.

The INTO-CPS Co-simulation Orchestration Engine (COE), called Mae-stro [27], manages the FMUs in accordance with various co-simulation algo-rithms. It is configured by a *multi-model* and a *configuration*. The multi-model defines the FMUs participating in a co-simulation, the dependencies between them, and their parameters. The configuration specifies the co-simulation exe-cution including details such as logging and step size (i.e., the time interval between value exchanges between the FMUs).

The tool chain also supports Design Space Exploration (DSE). This is the process of systematically executing co-simulations with a variety of values for specified design parameters, with the goal of maximising an objective such as energy efficiency or a performance measure [6,9] and part of the INTO-CPS Toolchain.

The tool chain is neutral about the sources of FMUs, but it has been instan-tiated with several formalisms and simulation engines. For example, DE mod-els can be developed in the Overture tool [16] which supports a dialect of the Vienna Development Method's modelling language for Real Time systems (VDM-RT [29]). Using Overture and the extension overture-fmu[1] one can export FMUs from a VDM-RT project [15,28]. CT models have been developed using 20-sim[2], which also can export conformant FMUs.

3   The Aarhus University Experience: Co-modelling and Co-simulation in the Systems Engineering Curriculum

In this section, we describe the introduction of co-modelling and co-simulation in the AU engineering curriculum. Students taking a Masters degree in elec-tronic engineering or computer engineering follow a mandatory course in systems engineering. Formerly largely focussed on document-based processes, the course is evolving to provide a stronger introduction to model-based techniques, with about half of the course using the new research results in MBSE, multi-modelling and co-simulation through the INTO-CPS tool chain. Since the students are novices in the technology, this demands user friendliness in the prototype tools resulting from the research.

3.1   Course Structure and Content

The systems engineering course includes practical examples. A student driven project spanning the entire semester is performed in close collaboration with two Danish companies, namely Terma and Beumer. Here, student teams develop different systems engineering artefacts while the companies act as the respective customers in particular to embrace the T-shaped characteristics mentioned in Sect. 1 above. During the course the students learn on one hand to use different tools to model and design their systems and on the other hand to combine

---

[1] https://github.com/overturetool/overture-fmu.
[2] https://www.20sim.com.

these tools in a single tool chain for engineering their systems efficiently using common terms. Hands-on tutorials as well as their ongoing group project guides them towards a deep understanding of MBSE and co-simulation.

To achieve this, the course is structured as follows: First the students get an overview on CPSs as well as co-simulation and the entire INTO-CPS tool chain. This overview allows us to structure the remainder of the lectures to dive into the relevant details. We use SysML, the industry standard for systems engineering, as graphical modelling language and VDM to formally specify software systems using the tools Modelio and Overture, respectively.

To teach students how to model dynamic systems, we utilise 20-sim, allowing students to define models via sets of equations or as graphical models, i.e., block diagrams.

Once students have the basis for constructing models of both cyber and physical systems elements, and have gained experience using industry tools such as 20-sim, they learn how to explore design parameters using the DSE features of the tool chain. This is followed by an introduction to the development of the software components, including automatic code generation.

3.2   Course Material

The INTO-CPS Association has created and maintains a series of tutorials on the installation and operation of the features of the INTO-CPS tool chain, using a simple running example based on the Line Following Robot (LFR) illustrated in Fig. 2. These are:

Tutorial 0: Setting up the environment. This covers the installation of INTO-CPS, its main dependencies, the Java runtime, and the use of the COE Maestro.

Tutorial 1: First Co-simulation. This provides a demonstration of a water-tank co-simulation followed by an introduction to the concepts involved e.g.

Fig. 2. Line Following Robot LFR used as a simple running example for co-simulation.

FMUs, models, multi-models, and an introduction on how to run a preset co-simulation.

Tutorial 2: Adding FMUs. This covers the deeper inner workings of a multi-model and co-simulation configuration, including the definition of parameters, which visual graphs to plot, which FMUs to use, and establishing the input/output connections between FMUs. Exercises help students to think about both the dynamics of the models being simulated and the effects of co-simulation parameters in the short- and long-term results of the co-simulation.

Tutorial 3: Using SysML. This introduces elements of SysML and the Modelio tool to develop the overall architecture of a multi-model. It covers the generation of a multi-model and its import into INTO-CPS.

Tutorial 4: FMU Export (Overture). The preceding tutorials have used a ready-made controller FMU. This tutorial explains where that FMU comes from. It includes the definition and export of a controller in VDM. Exercises allow the students to experiment with different control approaches.

Tutorial 5: FMU Export (20-sim). This focuses on the use of 20-sim to create and export the physical system FMU, allowing students to experiment with different physical models and observe how the controller behaves with each.

Tutorials 6 & 7: DSE configuration and execution. Building on Tutorial 3, students create a SysML representation of the DSE configuration (Tutorial 6) and learn how to use the DSE script to launch it and automatically compute fitness metrics for each design (Tutorial 7).

Tutorial 8: SysML for Co-Simulation. Students learn how use SysML to generate and import the description of the sub-components used in a co-simulation (Tutorial 3 was limited to using SysML to describe the overall multi-model architecture).

Tutorial 9: Building Controllers in VDM. This tutorial introduces techniques for designing controllers that are robust with respect to noise in the signals. Controllers are validated by co-simulation and are ready to be deployed.

Tutorial 10: Deploying the LFR Controller. At this point it is assumed that students have experienced how to develop the models of the LFR in a co-simulation (virtual) environment, and this illustrates how to deploy and validate a co-simulation unit using hardware performing in a real environment. The goal is to show how to export a VDM controller as an FMU, and subsequently use it to upload it as a sketch into the Arduino board controlling a hardware model of LFR.

Tutorial 11: Building Controllers in PVSio-Web. This tutorial teaches the students to write controllers in an PVSio-Web [21] and follows the approach in [23]. This tools enables the rapid prototyping of user interfaces and control code. The students then learn how to deploy their code into the hardware.

3.3 Course Delivery

We have applied the tutorials in the AU systems engineering course over the last three years. We group the tutorials into thematic units and deliver them throughout approximately five sessions depending on the students' progress. Sessions start with an exposition of the concepts behind the unit (e.g. co-simulation, DSE). Then hands-on tutorials allow students to interact with the tools while attempting to replicate the tutorial steps. A team of two to four teaching assistants helps troubleshoot problems students may find. Both software errors and repeated failed attempts to achieve the results of the steps prompt guidance using a case by case approach. Naturally, having newcomers using the prototype tools from the INTO-CPS project means that it gets used in ways not originally envisaged and this feeds back into further improvements of the tool chain elements. In the following, we provide an account of our experience of the sessions typical outcomes.

First Session. This is the students' first contact with the model-based approach and co-simulation concept. Usually students fully complete Tutorial 0, 1 and 2 and achieve an abstract understanding a co-simulation. The first challenge appears with Tutorial 0 and the installation of the Java virtual machine, which surprisingly poses troubles to a great group of students. Although theoretically a simple step for a master level student to perform, in practice we observe that the students often get frustrated while finding the links for the software package in the official provider downloads webpage. The problem is nowadays compounded with the display of complex licensing information and with the redirection to a registration page. It is awkward to observe that often students decide to install the virtual machine from non-official providers. This is a problem mostly affecting students without previous exposure to the Java and its development environment. In most cases, the completion of Tutorial 1 poses no trouble beyond tool glitches, or when the students miss accomplishing some of the previous steps. Commonly, a student may be unable to invoke the co-simulation orchestrator because they forgot to install the Java runtime or to download the `coe.jar` file. In contrast, the completion of Tutorial 2 is more complex and students often ask for assistance because the co-simulation is not launched (e.g., the misconfiguration of FMUs connections is detected by Maestro at launch time) or the results diverge from what is expected (e.g., the LFR animation displays a robot running in circles instead of following the line).

Second Session. After a shallow contact with co-simulation, the students are presented with Tutorials 3 and 4. Tutorial 3 is usually appreciated as it provides an appealing graphical approach to manipulating and visualising the co-simulation multi-model. On the downside, at some points, the Modelio tool is not user-friendly. In some cases, it crashes unexpectedly and steps need to be repeated. This tutorial takes most students time, which causes some students to move the completion of Tutorial 4 to the following session. The completion of Tutorial 4 goes without much trouble. This may be because that most of the steps involve the use of INTO-CPS features that are already familiar from previous tutorials. We find that the novel aspect of it – the generation of an FMU using Overture – is typically less prone to tool crashes, and most of our students have previous experience with Overture, which may simplify the task.

Third Session. This session is devoted to Tutorial 5 only. Installing and editing a CT model in 20-sim is usually accomplished with little assistance. In the second part, students are required to set up a C++ development environment in a Windows system, which involves the installation of tools such as Microsoft Build Tools and the troubleshooting of compilation errors. Usually students find this challenging and require more instructor support, for example because some students' systems do not accommodate the multi-Gigabyte demands of the installation, or the compilation script fails to find some of the registry entries.

Fourth Session. At this point, students have a working knowledge of the DE and CT models of the LFR. The session consists of Tutorials 6 and 7 which explore the DSE concept. Some students follow Tutorial 6 with some difficulty, as the graphical language is too abstract. But most are able to finish and progress to Tutorial 7. This tutorial is usually well-received when completed, as the students have a hands-on experience with DSE. Students are usually able to configure DSE launch scripts, but often have trouble because of misconfiguration of the Python dependency and the specific libraries required to run the scripts.

Fifth Session. To finalise the MBSE sessions we usually deliver one of the tutorials where the students develop the controller for the LFR example either using VDM (Tutorial 9) or PVSio-Web (Tutorial 11) and then deploy a controller into the hardware platform Tutorial 10. Tutorial 10 involves the compilation and upload of an Arduino sketch into LFR. Some of the steps are cumbersome because the standard compiler in the Arduino IDE tool chain version must be substituted by a different version. Also, the process involves several options and flags, which may at points be confusing. The interested students get hold of the LFR hardware and deploy it and run it on line tracks we set up for the experiments.

To what extent have we addressed the need for the more T-shaped skills identified in Sect. 1? In the context of this systems engineering course, *negotiating common terms and concepts across discipline models* is exercised both in the document-based part as well as in the model-based part of the course. "Real" negotiation is actually carried out in the document-based part where the different groups also act as sub-contractors to another group. *Identifying and performing system-level tests* is in particular exercised in the model-based part where co-simulation is used in the tests performed. Experience at *modifying and reassessing designs* is done mostly in the document-based part where a design change is introduced (on purpose but) unexpectedly for the students. If we had more time we would like to also use this in the model-based part of the course. *Performing design optimisation* is exercised using DSE in a co-simulation context, and here we think that there is an opportunity to run a small competition to deliver designs that deliver optimal performance against specified systems-level criteria.

4   The Newcastle University Experience: Co-modelling and Co-simulation for Computer Scientists

NU's School of Computing admits about 300 students per year to study for a six-semester Bachelor of Science (Honours) degree in Computer Science, or an eight-semester Master of Computing degree. As a university focussed on fundamental research that has a positive business, societal or environmental impact, there is a strong motivation to expose students to advances in technology that are on the horizon now, but may become significant in their professional careers.

The focus of the NU computer science degree programmes has traditionally been on software and systems rather than on engineering. Perhaps as a consequence of this, although the programmes require a high level of attainment by students on entry, they do not require pre-entry qualifications to be in particular subjects. Students enter having specialised at high school in almost any discipline, although all must have a basic level of mathematics and around half do have backgrounds in mathematical and physical sciences. The resulting diversity of intellectual background among students is seen as a strongly positive feature, but it does mean that mathematical and computing maturity varies across the cohort on entry. Some "levelling up" in mathematics for computing takes place in the first semester of study, and the mathematics needed for specialised subjects, such as basic number theory for cryptography, is taught close to the point of use.

The undergraduate programmes considered here are taught over six semesters. We here consider the current Stage 3 specialist module in real time and CPS delivered in Semester 6. Students with an interest in this area will have studied some basic formal modelling in VDM in Semesters 3 or 4, and may also have chosen to undertake a specialist project in the area in Semesters 5 and 6 alongside this pivotal module.

4.1   Course Structure and Material

CPSs typically have a significant real-time element as well as requiring the integration of physical and digital worlds. The MBSE approach taught at NU emphasises the real-time, concurrency and scheduling elements that Computing graduates need to know, alongside an appreciation of the multi-disciplinary cyber-physical integrations that give rise to temporal requirements.

The technical aims of the module are to understand the basic concepts of real time and embedded systems as well as CPSs; to understand the requirements and challenges of such systems, and how these have influenced the design of real-time languages; understand the implementation and analysis techniques for realisation of these systems; and to understand the concepts of model-based design, DE and CT models.

Introduction: The concepts of real-time, embedded and CPSs are clarified, and the integral role of dependability in such systems is introduced. In one classroom exercise, for example, students are asked to form teams responsible for the software, hardware or safety of a simple product (a personal transport device like a Segway). Concepts of larger-scale CPSs as systems-of-systems are introduced.

CT Modelling and Control of Physical Components: The motivations for CT modelling are introduced: this is particularly important for computer science students who have studied almost everything up to this point in an exclusively DE setting. In many cases, this is the point of reacquainting computer science students with physics and applied mathematics that they have not studied since high school. Concepts of controller characteristics (e.g., managing jerky acceleration) are illustrated using 20-sim and the standard example of the controller of a torsion bar in which a flexible axle connects two disks, one of which is rotated by a controlled motor. Elements of computer control (sample, compute and hold) are also introduced.

Discrete-event Modelling of Controllers: The idea of levels of control from loop to supervisory control are introduced by considering motorway driving. A review of VDM-RT includes a discussion of support for concurrency. Design patterns are introduced used as a basis for describing controller structures.

Multi-modelling and Co-simulation: The idea of a simple multi-model is introduced using the same LFR example as the AU course. This section discusses the pragmatics of co-model development and FMU integration. This is the point at which variable time step co-simulation semantics is first introduced. The full INTO-CPS tool chain is introduced, and DSE is first encountered, again using the LFR.

Dependability and Fault Tolerance: Key dependability concepts are introduced using traffic light control and a paper pinch control as examples. Students examine techniques for error detection, isolation and recovery and again use patterns to examine relevant solutions such as safety kernels and voter architectures.

Related Topics covered in the later classes of the module build on the core of control explored through co-modelling and co-simulation. For example, techniques for managing concurrency are discussed through the lock- and synchronisation-free communications mechanisms that are needed for example soft control systems. Resource sharing is explored through the Mars Pathfinder priority inversion problem.

4.2   Course Delivery

The module is delivered over a single semester. It is expected to require around 100 h of work from a student, of which about 36 are formal lectures or laboratory teaching. The remainder is independent study with access to labs, tools and learning materials including recordings of lectures. Contact hours are structured as a two-hour lecture followed by a one-hour practical session each week.

This timetabling can be tiring, but it does offer the opportunity to try techniques discussed in the classroom immediately in the laboratory. Small items of practical work are embedded within the main course material, to familiarise students with specific technologies. These are followed by more substantial assessed coursework which builds on these smaller exercises and broadens students' experience. The module is assessed by a combination of this assessed work and a written examination.

Practical sessions begin once CT modelling and 20-sim have been introduced in lectures. Since the cohort are largely familiar with VDM and DE modelling[3] from Stage 2, this material is presented upfront because it is the most different to what students have previously experienced.

Practical classes are supported by three demonstrators (PhD students) and the lecturer. Each of the first four practicals introduces a tutorial exercise that lets students try out the tools and techniques discussed in preceding classes, reinforcing the content and providing students with the experience needed to tackle the longer assessed coursework. Each exercise is designed to take about one hour and must be signed off for a small amount of credit. Since students work at different rates and not all students can attend all sessions, sign-off sheets help to track individual students' progress; any students who seem to be falling behind are contacted individually to identify problems. Once all sign-off deadlines has passed, the final practical sessions allow students to ask for help on the longer piece of assessed coursework. In the following we discuss the practical exercises and student experiences. These have been refined over a few years and we highlight important changes that were made.

Installation. Practical classes are held in computer clusters with access to 20-sim, Overture and INTO-CPS, so students can start rapidly. One problem with INTO-CPS is due to the co-simulation engine using HTTP connections. Firewalls occasionally block this traffic, resulting in failure to run a co-simulation without a useful error message. One year there was a problem where only some machines had the correct firewall exceptions, so the problem was intermittent. Another issue was the need for the FMU export plug-in for Overture to be installed manually by each user, causing problems with roaming profiles. In one case, a new version of the plug-in was released that was incompatible with the version of Overture, so an entire practical was lost pending a workaround.

Students are increasingly using their own devices, and we provide installation instructions. Installation is typically smooth, but some machines have network-specific firewall restrictions. In addition, some students using MacOS or Linux are unable to install the full tool suite (e.g., 20-sim). So, while students are not prevented from working, the nature of the tools might prevent some working in the way that suits them best.

Exercise 1 follows a lecture on CT modelling and simulation, and an introduction to 20-sim. Its aim is to familiarise students with the 20-sim interface

---

[3] Exchange students unfamiliar with VDM are provided with extra gsupport.

(making connections, changing parameters and running simulations) by recreating a model of the standard torsion bar based on a screenshot of the layout. This exercise is based on training material from Controllab Products, with the of addition material to help clarify engineering concepts to non-engineer computer scientists. A problem here is that some students are not sure what they are modelling, since the torsion bar concept is not immediately familiar to most computing students. This might be improved by finding a more familiar example (e.g., a bouncing ball).

Exercise 2 introduces tuning of PID controllers, again using the torsion bar. This aims to help students understand the nature of low-level real-time control – one of the main new concepts the course introduces. The Ziegler-Nichols method, which is a common heuristic for tuning a certain class of system, is used to guide students. The torsion bar was designed as an example for teaching and is therefore fairly forgiving, which can cause confusion when students are unsure when they have finished tuning. In addition, while the Ziegler-Nichols method keeps the exercise straightforward, it does not provide good intuition of the roles of P, I, and D. This exercise could be enhanced using a different example where students tune manually before applying Ziegler-Nichols.

Exercise 3 covers DE modelling using Overture and the LFR example. As the majority of the cohort has studied VDM-SL, the aim here is to highlight the differences with VDM-RT. The exercise uses a "DE-first" version of the LFR example where a simple VDM environment model represents the robot. The produces output to the console and a CSV file that can be used to visualise the robot path in Excel. Students build a controller to follow the line, coping with ambient light. Some students find it frustrating building a controller without seeing the robot, however this is somewhat intentional as it motivates co-simulation in the next exercise. Another issue is that some students take time to understand the paradigm of control loops, for example using loops inside a main VDM operation, instead of treating the operation as the body of a loop. This exercise typically takes the most time.

Exercise 4 uses INTO-CPS to run a co-simulation using the LFR example. Students take their controller from Exercise 3 and see it driving the virtual 3D robot, which most students seem to find satisfying. This builds familiarity with the INTO-CPS interface, and how to run and monitor a co-simulation. The exercise is often quick to complete, compensating somewhat for the length of Exercise 3. A frustration here is that the older LFR model crashes when completing a co-simulation (even a successful one). Although a note is included in the exercise description, some students still find this confusing.

Assessed Coursework Rather than use smaller exercises, the assessed coursework focuses on a scenario that is explored in greater depth. For example, the 2019/20 coursework is based on designing a controller for a driverless train and testing it using co-simulation. The train model includes a human passenger, the comfort of whose ride is important: the train cannot accelerate or brake too much if the passenger is to avoid falling. A model of train and passenger physics and a basic PID loop controller is given in 20-sim, and an outline supervisory controller in VDM-RT. A 3D visualisation is included to help test the controller. The tasks are:

1. Within 20-sim, tune the PID controller with respect to a permitted upper limit on passenger movement. Students explore a range of control parameters. Once tuned, the model is imported into the INTO-CPS application.
2. Create a VDM-RT model of a supervisory controller that manages train journeys subject to constraints on speed, stopping accuracy and passenger comfort. Students are given a base project in INTO-CPS that includes the necessary VDM-RT classes to read train position and speed, but which they may extend with features to structure the control logic as they see fit. An important requirement is the adaptability of the controller to a variety of train route scenarios.
3. Reflect on their experience of the task, considering how they went about tuning the controller, designing the controller to meet the constraints, and how their solution could be further improved.

4.3 Next Steps for the NU Curriculum

To what extent have we addressed the need for the more T-shaped skills that we identified in Sect. 1? Within the current NU module, students gain experience at *negotiating common terms and concepts across discipline models* from the outset because of the unfamiliarity of the kinds of CT model that we present. Concepts of controller architecture are, for example, quite new to students form this background. Experience at *identifying and performing system-level tests* is gained from the practical work. Experience at *modifying and reassessing designs*, and *performing design optimisation* is provided to some degree, e.g. in the coursework, but this is less systematic that we might wish.

The current module is moderately popular, attracting about 53 students in 2019-20 (about 20% of the available cohort). While those students who do take the course mostly report positive experiences, the relative unfamiliarity of the topic to classically trained computer scientists is potentially a deterrent.

In 2017 a complete review of the NU BSc computing curriculum was undertaken, influenced by two factors. First, there was a desire to expose students to active research topics earlier. Second, there was continuing recognition of the need to equip graduates with skills for employment [25]) in an increasing range of industries such as manufacturing that are not traditionally seen as destinations of software specialists [1]. The new curriculum takes a portfolio-based approach in which problem-based learning plays a significant role [2]. This suits CPS and MBSE perfectly. In order to ensure an introduction to research-inspired topics as early as practicable, a brief introduction to CPS will be given in Semester 4, giving students an opportunity to consider specialising in the area by taking the specialist module in Semester 5 and a capstone project in Semester 6. It is hoped that introducing topics in Stage 2 may demystify CPS engineering. The revised Semester 5 module will run in 2021–22 year with the following key changes:

1. The new Semester 4 module provides only a brief introduction to MBSE, CPS and VDM. This requires a change to the current delivery to teach more fundamentals at Semester 5, but it creates an opportunity to broaden students' MBSE experience in the CPS context by introducing a wider range of formalisms.
2. Two new academic staff will join the delivery team, bringing expertise in probabilistic modelling, machine learning and verification for CPS. This creates an opportunity to engage in further research-informed teaching and bring different perspectives on MBSE for a shared case study, for example.
3. The portfolio-based approach means students will be more familiar with larger pieces of coursework, team working and reflective writing. This creates an opportunity to expand assessment to more collaborative aspects such as assigning roles to students to create, share FMUs that could be integrated in assigned teams, or as a supplier-customer relationship between students supported by peer assessment and feedback to shape students' collaboration skills.

5   Discussion

In Sect. 1 we set ourselves the challenge of developing 'T-shaped' graduates, but doing so in the context of research-inspired curricula. The approaches we have taken at our two institutions are different in that one (AU) is situated in the context of a systems engineering course at Masters level, while the other (NU) is within a mono-disciplinary computer science programme at Bachelors level. In both cases we feel that this initiative can be considered successful if the graduates have both experienced the need for inter-disciplinary collaboration, and understood the need to develop and adapt professional practice as new research results become available, making companies innovative and competitive.

Although AU and NU have up to now placed the core modules on MBSE for CPS at different stages of study, it is notable that both institutions are now acting to place the first introduction of these topics earlier: both of them in Semester 4 of undergraduate programmes [14].

The NU module is part of a computer science degree delivered in a Computing school, rather than an Engineering degree in an Engineering education as at AU. This has influenced the content in that we are introducing students who have been thinking in largely discrete formalisms to the fact that their software will have – for good or ill – profound physical effects. Conversely, engineering students would benefit from greater awareness of the software engineering principles that will be critical to the success of innovations in many sectors. To that end, NU has created a new Masters programme in Smart Systems Engineering, aimed at both engineers and computer scientists.

Practical work plays a key role in both the AU and NU approaches to developing T-shaped skills for model-based CPS engineering. One of the most important lessons we have learned so far has been the need to create good ecosystems in which students practice and develop their skills. In our experience there are two such ecosystems to consider: first an ecosystem of disciplines; second, a business ecosystem in which roles such as contractors, integrators and end users are available. We have experienced pragmatic challenges in setting the disciplinary ecosystem up because discipline silos are often embedded in university structures. This makes it difficult to bring diverse groups together, often for prosaic reasons such as timetabling, but also because student and faculty expectations and forms of delivery differ between departments. As a result, we recommend developing an early-stage commitment to such multi-discipline projects. In creating a business ecosystem, we strongly recommend building relationships with external stakeholders to act as clients from outside the students' immediate technical environment. We have worked with real businesses, as well as other university professional departments for this purpose, chiming with the experience of Boehm and Mobasser [4]. The AU experience of creating subcontractors and integrator teams has been successful in creating a rich environment for understanding contractual relationships.

A lesson from both AU's and NU's experience is that successful deployment of research products in teaching hinges on having robust, well-documented tools with large bodies of examples aimed at users at a range of experience levels. This requires a very significant investment of effort in activities that rarely win academic plaudits. These include carefully structuring and refactoring tools, dealing with changes in platforms, developing, trialling, and improving materials (sometimes in several languages). Without these activities, tools and methods lack the credibility to influence more than a handful of the next generation of practitioners. Such an effort is typically only possible by maintaining a coherent series of research projects that keep key stakeholders involved.

6   Future Work

For 2021 we hope that we will be able to use a cloud-based version of the INTO-CPS Application [24] such that the students will have less installation necessary on their own laptops. In the future we hope to be able to use our research prototypes in a digital twin context [11]. Here we plan to make use of desktop version of the agricultural robot called Robotti [12]. This can be seen at Fig. 3 and it is a platform that can be equipped with additional sensors and explored in a digital twin context as well [11].

In this paper, we have considered examples of the influence of research on teaching in MBSE for CPSs. The underlying idea is that the best way to have a positive influence on industry and the wider environment is to develop graduates who keep abreast of research and allow it to influence their professional practice. In that context, it is worth universities considering their responsibility for lifelong learning [7]. What can we do to maintain the skills and knowledge of own alumni, and maintain the virtuous cycle in which graduates convey advances in practice to industry, which rewards universities in turn with new technological challenges for research and innovation.

Fig. 3. The Robotti agricultural robot (left), and desktop-sized version (right).

At both AU and NU we have taken the initiative of establishing not-for-profit Digital Innovation Hubs (DIHs) with missions to improve the take-up of innovative technology in the surrounding business ecosystems, particularly in MBSE for CPSs. There is a long way to go in helping companies to truly take advantage of the expertise and innovations to be found in our universities. This is the goal of future work with partners in the HUBCAP project[4] [19] which aims to use DIHs to lower barriers to innovation through easier platform-based access to MBSE tools, models and practitioner experience.

Acknowledgements. We are grateful to many colleagues and students at both our universities. We acknowledge the European Union's support for the INTO-CPS and HUBCAP projects (Grant Agreements 644047 and 872698). We are especially grateful to the Poul Due Jensen Foundation, which has funded subsequent work taking co-modelling and co-simulation forward into the engineering of digital twins.

References

1. Made Smarter Review: UK Government. Department for Business, Energy and Industrial Strategy (2017)
2. Barnes, J., et al.: Designing a portfolio-oriented curriculum using problem based learning. In: Proceedings of the 4th Conference on Computing Education Practice 2020, CEP 2020. Association for Computing Machinery, New York (2020). https://doi.org/10.1145/3372356.3372367
3. Bastian, J., Clauss, C., Wolf, S., Schneider, P.: Master for co-simulation using FMI. In: 8th International Modelica Conference (2011)
4. Boehm, B., Mobasser, S.K.: System thinking: educating T-shaped software engineers. In: Proceedings of IEEE/ACM 37th IEEE International Conference on Software Engineering, pp. 333–342 (2015)
5. Broenink, J.F., et al.: Design support and tooling for dependable embedded control software. In: Proceedings of Serene 2010 International Workshop on Software Engineering for Resilient Systems, pp. 77–82. ACM (2010)
6. Broenink, J.F., et al.: Methodological guidelines 3. Technical report, The DESTECS Project (INFSO-ICT-248134) (2012)
7. Field, J.: Social Capital and Lifelong Learning. The Policy Press (2005)

---

[4] See hubcap.eu.

8. Fitzgerald, J., Gamble, C., Larsen, P.G., Pierce, K., Woodcock, J.: Cyber-physical systems design: formal foundations, methods and integrated tool chains. In: FormaliSE: FME Workshop on Formal Methods in Software Engineering, ICSE 2015, Florence, Italy (2015)
9. Fitzgerald, J., Gamble, C., Pierce, K.: Method guidelines 3. Technical report, INTO-CPS Deliverable, D3.3a (2017)
10. Fitzgerald, J., Larsen, P.G., Verhoef, M. (eds.): Collaborative Design for Embedded Systems - Co-modelling and Co-simulation. Springer, Heidelberg (2014). https://doi.org/10.1007/978-3-642-54118-6
11. Fitzgerald, J., Larsen, P.G., Pierce, K.: Multi-modelling and co-simulation in the engineering of cyber-physical systems: towards the digital twin. In: ter Beek, M.H., Fantechi, A., Semini, L. (eds.) From Software Engineering to Formal Methods and Tools, and Back. LNCS, vol. 11865, pp. 40–55. Springer, Cham (2019). https://doi.org/10.1007/978-3-030-30985-5_4
12. Foldager, F., Larsen, P.G., Green, O.: Development of a driverless Lawn Mower using co-simulation. In: 1st Workshop on Formal Co-Simulation of Cyber-Physical Systems, Trento, Italy (2017)
13. Gomes, C., Thule, C., Broman, D., Larsen, P.G., Vangheluwe, H.: Co-simulation: a survey. ACM Comput. Surv. **51**(3), 49:1–49:33 (2018)
14. Hallerstede, S., Larsen, P.G., Boudjadar, J., Schultz, C.P.L., Esterle, L.: Frontiers in software engineering education. In: On the Design of a New Software Engineering Curriculum in Computer Engineering (2020)
15. Hasanagić, M., Fabbri, T., Larsen, P.G., Bandur, V., Tran-Jørgensen, P., Ouy, J.: Code generation for distributed embedded systems with VDM-RT. Des. Autom. Embed. Syst. (2019). https://doi.org/10.1007/s10617-019-09227-0
16. Larsen, P.G., Battle, N., Ferreira, M., Fitzgerald, J., Lausdahl, K., Verhoef, M.: The overture initiative - integrating tools for VDM. SIGSOFT Softw. Eng. Notes **35**(1), 1–6 (2010). https://doi.org/10.1145/1668862.1668864
17. Larsen, P.G., et al.: Integrated tool chain for model-based design of cyber-physical systems: the INTO-CPS project. In: CPS Data Workshop, Vienna, Austria (2016)
18. Larsen, P.G., Kristiansen, E.L., Bennedsen, J., Bjerge, K.: Enhancing non-technical skills by a multidisciplinary engineering summer school. Eur. J. Eng. Educ. **42**, 1076–1096 (2017)
19. Larsen, P.G., et al.: An online MBSE collaboration platform. In: SimulTech 2020 (2020)
20. Macedo, H.D., Sanjari, A., Villadsen, K., Thule, C., Larsen, P.G.: Introducing angular tests and upgrades to the INTO-CPS application. In: Submitted for Publication (2020)
21. Masci, P., Oladimeji, P., Zhang, Y., Jones, P., Curzon, P., Thimbleby, H.: PVSio-web 2.0: joining PVS to HCI. In: Kroening, D., Păsăreanu, C.S. (eds.) CAV 2015. LNCS, vol. 9206, pp. 470–478. Springer, Cham (2015). https://doi.org/10.1007/978-3-319-21690-4_30
22. Modelica Association: Functional Mock-up Interface for Model Exchange and Co-Simulation (2019). https://www.fmi-standard.org/downloads
23. Palmieri, M., Macedo, H.D.: Automatic generation of functional mock-up units from formal specifications. In: 3rd Workshop on Formal Co-Simulation of Cyber-Physical Systems, Oslo, Norway (2019, To appear)
24. Rasmussen, M.B., Thule, C., Macedo, H.D., Larsen, P.G.: Migrating the INTO-CPS application to the cloud. In: Gamble, C., Couto, L.D. (eds.) Proceedings of 17th Overture Workshop, pp. 47–61. Newcastle University Technical Report CS-TR-1530 (2019)

25. Shadbolt, N.: Shadbolt review of computer science degree accreditation and graduate employability. UK Government. Department for Business, Innovation and Skills, and Higher Education Funding Council for England (2016)

26. Thompson, H. (ed.): Cyber-Physical Systems: Uplifting Europe's Innovation Capacity. European Commission Unit A3 - DG CONNECT (2013)

27. Thule, C., Lausdahl, K., Gomes, C., Meisl, G., Larsen, P.G.: Maestro: the INTO-CPS co-simulation framework. Simul. Model. Pract. Theory **92**, 45–61 (2019). http://www.sciencedirect.com/science/article/pii/S1569190X1830193X

28. Thule, C., Lausdahl, K., Larsen, P.G.: Overture FMU: export VDM-RT models as tool-wrapper FMUs. In: Pierce, K., Verhoef, M. (eds.) The 16th Overture Workshop, TR-1524, pp. 23–38. Newcastle University, School of Computing, Oxford (2018)

29. Verhoef, M., Larsen, P.G., Hooman, J.: Modeling and validating distributed embedded real-time systems with VDM++. In: Misra, J., Nipkow, T., Sekerinski, E. (eds.) FM 2006. LNCS, vol. 4085, pp. 147–162. Springer, Heidelberg (2006). https://doi.org/10.1007/11813040_11

30. Walden, D.D., Roedler, G.J., Forsberg, K.J., Hamelin, R.D., Shortell, T.M. (eds.): Systems Engineering Handbook. A Guide for System Life Cycle Processes and Activities, Version 4.0., 4 edn. Wiley (2015)

Competitions and Workshops

Designing Interactive Workshops for Software Engineering Educators

Cécile Péraire[1](✉), Hakan Erdogmus[1](✉), and Dora Dzvonyar[2](✉)

[1] Carnegie Mellon University, Silicon Valley Campus,
Moffett Field, CA 94035, USA
{cecile.peraire,hakan.erdogmus}@sv.cmu.edu
[2] Faculty of Informatics, Technical University of Munich, 80333 Munich, Germany
dora.dzvonyar@tum.de

Abstract. Given the rapid pace of changes in the software industry, software engineering educators face the challenge of keeping up with emerging trends and technology and incorporating them into the classroom. Among other tools at their disposal, educators leverage software engineering education workshops to share knowledge and experiences, and hence further their own education. Unfortunately, information available to educators on how to run and organize these workshops is scarce. This paper is an attempt to fill the gap by sharing lessons learned. It is based on the authors' experience designing, facilitating, and participating in such workshops, an interview with a workshop organizer, and an exploration of software engineering education workshop websites. The paper documents the current state of software engineering education workshops, identifies workshop design challenges—including interactivity of the format—and proposes solutions to address the challenges.

Keywords: Software engineering education · Continuing education ·
Professional development · Software Engineering Workshop · Workshop design

1 Introduction

Given the rapid pace of changes in the software industry, Software Engineering (SE) educators face the challenge of keeping up with emerging trends and technology and bringing new ideas to the classroom. SE educators typically stay current by following the SE literature, attending SE conferences, participating in webinars organized by professional organizations such as ACM and IEEE Computer Society, taking online courses, and attending professional development events. These events often take place at conferences, or are sponsored by the educators' institutions or (inter)national bodies and granting organizations.

Some of the above channels cover higher education within a context larger than SE, typically in the much broader scopes of computer science or engineering education. For example, in the U.S., the Association for Engineering Education

© Springer Nature Switzerland AG 2020
J.-M. Bruel et al. (Eds.): FISEE 2019, LNCS 12271, pp. 217–231, 2020.
https://doi.org/10.1007/978-3-030-57663-9_14

organizes the National Effective Teaching Institutes (NETI), a series of workshops aimed at developing teaching skills of educators in engineering-related fields [18]. The annual technical symposium organized by ACM's Special Interest Group on Computer Science Education [14] also hosts a number of workshops and tutorials highly relevant to SE educators. The National Science Foundation, the main U.S. federal granting agency in science, engineering, and technology, also routinely sponsors professional development events and workshops for computer science educators, some of which are on topics highly relevant for SE educators—for instance, see [15]. In addition, many universities have established centers of teaching excellence to support their teaching faculty with continuing education opportunities. An example is Carnegie Mellon University's Eberly Center [12], which organizes annual *Teaching-As-Research* workshops to promote latest pedagogical strategies across the university, most of which are well-suited for the increasingly interactive and collaborative nature of SE education.

However, the above channels do not specifically focus on the unique needs and problems of SE education. They are not necessarily ideal to allow the smaller cohort of SE educators to share their common experiences and solutions and learn from each others. In this paper, we exclusively focus on workshops run by SE educators for SE educators with the goal of allowing dynamic exchange of knowledge among participants using approaches commonly used in the SE practice itself and specifically suited in the SE context.

Furthermore, how to organize and run SE education workshops is not typically addressed in the SE education literature, and information and advice available to educators willing to lead such workshops is scarce. This paper attempts to fill the gap by sharing the authors' experiences and lessons learned in this space, primarily based on two highly interactive workshops: the *First IEEE/ACM International Workshop on Software Engineering Curricula for Millennials* (SECM'17) [9] and the *Second IEEE/ACM International Workshop on Software Engineering Education for Millennials* (SEEM'18) [8]. The paper also reviews recent SE education workshops based on published workshop proceedings (e.g. [24]), reports (e.g. [23]), and websites (see Table 1) to establish common formats, strategies, and outcomes.

The above information is supplemented by an interview of one of the organizers of the *First International Workshop on Frontiers in Software Engineering Education* (FISEE'19) [10]. The semi-structured interview was conducted over video conference and lasted about an hour. It was based on a set of open-ended questions (e.g., *What was the workshop overall agenda? What are some workshop elements that worked well and will be reused next time? What are some workshop elements that did not work well and will be removed or replaced? How?*). Prepared questions were used as a guide, rather than forcing a strictly scripted sequence, allowing for discussions and additional topics to emerge. The interview's key insights are captured in the paper in a distributed fashion as they pertain to a point being discussed.

As a result, the paper covers the design of SE education workshops from multiple angles. Section 2 documents the current state of SE education workshops, using different workshops offered in 2019 as examples. Section 3 discusses a number of design challenges faced by workshop organizers and facilitators and proposes various solutions to address the challenges. Finally, Sect. 4 concludes with the paper's key contributions.

2 State of SE Education Workshops

Workshops have been used by SE educators to support their continuing education and professional development needs for quite some time. As early as 1976, Wasserman and Freeman facilitated a one-day *Interface Workshop on Software Engineering Education: Needs and Objectives* [24]. The goal was to create an "interface" between industry, government, and universities to discuss what SE concepts needed to be taught to both students and practicing professionals. About 40 participants attended the workshop. Discussions were based on short position papers submitted by participants and later published in the workshop proceedings.

Table 1. Examples of 2019 SE education workshops.

Acronym	Workshop	Country
SEISEWE'19	*16th SEI Software Engineering Workshop for Educators* [3]	USA
EASEAI'19	*First International Workshop on Education through Advanced Software Engineering and Artificial Intelligence* [4]	Estonia
FISEE'19	*First International Workshop on Frontiers in Software Engineering Education* [10]	France
WESEE'19	*Second Workshop on Emerging Software Engineering Education* [5]	India
ISEE'19	*Second Workshop on Innovative Software Engineering Education* [6]	Germany
SEED'19	*Software Engineering Education Workshop* [7]	Malaysia

Workshops for SE educators have been offered on a regular basis since the 1970s. A simple internet search reveals that they have become relatively popular in recent years. As examples, workshops offered in 2019 are presented in Table 1. These workshops, although they share a common goal, vary in scope, audience, admission process and outcomes, duration and agenda, level of interactivity, and organization structure:

- **Scope**. While most workshops advertised a broad initial scope on SE education, EASEAI'19 identified a narrower focus related to how artificial intelligence can support SE education. The scope of most other workshops ended up being shaped by participants' interests. For instance, a SEISEWE'19 organizer [3] mentioned *"Artificial intelligence, machine learning, and data science were high on the list of topics participants thought were important to introduce to the classroom."* As a result, those topics naturally emerged as central to the workshop, rather than being predetermined.

- **Audience**. Even-though the primary audience of most workshops was SE educators from academia, some—like EASEAI'19 and WESEE'19—explicitly called for industry participants. SECM'17 (discussed later) also invited student participants to get the perspectives of those on the receiving end.

- **Admission Process and Outcomes**. While WESEE'19 was open to all participants without up-front contributions, admission to most workshops was based on the submission of a paper formally reviewed by a program committee and later published in the workshop proceedings. Typical submissions included short four-page papers as well as long eight-page papers. The publication of these papers was the sole tangible outcome of most workshops. At SEISEWE'19 the educators' "entrance fee" for attending the workshop was the submission of an artifact aimed at introducing SE topics into the college curriculum, such as course slides and syllabi.

- **Duration and Agenda**. While most workshops were one-day long, their duration varied from half a day for SEED'2019 and WESEE'2019 to three days for SEISEWE'19. While the SEED'2019 half-day workshop followed a mini-conference format based mostly on paper presentations, the WESEE'2019 half-day workshop was structured around one expert talk and two interactive activities. The SEISEWE'19 three-day workshop offered two days of instruction and a final day of invited talks and group sessions.

- **Level of Interactivity**. A number of workshops—ISEE'19, EASEAI'19, and SEED'19—adopted a mini-conference format based mostly on paper or poster presentations. In this format, discussions among participants happen primarily during *Question-and-Answer* sessions during or after the presentations. Other workshops introduced various activities to more actively engage participants and make the workshop more interactive. For instance, WESEE'19 incorporated an interactive activity where participants leveraged the *Wall of Ideas* [1] brainstorming technique: starting with trigger questions, the goal was to generate as many ideas as possible to fill up an entire wall. At FISEE'19, the organizers included a couple of *Panel Discussions* (see also Sect. 3.3).

- **Organizing Structure**. Some workshops were co-located with larger SE conferences while others were held independently. For instance, WESEE'19 was co-located with the *12th Innovations in Software Engineering Conference* (ISEC'2019), while FISEE'19 was an independent event. SEISEWE'19 was also an independent event hosted by the Software Engineering Institute (SEI).

Outside of the 2019 workshops listed in Table 1, the *First IEEE/ACM International Workshop on Software Engineering Curricula for Millennials*

(SECM'17) [9] and *Second IEEE/ACM International Workshop on Software Engineering Education for Millennials* (SEEM'18) [8], organized by two of the authors, are notable in terms of their strong focus on interactivity and how they address design challenges. In the next section we will use these two workshops as concrete examples while discussing design challenges and solutions.

3   Workshop Design Challenges and Solutions

This section discusses a number of design challenges faced by organizers and facilitators of SE education workshops. The challenges relate to (1) involving all participants during the workshop, (2) selecting the workshop topics, (3) making the workshop interactive, (4) generating tangible workshop outcomes, (5) closing the workshop, and (6) setting up the workshop physical space.

3.1   Involving All Participants

Workshops benefit from the perspectives of all participants. Some of us have witnessed workshops where discussions were mostly among the workshop organizers, presenters, and a few vocal participants in the audience. The other participants remained mostly silent. To avoid such situations, we believe that it is important to provide all participants with a space to introduce themselves and build credibility at the beginning of a workshop. This way, participants feel empowered to actively participate during the rest of the workshop.

During SECM'17 [9], we used a simple round-table format to provide each participant with one minute to briefly introduce themselves. Unfortunately, this did not prevent us from having a few silent participants. Without visuals and time to prepare, the introductions were generally dull and quickly forgotten. With this common approach, shy or reserved participants do not build the credibility that they need to feel confident to actively participate later.

During SEEM'18 [8] we adopted a different format that proved more effective. We asked participants to prepare a single *Visual Introduction Slide* including their photo, name, title, affiliation, and a pictorial representation of their favorite topics of interest when it comes to SE education. Each participant was given one minute at the beginning of the workshop to present their slide in front of the room. Figure 1 shows some examples of visual introduction slides. Furthermore, we encouraged all participants to create a blog post at se-edu.org to advertise their work before the workshop. We later observed that all 20 participants were actively engaged during the rest of the workshop. Although we cannot know for sure whether it was the introduction format and/or the blog posts that made the difference versus the particular make-up of the participants, we believe that strategies similar to those of SEEM'18 that promote stronger early presence may be more effective at encouraging consistent participation than those that promote only cursory early presence.

Fig. 1. Examples of visual introduction slides

3.2   Selecting the Workshop Topics

Selecting the main workshop topics can be challenging. A narrow scope reduces the target population of participants. A broad scope makes it difficult to run a workshop that is of interest to all participants. To identify topics of common interest ahead of time, the organizers of the *Software Engineering Education Workshop* (SEEW'12) [23] asked participants to submit a position statement, respond to an online survey, and participate in an online discussion before the workshop. In the workshop report, they describe their approach as somehow successful, while acknowledging the need for a more effective way of analyzing the collected data to better capture common participant interests ahead of the workshop.

Attracting participants can also be challenging, especially for new and independent workshops. The organizer of FISEE'19 [10]—a new and independent workshop—mentioned during the interview that attracting participants was a key challenge. To solve this problem, some workshops co-locate with well-known international conferences, such as the *International Conference on SE* (ICSE) and the *Conference on Software Engineering Education and Training* (CSEE&T). That way, workshop organizers can draw participants from a large and diverse pool of conference attendees from all over the world.

A further attendance factor is that most SE educators from academia are evaluated by their department based on publications. These educators might be more inclined to participate in workshops providing publication opportunities. This poses another dilemma for workshop organizers: To attract participants from academia they must solicit and formally review paper submissions and include formal presentations in their agenda, while trying to conduct interactive activities at the same time.

During both SECM'17 [9] and SEEM'18 [8], we addressed the scope and attendance challenges by being co-located with ICSE, using a format allowing participants to select topics during the workshop itself, and balancing interactivity and presentations.

The initial workshop scope was intentionally left very broad, covering *"the unique needs and challenges of SE education for Millennials"*. The proposed topics included, but were not limited to:

- SE education for new and emerging technologies;
- Needs and expectations of the next generation of students aspiring to be software engineers;
- Skills and continuing education for SE educators;
- Classroom formats that cater to diverse learning styles;
- Teaching approaches that leverage technology-enhanced education in SE courses;
- Balancing teaching of soft and hard skills;
- Balancing rigor and practicality;
- Experiential and hands-on learning for software engineers; and
- Gaps and challenges in professional graduate SE programs.

To balance the academic participants' needs and workshop goals, we solicited three kinds of contribution: *research papers* (maximum 8 pages for case studies and original research results), *experience reports* (maximum 8 pages for experiences related to SE courses with a focus on insights and lessons learned), and *position papers* (maximum 4 pages for original ideas or opinions).

Fig. 2. Affinity mapping activity: Whiteboard with unorganized sticky notes generated during presentations (top); Participant grouping sticky notes by affinity (bottom left); Sticky notes organized by affinity with dots from prioritization; each cluster represents a discussion topic (bottom right).

During the workshop, authors of accepted papers gave brief (five-minute long) presentations highlighting the key points of their papers. The audience was asked not to interrupt, and only short clarification questions were allowed at the end of each presentation. Instead, participants were tasked with capturing interesting insights, follow-on questions from the presentations, and fundamental discussion points on sticky notes to be used later in a more collaborative session.

Using the sticky notes generated during the short presentations, participants later conducted an *Affinity Mapping* activity [2] as illustrated in Fig. 2. On a large whiteboard participants collectively grouped related sticky notes into clusters that they repeatedly re-arranged until the emergence of a number of cohesive clusters. Each resulting cluster represented a discussion topic.

Community Dot-Voting [19] was used to prioritize the topics, with participants placing colored dots on their favorite topics. High-priority topics—with the highest numbers of dots—became the main topics. These topics were further addressed during the rest of the workshop in the context of a highly interactive activity.

3.3   Making the Workshop Interactive

Interaction among participants is a critical ingredient of a successful workshop. Depending on the audience, the interaction can happen spontaneously and lead to productive discussions without much work from the workshop facilitators. Unfortunately, this is not always the case. Unstructured discussions can die, go in circles, or go nowhere interesting with participants ultimately losing interest.

While some workshops rely solely on unstructured discussions following presentations to support interaction among workshop participants, others introduce structured activities to better control and promote interaction. This section provides some examples of activities that could be incorporated into workshops to make them more interactive: *Panel Discussion*, *Park Bench Panel*, *Mad-Sad-Glad Reflection*, and *Mind Mapping a Big Hairy Audacious Goal*. Many other techniques are also available [20]. However, in this section we focus on examples that are based on our experience at SECM'17 [9] and SEEM'18 [8], as well as the interview with a FISEE'19 [10] organizer.

Panel Discussion and Park Bench Panel: A *Panel Discussion* is a moderated discussion on a specific topic by a selected group of panelists who share differing perspectives in front of an audience [11]. Panels have been used in several SE education workshops.

For instance, FISEE'19 included a couple of panel discussions. Each was facilitated by a moderator. Each panel was formed by a group of about three educators who shared facts and opinions and responded to questions from the audience. Each had a specific topic defined by the workshop organizers (e.g. *"Assessment of teaching approaches"*). The panel sessions lasted about one hour. During the interview, which was conducted a few months after the workshop, a FISEE'19 organizer declared that *"Panels are a must!"* and that the organizers are planning to use panel discussions again in the next edition of the workshop.

The central activity of SECM'17 was a *Park Bench Panel.* A park bench panel is similar to the panel discussion presented above, but with one key difference: an open chair in the panel. It works better in situations where *"the panel can't get it together and the real expert is in the audience"* [16]. If a member of the audience wants to share her perspective on the currently discussed topic, she joins the panel by taking the open chair. Since the rule is to always have one open chair, another panelist must leave his chair—which becomes the new open chair—and rejoin the audience. That way, the panel is made of a fluid set of experts that evolves naturally based on the collective expertise of all the workshop participants. During SECM'17, several topics were covered during the park bench panel, selected out of the high priority topics that emerged during the affinity mapping activity.

While a panel, whether regular or of parkbench variety, is an effective way of generating productive discussions among participants, one drawback raised during the SECM'17 workshop retrospective is the fact that all the participants have to discuss the same topics together. To address this issue, we decided to replace the panel with structured breakout sessions in SEEM'2018, allowing participants to work on the topic they are interested in the most. This approach is presented below.

Fig. 3. Breakout group conducting a Mad-Sad-Glad reflection.

Mad-Sad-Glad Reflection: The central activity of SEEM'18 was a *Mad-Sad-Glad Reflection* done in breakout groups. The participants self-selected breakout groups to discuss the highest-priority topics identified during the affinity mapping activity. Each discussion was structured around the *"Mad-Sad-Glad"* format [21], where participants reflect on their topic by answering the following questions (as illustrated in Fig. 3):

1. What makes you *glad* about the topic? What are some encouraging aspects and grounds gained?

2. What makes you *sad*? What disappoints you about the topic, for example, certain angles not being addressed sufficiently, occasional misrepresentation of underlying issues, or insufficient interest?
3. What makes you *mad*? What makes you passionately furious about the topic, for example, lack of leadership, chronic student disinterest, systemic obstacles, or inherent difficulty and complexity of the underlying problems?
4. What could be some improvements focusing on the issues identified, in order of priority, under the *mad* and *sad* categories?

At the end of the activity, each breakout group summarized the outcomes of their discussion to the rest of the audience. Figure 4 shows a breakout group presenting the outcome of their Mad-Sad-Glad reflection.

Fig. 4. Breakout group presenting the outcome of their Mad-Sad-Glad reflection.

This format encourages participants to cover and share both positive and negative aspects of their topic, and brainstorm possible solutions to contentious issues and improvements to existing strategies.

Mind Mapping a Big Hairy Audacious Goal: Out of the four SEEM'18 breakout groups, one took a different approach (compared to the approach described above) and conducted a *Mind Mapping* activity based on a *Big Hairy Audacious Goal* (BHAG). A BHAG is a clear and compelling goal that serves as a unifying focal point of effort [13]. By being bold, and with a clear finish line, the BHAG stimulates progress by encouraging people to think outside the box. For instance, during the workshop, the breakout group's BHAG was *to turn every student team into a high-performance team*. They called their goal *"Team Magic"* for short. Then they brainstormed how to reach their goal by creating a

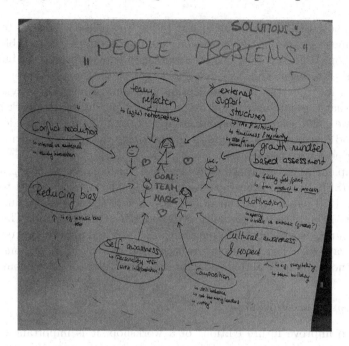

Fig. 5. Mind Map for the *"Team Magic"* Big Hairy Audacious Goal (BHAG).

mind map. A mind map [22] is a graphical way of representing related ideas. It is a visual thinking tool that helps structure information while analyzing, comprehending, synthesizing, recalling and generating new ideas. The group's mind map is shown in Fig. 5 as an example.

This format encourages participants to think in a solution-oriented manner by providing support for articulating a vision as well as a tool to brainstorm and visualize how to achieve that vision.

3.4   Generating Tangible Workshop Outcomes

Typical workshop outcomes include the publication of papers submitted before the workshop in the workshop proceedings, as well as new knowledge acquired by participants during the workshop itself. In addition, a workshop is by design a networking event. Hence the natural outcome of a workshop is also an extended network for participants and the hope that new collaborations might somehow emerge. However, generating tangible outcomes during the workshop itself, with real artifacts of value to the community, is difficult: this requires intentional actions from the workshop organizers.

Facilitating activities, as described in the previous section, provides workshop organizers with more control over the outcomes. For instance, asking participants to generate a mind map (as presented in Fig. 5) ensures that most participants have something tangible to share at the end of the workshop.

During both SECM'17 [9] and SEEM'18 [8], we asked participants to publish the outcomes of their breakout sessions online, at our se-edu.org blog, after the workshop. Unfortunately, once the workshop is over, people get busy, their motivation dies down, and they tend to forget to do their homework. Hence, we plan on incorporating this publication step into an explicit activity in the future so that the outcomes could be produced right during the workshop. For instance, we could ask each breakout group to take a picture of their deliverable (e.g. a mind map), write a paragraph summarizing the takeaways, and create a short blog post with this content.

A complementary approach is to leverage the concept of *post-proceedings* used by FISEE'19 [10]. Even-though all participants are encouraged to submit a proposal (full paper or extended abstract) before the workshop, final contributions are submitted and formally reviewed after the workshop. This format might encourage workshop participants to join forces and publish papers together or incorporate their learning from the workshop into the final versions of their papers, hence leading to actual collaborations and value-added outcomes.

3.5 Closing the Workshop

In order to improve future editions of a workshop, it is important to collect feedback and improvement ideas from the participants.

At the end of SECM'17 [9] and SEEM'18 [8], we conducted a *Retrospective* [17] to identify what went well during the workshop, what went wrong, what could be improved, and what the next steps should be. This activity aimed at identifying opportunities for improvement as well as potential follow-up action items, events, and collaborations. Insights from participants and organizers gathered during the SECM'17 retrospective were incorporated in SEEM'18, and what was learned during the SEEM'18 retrospective is presented as recommendations here.

An example agenda of a one-day workshop, with the retrospective scheduled just before the closing, is shown below:

- 08:15 Welcome
- 08:45 Introduction (with visual introduction slides)
- 10:00 Short Presentations (5 min each)
- 10:30 Coffee Break
- 11:00 Short Presentations (5 min each)
- 12:30 Lunch
- 14:00 Topics Selection (Affinity Mapping)
- 14:30 Breakout Sessions (Mind Mapping a Big Hairy Audacious Goal)
- 15:30 Coffee Break
- 16:00 Breakout Sessions Outcome Reporting
- 16:30 Retrospective
- 17:00 Closing
- 18:30 Dinner Social (at a local restaurant, optional)

Note that the workshop closes with an optional dinner social at a local restaurant. At FISEE'19 [10], the social event was a wine-tasting tour at a local winery. Such social events allow participants to continue discussions started during the workshop and forge collaborations in a convivial and unstructured setting.

3.6 Setting up the Workshop Physical Space

Traditional lecture-style classrooms are often optimized to accommodate a maximum number of people within a limited space. They sometimes have fixed tables and chairs. Such a space does not fit the needs of an interactive workshop.

The workshop meeting room should be large enough to accommodate highly interactive activities. For instance, with 25 participants, an interactive workshop that allows people to move around freely during activities would require a room that ordinarily accommodates up to 40 participants with an otherwise static setup.

The room should be equipped with at least one large whiteboard or wall, as well as movable chairs and tables. Organizers should configure the meeting room before the event—and potentially reconfigure the room during the day—based on the specific needs of the workshop activities. Fig. 6 shows an example of workshop meeting room.

In addition, the organizers should consider needed supplies, props, and audiovisual support, including flip-charts, markers, sticky notes, digital projector, and microphones for plenary speakers, as applicable.

Fig. 6. Example of a workshop meeting room including a large whiteboard, walls with workshop artifacts, and tables organized as islands for breakout groups discussions.

4   Conclusion

This paper covered the design of interactive workshops for SE educators. It provides three main contributions.

- The paper documents the current state of SE education workshops by comparing a representative sample of workshops offered in 2019. Despite a common goal of supporting continuing education for software engineering educators, the covered workshops vary in terms of scope, audience, admission process, outcomes, duration, agenda, level of interactivity, and organization structure.
- The paper discusses central design challenges faced by workshop organizers and facilitators. The challenges relate to involving all participants during the workshop, selecting the workshop topics, making the workshop interactive, generating tangible workshop outcomes, closing the workshop in a way that supports continuity, and setting up the physical space.
- The paper proposes various solutions addressing the identified design challenges. These solutions could be leveraged by future organizers of SE education workshops. We recognize however that every situation is unique and we do not expect the proposed solutions to be applicable in all contexts. Instead, we offer them as starting points for SE educators planning on organizing a workshop for the first time, or as comparison points for experienced workshop organizers.

These contributions matter since success factors for SE workshops for educators are not typically covered in the literature and the information available to SE educators willing to lead such workshops is scarce. More experiences are needed to validate or invalidate the practices and strategies presented in this paper. The SE community needs to accumulate and share more content to support pedagogical solutions and ways of propagating these solutions among SE educators. By further building on existing knowledge, the community should be able to more effectively support professional development of SE educators. This would enable educators to more rapidly adapt to our fast-paced industry, and hence better serve our student population.

References

1. Wall of ideas. Design a better business. https://www.designabetterbusiness.tools/tools/wall-of-ideas
2. The affinity diagram tool. Six Sigma Daily, your everyday fix (2012). http://www.sixsigmadaily.com/the-affinity-diagram-tool
3. 16th SEI Software Engineering Workshop for Educators. Software Engineering Institute, Pittsburgh, USA (2019). https://www.sei.cmu.edu/news-events/news/article.cfm?assetid=553448
4. First International Workshop on Education Through Advanced Software Engineering and Artificial Intelligence (EASEAI 2019). Co-located with the 27th ACM Joint European Software Engineering Conference and Symposium on the Foundations of Software Engineering (ESEC/FSE), Estonia (2019). https://easeai.github.io/

5. Second Workshop on Emerging Software Engineering Education (WESEE 2019). Co-located with the 12th Innovations in Software Engineering Conference (ISEC), India (2019). https://sites.google.com/view/wesee2019
6. Second Workshop on Innovative Software Engineering Education (ISEE 2019). Co-located with the German Software Engineering conference SE 2019 in Stuttgart, Germany (2019). https://ase.in.tum.de/isee2019/
7. Software Engineering Education Workshop (SEED 2019), Putrajaya, Malaysia (2019). https://seed-2019.info/
8. Second IEEE/ACM International Workshop on Software Engineering Education for Millennials (SEEM 2018). Co-located with the 40th International Conference on Software Engineering (ICSE 2018), Gothenburg, Sweden, June 2018. http://seem2018.se-edu.org/
9. First IEEE/ACM International Workshop on Software Engineering Curricula for Millennials (SECM 2017). Co-located with the 39th International Conference on Software Engineering (ICSE 2017), Buenos Aires, Argentina, May 2017. http://secm2017.se-edu.org/wp/
10. First International Workshop on Frontiers in Software Engineering Education (FISEE 2019). Château de Villebrumier, Toulouse, France, November 2019. https://www.laser-foundation.org/fisee/fisee-2019/
11. Arnold, K.: The definition of a panel discussion. Powerful Panels. https://powerfulpanels.com/definition-panel-discussion/
12. Carnegie Mellon University, Eberly Center: Eberly center faculty series. https://www.cmu.edu/teaching/facultyprograms/index.html
13. Collins, J.: Bhag. https://www.jimcollins.com/concepts/bhag.html
14. Association for Computing Machinery: ACM SIGCSE Technical Symposium. https://sigcse.org/sigcse/events/symposia/index.html
15. Association for Computing Machinery: Empirical CS education. EmpiricalCSEd. http://empiricalcsed.org/
16. Cunningham, W.: Park bench panel. The WikiWikiWeb (also known as Wiki). https://wiki.c2.com/?ParkBenchPanel
17. Derby, E., Larsen, D.: Agile Retrospectives: Making Good Teams Great. Pragmatic Bookshelf, Raleigh (2006)
18. American Society for Engineering Education: National Effective Teaching Institutes. https://www.asee.org/education-careers/continuing-education/courses-and-workshops/neti
19. Gibbons, S.: Dot voting: a simple decision-making and prioritizing technique in UX. Nielsen Norman Group (2019). https://www.nngroup.com/articles/dot-voting/
20. Gray, D., et al.: Gamestorming: A Playbook for Innovators, Rulebreakers, and Changemakers. O'Reilly, Sebastopol (2010)
21. Linders, B.: Retrospective classic: Mad sad glad. Ben Linders Consulting (2017). https://www.benlinders.com/2017/retrospective-classic-mad-sad-glad/
22. Passuello, L.: What is mind mapping? (and how to get started immediately). Litemind. https://litemind.com/what-is-mind-mapping/
23. Shukla, R., Sureka, A., Joshi, R., Mall, R.: A report on software engineering education workshop. ACM SIGSOFT Softw. Eng. Notes 37(3), 26–31 (2012)
24. Wasserman, A., Freeman, P. (eds.): Software Engineering Education. Needs and Objectives Proceedings of an Interface Workshop. Springer, New York (1976). https://doi.org/10.1007/978-1-4612-9898-4

Hackathons as a Part of Software Engineering Education: CASE in Tools Example

Andrey Sadovykh[✉], Maria Beketova, and Mansur Khazeev

Innopolis University, Innopolis, Russia
{a.sadovykh,m.khazeev}@innopolis.ru, m.beketova@innopolis.university

Abstract. Software engineering programs intend to connect with industry practices to provide the most relevant up to date knowledge to the students. Students tend to pay more attention and attach more credibility to the academic knowledge when they see the endorsement of the program by the industry. For various reasons, faculty members find it difficult to connect to the industry, while as we noted those relations are essential both for education and research. Companies, while generally keen for recruitment of fresh graduates, may experience difficulty to convey their needs in terms of required capabilities and to influence education programs. We address these issues by introducing a hackathon as a part of the software engineering program curriculum and proposing a particular setup of this event. Incorporating educational hackathons into software engineering programs will ensure a connection between academic educational programs and current industrial practice.

Keywords: Hackathon · Education · Software Engineering

1 Introduction

Co-located with the TOOLS 50+1 conference, the CASE in Tools hackathon [2] joined students, companies, and researchers to experiment together with all kinds of tools for Software Engineering (SE). This event intended to help to gather expertise and new ideas on interesting practices, expose students to various business domains and modern challenges in Software Engineering. The overall goal was to open a dialogue among companies, researchers and students on hot topics in Software Engineering supported by hands-on experiments delivered in an entertaining manner in a time-boxed brainstorming format. As faculty, we designed this event to enhance the course on Management of Software Development in order to motivate and encourage students.

In this paper, we provide a brief literature review of hackathons in education, present our specific design of a hackathon that increases the outcomes for all stakeholders, discuss our experience of implementing the hackathon - both success and challenges, and present the results evaluated with a survey. We believe that this approach will be interesting to a wide audience of instructors in Software Engineering.

© Springer Nature Switzerland AG 2020
J.-M. Bruel et al. (Eds.): FISEE 2019, LNCS 12271, pp. 232–245, 2020.
https://doi.org/10.1007/978-3-030-57663-9_15

2   Literature Review

The hackathons have been applied in education for over a decade, Porras et al. [8] describe the history, discuss challenges and benefits of hackathons in various forms. They report that hackathons are a means to teach soft skills to engineers and improve the engagement of students with the course material. In particular, the hackathons provide a stimulating environment to practice teamwork, leadership, communication, presentation skills. Hackathons expose students to business domains, customers requirements and expectation management, that way encouraging awareness about end-users' preoccupations. Overall, hackathons represent a gamification of the education process that may positively impact learning outcomes. In the same paper, Porras et al. give a basic taxonomy of hackathons with 24-h events, week-long code camps, hacks as an exam, competitions and industry hacks. The goals may differ from a fast track to a new topic or a technology, to testing skills in a real project or emphasizing innovation and creativity in a context given by a customer.

Nandi and Mandernach [7] looked at hackathons from the informal learning standpoint and emphasized the benefits from informal peer learning that helps participants to acquire new skills. Anslow et al. [1] proposed datatons - data analytics hackathons as a way to boost the software engineering curricula. At datatons the students and data scientists explore together customers datasets. In [3] Decker et al. proposed a community-based format for hackathons - Think Global Hack Local (TGHL) to alleviate the intimidating culture of hackathons and make hackathons more fun and inclusive. They successfully run two TGHL events with students helping non-profit organizations. Gama et al. described an experience of introducing a hackathon as a part of an undergraduate course: the final course projects were developed during the 24-h hackathon event [5]. Uys introduced 24-h hackathon into an undergraduate capstone course. During the preparation phase that took about 12 weeks, teams formation, business case development, requirements elicitation were completed. One of the teams was also responsible for administrative tasks of the hackathon organization. During the hackathon event, students were encouraged to stay awake through the entire 24-h period and had to submit a working system by the end of the event. The final documentation and presentations had to be developed in the past-hackathon stage that lasted for four weeks [10].

Researchers admit that in education hackathons are helpful to extend core content without over-stressing the curriculum [8]. Instructors obtain new means to evaluate students' skills and teach soft skills in a real environment. Students learn faster, get appreciation and acknowledgment for their contributions by their peers, companies, and community. Hackathons augment hiring perspectives as students and companies closely collaborate in work-related areas. Companies further benefit from crowdsourcing for new creative product ideas and solutions. As pointed by J. Duhring, hackathons can be also used in academic course design as a means to identify students' interests, to reveal hidden students' talents, to benchmark students and identify their learning objectives [4].

Nevertheless, researchers indicate that hackathons may also have negative effects. They require significant additional effort by faculty on top of their regular duties. The intensity of hackathons and associated stress may affect participants' study-life balance and in worse cases be harmful to health. When evaluating the group work, it is difficult to cope with the "free rider" problem. Finally, the outcomes for companies are uncertain since they depend on many factors that are hard to control or unify such as the team's qualification and experience with a particular technology.

3   Proposed Design of Hackathon for SE Education

While teaching a Master's program at Innopolis University, we faced several challenges that led us to apply the hackathon approach. In this section we discuss the teaching challenges, the goals for the educational hackathon and the particular hackathon setup that we designed in order to maximize the benefits and alleviate the risks mentioned above.

3.1   Specific Challenges on Example of MSD Course

The CASE in Tools hackathon was designed for students of Masters programs at Innopolis University, as a part of the "Managing Software Development" (MSD) course. This course, originally created by David Root and Eduardo Miranda from Carnegie Mellon University, is focused on such aspects of software development as processes, planning, people management, etc. The course is organized as follows: 2 lectures per week, individual assignments (reading questions, essays), and group assignments (case studies). Overall, the course has a high workload: twice as many lectures as in a regular course; heavy home assignments requiring much writing resulting in up to 20 h weekly working effort.

The course is taught for students of two master's programs: Software Engineering and Data Science. The enrollment requirements for these programs differ significantly: The Software Engineering program requires 1+ years of industrial experience, while the Data Science program does not have such a requirement. Lack of industrial experience causes difficulties in understanding of concepts and techniques taught in the course. Another challenge comes from the theoretical set-up of the course: although the course is packed with practical assignments, they are built around papers that were written years ago, and discussing some case studies in a form of essays; lack of real-life practice decreases students' motivation and makes it harder to convey the relevance of the course. The survey conducted with the students of Software Engineering program has shown that students are not enthusiastic and lack effort when learning tools and methodologies they believe to be invaluable for their future careers [6].

3.2   Overall Goals for Educational Hackathon

While designing the hackathon as a part of the "Managing Software Development" (MSD) course, we set the following goals:

Expose Students to Various Business Domains. Students need to get acquainted with various business domains so that they can find a sphere of their interest and aspiration.

Stimulate Soft Skills Development. Participation in the hackathon facilitates the development of creativity, critical thinking, teamwork, leadership, communication and presentation skills.

Stimulate Communication with Real Customers. Facing a real customer provides students with a deeper understanding of the importance of communication in software development and the issues that it brings along.

Expose Students to Modern Challenges in Software Engineering. The problems offered by customers represent a state of practice in software engineering.

Provide Tangible Benefits to Customers. The hackathon was designed to provide customers with such benefits as the connection of students with potential future employers, insights on technical challenges, promotion of the company and its technologies.

Re-enforce Faculty-Industry Communication. Communication with the industry, even though perceived by the faculty as important and beneficial, is often insufficient due to the busyness of the faculty members or lack of soft skills. The hackathon induces the researchers to connect and communicate with people from the industry and face pertinent issues in software development.

3.3   Education "Hackathon" Process

The authors of the current paper designed and successfully conducted four specialized hackathons to boost collaboration in a large research project as reported in [9]. We intended to transpose our experience to the education domain as many characteristics were deemed extremely relevant. First, the hackathon was restricted to 8 h of intensive work that limited the effort required by the organizers, students, and companies. Second, the customer was not just a stakeholder, but an integral part of a team - that enhanced the collaboration between students, companies and faculty. The "homework" - preparation activities by the teams before the hackathon - helped to diminish stress, effectively plan the Hackathon Day, and improved the outcomes. Third, entertainment was the necessary part to stimulate creativity, facilitate communication and induce positive experience for all participants. Finally, we opted for a frugal administrative approach to limit the load on organizers. That was to choose the simplest and the most affordable options for the registration, coffee breaks, lunch, rooms and presentation equipment.

In the table below we compare the main characteristics in comparison with a "Traditional" hackathon - the most frequent form of a hackathon as summarized from the literature review above (Table 1).

With regards to the process and timeline, the CASE in Tools was designed in three stages as depicted in Fig. 1:

Table 1. Comparing hackathon approaches.

Properties	"Traditional" hackathon	CASE in tools	Intended benefits
Duration	From 24 h	8 h - intensive work, Several days of "Homework"	Less stress, Better work-life balance, Individual pace, Improving the outcomes through shaping the topics
Teams	Students only	Students, Industry representative, Mentor from Faculty	Extensive communication and working relations: - Student-Industry - Faculty-Industry
Topic	Product prototype	Focused experiment	More predictable outcomes to companies
Evaluation	Jury	All participants, audience favorite	Better participation, Students learn from other teams' results
Awards	Monetary	Symbolic goodies, Course grades	Less stress, Less control needed, Less burden on event budget

- **Stage 1: Call for topics** - starting three months before the Hackathon Day. Sourcing potential customers and defining a topic: a focused experiment feasible within 4–6 h.
- **Stage 2: Team forming** - a preparation stage, starting three weeks before the Hackathon Day. Topics announcement is followed by students' registration and gathering their interest in a set of particular topics. The teams are formed and they have about two weeks to organize the first meeting with a customer, ask questions about the topic, prepare a technical environment and get familiar with background concepts.
- **Stage 3: Hackathon Day** - 8-h event with lunch and 2 coffee-breaks.
  Competition The day starts with topic pitches, presented by customers. Then the teams' forming is finalized and the teams spread in various locations to work together on selected topics.
  Demo time - presentations of the teams' results at the end of the Hackathon Day. Evaluation of the technical progress, business impact and entertainment level of the final demonstration. Award ceremony with symbolic prizes for participants and winners, followed by an afterparty.

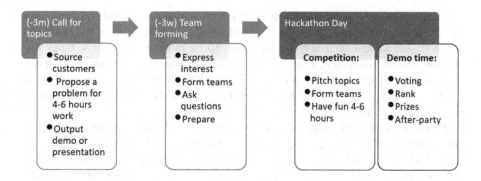

Fig. 1. Three stages of the CASE in Tools hackathon.

4   CASE in Tools in Practice

The hackathon design presented in the previous section was implemented at the TOOLS 50+1 Conference. In this section, we discuss our experience with regards to implementation and elaborate on the hackathon outcomes based on the evaluation survey.

4.1   Implementation

We started sourcing customers 3 months before the Hackathon Day. We used direct connections and mailing to the Innopolis University network. It was hard to convey benefits for potential customers: only direct connections worked, we have not received answers to cold emails. Nonetheless, we managed to find eight customers paying for participation in the hackathon. We conducted interviews with each customer to discuss the potential benefits of participation, explain the process and organization and define a feasible scope of a proposed challenge. The duration of the interviews ranged between 1 and 3 h. The output of this stage was the description of challenge topics that we published on the Hackathon website[1].

The next stage was teams formation. Participation in the hackathon was voluntary yet the students of MSD course were offered bonus points for participation, which accounted for 10% of the MSD course final grade. For these points only participation was taken into account, regardless of the team's final ranking in the Hackathon. As a result, 34 out of 44 MSD students took part in the event. We used an online poll to collect students' preferred projects - they prioritised the challenges on their 1st, 2nd and 3rd choice. Organizers allocated students to teams according to the preferences collected. Some challenges attracted more interest than the others, so manual balancing was required, and there were challenges that were not the first choice of any of its participants. A mentor from the academic staff was added to each team.

---

[1] https://www.caseintools.info/challenges.

The preliminary work stage started 2 weeks before the Hackathon Day. During this stage, the teams had to organize at least one meeting with the customer and to collect all the necessary information. Mentors were expected to track this process. During this stage, 4 out of 8 customers conducted a tutorial so that the hackathon participants could get acquainted with the technology to be used in a respective challenge. We checked the teams status with online polls to ensured that they had started working.

The Hackathon Day was the core part of the hackathon. After the opening speech delivered by organizers, the customers presented their challenges. The teams had 4 h, excluding lunch and coffee breaks, to provide a solution for their challenge and prepare a presentation. A customer and a mentor worked together with their team, providing guidance when necessary.

The Hackathon Day ended with the presentations, voting and award ceremony. Each team presented its results in a 10–15 min speech. Each presentation was followed by voting: mentors, customers and students from other teams evaluated the presentation on a 5-point scale based on four criteria: importance for the company or society, technical contribution of the team, potential for future work, entertainment. The Mentimeter[2] tool was used for voting. All participants in the audience could follow the results on an interactive dashboard showing the presenting team progress. Teams' final scores were computed as the average of four criteria. Example of the voting dashboard for the audience is presented in Fig. 2. The winner was defined by the highest final score.

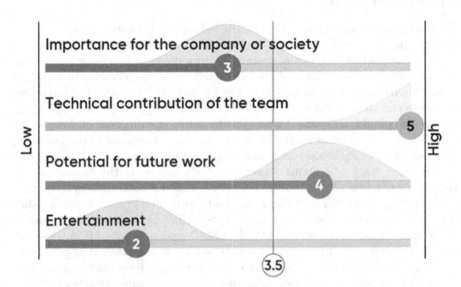

Fig. 2. Example of the voting dashboard as visible by the audience. The final score is 3.5.

---

[2] https://www.mentimeter.com/.

4.2   Survey Results

We conducted a survey to evaluate the outcomes. The dataset collects replies of 28 out of 34 student participants, 5 out of 7 participating customers and all 9 mentors from researchers and faculty. Although the dataset is not representative enough to draw definite conclusions, the results may give interesting insights about the appropriateness of hackathons for education purposes.

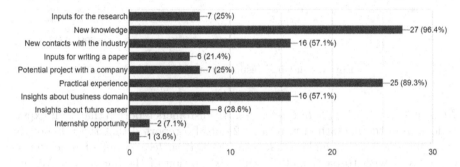

Fig. 3. Students' responses on the hackathon outcomes.

The majority of students reported acquiring new knowledge and practical experience. More than half of students report contacts with industry and insights about the business domain as an outcome. A minor part of students reported that they obtained inputs for their research, potential projects for the company and insights for their future career.

With regards to the hackathon objectives, we can conclude that they were mostly met:

Expose Students to Various Business Domains. 57% of students reported that they obtained insights into the business domain (Fig. 3).

Stimulate Soft Skills Development. The hackathon helped students to practice creativity, critical thinking, teamwork, leadership, communication and presentation skills. In particular, 78% of students indicated that teammates' contribution was adequate (Fig. 4). Moreover, our observations after the hackathon made us believe that the distance within the teams significantly diminished.

Stimulate Communication with Real Customers. 89% of students reported that the customer provided all necessary information and feedback (Fig. 3). 4 of 5 customers reported that all team members were engaged in the work (Fig. 5).

Expose Students to Modern Challenges in Software Engineering. 96% of students reported an exposure to new technologies and 89% reported to obtain a practical experience (Fig. 3).

Tell us about your team

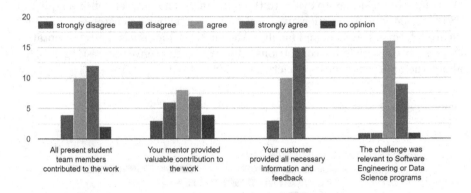

Fig. 4. Students' responses on the teamwork.

Provide Tangible Benefits to Customers. All customers reported that their expectations from the hackathon were met. 2 out of 5 reported that the value of the outcome was 3 times higher than the registration fees. 3 out of 5 customers expressed a wish to participate in the next edition of the hackathon. All customers will recommend the hackathon to a colleague (Fig. 5).

Re-enforce Faculty-Industry Communication. 77% of researchers reported getting new contacts with the industry. 55% reported obtaining inputs for their research. 33% indicated a possibility for a follow-up project with a customer (Fig. 6).

All in all, we can safely claim that the event was very successful. Students were exposed to different advanced subjects in software engineering, while companies could explore the solution for their problems with the help of students and researchers. Overall the ambiance at the event and after made us believe that we were on the right track for improving the education process.

As a concluding remark for the survey results, we would like to cite one of the students: *"Mr. Sadovykh, thank you for organizing this Hackathon. It was really inspiring for me and I am happy to have one more wonderful day in my life. At first, I was doing it for the grades but it turned out much more than that. I **learned so much** from it."*

5   Discussion

The main challenge in the organization was sourcing customers that would be interested in participating in the educational hackathon. The cold mailing among partner companies did not provide any results. Ten companies responded to our 23 personal invitations, and all responded were our direct contacts. Among those few, two organizations had difficulty understanding their professional benefits in participating in this event. One of the obstacles was the preconception on

Were you satisfied with the event?

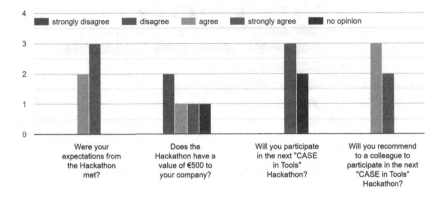

Fig. 5. Customers' responses on the hackathon outcomes.

students' qualifications and ability to solve business problems. Three organizations found it difficult to formulate a compact business problem and define its scope so that students would solve it in such a limited time. The interviews and workshops between organizers and customers helped to bootstrap that process. Overall, there was always a possibility to extract the right problem with an effort of a 2 h workshop. The feasibility of solving the proposed problems within the hackathon time frame was estimated based on the MSD course instructors experience.

The soft skills learning and much of knowledge transfer about the business domain rely on the involvement of customers in teamwork. We had a team with a remote customer due to travel restrictions. While the team and the customer reported overall satisfaction with the process and the event in general, our observations showed a limited success for the team, since the team would have had difficulty conveying the business impact of their findings. Ability to collaborate remotely is an important skill nowadays, especially in the information technologies field. So we believe that work with the remote customer is a valuable experience even if it implies some complications.

One of the customers sent a representative, who had limited expertise in the topic and lower personal engagement since he was not involved in the preparation workshop. That presumably harmed the team's learning outcomes and ultimately chances at the final presentations contest. Therefore for the future hackathons we believe it is crucial to ensure that the customer demonstrates the appropriate level of engagement during the preparation stage.

Team formation is a tricky task as some challenges might attract more interest than the others. We believe that we found an effective solution to this issue. We used an online poll to collect students' preferred projects - they marked the challenges of their 1st, 2nd and 3rd choice. Organizers allocated students to teams according to the preferences collected. This process ensures that students

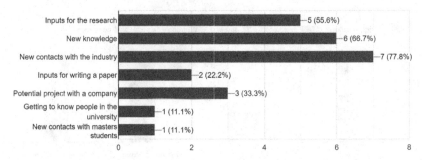

What are the outcomes for you from the event?

9 responses

Fig. 6. Researchers' responses on the hackathon outcomes.

are allocated uniformly to the challenges, and that they work on a challenge that is of interest to them.

Managing an international event required an unintended amount of administrative effort, for example ordering branded hand-outs, badges, collecting registration fees, controlling the budget revenues and expenses. While we received considerable help from volunteers and the Innopolis University administrative staff, this imposed a significant unplanned distraction and added up on top organizers' regular daily duties. Admittedly, these complications arise only when organizing hackathon for the first time, for the future hackathons it will be much easier, as both the organisers and the administrative staff learnt what should be done and how. Another opportunity would be to delegate the administrative tasks to students to let them practice organisational, leadership and other soft skills.

The role of a "customer" was clear for all the participants, yet the mentors' communication with their teams was not always efficient. We think it is necessary to select mentors well in advance (preferably among the current and probably the former teaching assistants of the relevant courses) and to educate them on their role in teams' success.

We hoped that the voting process, when the audience evaluated each presenting team would stimulate attention to the final presentations and would help all the participants to learn from each other's experience. These hopes were not fully realized due to several reasons. First, the available project equipment was not adequate for a large space. The presenters had very different presentation skills. The audience was overly tired after a stressful day of intensive work. The presentations took twice as long as it was planned. It was difficult to constantly maintain the focus due to a large number of highly technically dense and diverse topics. As a consequence, the participants reported their overall frustration with the evaluation process. This all prevented the audience from getting maximum from presentations. Thus, the evaluation may take an unreasonable amount of time after a long working day. To avoid this, it is important to plan well the agenda, to be strict with timing (8–10 min per presentation), and to make sure that teams are prepared to deliver their presentations in a timely manner by practicing the delivery, foreseeing possible technical issues and addressing them in advance. Meeting space and equipment is also very important - it is preferable to use a room of appropriate size with pre-installed equipment. We also have to admit that the scalability of the event is limited since the time needed for final presentations grows with the number of teams. As for the voting process, after analyzing the feedback from the students, we believe that the evaluation of the teams' presentations should be done by the customers and mentors, and students should not be a part of this corps. Besides, it would be beneficial to acquaint the evaluators with the grading rubric in advance.

Despite all the issues discussed above, we were quite pleased to witness that our main goals were met. The customers presented a variety of business challenges that were quite relevant to the curriculum. The students and customers actively communicated on the task-related topics. That had a positive impact on learning outcomes for students and improved the outcomes for the customers. Both groups reported high satisfaction with the event. We also observed a higher motivation by students to attend sessions specific to their challenges at the TOOLS conference.

In future we would like to extend our experience and experiment with the hackathon as an integrative part of the software engineering program that would assess the learning outcomes spreading over several courses at once. That way, the students would practice their skills acquired at various courses applying them to practical challenges provided by organizations as a replacement of traditional course evaluation. As an example, in terms of timing, one Hackathon Day is an equivalent of a series of mid-term exams at 4 courses lasting 2 h each. We would argue that the Hackathon may be more motivating and engaging thus resulting in better learning outcomes.

6   Conclusions

Hackathons have become an important means for educational purposes. The gamification aspect of hackathons promotes faster learning of new technologies, encourages the practice of soft skills and engagement with curricula. Students get exposed to the business domain and technology challenges of companies in real-life settings in an entertaining and stimulating environment. In the meantime, hackathons may reveal certain drawbacks such as associated stress, time and administrative effort as well as uncertain outcomes to the participating companies.

The connection between academic educational programs and the current industrial practice is valuable for faculty, students and industry, yet not easy to implement. Based on our experience with collaborative research hackathons, we designed a specialized educational hackathon to accelerate learning and promote collaboration between faculty, industry and students in a time-boxed event.

The hackathon setup has the following distinct features. First, the hackathon is restricted to 8 h of intensive work that limits the effort required by the organizers, students, and companies. Second, the customer is an essential part of the team - that enhanced the collaboration between students, companies and faculty. Third, we introduce a set of preparation activities before the Hackathon Day, such as meeting with a customer and tutorials, to help to diminish stress, effectively plan the Hackathon Day and improve the outcomes. Fourth, entertainment was the necessary part to stimulate creativity, facilitate communication and induce positive experience for all participants. Finally, we propose a frugal administrative approach to limit the load of organizers.

The hackathon organization revealed a number of challenges, such as difficulty to find paying customers and define a feasible scope of a proposed topic, high administrative effort of the organizers on top of their regular duties, shortcomings of Demo time organization. The discussion of these issues lays the foundation for a more efficient organization of future hackathons.

Despite the challenges mentioned above, the event was very successful. Students were exposed to different advanced subjects in software engineering, while companies could explore the solution for their problems with the help of students and researchers. The outcome of the hackathon is evaluated based on a survey completed by students, mentors and industry representatives after the event. All groups reported high satisfaction with the event. Students reported that they obtained insights about the business domain (57%), exposure to new technologies (96%) and practical experience (89%). Researchers reported getting new contacts with the industry (77%), obtaining inputs for their research (55%), obtaining a possibility for a follow-up project with a customer (55%). All customers reported that their expectations from the hackathon were met. The results make us believe that hackathons should become a part of the curriculum.

Acknowledgment. The authors would like to express their gratitude to Dr. A. Naumchev for his significant contribution to the hackathon organization, to Dr. V. Ivanov, O. Bulichev for the mentorship of teams as well as to administrative staff and in particular Inna Baskakova for providing support on administrative matters.

References

1. Anslow, C., Brosz, J., Maurer, F., Boyes, M.: Datathons: an experience report of data hackathons for data science education. In: Proceedings of the 47th ACM Technical Symposium on Computing Science Education. SIGCSE 2016, pp. 615–620. Association for Computing Machinery, New York (2016). https://doi.org/10.1145/2839509.2844568
2. Case in tools hackathon 2019. https://www.caseintools.info. Accessed 22 Oct 2019
3. Decker, A., Eiselt, K., Voll, K.: Understanding and improving the culture of hackathons: think global hack local. In: Proceedings of the 2015 IEEE Frontiers in Education Conference (FIE). FIE 2015, pp. 1–8. IEEE Computer Society, USA (2015). https://doi.org/10.1109/FIE.2015.7344211

4. Duhring, J.: Project-based learning kickstart tips: hackathon pedagogies as educational technology. In: VentureWell. Proceedings of Open, the Annual Conference, pp. 1–8. National Collegiate Inventors & Innovators Alliance (2014)

5. Gama, K., Alencar Gonçalves, B., Alessio, P.: Hackathons in the formal learning process. In: Proceedings of the 23rd Annual ACM Conference on Innovation and Technology in Computer Science Education. ITiCSE 2018, pp. 248–253. Association for Computing Machinery, New York (2018). https://doi.org/10.1145/3197091.3197138

6. Khazeev, M., Aslam, H., de Carvalho, D., Mazzara, M., Bruel, J.M., Brown, J.A.: Reflections on teaching formal methods for software development in higher education. In: Bruel, J., Capozucca, A., Mazzara, M., Meyer, B., Alexandr Naumchev, A.S. (eds.) First International Workshop on Frontiers in Software Engineering Education. LNCS, vol. 12271, pp. 28–41. Springer, Cham (2020)

7. Nandi, A., Mandernach, M.: Hackathons as an informal learning platform. In: Proceedings of the 47th ACM Technical Symposium on Computing Science Education. SIGCSE 2016, pp. 346–351. Association for Computing Machinery, New York (2016). https://doi.org/10.1145/2839509.2844590

8. Porras, J., et al.: Hackathons in software engineering education: lessons learned from a decade of events. In: Proceedings of the 2nd International Workshop on Software Engineering Education for Millennials. SEEM 2018, pp. 40–47. Association for Computing Machinery, New York (2018). https://doi.org/10.1145/3194779.3194783

9. Sadovykh, A., et al.: On the use of hackathons to enhance collaboration in large collaborative projects: - a preliminary case study of the MegaM@Rt2 EU project. In: 2019 Design, Automation Test in Europe Conference Exhibition (DATE), pp. 498–503 (2019). https://doi.org/10.23919/DATE.2019.8715247

10. Uys, W.F.: Hackathons as a formal teaching approach in information systems capstone courses. In: Tait, B., Kroeze, J., Gruner, S. (eds.) SACLA 2019. CCIS, vol. 1136, pp. 79–95. Springer, Cham (2020). https://doi.org/10.1007/978-3-030-35629-3_6

Teaching Efficient Recursive Programming and Recursion Elimination Using Olympiads and Contests Problems

Nikolay V. Shilov$^{(\boxtimes)}$ and Danila Danko

Innopolis University, 1, Universitetskaya Str., 420500 Innopolis, Russia
`shiloviis@mail.ru`, `d.danko@innopolis.university`

Abstract. Olympiads and contests are popular with bachelor students of Software Engineering, Computer Science and other departments educating professionals to be involved software development. But educational role and potential of these activities are under-evaluated and poorly used in the education. In the present paper we address one particular topic that can be introduced using problems from Olympiads and Contests, namely — efficient recursive programming and recursion elimination. Here we understand efficient recursive programming as problem solving with recursive algorithm design. Recursion elimination studies how to construct (functional) equivalent iterative (imperative) program for a given recursive (functional) preferably with use of fix-size static memory. Great computer scientists have contributed to the recursion elimination studies — John McCarthy, Amir Pnueli, Donald Knuth, etc., many fascinating examples have been examined and resulted in recursion elimination techniques known as *tail-recursion* and as *corecursion*. We base our study on examples borrowed from the worlds of Mathematical Olympiads and Programming contests. At the same time we use these examples to stress importance of the recursion elimination studies not only for better education but for better and more efficient program specification, verification, optimization and compiler design.

Keywords: Recursive programming · Iterative programming · Functional equivalence · Recursion elimination · Ascending and descending dynamic programming · International Mathematical Olympiad · International Collegiate Programming Contest

1 Introduction

Almost two decades passed since publication of the article [19] on *Engaging Students with Theory through ACM Collegiate Programming Contests*. The article was published soon after publication 2001 of Computer Science curricular [22] by Association for Computing Machinery (ACM). One of primary purposes of the article [19] was to draw attention of CS educators to educational role and potential of Olympiads and contests that are popular with bachelor students

© Springer Nature Switzerland AG 2020
J.-M. Bruel et al. (Eds.): FISEE 2019, LNCS 12271, pp. 246–264, 2020.
https://doi.org/10.1007/978-3-030-57663-9_16

(like *International Collegiate Programming Contest ICPC* [26]). Unfortunately, the current version of the ACM Computer Science curricular [23] (published in 2013) still ignore *sport programming* as curricular topic or as educational approach.

Because of the above we would like to try again to draw attention of the SE and CS educators to educational role and potential of Olympiads and contests. This time we would like to present recursive programming and recursion elimination using problems borrowed from different Olympiad and contests. At the same time we use these examples to stress importance of the recursion elimination studies not only for better education but for better and more efficient program specification, verification, optimization and compiler design.

1.1 Structure of the Paper

In the following-up Subsect. 1.2 we give a simple but fascinating example of recursion elimination to solve a problem from the mot recent *International Mathematical Olympiad* (IMO)

In the next Sect. 2 we address recursion elimination for/in a problem that is very popular for training students *dynamic programming* in preparation for different programming contests.

Then in the Sect. 3 we discuss dynamic programming in more general settings and introduce *ascending dynamic programming*.

In the Sect. 4 we study when fix-size memory is sufficient to implement ascending dynamic programming and give examples of recursion elimination (including an example borrowed from a popular contest and training resource *Code Forces* [34]).

In the last Sect. 5 we sum up our results, discuss paper' contribution, educational importance of popular Olympiads and contests, SE, CS and Artificial intelligence for Olympiads and contests progress, and importance of further studies of recursion elimination.

1.2 Why Math Students Should Learn Programming Theory

A discourse about historical, cultural, educational relations and connections between Mathematics and Science and Art of Programming (exactly Programming not Computer Science) is quite old: it started in early days of computing machinery more than 70 years ago (since, at least, since ENIAC was completed and first put to work in 1945). Many programming pioneers — e.g. Edsger W. Dijkstra, Andrey P. Ershov, Donald E. Knuth — had published their reflections on this topic [4–6,10]. (Unfortunately, we are not aware about reflections of mathematicians on this topic while we know and highly recommend a book of outstanding Russian mathematician Vladimir A. Uspensky [20] where he had promoted and advocated a view on Mathematics as a humanitarian science.)

In our opinion it is very important introduction of programming art and science [7,8,11] to mathematical education. It isn't just because of industrial demand and/or employment opportunities for graduates but because of a need of programming culture for solving mathematical problems. We would like to advocate this claim by analysis of the problem set [25] of the most recent International Mathematical Olympiad 2019 (IMO-2019) [24] (which was the 60th in the series).

The Olympiad set [25] comprises 6 problems from which *at least one* is good examples to demonstrate programming art and science. Namely, we speak about the following problem 1 from the set:

Let $\mathbb{Z}$ be the set of integers. Determine all functions $f : \mathbb{Z} \to \mathbb{Z}$ such that, for all integers a and b, $f(2a) + 2f(b) = f(f(a+b))$.

The problem can serve as an example of recursion elimination via reduction (corecursion) of a monadic recursion to a tail recursion, we discuss this programming technique and its application to the problem 1 in the next subsection.

A classic example monadic recursion elimination by reduction to the tail recursion [30] via corecursion [2,29] is a so-called John McCarthy function M_{91} : $\mathbb{N} \to \mathbb{N}$ [11,17] that is defined as follows below:

$$M_{91}(n) = \ if \ n > 100 \ then \ (n - 10) \ else \ M_{91} \ (M_{91}(n + 11)).$$

It turns out that $M_{91}(n) = \ if \ n > 101 \ then \ (n - 10) \ else \ 91$. A key idea in recursion elimination is move from a monadic function $M_{91} : \mathbb{N} \to \mathbb{N}$ to a binary function $M2 : \mathbb{N} \times \mathbb{N} \to \mathbb{N}$ such that $M2(n, k) = (M_{91})^k(n)$ for all $n, k \in \mathbb{N}$ (where $(M_{91})^k(n)$ is k-time application of the function, i.e. $(M_{91})^k(n) = \overbrace{M_{91}(\ldots M_{91}(n)\ldots)}^{k}$); of course, $M2(n, 0) = (M_{91})^0(n) = n$ for every $n \in \mathbb{N}$.

Let us apply the idea presented in the previous paragraph to the problem 1 of the International Mathematical Olympiad. Since $f(2a) + 2f(b) = f(f(a+b))$ is true for all $a, b \in \mathbb{Z}$, then $f(0) + 2f(b) = f(f(b))$ for all $b \in \mathbb{Z}$. Let us define a binary function $F : \mathbb{Z} \times \mathbb{N} \to \mathbb{Z}$ such that $F(b, k) = f^k(b)$ and $F(b, 0) = f^0(b) = b$ for all $a \in \mathbb{Z}$ and $k \in \mathbb{N}$. Then for all $a \in \mathbb{Z}$ and $k \in \mathbb{N}$

$$F(b, (k+1)) = \ 2F(b, k) + f(0) = 2(2F(b, (k-1)) + f(0)) + f(0) = \ldots$$
$$= 2^{(k+1)} F(b, 0) + (2^{(k+1)} - 1)f(0) = 2^{(k+1)}b + (2^{(k+1)} - 1)f(0),$$

and, hence, $f(b) = f^1(b) = F(b, 1) = 2b + f(0)$ and thus the problem 1 from IMO-2019 is solved!

2 Dynamic Programming Case Study

2.1 The Hull Strength Puzzle

In this section we discuss a so-called *The Hull Strength Puzzle* (HSP) [17], which is just a literary version of *The Dropping Bricks Problem* [18] or *The Egg Dropping Puzzle* from Wikipedia article on *Dynamic Programming* [28].

Let us characterize the mechanical stability (strength) of a phone case (the hull of a mobile phone) by an integer h that is equal to the height (in meters) safe for the case to fall down, while height $(h+1)$ meters is unsafe (i.e. the hull breaks). You have to determine the stability of hulls of a particular kind by dropping them from different levels of a tower of H meters. (One may assume that mechanical stability does not change after a safe fall.) How many times do you need to drop hulls, if you have 2 hulls in the stock? What is the optimal number (of droppings) in this case?

The Hull Strength Puzzle is an example of optimization problems. For every $x \in [0..H]$ let T_H be the number of test (droppings) that is the optimal (i.e. a necessary but sufficient) to determine the (mechanical) strength up to level x using 2 hulls (at most) Any optimal method to define the mechanical stability for $H > 0$ should start with some step (command) that prescribes to drop the first phone from some particular (but optimal) level h. Hence the following equality must hold for this particular level h:

$$T_H = 1 + \max\{(h-1), T_{H-h}\},$$

where (in the right-hand side)

1. $1+$ corresponds to the first test (dropping),
2. $(h-1)$ corresponds to the case when the hull of the first phone breaks after the first dropping (and we have to drop the remaining second phone from the levels $1, 2, \ldots (h-1)$ in a series),
3. T_{H-h} corresponds to the case when the hull of the first phone is safe after the first dropping (and we have to define stability by dropping the pair of phones from $(H-h)$ levels in $[(h+1)\ldots H])$,
4. 'max' corresponds to the worst in two cases above.

Since the particular value h is *optimal*, and *optimality* means *minimality*, the above equality transforms to the following one:

$$T_H = \min_{1 \leq h \leq H} (1 + \max\{(h-1), T_{H-h}\}) = 1 + \min_{1 \leq h \leq H} \max\{(h-1), T_{H-h}\}.$$

Besides, we can add one obvious equality $T_0 = 0$.

Remark that the sequence of integers $T_0, T_1, \ldots T_H, \ldots$ that meets two equalities above is unique since T_0 has an explicit definition, T_1 is defined by T_0, T_2 is defined by T_0 and T_1, T_H is defined by $T_0, T_1, \ldots T_{H-1}$. Hence it is possible to move from the sequence $T_0, T_1, \ldots T_H, \ldots$, to a function $T : \mathbb{N} \to \mathbb{N}$ that maps every natural x to T_H and satisfies the following *functional equation* for the *objective function* T:

$$T(x) = if \ h = 0 \ then \ 0 \ else \ 1 + \min_{1 \leq h \leq x} \max\{(h-1), T(x-h)\}. \qquad (1)$$

This equation has a unique solution as it follows from the uniqueness of the sequence $T_0, T_1, \ldots T_H, \ldots$ let us summarize the above discussion as follows:

Functional equation (1) has unique solution in $\mathbb{N}^{\mathbb{N}}$; *moreover we can go further: The equation (1) can be adopted as a recursive definition of a function, (i.e. a recursive algorithm presented in a functional pseudo-code) that solves the Hull Strength Puzzle.*

The primary purpose of this section is to prove the following simple formula

$$T(x) = \arg\min t : \frac{t(t+1)}{2} \geq x \tag{2}$$

that is easy to implement as iterative imperative program.

A proof of the formula (2) can be found in [17], but the derivation in [17] relies rather upon human analysis of the Hull Strength Puzzle than formal manipulations and transformations. Because of it, in the next Subsect. 2.2 we present a new (easier) derivation of this formula by means of corecursion (i.e. via problem generalization and inductive proof).

2.2   HSP via Corecursion

Let us start with the following reformulation of the HSP question:

For every integer tight $h \geq 0$ *what is a necessary and sufficient number of (dropping) tests* $T(h)$ *to determine the (mechanical) strength in the range* $[0..h]$ *of the hull (of the mobile phones) if you have* $n = 2$ *hulls in the stock?*

Next let us introduce another function $H : \mathbb{N} \times \mathbb{N} \to \mathbb{N}$ that solves the following problem:

For any number $n \geq 0$ *of hulls in stock and any number* $t \geq 0$ *of allowed (dropping) tests what is the largest* $H(n, t)$ *such that* n *hulls and* t *tests are sufficient to determine any mechanical strength in the range* $h \in [0..H(n, t)]$?

Then it is easy to see that for every $x \geq 0$

$$T(x) = \arg\min t : H(2, t) \geq x. \tag{3}$$

Hence the only we need to prove the formula (2) is to prove that

$$H(2, t) = \frac{t(t+1)}{2}. \tag{4}$$

Let us derive recursive equation for $H : \mathbb{N} \times \mathbb{N} \to \mathbb{N}$.

– It is quite obvious that $H(0, t) = H(n, 0) = 0$ for all $n, t \in \mathbb{N}$.
– If $n > 0$ and $t > 0$ then any test trial starts with the first dropping from some particular level $h \in [1..H(n, t)]$;
  - since the first tested hull can break in the first test in the trial (i.e. we lose one hull and one test) then $(h - 1)$ can be as large as $H((n - 1), (t - 1))$;

- since the first tested hull can return safe after the first test in the trial (i.e. we don't lose any hull but one test) then there can be up to $H(n, (t-1))$ levels above h;

hence $H(n,t) = (H((n-1), (t-1)) + 1) + H(n, (t-1))$ in this case.

To sum-up the above arguments, we come to the following equation:

$$H(n,t) = \ if \ (n = 0 \ or \ t = 0) \ then \ 0$$
$$else \ (H((n-1), (t-1)) + H(n, (t-1)) + 1). \quad (5)$$

Now we can prove (4) and (2) as follows. First, according to (5) for every $t \geq 0$ we have

$$H(1,t) = \ if \ t = 0 \ then \ 0 \ else \ (H(1, (t-1)) + 1) = \sum_{k=1}^{k=t} 1 = t. \quad (6)$$

Next, according to (5) and to (6) for every $t \geq 0$ we have

$$
\begin{aligned}
H(2,t) &= \\
&= if \ t = 0 \ then \ 0 \ else \ (H(1, (t-1)) + H(2, (t-1)) + 1) = \\
&= if \ t = 0 \ then \ 0 \ else \ (t + H(2, (t-1))) = \sum_{k=1}^{k=t} k = \\
&= \frac{t(t+1)}{2}.
\end{aligned} \quad (7)
$$

Hence, according to (3) and (7) we get (4) and then (2).

The following proposition give explicit (recursion-free) definition (8) for the function $H : \mathbb{N} \times \mathbb{N} \to \mathbb{N}$ defined by recursive equation (5). Let us remark that the explicit definition (8) is easy to implement using iterative imperative programming with fixed size finite memory. (Remark also that the implementation can be even loop-free if integer multiplication is provided!)

Proposition 1.

$$H(n,t) = \sum_{k=1}^{k=n} C_t^k \quad (8)$$

where C_t^k are the standard binomial coefficients.

Proof. Let us proceed by mathematical induction on $t \geq 0$.

Base case $t = 0$ is trivial: For all $n \geq 0$, according to (5), $H(n, 0) = 0$, as well as $H(n, 0) = 2^t - 1 = 0$ according to (8).

Induction hypothesis: Let us assume that for some $T \geq 0$ equality (8) is true for all $t \in [0..T]$ and all $n \geq 0$.

Induction step:

$$H\left(n, (T+1)\right) = (\text{according to } (5)) = H\left((n-1), T\right) + H\left(n, T\right) + 1 =$$
$$= (\text{according the induction hypothesis}) = \left(\sum_{k=1}^{k=n-1} C_T^k\right) + \left(\sum_{k=1}^{k=n} C_T^k\right) + 1 =$$
$$= (\text{index substitution in the first sum}) = \left(\sum_{k=2}^{k=n} C_T^{k-1}\right) + \left(\sum_{k=1}^{k=n} C_T^k\right) + 1 =$$
$$= (\text{because } 1 = C_T^0) = \left(\sum_{k=1}^{k=n} C_T^{k-1}\right) + \left(\sum_{k=1}^{k=n} C_T^k\right) + 1 =$$
$$= (\text{re} - \text{grouping both sums}) = \sum_{k=1}^{k=n} \left(C_T^{k-1} + C_T^k\right) =$$
$$= (\text{because } C_{T+1}^k = C_T^{k-1} + C_T^k \text{ for all } k) = \sum_{k=1}^{k=n} C_{T+1}^k,$$

i.e. $H\left(n, (T+1)\right) = \sum_{k=1}^{k=n} C_{T+1}^k$.

Hence, according to principle of mathematical induction, equality (8) is true for all $t \geq 0$ and all $n \geq 0$. — Q.E.D.

Remark that according to this Proposition 1, for all $k, t \in \mathbb{N}$, if $k \geq T$ then $H(n, t) = 2^t - 1$. Also, the proposition implies equality (4):

$$H(2, t) = \sum_{k=1}^{k=2} C_t^k = t + \frac{t(t-1)}{2} = \frac{t(t+1)}{2}.$$

Together with (3) it gives another proof for (4) and (2).

We believe that both proofs of (2) as a solution for the Hull Strength Problem are much more transparent and formal than a proof from [17]).

3 Ascending Dynamic Programming

3.1 Recursive Dynamic Programming

In the previous section 2 we discuss recursion elimination for a particular example of dynamic programming, in the present section we discuss recursion elimination for dynamic programming in more general settings. The term *Dynamic Programming* was introduced by Richard Bellman in the 1950s to tackle optimal planning problems. *Bellman equation* is a name for recursive functional equation for the objective function that expresses the optimal solution at the "current" state in terms of optimal solutions at next (changed) states, it formalizes a so-called *Bellman Principle of Optimality: an optimal program (or plan) remains optimal at every stage.*

In papers [16,18] we study a class of Bellman equations that matches the following recursive pattern:

$$G(x) = \textit{if } p(x) \textit{ then } f(x) \textit{ else } g\left(x, \left\{h_i\big(x, G(t_i(x))\big), \ i \in [1..n(x)]\right\}\right) \quad (9)$$

We consider the pattern as a *recursive program scheme* (or template) [15], i.e. a recursive control flow structure with *uninterpreted symbols*:

- G is the *main* function symbol representing (after interpretation of *ground* functional and predicate symbol) the objective function $G : X \to Y$ for some X and Y;
- p is a ground predicate symbol representing (after interpretation) some *known*[1] predicate $p \subseteq X$;
- f is a ground functional symbol representing (after interpretation) some known(see footnote 1) function $f : X \to Y$;
- g is a ground functional symbol representing (after interpretation) some known(see footnote 1) function $g : X \times Z^* \to X$ for some appropriate Z (with a variable arity $n(x) : X \to \mathbb{N}$);
- all h_i and t_i ($i \in [1..n(x)]$) are ground functional symbols representing (after interpretation) some known(see footnote 1) function $h_i : X \times Y \to Z$, $t_i : X \to X$ ($i \in [0..(n(x) - 1)]$).

Let us remark that both recursive function definitions (1) and (5) match the pattern (9). Please refer [18] for detailed discussion how (1) does match the pattern (9), but let us discuss here why (5) does match the pattern (9):

- G is H, X is $\mathbb{N} \times \mathbb{N}$, Y is $\mathbb{N}$ (i.e. $H : \mathbb{N} \times \mathbb{N} \to \mathbb{N}$);
- p is ($n = 0$ *or* $t = 0$) — a subset of $\mathbb{N} \times \mathbb{N}$;
- f is a constant 0 (i.e. a function $f : (x, y) \mapsto 0$ that always return 0);
- g is 1 plus the sum of the elements of the second component (i.e. $g : (x, (y_0, y_1, \ldots)) \mapsto (1 + (y_0 + y_1 + \ldots)))$;
-
  - n is a constant 1 (i.e. a function $n : (x, y) \mapsto 1$ that always return 1),
  - both functions h_0 and h_1 are second component of a pair (i.e. $h_0, h_1 : (x, y) \mapsto y$),
  - functions t_0 and t_1 are defined as $t_0 : (x, y) \mapsto ((x - 1), (y - 1))$ and $t_1 : (x, y) \mapsto (x, (y - 1))$.

3.2 Using One-Time Allocated Associative Array

Let us consider a function $G : X \to Y$ that is defined by the interpreted recursive scheme (9). Let us define two sets $bas(v), spp(v) \subseteq X$:

- base $bas(v) = $ *if $p(v)$ then $\emptyset$ else $\{t_i(v) : i \in [1..n(v)]\} \subseteq X$* comprises all values that are immediately needed to compute $G(v)$;
- support $spp(v)$ is the set of all values that appear in the call-tree of $G(v)$.

For example,

- for function T defined by (1), $bas(x) = spp(x) = [0..(x - 1)]$ for all $x \in \mathbb{N}$;
- for function H defined by (5) $bas(x, y) = \{((x - 1), (y - 1)), (x, (y - 1))\}$ and $spp(x, y) = [0..x] \times [0..(y - 1)]$ for all $x, y \in \mathbb{N}$.

Note that

- $bas(v)$ is always finite;

---

[1] i.e. that we know how to compute .

- G is defined on v then the support $spp(v)$ is finite;
- $spp(v)$ can be computed by the following algorithm:

$$spp(x) \ = \ if \ p(x) \ then \ \{x\} \ else \ \{x\} \cup (\bigcup_{y \in bas(x)} spp(y)). \tag{10}$$

(Remark also that (10) has recursive dynamic programming pattern (9).)

Let us specify and verify below the following iterative annotated template for/of (ascending) dynamic programming:

- Precondition $PRE(v)$ parameterized by an "input" value v:
    1. v is a value in X (i.e. $v \in X$);
    2. function G is defined by (9);
    3. $spp : X \to 2^X$ is the support function for G;
    4. NiX is a distinguishable fixed indefinite value[2] for X;
- Template Pseudo-Code $TPC(v)$ parameterized by an "input" value v:

1 : $VAR \ LUT \ : assosiative \ array \ indexed \ by \ values \ in \ spp(v)$
            $containing \ values \ in \ Y;$

2 : $LUT := \ array \ filled \ with \ NiX;$

3 : $for \ all \ u \in spp(v) \ do$

4 : $if \ p(u) \ then \ LUT[u] := f(u);$

   // Annotation-1: for all $u \in spp(v)$:

       // $((p(u) \Leftrightarrow LUT[u] = f(u)) \ \& \ (\neg p(u) \Leftrightarrow LUT[u] = NiX))$

5 : $while \ LUT[v] = NiX \ do$

   // Annotation-2: for all $u \in spp(v)$:

       // $(p(u) \Rightarrow LUT[u] = G(u)) \ \&$

       // $\& \ (LUT[u] = G(u) \Leftrightarrow LUT[u] \neq NiX)$

6 : $let \ u \in spp(v) \ be \ any \ element$

7 : $such \ that \ LUT[u] = NiX \ and$

8 : $LUT[t_i(u)] \neq NiX \ for \ all \ i \in [1..n(u)]$

9 : $in \ LUT[u] := \ g\left(u, \ \{h_i\left(u, LUT[t_i(u)]\right), \ i \in [1..n(u)]\}\right).$

Note that the template uses one time allocated *associative array LUT* (stays for *Look Up Table*) that size depends on the parameter value v.

Proposition 2. *For every* $v \in X$, *if* $PRE(v)$ *then the following holds:*

1. *if* $G(v)$ *is defined then* $TPC(v)$ *terminates after* $|spp(v)|$ *iterations of both loops, and* $LUT[v] = G(v)$ *by termination;*
2. *if* $G(v)$ *is not defined then* $TPC(v)$ *never terminates.*

Proof. 1. If $PRE(v)$ then Annotation-1 and Annotation-2 are invariants of the control points of their location; because of it and because $v \in spp(v)$, $LUT[v] = G(v)$ upon $TPC(v)$ termination.

Recall that if $G(v)$ is defined then $spp(v)$ is finite; termination of both loops in $TPC(v)$ is guaranteed in this case, because each iteration of each of these loops decreases the number of elements $u \in spp(v)$ where $LUT[u] = NiX$.

---

[2] *NiX—Non in any type* X, *similarly to Non a Number —* NaN.

2. Recall that if $G(v)$ isn't defined then $spp(v)$ is infinite; hence (at least) the second loop never terminates.
 — Q.E.D.

For example, let us specialize (and optimize a little bit) the template TPC to compute value $H(n,t)$ of the function H defined by (5) for given $n, t \in \mathbb{N}$:

1 : $VAR\ LUT\ :\ array\ [0..n;\ 0..(t-1)]\ of\ integers;$
2 : $for\ all\ (x,y) \in [0..n] \times [0..(t-1)]\ do$
3 : $if\ ((x=0)\ \vee\ (y=0))\ then\ LUT[x,y] := 0$
4 : $else\ LUT[x,y] := NaN;$
5 : $while\ LUT[n,t] = NaN\ do$
6 : $let\ (x,y) \in [0..n] \times [0..(t-1)]\ be\ any\ element$
7 : $such\ that\ LUT[x,y] = NaN\ and$
8 : $LUT[(x-1),(y-1)] \neq NaN\ and\ LUT[x,(y-1)] \neq NaN$
9 : $in\ LUT[x,y] :=\ (LUT[(x-1),(y-1)] + LUT[x,(y-1)] + 1).$

Let us refer this iterative algorithm as $TPC - H$ in the sequel; remark that it uses a standard (indexed by integers) array instead of an associative array (indexed by elements of a fixed but arbitrary type) that is used in general case in the template TPC.

4   Using Fix-Size Static Memory

4.1   When Fix-Size Memory Is Enough

Nevertheless, the above algorithm $TPC - H$ uses array while the function H defined by (5) and computed by this algorithm may be computed by an iterative program (according to Proposition 1) without array at all. Hence, a natural question arises: is a finite fix-size static memory sufficient when computing a recursive function that matches recursive dynamic programming pattern (9)? Unfortunately, in general, the answer is negative according to the following proposition by M.S. Paterson and C.T. Hewitt [15].

Proposition 3. *The following special case*

$$F(x) = \ if\ p(x)\ then\ x\ else\ f(F(g(x)), F(h(x))) \tag{11}$$

of the recursive template (9) is not equivalent to any standard program scheme (i.e. an uninterpreted iterative program scheme with finite fix-size static memory).

Proposition 3 does not imply that dynamic memory is *always* required; it just says that for some interpretations of *uninterpreted* symbols p, f, g and h the size of required memory depends on the input data. But if p, f, g and h are *interpreted*, it may happen that function F can be computed by an iterative program with a finite static memory. For example, Fibonacci numbers

$$Fib(n) = \ if\ (n=0\ or\ n=1)\ then\ 1\ else\ Fib(n-2) + Fib(n-1) \tag{12}$$

matches the pattern of the scheme in the above Proposition 3, but just six (three actually) integer variables suffice to compute it by an iterative program.

Proposition 4. *Assume that $PRE(v)$ holds altogether with the following additional conditions:*

- *the arity function $n : X \to \mathbb{N}$ is some constant $n \in \mathbb{N}$;*
- *base functions $t_1, \ldots t_n$ are invertible and $t_i = (t_1)^i$ for all $i \in [1..n]$;*
- *predicate p is t_1-closed in the following sense: $p(u) \Rightarrow p(t_1(u))$ for all $u \in X$.*

Let $m \in \mathbb{N}$ be number of static variables that suffice to implement imperative iterative algorithms to compute ground predicate and functions p, f, h_i ($i \in [1..n]$), t_1 and t_1^- for any input value. Then the objective function G may be computed by an imperative iterative algorithm with $2n + m + 2$ static variables.

Let us simply present below one particular array-free template $AFT(v)$ that proves the proposition:

```
1 :     var x, x₁, ... xₙ : X;
2 :     var y, y₁, ... yₙ : Y;
3 :     x := v;
4 :     if p(x) then y := f(x)
5 :        else { do x := t₁(x) until p(x);
6 :                 x₁ := x; x₂ := t₁(x₁); ... xₙ := t₁(xₙ₋₁);
7 :                 y₁ := f(x₁); y₂ := f(x₂); ... yₙ := f(xₙ);
8 :                 do x := t₁⁻(x);
```

$$// \text{ Annotation: } x = t_1^-(x_1) \ \& \ bas(x) = \{x_1, \ldots x_n\} \ \&$$
$$// \ \& \ y_1 = G(x_1) \ \& \ldots \& \ y_n = G(x_n)$$

```
9 :                 y := g( x, (h₁(x,y₁), ... hₙ(x,yₙ)) );
10 :                yₙ := yₙ₋₁; ... y₃ := y₂; y₂ := y₁;
11 :                y₁ := y;
12 :                x₁ := t₁⁻(x₁); ... xₙ := t₁⁻(xₙ)
13 :             until x = v }.
```

Formally correctness of the Proposition 4 follows from the observation that the Annotation is an invariant of the point where it is specified. The idea behind this template $AFT(v)$ is quite simple:

- let $m = \arg\min \ m : p(g_1^m(v))$;
- let $prf = \{g_1^k(v) \ : \ 0 \leq k < m\}$;
- let $suf = \begin{cases} \{v\}, \text{ if } m = 0 \\ \{g_1^m(v), \ldots, g_1^{m+n-1}(v)\}, \text{ if } m > 0 \end{cases}$;

then $spp(v) = prf \cup suf$, prf is traversed in the line 5 of $AFT(v)$, and suf — in the line 4 xor in the line 6 of $AFT(v)$.

4.2   Example: Fibonacci Numbers

Let us remark that there is no contradiction between Propositions 3 and 4 because functions g and h in (11) that correspond to functions t_i, $i \in [1..n]$

in (9) (i.e. $n = 2$ and either g is t_1 and h is t_2 or h is t_1 and g is t_2) aren't expressible one in terms of another, but are considered as unrelated functions.

Fibonacci numbers (12) matches the template (11) but satisfy conditions of the Proposition 4: let

- $t_1, t_2 : \mathbb{N} \to \mathbb{N}$ be
    - $t_1 : x \mapsto (if\ x > 0\ then\ (x - 1)\ else\ 0)$,
    - $t_2 : x \mapsto (if\ x > 1\ then\ (x - 2)\ else\ 0)$,
- $p \subseteq \mathbb{N}$ be $(x = 0\ or\ x = 1)$;

then

- $t_2 = t_1^2$ and $t_1^- : x \mapsto (x + 1)$,
- $p(x) \Rightarrow p(t_1(x))$ for all $x \in \mathbb{N}$.

Hence iterative program with a fix-size finite memory to compute Fibonacci numbers can result from specialization of the *AFT*:

```
1 :    var x, x₁, x₂ : ℕ;
2 :    var y, y₁, y₂ : ℕ;
3 :    x := v;
4 :    if (x = 0 or x = 1) then y := 1
5 :      else { do x := (x − 1) until (x = 0 or x = 1);
6 :            x₁ := x; x₂ := (x₁ − 1);
7 :            y₁ := 1; y₂ := 1;
8 :            do x := (x + 1);
                 // Annotation: x = (x₁ + 1) & bas(x) = {x₁, x₂} &
                 //  & y₁ = Fib(x₁) & y₂ = Fib(x₂)
9 :              y := (y₁ + y₂);
10 :             y₂ := y₁;
11 :             y₁ := y;
12 :             x₁ := (x₁ + 1); x₂ := (x₂ + 1)
13 :      until x = v }.
```

4.3   Example: Fibonacci Words

The example below was presented on the workshop *Fun With Formal Methods* FWFM-2013 [31], the first workshop in a series FWFM-2013, FWFM-2014 FWFM-2019. The example is closely related to the Fibonacci numbers but is about the Fibonacci words.

An infinite sequence of Fibonacci words $w_0, w_1, \ldots$ is defined [13] very similar as the infamous sequence of Fibonacci numbers: let a and b be two distinguishable symbols ("letters"); then $w_0 = b$, $w_1 = a$, and $w_{i+2} = w_i \circ w_{i+1}$ for all $i \geq 0$ where "$\circ$" is concatenation on words. In other words, Fibonacci words are defined by the following recursion:

$$W(n) = \ if\ (n = 0\ or\ n = 1)\ then\ \{if\ n = 0\ then\ b\ else\ a\} \\ else\ W(n - 2) \circ W(n - 1). \tag{13}$$

It is easy to see that the sequence of Fibonacci words starts as b; a; ba; aba; $baaba$; $ababaaba$; $baabaababaaba$.

One can observe that none of the first seven Fibonacci words listed above contains two b's or three a's in a row (i.e. no sub-words bb or aaa). This observation leads to a hypothesis that all Fibonacci words contain neither two b's nor three a's in a row. But then the next question arises: how to prove (or refute) the hypothesis?—The paper [13] discusses how to prove these two hypothesis in two steps:

1. first-order sound axiomatization of algebraic systems (first-order models) where all elements of the domain may be generated using Fibonacci words
2. and then automatic generation of finite countermodels that meet the axiomatization but refute that some element may be generated using two b's or three a's in a row.

Surprisingly, the countermodels for each of these properties are quite small, — just 5 elements to refute a possibility of two b's and 11 element to refute a possibility three a's in a row [13].

But we are interested exclusively in recursion elimination, i.e. how to compute (13) iteratively using finite fix-size memory. This time base functions t_1, t_2 and predicate p are the same as for Fibonacci numbers above (see Subsect. 4.2). But the function f is a little bit more complicated because it gets different values for 0 and for 1. Hence iterative program with a fix-size finite memory to compute Fibonacci words isn't just specialization of the AFT but requires some modification (in contrast to Fibonacci numbers):

$1:$ $var\ x, x_1, x_2 : \mathbb{N};$

$2:$ $var\ y, y_1, y_2 : \{a, b\}^*;$

$3:$ $x := v;$

$4:$ $if\ (x = 0\ or\ x = 1)\ then\{if\ x = 0\ then\ y := b\ else\ y := a\}$

$5:$ $else\ \big\{\ do\ x := (x-1)\ until\ (x = 0\ or\ x = 1);$

$6:$ $x_1 := x;\ x_2 := (x_1 - 1);$

$7:$ $y_1 := a;\ y_2 := b;$

$8:$ $do\ x := (x+1);$

           // Annotation: $x = (x_1 + 1)\ \&\ bas(x) = \{x_1, x_2\}\ \&$

           // $\&\ y_1 = W(x_1)\ \&\ y_2 = W(x_2)$

$9:$ $y := (y_2 \circ y_1);$

$10:$ $y_2 := y_1;$

$11:$ $y_1 := y;$

$12:$ $x_1 := (x_1 + 1); x_2 := (x_2 + 1)$

$13:$ $until\ x = v\ \big\}.$

4.4   Example: Beyond Hull Strength Puzzle

Proposition 1 gives an explicit expression (8) for the function $H : \mathbb{N} \times \mathbb{N} \to \mathbb{N}$ defined by recursive equation (5). Remark that this explicit expression (8) is easy to implement by an iterative imperative program with finite fix-size memory, but with loops (to accumulate sum). We also know an explicit expression (4) for function $H(2,t) : \mathbb{N} \to \mathbb{N}$. Because of it we can construct an iterative imperative program with finite fix-size memory to compute function $H(3,t) : \mathbb{N} \to \mathbb{N}$ in two ways:

- either specializing a program that computes $H : \mathbb{N} \times \mathbb{N} \to \mathbb{N}$ for the first argument being equal to 2,
- or specializing the recursive definition (5) for the first argument being equal to 2 and using Proposition 4.

Below we present the latter approach.

According to (5) for every $t \geq 0$ we have

$$
\begin{aligned}
H(3,t) &= \\
&= if\ t = 0\ then\ 0\ else\ (H\,(2,(t-1)) + H\,(3,(t-1)) + 1) = \\
&= if\ t = 0\ then\ 0\ else\ \left(\tfrac{(t-1)((t-1)+1)}{2} + H\,(3,(t-1)) + 1\right) = \\
&\quad = if\ t = 0\ then\ 0\ else\ \left(1 + \tfrac{t(t-1)}{2} + H\,(3,(t-1))\right).
\end{aligned}
\tag{14}
$$

Remark that this equation is not an instance of the tail recursion but satisfies conditions of the Proposition 4 if

- $t_1 : \mathbb{N} \to \mathbb{N}$ is $t_1 : x \mapsto (if\ x > 0\ then\ (x-1)\ else\ 0)$.
- and $p \subseteq \mathbb{N}$ is predicate $x = 0$.

Because of it, $H(3,t)$ can be computed by the following specialization of the template $AFT(t)$:

```
1:    var x, x₁ : ℕ;
2:    var y, y₁ : ℕ;
3:    x := t;
4:    if x = 0 then y := 0
5:      else { do x := x − 1 until x = 0;
6:        x₁ := x;
7:        y₁ := 0;
8:        do x := x + 1;
         // Annotation: x = (x₁ + 1) & bas(x) = {x₁} & y₁ = H(3, x₁)
9:          y := 1 + x(x−1)/2 + y₁;
11:         y₁ := y;
12:         x₁ := x₁ + 1;
13:        until x = t }.
```

(Remark that line 10 has vanished because in the template $AFT(v)$ the template for this line is $y_n := y_{n-1}; \ldots y_2 := y_1$, but $n = 1$ in our case.)

4.5   Example: Permutation Concatenation

Wikipedia reads [33] about Code Forces [34]: *Codeforces is a website that hosts competitive programming contests. It is maintained by a group of competitive programmers from ITMO University led by Mikhail Mirzayanov.*

Below we are going to discuss the following problem *New Year and the Permutation Concatenation* (PCP) [35]:

Let n be an integer. Consider all permutations on integers 1 to n in lexicographic order, and concatenate them into one big sequence p. For example, if $n = 3$, then $p = [1, 2, 3, 1, 3, 2, 2, 1, 3, 2, 3, 1, 3, 1, 2, 3, 2, 1]$. The length of this sequence will be $n \cdot n!$.

*Let $1 \leq i \leq j \leq n \cdot n!$ be a pair of indices. We call the sequence $(p_i, p_{i+1}, \ldots, p_{j-1}, p_j)$ a **subarray** of p. Its **length** is defined as the number of its elements, i.e., $j - i + 1$. Its **sum** is the sum of all its elements, i.e., $\sum_{k=i}^{j} p_k$.*

You are given n. Find the number of subarrays of p of length n having sum $\frac{n(n+1)}{2}$.

In the above we skip the ending of the problem statement because it is important only for solution of the problem using integers of a fix size. Also we need to expand the formulation by the assumption that $n > 0$ (since case $n = 0$ doesn't make sense for permutations).

Algorithm of the solution is also available on Code Forces [36]:

The answer is:

$$n \cdot n! - \sum_{k=1}^{n-1} \frac{n!}{k!}$$

This can be calculated in $O(n)$ without the need of modular division.
There is also a simple recurrence counting the same answer, found by arsijo:

$$d(n) = \Big(d(n-1) + (n-1)! - 1 \Big) \cdot n.$$

Of course, the above recurrent relation must be completed by the basic case $n = 1$:

$$d(n) \;=\; if \; n = 1 \; then \; 1 \; else \; \Big(d(n-1) + (n-1)! - 1 \Big) \cdot n. \qquad (15)$$

Below we first explain the recurrent formula (15), then extract iterative algorithm to compute function $d : \mathbb{N} \to \mathbb{N}$ using Proposition 4 assuming that the factorial is one of known functions, and finally discus a variation of the recurrent equation (15) and equivalent iterative algorithm without assumption that we know how to compute factorial.

Remark that the equation (15) satisfies conditions of the Proposition 4 if

- $t_1 : \mathbb{N} \to \mathbb{N}$ is $t_1 : x \mapsto (if \; x > 1 \; then \; (x-1) \; else \; 1$.
- and $p \subseteq \mathbb{N}$ is predicate $x = 1$.

Because of it, $d(n)$ can be computed by the following specialization of the template $AFT(n)$:

```
 1 :    var x, x₁ : ℕ;
 2 :    var y, y₁ : ℕ;
 3 :    x := n;
 4 :    if x = 1 then y := 1
 5 :      else { do x := x − 1 until x = 1;
 6 :            x₁ := x;
 7 :            y₁ := 1;
 8 :            do x := x + 1;
               // Annotation: x = (x₁ + 1) & bas(x) = {x₁} & y₁ = d(x₁)
 9 :              y := x(y₁ + x₁! − 1);
11 :              y₁ := y;
12 :              x₁ := x₁ + 1;
13 :            until x = n }.
```

(Remark that again the line 10 has vanished because in the template $AFT(v)$ the template for this line is $y_n := y_{n-1}; \dots y_2 := y_1$, but $n = 1$ in our case.)

5   Conclusion

We started this paper with an example of recursion elimination in a problem from International Mathematical Olympiad of 2019. Unfortunately, competitions like IMO or ICPC are still not involved into education process but we hope that competitions of this kind may be used for engaging students with Theory of Computer Science and Formal Methods in Software Engineering [19].

We also would like to stress that our example for recursion elimination as an unified approach to some mathematical Olympiad problems can be considered as a step towards a so-called *IMO Grad Challenge* [27]:

> The International Mathematical Olympiad (IMO) is perhaps the most celebrated mental competition in the world and as such is among the ultimate grand challenges for Artificial Intelligence (AI).
>
> The challenge: build an AI that can win a gold medal in the competition. To remove ambiguity about the scoring rules, we propose the formal-to-formal (F2F) variant of the IMO: the AI receives a formal representation of the problem (in the Lean Theorem Prover), and is required to emit a formal (i.e. machine-checkable) proof. We are working on a proposal for encoding IMO problems in Lean and will seek broad consensus on the protocol.
>
> . . .
>
> Challenge. The grand challenge is to develop an AI that earns enough points in the F2F version of the IMO (described above) that, if it were a human competitor, it would have earned a gold medal.

But we didn't bound our study of recursion elimination by educational examples like IMO problems or the Hull Strength Puzzle (i.e. the Egg Dropping Puzzle [28]). We also studied use of associative arrays (with one-time memory allocation) for recursion elimination in descending dynamic programming (see Sect. 3), conditions that are sufficient for finite fixed-size static memory in ascending dynamic programming (see Sect. 4), and gave examples of recursion elimination to illustrate these mentioned results.

To the best of our knowledge, use of integer arrays for efficient translation of recursive functions of integer argument was suggested first in [1]. In the cited paper this technique of recursion implementation was called *production mechanism*. The essence of the production mechanism consists in support evaluation (that is a set of integers), array declaration with a proper index range, and fill-in this array in bottom-up (i.e. ascending) manner by values of the objective function. Use of auxiliary array was studied also in [14]. The book [14] doesn't use templates but translation techniques that is asymptotically more space efficient that our approach.

Some topics for further studies are presented below (from the nearest to that which require more time).

– To prove using a proof-assistance (ACL2 most probably) that iterative and recursive versions of the function $H(n, t)$ are equivalent.
– To investigate how to generalize the pattern of the recursive function and very particular manipulations used/presented in this paper for recursion elimination in more general cases.
– Investigate methods to find recursive patterns admitting recursion elimination. Maybe, we need to design a type system or/and use machine learning to advance in this direction.
– To design and implement a plugin for some IDE (Integrated Development Environment) that analyses program code to find recursive patterns admitting recursion elimination and eliminates these cases of recursion at object code level.

References

1. Berry, G.: Bottom-up computation of recursive programs. RAIRO - Informatique Théorique et Applications (Theoret. Inform. Appl.) **10**(3), 47–82 (1976)
2. Bird, R.S.: Using circular programs to eliminate multiple traversals of data. Acta Informatica **21**(3), 239–250 (1984). https://doi.org/10.1007/BF00264249
3. Bird, R.S.: Zippy tabulations of recursive functions. In: Audebaud, P., Paulin-Mohring, C. (eds.) MPC 2008. LNCS, vol. 5133, pp. 92–109. Springer, Heidelberg (2008). https://doi.org/10.1007/978-3-540-70594-9_7
4. Dijkstra, E.W.: On a cultural gap. Math. Intell. **8**(1), 48–52 (1986). https://doi.org/10.1007/BF03023921
5. Ershov, A.P.: Aesthetics and the human factor in programming. Commun. ACM **15**(7), 501–505 (1972)
6. Ershov, A.P.: Programming as the second literacy (1980). http://ershov.iis.nsk.su/ru/second_literacy/article. Accessed 20 Jan 2020 (in Russian)

7. Ershov, A.P., Knuth, D.E. (eds.): Algorithms in Modern Mathematics and Computer Science. LNCS, vol. 122. Springer, Heidelberg (1981). https://doi.org/10.1007/3-540-11157-3
8. Gries, D.: The Science of Programming. Monographs in Computer Science. Springer, Heidelberg (1981). https://doi.org/10.1007/978-1-4612-5983-1
9. Hoare, C.A.R.: An axiomatic basis for computer programming. Commun. ACM **12**(10), 576–580 (1969)
10. Knuth, D.E.: Computer science and its relation to mathematics. Am. Math. Monthly **81**(4), 323–343 (1974)
11. Knuth, D.E.: Textbook Examples of Recursion (1991). https://arxiv.org/pdf/cs/9301113.pdf. Accessed 20 Jan 2020
12. Knuth, D.E.: The Art of Computer Programming, Volumes 1–3 Boxed Set, 2nd edn. Addison-Wesley, Boston (1998)
13. Lisitsa, A.: Tackling Fibonacci words puzzles by finite countermodels. Contributed talk at the CAV Workshop Fun With Formal Methods, St. Petersburg, Russia, 13 July 2013. http://cgi.csc.liv.ac.uk/~alexei/Fibonacci_Challenge/fun2013.pdf. Accessed 20 Jan 2020
14. Liu, Y.A.: Systematic Program Design: From Clarity to Efficiency. Cambridge University Press, Cambridge (2013)
15. Paterson, M.S., Hewitt C.T.: Comparative schematology. In: Proceedings of the ACM Conference on Concurrent Systems and Parallel Computation, pp. 119–127 (1970)
16. Shilov, N.V.: Study of recursion elimination for a class of semi-interpreted recursive program schemata. In: Abstracts of 31st Nordic Workshop on Programming Theory NWPT 2019, Tallinn, Estonia, 13–15 November 2019, pp. 54–58 (2019)
17. Shilov, N.V.: Etude on recursion elimination. Model. Anal. Inf. Syst. **25**(5), 549–560 (2018)
18. Shilov, N.V.: Algorithm design patterns: program theory perspective. In: Proceedings of Fifth International Valentin Turchin Workshop on Metacomputation (META-2016), University of Pereslavl, pp. 170–181 (2016)
19. Shilov, N.V., Yi, K.: Engaging students with theory through ACM collegiate programming contests. Commun. ACM **45**(9), 98–101 (2002)
20. Uspensky, A.V.: Mathematics Apology. Amphora, Sant-Petersburg (2009). (in Russian)
21. Shilov, N.V., Shilova, S.O.: On mathematical contents of computer science contests. In: Enhancing University Mathematics: Proceedings of the First KAIST International Symposium on Teaching. CBMS Issues in Mathematics Education, vol. 14, pp. 193–204. American Society (2007)
22. Computing Curricula 2001. Computer Science. https://www.acm.org/binaries/content/assets/education/curricula-recommendations/cc2001.pdf. Accessed 01 July 2020
23. Computer Science Curricula (2013). https://www.acm.org/binaries/content/assets/education/cs2013_web_final.pdf. Accessed 01 July 2020
24. International Mathematical Olympiad. https://www.imo-official.org/default.aspx. Accessed 20 Jan 2020
25. Problems (with solutions). 60th International Mathematical Olympiad. Bath - UK, 11th–22nd July 2019. https://www.imo2019.uk/wp-content/uploads/2018/07/solutions-r856.pdf. Accessed 20 Jan 2020
26. ICPC. International Collegiate Programming Contest. https://icpc.baylor.edu/. Accessed 20 Jan 2020

27. IMO Grand Challenge. https://imo-grand-challenge.github.io/. Accessed 20 Jan 2020
28. The Egg Dropping Puzzle. From Wikipedia, the free encyclopedia, article on Dynamic Programming. https://en.wikipedia.org/wiki/Dynamic_programming#Egg_dropping_puzzle. Accessed 20 Jan 2020
29. Corecursion. From Wikipedia, the free encyclopedia. https://en.wikipedia.org/wiki/Corecursion. Accessed 20 Jan 2020
30. Tail call. From Wikipedia, the free encyclopedia. https://en.wikipedia.org/wiki/Tail_call. Accessed 20 Jan 2020
31. Fun With Formal Methods (2013). http://www.iis.nsk.su/fwfm2013. Accessed 20 Jan 2020
32. Fun With Formal Methods (2019). https://persons.iis.nsk.su/en/FWFM19. Accessed 20 Jan 2020
33. Codeforces. From Wikipedia, the free encyclopedia. https://en.wikipedia.org/wiki/Codeforces. Accessed 22 June 2020
34. Code Forces. Sponsored by Telegram. https://codeforces.com/. Accessed 22 June 2020
35. D. New Year and the Permutation Concatenation. https://codeforces.com/contest/1091/problem/D?locale=en. Accessed 22 June 2020
36. 1091D - New Year and the Permutation Concatenation. https://codeforces.com/blog/entry/64196. Accessed 22 June 2020

Empirical Studies

An Experience in Monitoring EEG Signals of Software Developers During Summer Student Internships

Rozaliya Amirova[1], Vladimir Ivanov[1], Sergey Masyagin[1], Aldo Spallone[2], Giancarlo Succi[1], Ananga Thapaliya[1(✉)], and Oydinoy Zufarova[1]

[1] Innopolis University, Innopolis 420500, Russia
a.thapaliya@innopolis.ru
[2] RUDN University, Moscow 117198, Russia

Abstract. Given the emerging importance of individual biophysical data for understanding software development activities, an internship was organized to provide the students with first hand experience on the collection of such data. The specific goal of the internship was to offer students the possibility to collect, analyse, understand, and draw conclusions from EEG signals. The overall internship spanned about 3 months and involved about 17 students. The results have been very positive in terms of the specific knowledge gained by each student and also of the value of the collected data. In this paper we detail the structure of the internship, the tasks carried out, the challenges faced, and how such challenges have been overcome.

Keywords: EEG · Brain waves · ERD · Correlation

1 Introduction

Electroencephalography (EEG) is a device to record electrical activity with a high spatial resolution that provides non-obtrusive access to neuronal dynamics at the population level on virtually any transient scale that is now considered essential for cognition [15]. It's more accessible and inexpensive than various devices, such as MEG, and facilitates cognition research in a broader variety of circumstances [30]. This internship was related to the field of software engineering which requires using EEG device to analyze the brain waves of programmers under conditions such as pair programming and programming with (without) music which was completed over the time period of 3 months carrying out experiments with 17 participants, both undergraduate and graduate students.

The goal of the internship was to collect the brain waves of the programmers using EEG and analyze their data to measure the difference in concentration level given under different physical situations [14,17,39] or for carrying out special tasks in coding [19,40]. In this paper, we describe the overall process of how the internship was carried out, how the process of collecting & analyzing the

© Springer Nature Switzerland AG 2020
J.-M. Bruel et al. (Eds.): FISEE 2019, LNCS 12271, pp. 267–278, 2020.
https://doi.org/10.1007/978-3-030-57663-9_17

data worked and also including the organizational report about what happened before the start of the internship. This paper is organized as follows: Sect. 2 gives the overall idea of the internship, organizational tasks, methods of data management, experiment procedure, data collection procedures and the tools for data collection, analysis & visualization. Section 3 gives the brief description about the settings of the device and how the experiment was carried out. Section 4 give the evaluation and preliminary outcomes of the internship. Section 5 talks about the technical & organizational challenges faced during the internship and finally on Sect. 6 we give our final thoughts and point out about the future research that can be done based on this internship.

2 Preliminaries

In this study, we identify a complete workflow using EEG to examine the subject's brain activities during the programming process. The data consists of continuous EEG recordings executing a programming task from 17 participants. These participants were computer scientists (undergraduate or graduated) from the age 18 to 35. Subjects were faced with various levels of programming assignments, from which they had to select and continue with the task according to their experience. The dataset offers a rich framework for researching various brain behavior and cognitive problems, such as: What brain signals activate the behavior at what particular point? At the same time, it introduces a well-studied model that can be advantageous for the growth of communication and reference localisation processes [1]. Experiments were performed under two factors: pair programming and music (without music). These factors are the most common factors practiced in industry and academia used by developers while solving problems and developing software [2,25]. The relevance of this study goes beyond the simple understanding of a practice, but fits the overall evolution of the discipline of metrics and empirical software engineering through the last 25 years of experiments always providing a better understanding of the complex phenomena of the development of software [3, 4, 10, 20–23, 26, 27, 32, 33, 36–38, 43–45, 47, 48].

2.1 Organizational Tasks of the Internship

This section describes the initial stage of the internship where we discussed how the internship can initiate, how to proceed with the experiments and conduct meetings. Like every other internship, first we set the organizational structure (basic rules, initiation of the internship) about the meetings and divided the tasks as required by the internship.

First we decided to formalize everything (word by word) that was discussed during the meeting. Then we got the references and opinions from experts in the field about the EEG device, data collection and analysis. This was done for the theoretical knowledge of the keywords, device and ways to conduct and collect the experiment data. Also, we talked about the organization of weekly meetings for the discussion of weekly progress of interns. We finalized the goals, metrics, protocol of the experiment and about porting all the data collected to the new storage and classifying the data according to the protocol.

2.2 Method of Data Management

Format of Saving: After the collection of data from the subject, it was decided to save it on *edf* format describing all the metadata such as name and birth date in regardless of the tools and data format used [16].

Naming Convention: For the naming convention, we wanted to make it as self explanatory as possible for the ease of read. The following convention was used:

- NameOfSubject.DateOfExperimentDay.Goal.Mode.edf
- NameOfSubject.DateOfExperimentDay.Goal.Calibration.Condition.edf

2.3 Experiment Procedure

Before the start of the experiment there were certain procedures that should be applied to the device, for the better quality of the data [9]. This procedure includes to clean the EEG cap (the device), put the cap on the test subject and making it comfortable for the subject, put the ear electrodes on the test subject's earlobes, fill the electrodes with conductive gel (also ear electrodes) and connect the transmitter of the device to personal computer using bluetooth. Then, choose the reference electrode as the referent and Mono 21 as the montage and make sure that every electrode is running in it's own range and there are no spikes nor noises on the signal. Finally, if the electrode is not working properly then put additional gel on it or try to make the cap fit better.

During the experiment it was necessary to follow the specific procedure and protocol in a systematic way so that it would be beneficial for both the researcher and the subject [13]. First, run the calibration procedures (eyes closed and open for 2 min before the initiation). Then, we let the subjects set up the environment on their computer, start working on the given tasks and start recording. The record session should be at least 60 min long. During the recording the subject should not leave his/her working place and he/she should move and talk as less as possible (if it is not a part of the experiment).

2.4 Tools for Data Collection, Analysis and Visualization

The programming tools and libraries that were used for the experiment was Anaconda 3 with Python 3, Numpy Packs, Scipy Packs, MNE 0.16.1 and Jetbrains Pycharm IDE. For filtering the data, we used finite impulse response method which is provide by MNE library. For all the recording, processing and imaging we used Mitstar EEG studio.

3   Approach to the Experiment

3.1   Device and Experiment Settings

We have used a lightweight 24-channel portable EEG Smart BCI cap which is offered by Mitsar company in the study. Electrode positioning is achieved by a regular 10–20 scheme. The frequency of measurements is 250 Hz, and the amplitude range is 0–70 Hz. Since we are using a dual-channel EEG tool, the first step to take is to select the channels that are the most appropriate for the study. On the one side, most channels offer a wide range of data from the entire scalp. Anyway this detail may be redundant. Furthermore, various kinds of EGG objects affect electrodes mounted on different areas of the scalp, such as cortical electrodes which are expected to be affected by body and eye motions. The following 18 electrodes, Fp1, Fp2, F7, F3, Fz, F4, F8, T3, C3, C4, T4, T5, P3, Pz, P4, T6, O1 and O2 with the reference electrode being Cz were used. For the primer data investigation on the music analysis, all electrodes were utilized. During the test set-up of the structure for the pair programming, we found that with EEG pre-processing strategies, for example, particular segment investigation and manual separating, a sign from the frontal terminals can't be cleaned. We didn't propose any procedures other than these two for frontal electrodes as we found that central electrodes would be sufficient for examination and results for this particular little scope try. Before the trial terminals were cleaned with liquor, we additionally utilized conductive gel during information recording to give a superior association among electrodes and scalp. The Mitsar EEG studio programming was utilized to record, pre-process and perform frequency tests.

A pair was formed between each participant of driver (programmer) and navigator (tells the programmer what to do). Each trial was performed on a daily basis in one month's time frame with comparable conditions. The analysis consists of two stages. The underlying stage is the two-section modification period. The first is the member sits in a relaxed state with the shut eyes doing nothing and the second is the same with the eyes opened. The coordination stage tests the synchronization of alpha and theta waves. The next step is the step where real employment and undertakings take place. Members are actually beginning to program in solo. It is going on only for an hour. Currently after the completion of the solo programming, participants are given five minutes of replay before the start of pair programming. One carries on as a driver throughout pair programming, and another as a pilot. The jobs don't make any difference because the two participants need to resume the test with separate jobs again. Equally, this goes on for an hour. Members are given 30 min of reprieve after the second cycle of pair programming. Members are in complete state of rest during the break. After the break, the pair programming cycle starts only with navigator's and driver's changing roles.

The same experimental setting is repeated with the music factor. The only new setting is that the participants work with (without) music to complete the given task. The music was already selected, a typical instrumental music for work [12]. Participants used the earphone provided by us.

4   Evaluation and Preliminary Results

The preliminary assessment using Mitsar EEG Studio software was finalized for the music experiment. Analysis of power spectra [42] was per-shaped by taking spectral qualities from the unit. Band esteems acquired from a similar subject programming were analyzed at that stage, with and without music. The idea was to identify variations in power spectra for a specific unit, and to differentiate common designs from different topics. For pair programming, investigation was performed using Event Related Desynchronization (ERD) techniques and correlation analysis [13]. The main machine gauges the different neuron movements between the state of rest and programming as a sign of the undertaking's trouble performed. The relation quantifies the association between different waves. Strong wave relation clarifies various mental exercises and studies. ERD and relationship were used along those lines to break down the experimental details for Pair Programming.

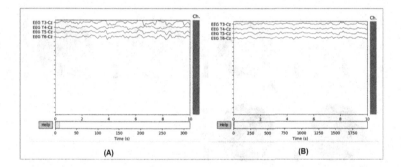

Fig. 1. Image A shows us the waves produced while closing eyes and Image B shows us the waves produced during open eyes. We can see from the waves that we can see that amplitude on the eyes closed is higher than on eyes open (coding) part.

Regarding pair programming, we got higher pair-navigator ERD and equal qualities for solo and pair-driver mode. This result is like the results of a correlation analysis. This can conclude that pair programming in pilot mode needs more thought, as they have to evaluate and direct as of now theorized by during code composition. Figure 1 shows the comparison of amplitude between eyes closed and eyes open (programming). Figure 2, 3, 4 shows the brain maps of the programmers in their own state which is visualized using EEG spectral wizard. The brain maps can be compared to detect the areas of the brain, were the different waves are generated. At first glance, you can see there are differences in the power of the waves between the different situations, with a higher brain activation in solo compared to both pair programming.

For programming with (without music), after analyzing the details, we discovered that in all the subjects a huge distinction was documented in the cerebrum movement as the force spectra are diverse programming and music contrasting,

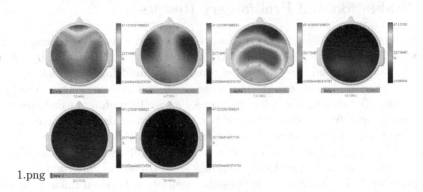

Fig. 2. Brain maps of the waves of solo programming (spectra wizard, power percentage)

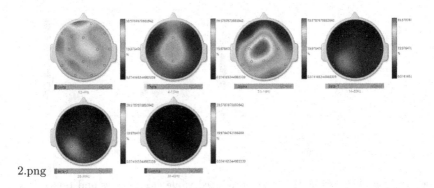

Fig. 3. Brain maps of the waves of navigator (spectra wizard, power percentage)

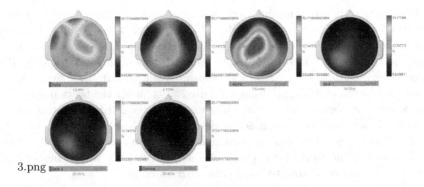

Fig. 4. Brain maps of the waves of driver (spectra wizard, power percentage)

and without. In any case, an unusual illustration of cerebrum activity could not be identified in our datasets, nor could we differentiate engineering gatherings with comparable examples: some subjects had lower delta waves with music and some had higher delta waves with music comparing with control gathering, and similar circumstances existed with other wave types, similar to theta, alpha, beta, and gamma. Over and over, but we can't close out an outstanding music effect over the entire datasets. Later on, by making the datasets accessible, we want to discern rational co-variations that can help profile the music's effect on specific developer groups even more successfully.

5   Challenges

The primary objective of this internship was to test the methodology and the nature of the study to decide if EEG is an appropriate way to research programmers' behavior. Although this methodology appears ideal for evaluating brain involvement during training, we have faced the difficulties and shortcomings. During the internship, students came across different challenges and we have grouped them into two types: technical and organizational challenges.

5.1   Technical Challenges

– Depending on the design of the study used, before starting the actual experiment researchers should plan both the collection of data and the review of protocols fully at individual experiments as well as specific groups of individuals [31].
– This evaluation of the study will potentially alter how the stimulus should be communicated or how problematic the activation function may be, for example, to ensure that adequate preliminaries and signal-to-noise ratio are present in preliminary proper behavior [49].
– During the data gathering, we gained extreme muscle action which muddied our results. Subjects also had to stay as silent as possible and to wince as sparingly as possible [1].
– The skull passes on like a minimal-pass network and defects the fundamental electrical activity of the brain over a vast scalp region. In addition, the scenarios reported on the scalp are expected to be generated by multiple groups of cerebral and post-cortical producers distributed over a reasonably large region [46].
– It is difficult to distribute with EEG report bits which are devalued by motor skill motions or eye blinks accompanying data processing because the EEG signal is of very low intensity as these motor skill gestures appear to overwhelm the EEG signal [35].
– EEG needs intensive analysis only to speculate what regions are implemented by a particular reaction, because EEG reveals very poor cortical temporal resolution [41].

5.2 Organizational Challenges:

- This took a considerable amount of time to start the test, as the system required a complex configuration of multiple electrodes across the head using different gels.
- Because the number of individuals who participated in the project is quite small and is restricted to participants at Innopolis University, a very minimal amount of data has been obtained. It results in the study findings being of no statistical significance. There are no publicly accessible databases which can be included in our experiments.
- Similar to the above, the limited number of individuals does not provide a credible assurance that all people will obtain confirmation of the results. Since only male students were tested, the results can be biased.
- The EEG machine itself is extremely susceptible to ambient noise, and needs to be adjusted very carefully. The good results are obtained once the subject of the study is not shifting, is not communicating and there is no electrification. But in real life and in the circumstances of our study design, those requirements are not achievable.
- Students in the study have not undergone a formal medical assessment, and most of them will have concealed issues with the blood flow, brain, and other irregularities that may affect EEG scan tests. Many anatomical characteristics can also add prejudice, such as long hair.
- During the test, the atmosphere could influence the results, too. The light may be too intense for example, or the activity around the subject. Therefore the setting for the study should be carefully constructed to remove external variables that can influence the signals from the samples collected.
- This is also an observational analysis, a summer internship, with the goal of deciding if the work will go forward. As such, it does not have the purpose or the potential of making a definite statement on whether computing with music or with pair programming produces different impacts in developers' brains that can be identified using EEG tools.

6 Conclusion and Future Research

The utilization of biological signs to break down engineers' activities and yield is getting perpetually normal. The findings correlated with brain function are of special interest as they can measure the response to various stimuli which are not readily identified by the human eye. Students in this internship have studied EEG approach to evaluate people's job programming with (without) music and in pair programming. We may reason that the EEG approach is feasible to the end of our expectations and it helped us to see the effect of the programming circumstances on cerebrum behavior. EEG designs for programming with (without) music and during pair programming are distinctive. The actual meaning of such cases is not well known. Further studies are expected to support the effect of music and pair programming on mind movement all the more probable.

Thus from the internship, the extent of further work was recognized, a convention for the investigation was grown, new apparatuses, settings, and issues were introduced. Playing out the analysis for a bigger scope may prompt better outcomes and open new territories of enthusiasm for considering designers' profile signals. To summarize, contingent upon all the results, our future research will be founded on progressively engaged analyses with specific programming circumstances utilizing bigger understudy informational collections and afterward, actually, endeavoring to move our assessment to the business. Future work would be directed in understanding better also specific application domains that are particularly important, such as mobile systems [5–8] and open source systems [11,18,24,29,34], and in applying techniques from machine learning and computational intelligence [28].

Acknowledgment. We thank Innopolis University for generously supporting this research.

References

1. Bell, M.A., Cuevas, K.: Using EEG to study cognitive development: issues and practices. J. Cogn. Dev. **13**(3), 281–294 (2012)
2. Busechian, S., et al.: Understanding the impact of pair programming on the minds of developers. In: 2018 IEEE/ACM 40th International Conference on Software Engineering: New Ideas and Emerging Technologies Results (ICSE-NIER), pp. 85–88. IEEE (2018)
3. Clark, J., et al.: Selecting components in large cots repositories. J. Syst. Softw. **73**(2), 323–331 (2004)
4. Coman, I.D., Robillard, P.N., Sillitti, A., Succi, G.: Cooperation, collaboration and pair-programming: field studies on backup behavior. J. Syst. Softw. **91**, 124–134 (2014)
5. Corral, L., Georgiev, A.B., Sillitti, A., Succi, G.: A method for characterizing energy consumption in Android smartphones. In: 2nd International Workshop on Green and Sustainable Software (GREENS 2013), pp. 38–45. IEEE, May 2013
6. Corral, L., Georgiev, A.B., Sillitti, A., Succi, G.: Can execution time describe accurately the energy consumption of mobile apps? An experiment in Android. In: Proceedings of the 3rd International Workshop on Green and Sustainable Software, pp. 31–37. ACM (2014)
7. Corral, L., Sillitti, A., Succi, G.: Software assurance practices for mobile applications. Computing **97**(10), 1001–1022 (2015)
8. Corral, L., Sillitti, A., Succi, G., Garibbo, A., Ramella, P.: Evolution of mobile software development from platform-specific to web-based multiplatform paradigm. In: Proceedings of the 10th SIGPLAN Symposium on New Ideas, New Paradigms, and Reflections on Programming and Software, Onward! 2011, pp. 181–183. ACM, New York (2011)
9. Daly, I., et al.: What does clean EEG look like? In: 2012 Annual International Conference of the IEEE Engineering in Medicine and Biology Society, pp. 3963–3966. IEEE (2012)
10. Di Bella, E., Sillitti, A., Succi, G.: A multivariate classification of open source developers. Inf. Sci. **221**, 72–83 (2013)

11. Fitzgerald, B., Kesan, J.P., Russo, B., Shaikh, M., Succi, G.: Adopting Open Source Software: A Practical Guide. The MIT Press, Cambridge (2011)
12. Hyde, K., et al.: The effects of musical training on structural brain development. Ann. N. Y. Acad. Sci. **1169**(1), 182–186 (2009)
13. Ikramov, R., et al.: Initial evaluation of the brain activity under different software development situations. In: SEKE, pp. 741–777 (2019)
14. Janes, A., Succi, G.: Lean Software Development in Action. Springer, Heidelberg (2014). https://doi.org/10.1007/978-3-642-00503-9
15. Jas, M., et al.: A reproducible MEG/EEG group study with the MNE software: recommendations, quality assessments, and good practices. Front. Neurosci. **12**, 530 (2018)
16. Kemp, B., Olivan, J.: European data format 'plus'(EDF+), an EDF alike standard format for the exchange of physiological data. Clin. Neurophysiol. **114**(9), 1755–1761 (2003)
17. Kivi, J., Haydon, D., Hayes, J., Schneider, R., Succi, G.: Extreme programming: a university team design experience. In: 2000 Canadian Conference on Electrical and Computer Engineering. Conference Proceedings. Navigating to a New Era (Cat. No.00TH8492), vol. 2, pp. 816–820, May 2000
18. Kovács, G.L., Drozdik, S., Zuliani, P., Succi, G.: Open source software for the public administration. In: Proceedings of the 6th International Workshop on Computer Science and Information Technologies, October 2004
19. Marino, G., Succi, G.: Data structures for parallel execution of functional languages. In: Odijk, E., Rem, M., Syre, J.-C. (eds.) PARLE 1989. LNCS, vol. 366, pp. 346–356. Springer, Heidelberg (1989). https://doi.org/10.1007/3-540-51285-3_51
20. Maurer, F., Succi, G., Holz, H., Kötting, B., Goldmann, S., Dellen, B.: Software process support over the internet. In: Proceedings of the 21st International Conference on Software Engineering, ICSE 1999, pp. 642–645. ACM, May 1999
21. Moser, R., Pedrycz, W., Succi, G.: A comparative analysis of the efficiency of change metrics and static code attributes for defect prediction. In: Proceedings of the 30th International Conference on Software Engineering, ICSE 2008, pp. 181–190. ACM (2008)
22. Moser, R., Pedrycz, W., Succi, G.: Analysis of the reliability of a subset of change metrics for defect prediction. In: Proceedings of the Second ACM-IEEE International Symposium on Empirical Software Engineering and Measurement, ESEM 2008, pp. 309–311. ACM (2008)
23. Musílek, P., Pedrycz, W., Sun, N., Succi, G.: On the sensitivity of COCOMO II software cost estimation model. In: Proceedings of the 8th International Symposium on Software Metrics, METRICS 2002, pp. 13–20. IEEE Computer Society, June 2002
24. Paulson, J.W., Succi, G., Eberlein, A.: An empirical study of open-source and closed-source software products. IEEE Trans. Softw. Eng. **30**(4), 246–256 (2004)
25. Pauws, S., Bouwhuis, D., Eggen, B.: Programming and enjoying music with your eyes closed. In: Proceedings of the SIGCHI Conference on Human Factors in Computing Systems, pp. 376–383 (2000)
26. Pedrycz, W., Russo, B., Succi, G.: A model of job satisfaction for collaborative development processes. J. Syst. Softw. **84**(5), 739–752 (2011)
27. Pedrycz, W., Russo, B., Succi, G.: Knowledge transfer in system modeling and its realization through an optimal allocation of information granularity. Appl. Soft Comput. **12**(8), 1985–1995 (2012)

28. Pedrycz, W., Succi, G.: Genetic granular classifiers in modeling software quality. J. Syst. Softw. **76**(3), 277–285 (2005)
29. Petrinja, E., Sillitti, A., Succi, G.: Comparing OpenBRR, QSOS, and OMM assessment models. In: Ågerfalk, P., Boldyreff, C., González-Barahona, J.M., Madey, G.R., Noll, J. (eds.) OSS 2010. IAICT, vol. 319, pp. 224–238. Springer, Heidelberg (2010). https://doi.org/10.1007/978-3-642-13244-5_18
30. Pfurtscheller, G., Da Silva, F.L.: Event-related EEG/MEG synchronization and desynchronization: basic principles. Clin. Neurophysiol. **110**(11), 1842–1857 (1999)
31. Puce, A., Hämäläinen, M.S.: A review of issues related to data acquisition and analysis in EEG/MEG studies. Brain Sci. **7**(6), 58 (2017)
32. Ronchetti, M., Succi, G., Pedrycz, W., Russo, B.: Early estimation of software size in object-oriented environments a case study in a CMM level 3 software firm. Inf. Sci. **176**(5), 475–489 (2006)
33. Rossi, B., Russo, B., Succi, G.: Modelling failures occurrences of open source software with reliability growth. In: Ågerfalk, P., Boldyreff, C., González-Barahona, J.M., Madey, G.R., Noll, J. (eds.) OSS 2010. IAICT, vol. 319, pp. 268–280. Springer, Heidelberg (2010). https://doi.org/10.1007/978-3-642-13244-5_21
34. Rossi, B., Russo, B., Succi, G.: Adoption of free/libre open source software in public organizations: factors of impact. Inf. Technol. People **25**(2), 156–187 (2012)
35. Schlögl, A., Slater, M., Pfurtscheller, G.: Presence research and EEG. In: Proceedings of the 5th International Workshop on Presence, vol. 1, pp. 9–11 (2002)
36. Scotto, M., Sillitti, A., Succi, G., Vernazza, T.: A relational approach to software metrics. In: Proceedings of the 2004 ACM Symposium on Applied Computing, SAC 2004, pp. 1536–1540. ACM (2004)
37. Scotto, M., Sillitti, A., Succi, G., Vernazza, T.: A non-invasive approach to product metrics collection. J. Syst. Architect. **52**(11), 668–675 (2006)
38. Sillitti, A., Janes, A., Succi, G., Vernazza, T.: Measures for mobile users: an architecture. J. Syst. Architect. **50**(7), 393–405 (2004)
39. Sillitti, A., Succi, G., Vlasenko, J.: Understanding the impact of pair programming on developers attention: a case study on a large industrial experimentation. In: Proceedings of the 34th International Conference on Software Engineering, ICSE 2012, pp. 1094–1101. IEEE Press, Piscataway, June 2012
40. Sillitti, A., Vernazza, T., Succi, G.: Service oriented programming: a new paradigm of software reuse. In: Gacek, C. (ed.) ICSR 2002. LNCS, vol. 2319, pp. 269–280. Springer, Heidelberg (2002). https://doi.org/10.1007/3-540-46020-9_19
41. Srinivasan, R.: Methods to improve the spatial resolution of EEG. Int. J. Bioelectromagnetism **1**(1), 102–111 (1999)
42. Stoica, P., Moses, R.L., et al.: Spectral analysis of signals (2005)
43. Succi, G., Benedicenti, L., Vernazza, T.: Analysis of the effects of software reuse on customer satisfaction in an RPG environment. IEEE Trans. Softw. Eng. **27**(5), 473–479 (2001)
44. Succi, G., Paulson, J., Eberlein, A.: Preliminary results from an empirical study on the growth of open source and commercial software products. In: EDSER-3 Workshop, pp. 14–15 (2001)
45. Succi, G., Pedrycz, W., Marchesi, M., Williams, L.: Preliminary analysis of the effects of pair programming on job satisfaction. In: Proceedings of the 3rd International Conference on Extreme Programming (XP), pp. 212–215, May 2002

46. Tarasau, H., Thapaliya, A., Zufarova, O.: Problems in experiment with biological signals in software engineering: the case of the EEG. In: Mazzara, M., Bruel, J.-M., Meyer, B., Petrenko, A. (eds.) TOOLS 2019. LNCS, vol. 11771, pp. 81–88. Springer, Cham (2019). https://doi.org/10.1007/978-3-030-29852-4_6

47. Valerio, A., Succi, G., Fenaroli, M.: Domain analysis and framework-based software development. SIGAPP Appl. Comput. Rev. **5**(2), 4–15 (1997)

48. Vernazza, T., Granatella, G., Succi, G., Benedicenti, L., Mintchev, M.: Defining metrics for software components. In: Proceedings of the World Multiconference on Systemics, Cybernetics and Informatics, vol. XI, pp. 16–23, July 2000

49. Wendel, K., et al.: EEG/MEG source imaging: methods, challenges, and open issues. Comput. Intell. Neurosci. **2009** (2009)

A Study of Cooperative Thinking

Paolo Ciancarini[1,2(✉)], Marcello Missiroli[1], and Daniel Russo[3]

[1] University of Bologna, Bologna, Italy
`paolo.ciancarini@unibo.it`
[2] Innopolis University, Innopolis, Russia
[3] University of Aalborg, Aalborg, Denmark

Abstract. Computational Thinking is a competence in computational problem solving. Cooperative Thinking (CooT) is an enhancement of Computational Thinking, supporting team-based computational problem solving. CooT is actually grounded on both Computational Thinking (CT) and Agile Values (AV) competencies, which focus respectively on the individual capability to think in a computational-oriented way (CT), and on the social dimension of software development (AV). However, CooT is not just the sum of CT and AV, rather it is a new overarching competence suitable to deal with complex software engineering problems. Previous papers focused on the conceptualization and the validation of Cooperative Thinking. We now analyze in depth the characteristics and consequences of this construct, with respect to the level of seniority and coding experience. Consequently, we run a Multi–Group Analysis of a representative stratified sample of High–School students, University students, and practitioners, through a Structural Equation Modeling technique. Our goal is to identify if there is a significant difference among groups with respect to the CooT model. Results show that seniority is a significant factor, suggesting as beneficial an early exposure of students to Cooperative Thinking practices.

Keywords: Computational Thinking · Cooperative Thinking · Agile · SEM-PLS

1 Introduction

Cooperative Thinking is an educational construct which enhances Computational Thinking with Agile Values and practices [41]. Since the scope and the tasks solved by software systems are becoming more complex day by the day, Computer Science education should evolve to train new generations of students which are fit to deal with real world complex tasks i.e., *wicked problems*. These problems do not have usually an unique solution but many Pareto-optimal ones [47]. This goal is largely shared also by governments, which recognize *Computer Science (CS) as a "new basic" competency necessary for economic opportunity and social mobility*[1]. This awareness is also shared by the European Commission [15].

---

[1] https://obamawhitehouse.archives.gov/blog/2016/01/30/computer-science-all.

© Springer Nature Switzerland AG 2020
J.-M. Bruel et al. (Eds.): FISEE 2019, LNCS 12271, pp. 279–292, 2020.
https://doi.org/10.1007/978-3-030-57663-9_18

In consideration of the complex nature of the disciplines of Computer Science, critical thinking, as opposed to mere memorization, is a crucial competence for future professionals. Some *ad hoc* teaching practices, such as Cooperative Learning [31] and Problem-based learning [29] do support the development of critical thinking, introducing also organizational and social skills in the pedagogical process.

Several scholars have argued that Computational Thinking (CT) [57] and Agile Values (AV) [5] are both core competencies for software developers. For instance, Denning and Tedri in their recent book [10] argue that two Computational Thinking competencies exist, a basic one for students and an advanced one for ICT professionals. We combine CT and AV into Cooperative Thinking, intended as *the ability to describe, recognize, decompose problems and computationally solve them in teams in a socially sustainable way* [41]. With particular regard to Software Engineering education, CT and AV represent core skills of software development: the individual ability to produce computationally efficient code and the social ability to interact with peers and stakeholders to deliver effective software.

A model of Cooperative Thinking has been recently conceptualized [48]; it was validated through an extensive empirical study [9]. In this paper we build on this research stream in order to explore the pedagogical implications of Cooperative Thinking, digging deeper into the analysis of such a construct.

This paper focuses on the level of seniority of software developers. A typical problem for educators is *when* to introduce new learning frameworks to students, i.e., which is the best age to start? More precisely, we are interested to find out these two issues: i) does seniority have any influence on CooT, and ii) if so, how does seniority influence CooT? This raises the following research question:

RQ$_1$: Does seniority influence the *Cooperative Thinking* model?

In other words, can we affirm that groups of informants with a different level of seniority fit the CooT model in a significant different way? If this is the case, how does seniority influence CooT? Does the model fit improve or decrease with more mature informants? At which education grade should we start implementing the Cooperative Thinking learning framework?

Thus, our second RQ is:

RQ$_2$: How does *Cooperative Thinking* evolve with seniority?

To answer these questions we run a Multi–Group Analysis [50] on Structural Equation Modeling with Partial Least Squares (SEM–PLS) [21]. This technique is grounded in Karl Popper's postpositivist view, according to social observations should be treated as entities like physical phenomena [43].

In order to compute the SEM–PLS model, we surveyed three samples: a representative sample of European K–12 students (lowest seniority), some University students (moderate seniority), and a number of practitioners (highest seniority).

The analysis found significant differences among these groups. Hence, this paper provides the following contributions:

- Segmentation by seniority of the Cooperative Thinking model.
- Evidence of the importance of an early exposure to the Cooperative Thinking learning framework.
- Validation of the Cooperative Thinking construct through Structural Equation Modeling – Partial Least Square Analysis (SEM–PLS).

This paper is organized as follows. In Sect. 2 we present the related literature. Then, we describe our research design in Sect. 3, along with a short explanation of PLS. Afterwards, in Sect. 4 we validate the results obtained with PLS. The analysis of our findings with the study limitations is in Sect. 5. Finally, we outline future works and our conclusions in Sect. 6.

2   Related Work

In 2001 the Agile Manifesto [27] was published, envisioning an alternative approach to the established software practices of the time. The agile vision puts much more emphasis on the social issues when developing some software product. Current agile development models provide opportunities to assess the direction of a project throughout the software lifecycle, focusing on the repetition of abbreviated workflows and stressing the importance of teamwork. This is formalized in a family of related methods such as Scrum [51] and Extreme Programming [4]. The latter work has arguably a more theoretical approach, clearly defining the agile values, practices, and principles that collectively define the Agile movement. In this work, we will collectively refer to them as Agile Values (AV).

A few years later, Jeannette Wing's paper defined the concept of Computational Thinking [57], portrayed as a fundamental skill in *all* fields, not only in Computer Science. It is a way to approach complex problems, breaking them down in smaller ones (decomposition), taking into account how similar problems have been solved (pattern recognition), ignoring irrelevant information (abstraction), and producing a general, deterministic solution (algorithm).

After more than 10 years, the influence of Wing's paper is still strong in the education field. In fact, only recently governments have begun to update school programs including CT elements in every order of schools (in the US, for example [19]). In general, computing education has been too slow moving from pure coding to more general considerations, CT included [24].

On the other hand, for the moment Agile has not had a disruptive effect on education practices. Though universities have started teaching Agile methods [37,45,53], little has been done at the K-12 level, barring a few exceptions [30,38,39]. This is all the more intriguing since K-12 education has already accepted and embraced Cooperative Learning [31], Collaborative Learning [12],

Problem-Based Learning [2], and Project Based Learning [36], even in the specific field of Computer Science [7,13,35,54]. These two teaching strategies focus on social skills and goal-oriented skills, two key elements of the Agile philosophy. Still, AV and CT remained quite unrelated concepts both in general and in Education; in particular, CT has always been considered an individual skill, and taught as such.

From the on-boarding and novice and senior developers performance perspective, literature already provided several different insights such as the role of on-boarding and providing support to new hires [6,32,44,52]. Similar studies have also been conducted in other disciplines [33], providing *ad hoc* on-boarding models [3].

With this paper we do not address the on-boarding process as such. Instead, we want to assess the degree to which the cooperative thinking competence is present among different seniority groups. Nevertheless, the implications of previous research are decisive to frame better pedagogical strategies to support CooT.

This stream of research is based on several research experiments [39,40,42] whose results suggest that effective coding teamwork in educational environments leads to quality software and improved learning outcomes. Nevertheless, good teamwork is not sufficient, *per se*, to solve complex tasks - individual problem solving competencies are also needed. We found that the best outcomes were provided in cases where both such competences (i.e., teamwork and problem solving skills) were effectively implemented [39].

Similarly, there is a growing belief that complex problem solving, critical thinking, creativity, people management, and coordinating with others will become the most important job skills [17]. According to the World Economic Forum, companies will actively search for employees who can master "capacities used to solve novel, ill-defined problems in complex, real-world settings" and "motivate, develop and direct people as they work, identifying the best people for the job, also adjusting actions in relation to others' actions" [17]. So, skills to think in a computational friendly way and to solve them in a social and sustainable manner are both required. Apparently, CT and AV skills are strictly connected for companies, as suggested by the World Economic Forum [17].

3   Research Design

Partial Least Squares Structural Equation Modeling is a *soft theory* statistical approach for the validation of latent variables [49]. It has been used in the first validation study of CooT [9]; we are extending it here with a Multi-Group analysis. This research technique has been already used in Computer Science Education [56], and also by other research communities as a model validation, in Management [28], Information Systems Research [11], and Organizational Behavior [26]. There is a general agreement that "SEM has become *de rigueur* in validating instruments and testing linkages between constructs" [18, p. 6], since it allows to distinguish between measurement and structural models, taking also the measurement error into account.

SEM is based on two different approaches: the first one includes covariance-based techniques (LISREL – CB-SEM); the second one includes variance-based techniques i.e., among which partial least squares (PLS) path modeling is the most used one [25]. So, CB-SEM estimates model parameters to minimize the estimated and sample covariance matrices differences; while PLS-SEM estimates model parameters to maximize the variance of endogenous constructs. Therefore, CB assumes multivariate normality with high sample sizes and PLS works with small sample sizes, since it makes no distributional assumptions. Accordingly, model convergence is in PLS the point at which no substantial difference happens from one iteration to the next one; while in CB it is the increase or decrease in the function value beyond a certain threshold. The PLS technique is used to test relations among variables, maximizing the explained variance of the dependent latent constructs. It offers several advantages compared to CB, beyond those already stressed. Notably for complex models CB seldom converges, especially while dealing with small sample sizes or non-normal data; this is not the case of PLS. Operational Research scholars consider PLS as a "silver bullet" for estimating causal models in many theoretical models and empirical data situations [22].

Data have been collected through a cross-sectional study using a survey. The scale development, as the structural model are taken from [9]. Those items were deeply-rooted in the existing literature and a 7-point Likert scale was used to collect informants statements. For all groups we used the same questionnaire to support construct validity and reliability [55], and allowed us to make trustworthy comparisons between groups.

To define the minimum sample size for a linear multiple regression t–test, which is a good approximation for a PLS analysis, we run an *a priori* power test [16]. In our model we have up to seven predictors for one latent variable (Agile Values). Therefore, considering average effect sizes of 0,15, error probability of 5%, and a Power of 80%, the minimum sample size required to compute the model is 103.

To define the different groups we used a convenience stratified sampling technique. Strata and demographics variables relevant to the context were controlled and represented in Table 1. In total we had 138 respondents, above the minimum power requirement.

Since the aim of this study is to provide a deeper understanding of an already validated model, the basic models assumptions do not change from the work of Ciancarini et al. [9]. Accordingly, we share the same three hypotheses:

H_1: *Computational Thinking positively influences Cooperative Thinking*

H_2: *Agile Values positively influence Cooperative Thinking*

H_3: *Cooperative Thinking positively influences Complex Problem Solving*

The difference will be the degree to which different groups will load on these three hypotheses.

Table 1. Demographics

	%	#
Population		
Grad. & Undergrad. students	44.20%	61
High School students	30.43%	42
Practitioners	25.36%	35

Programming experience		
Less than 1 year	7.97%	11
2-3 years	40.58%	56
4-6 years	22.46%	31
7-10 years	5.07%	7
11-20 years	13.04%	18
21-35 years	7.97%	11
More than 35 years	2.90%	4

Completed software projects		
1	10.14%	14
2-4	38.41%	53
5-10	27.54%	38
11-20	10.87%	15
20+	13.04%	18

Agile methods experience		
No experience	0.00%	0
Beginner or theoretic	30.43%	43
Moderate to expert	69.57%	98

Largest team participated in		
2	3.63%	5
3	4.35%	6
4	10.34%	14
5	27.54%	38
6	37.68%	52
7+	16.67%	23

4   Results

Since the measurement model has been positively validated [9], according to state of the art procedures [21,23], the focus of this paper is on Multi–Group Analysis [50], after a simplified assessment of the structural model. We remind that all measurements are reflective [21]. Our aim here is not to validate the model *per se*, rather to find significant differences among groups. Therefore, we took for granted the theoretical and empirical outcomes of the previous studies. Accordingly, we compute our model with Smart PLS 3.2.7 [46] to estimate the path weighting scheme. The Multi–Group Analysis allows to test if pre-defined data groups have significant differences in their group-specific parameter estimates (e.g., outer weights, outer loadings and path coefficients). Correspondingly, data groups were generated according to the demographics, assigning 1 for K–12 students, 2 for University students, and 3 for practitioners. Finally, we applied also non-parametric bootstrapping with 5000 replications to obtain standard error's estimates [8,14].

4.1   Model Validation

Briefly, we exploit the validity and exploratory power of the structural model proposed in [9]. We assert the robustness of the model based on different statistical parameters. The inner variance inflation factor values (VIF) are below the critical value of 5 to discard redundant inner–model constructs [21]. We see that those values are between 1,05 and 2,03, well below the critical value. Also the path's significance through biased–corrected and accelerated bootstrapping is robust. With a two–tailed test with a significance level of 10% all indicators are within critical values, as we can see from Table 2. So, T–statistics are above 1,96 for all paths and the p–values are below the reference level of 0,1 (for 10% significance), suggesting that all paths in the model are significant. This supports all the three hypotheses H_1, H_2, and H_3.

Likewise, R-square values of the two endogenous variables have a good fit with 0,43 for Cooperative Thinking and 0,083 for Complex Problem Solving. These results are in line with those shown in [9]. Overall, our structural model, represented in Fig. 1, is comparable to previous studies [9]. Thus, we conclude that the model is significant and predicts all tested constructs.

Table 2. Paths coefficients

Paths	Orig. sample	Mean	St. dev.	T	p
AV → CooT	0,540	0,548	0,070	7,722	0,000
CT → CooT	0,214	0,299	0,074	2,874	0,004
CooT → CPS	0,288	0,312	0,074	3,865	0,000

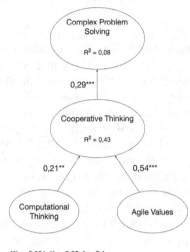

*** $p<0,001$, ** $p<0,05$, * $p<0,1$

Fig. 1. Structural model with Path coefficients and p values

4.2   Multi–Group Analysis

The MGA was run with a percentile bootstrapping of 5000 samples. We used a two tailed test with a significance level of 10%.

The aim is to see if there is a statistically significant difference between the paths of the three groups. So, we compared group–wise GROUP 1 (High School students), GROUP 2 (University students), and GROUP 3 (practitioners). Results are displayed in Table 3.

Table 3. PLS Multi–Group Analysis

Paths	Path Coeff.-diff (1-3)	Path Coeff.-diff (1-2)	Path Coeff.-diff (1-3)	p (1-3)	p (1-2)	p (2-3)
AV → CooT	0,398	0,305	0,093	0,923	0,862	0,780
CT → CooT	0,069	0,048	0,117	0,388	0,468	0,349
CooT → CPS	0,671	0,642	0,028	0,921	0,941	0,649

Interestingly, we notice how several relations are significantly different. In fact, the different groups High School students and practitioners for Agile Values and Cooperative Thinking, as also Cooperative Thinking and Complex Problem Solving, have a p–value above 0,9 (threshold value for 10% significance). Also the two groups High School students and University students are significantly different in the relationships Cooperative Thinking and Complex Problem Solving.

Therefore, these three relationships are statistically different between groups.

To analyze how Cooperative Thinking evolves with seniority, we have to look now at the absolute group–wise path weights. Accordingly, we run the PLS algorithm per data groups to see the different path coefficients per seniority groups. Looking at the results, shown in Table 4, we notice that with respect to the differences between High School students and practitioners, path weighs of practitioners are significantly greater in the model. This means that they fit the model better than students. Similarly, we notice more maturity also in University students, with respect to High School students for the relationship CooT → CPS.

All other relationships are not significantly different, as suggested by the p–values in Table 3.

Table 4. Group paths coefficients

Paths	GROUP 1	GROUP 2	GROUP 3
AV → CooT	0,300	0,605	0,698
CT → CooT	0,288	0,336	0,219
CooT → CPS	0,247	0,396	0,424

Hence, after this analysis we can conclude that the Cooperative Thinking model is empirically grounded, and the model fit improves with seniority.

5 Discussion

A first relevant finding of this paper is the further validation of the structural model of Cooperative Thinking through the positive assessment of H_1, H_2, and H_3.

With reference to our Research Questions, we can answer them both positively, according to these statistical considerations:

- RQ_1: seniority has a significant influence on the Cooperative Thinking model. Our Multi–Group Analysis highlighted a statistically significant difference between groups. In particular, those differences are among novice developers (i.e., GROUP 1) and more senior ones (i.e., GROUP 2, and 3). The p–value (above the threshold value of 0,9) is observed three times.
- RQ_2: the PLS analysis per data groups shows different path coefficients per groups. Therefore, coefficients of more senior developers (i.e., GROUP 2, and 3) are higher with respect to novice ones (i.e., GROUP 1). Accordingly, the Cooperative Thinking model *fits* better with senior developers.

Consistently with our research design, we outline now the educational implications of this study and its limitations.

5.1 Implications

We can affirm that the level of seniority has a significant positive impact on the Cooperative Thinking model. Therefore, the support for an early exposure to the CooT paradigm is the primer implication of this study. Taking for granted the pedagogical value of CooT, we see how non–trained developers perform sub-optimally, with respect to senior ones. We may explain this observation with the fact that the CooT construct is internalized by developers along with their practice, although not specifically trained for.

This aspect is also of great interest, suggesting that CooT is not an artificial construct, but an emerging competence important for every software developer. Accordingly, the attention should be focused on the teaching aspects, to enhance it from the earliest educational stages. Practicing activities related to CooT since High School (or even earlier) may introduce several benefits. The most relevant one regards the ability to work in teams to solve complex problems [17]. Indeed, the CooT model has been designed to specifically address those issues [9].

We are developing an approach to teaching Cooperative Thinking competency exploiting team building and serious games for agile developers; this is the subject of a future report.

The idea that "Groups are better and more efficient that individuals" is supported by both modern educational and organizational theories, but also by common sense. Teaching to teams is more fun and engaging—when properly executed—though arguably more difficult to execute. Moreover, the ultimate goal of developers is to solve new, complex problems, not to reinvent some existing solutions; the link between CoopT and Complex Problem Solving suggests that Cooperative Thinkers are potentially more suited to these tasks. Collaborative tools are also important [1]; most modern tools for software development need people expert in working in team, but these tools are expensive and usually not used by high school or university educators. This lays a heavy burden on educators. CS has traditionally been taught as a strictly individual activity, in general using directed education models. Group interaction only begins once the students starts programming "for real", and social skills inside a development team must be (re)learned from scratch.

5.2 Limitations

We summarize the limitations of this study, as inherent of any scientific investigation [58].

The use of cross–sectional data (i.e., observation of the population through data collection of many subjects at the same point of time) for the empirical assessment of the model has been addressed through a sound theoretical derivation, which is the best way to minimize these limitations [21]. In detail, we based our model on an existing one, already validated in literature.

Our constructs were measured from a subjective perspective through a single–informant approach with a sample size of 138 observations through different European environments to minimize the common method bias [34].

The use of perceptual measures, rather than objective ones, asking students to state their level of agreement on literature–derived items may not fully reflect the real world accurately due to potential respondent bias and random errors. We adapted, for this reason, items from previous studies, to minimize this limitation, following the recommendation of [21].

Sampling technique biases have also been taken into consideration: we used stratified sampling, were strata were defined accordingly to the level of seniority. However, we have to state that our research overlooked non–European countries; this may weaken the generalizability of our results, since the empirical results might not fully represent the constructs elsewhere.

In sum, we consider our limitations acceptable for this exploratory study, since we took several precautions to minimize them.

6   Conclusions

This paper suggests to introduce Cooperative Thinking practices in the early stages of education. This conclusion is supported by a Multi–Group Analysis based on Structural Equation Modeling with Partial Least Squares. Groups were defined per seniority level (High School students, University Students, and practitioners). Indeed, we found several statistically differences within the CooT model, suggesting a better fit of senior informants with respect to novice ones.

Future work will continue to analyze various specific aspects of the emerging Cooperative Thinking construct. Multi Group–Analysis will be performed on the following independent variables: gender, culture, and geographical regions. Moreover, a Finite Mixture Partial Least Squares (FIMIX-PLS) segmentation test will captures heterogeneity by estimating the probabilities of segment memberships, to better understand the construct performance on different segments [20]. We are also planning a similar analysis for the original construct of Computational Thinking. Also, through a controlled experiment we could confirm the findings of this study, using randomized control groups to test whenever treated groups have the same performance of non-treated ones. Finally, the pedagogical perspective of Cooperative Thinking should be fostered through teaching practices and rubrics, to provide teachers with an actionable didactic tool set.

Acknowledgment. This work was partially funded by the Consorzio Interuniversitario Nazionale per l'Informatica (CINI) and by CNR-ISTC. The authors thank all the colleagues who helped us spreading the survey, and the students who answered it.

References

1. Abeti, L., Ciancarini, P., Moretti, R.: Wiki-based requirements management for business process reengineering. In: Proceedings of the ICSE Workshop on Wikis for Software Engineering, pp. 14–24. IEEE Computer Society, Vancouver, May 2009
2. Barrows, H.S.: Problem-based learning in medicine and beyond: a brief overview. New Dir. Teach. Learn. **1996**(68), 3–12 (1996)

3. Bauer, T., Bodner, T., Erdogan, B., Truxillo, D., Tucker, J.: Newcomer adjustment during organizational socialization: a meta-analytic review of antecedents, outcomes, and methods. J. Appl. Psychol. **92**(3), 707 (2007)
4. Beck, K.: Extreme Programming Explained: Embrace Change. Addison-Wesley Professional, Boston (2000)
5. Beck, K., Andres, C.: Extreme Programming Explained: Embrace Change. Addison-Wesley, Boston (2004)
6. Begel, A., Simon, B.: Novice software developers, all over again. In: Proceedings of the Fourth International Workshop on Computing Education Research, pp. 3–14. ACM (2008)
7. Chase, J., Okie, E.: Combining cooperative learning and peer instruction in introductory computer science. In: ACM SIGCSE Bulletin, vol. 32, pp. 372–376. ACM (2000)
8. Chin, W.W.: Issues and opinion on structural equation modeling. MIS Q. **22**(1), vii–xvi (1998)
9. Ciancarini, P., Missiroli, M., Russo, D.: Cooperative thinking: analyzing a new framework for software engineering education. J. Syst. Softw. **157**, 1–12 (2019)
10. Denning, P., Tedre, M.: Computational Thinking. MIT Press, Cambridge (2019)
11. Dibbern, J., Goles, T., Hirschheim, R., Jayatilaka, B.: Information systems outsourcing: a survey and analysis of the literature. ACM SIGMIS Database **35**(4), 6–102 (2004)
12. Dillenbourg, P.: Collaborative learning: cognitive and computational approaches. Advances in Learning and Instruction Series. ERIC (1999)
13. Dillenbourg, P., Järvelä, S., Fischer, F.: Technology-Enhanced Learning. Springer, Heidelberg (2009)
14. Efron, B., Tibshirani, R.J.: An Introduction to the Bootstrap. CRC Press, Boca Raton (1994)
15. EU: Key competences for lifelong learning: European reference framework (2007). http://eur-lex.europa.eu/legal-content/EN/TXT/HTML/?uri=LEGISSUM: c1109
16. Faul, F., Erdfelder, E., Buchner, A., Lang, A.: Statistical power analyses using g* power 3.1: tests for correlation and regression analyses. Behav. Res. Methods **41**(4), 1149–1160 (2009)
17. Forum, W.E.: The future of jobs: employment, skills and workforce strategy for the fourth industrial revolution, January 2016. http://www3.weforum.org/docs/ WEF-Future-of-Jobs.pdf
18. Gefen, D., Straub, D., Boudreau, M.C.: Structural equation modeling and regression: guidelines for research practice. Commun. AIS **4**(1), 7 (2000)
19. Great Schools Partnership: The Glossary of Education Reform - 21st century skills (2016). http://edglossary.org/21st-century-skills/
20. Hahn, C., Johnson, M.D., Herrmann, A., Huber, F., et al.: Capturing customer heterogeneity using a finite mixture PLS approach. Schmalenbach Bus. Rev. **54**(3), 243–269 (2002)
21. Hair, J.F., Hult, G.T., Ringle, C., Sarstedt, M.: A Primer on Partial Least Squares Structural Equation Modeling (PLS-SEM). Sage Publications, New York (2016)
22. Hair, J.F., Ringle, C., Sarstedt, M.: PLS-SEM: indeed a silver bullet. J. Mark. Theory Pract. **19**(2), 139–152 (2011)
23. Hair, J.F., Sarstedt, M., Ringle, C., Gudergan, S.: Advanced Issues in Partial Least Squares Structural Equation Modeling. SAGE Publications, New York (2017)
24. Henderson, P.B.: Ubiquitous computational thinking. Computer **42**(10), 100–102 (2009)

25. Henseler, J., Ringle, C., Sinkovics, R.R.: The use of partial least squares path modeling in international marketing. In: New Challenges to International Marketing, pp. 277–319. Emerald Group Publishing Limited (2009)
26. Higgins, C.A., Duxbury, L.E., Irving, R.H.: Work-family conflict in the dual-career family. Organ. Behav. Hum. Decis. Process. **51**(1), 51–75 (1992)
27. Highsmith, J., Fowler, M.: The agile manifesto. Softw. Dev. Mag. **9**(8), 29–30 (2001)
28. Hulland, J.: Use of partial least squares (PLS) in strategic management research: a review of four recent studies. Strateg. Manag. J. **20**, 195–204 (1999)
29. Hung, W., Jonassen, D.H., Liu, R., et al.: Problem-based learning. Handb. Res. Educ. Commun. Technol. **3**, 485–506 (2008)
30. de Jager, T.W.: Using eduScrum to introduce project-like features in Dutch secondary Computer Science Education (2015). http://dspace.library.uu.nl/handle/1874/307201
31. Johnson, D., et al.: Cooperative learning in the classroom. ERIC (1994)
32. Johnson, M., Senges, M.: Learning to be a programmer in a complex organization: a case study on practice-based learning during the onboarding process at google. J. Workplace Learn. **22**(3), 180–194 (2010)
33. Jones, G.: Socialization tactics, self-efficacy, and newcomers' adjustments to organizations. Acad. Manag. J. **29**(2), 262–279 (1986)
34. Kim, D., Cavusgil, E.: The impact of supply chain integration on brand equity. J. Bus. Ind. Market. **24**(7), 496–505 (2009)
35. Köse, U.: A web based system for project-based learning activities in "web design and programming" course. Procedia-Soc. Behav. Sci. **2**(2), 1174–1184 (2010)
36. Krajcik, J., Blumenfeld, P.: Project-Based Learning. Oxford University Press, Oxford (2006)
37. Kropp, M., Meier, A.: Teaching agile software development at university level: values, management, and craftsmanship. In: Proceedings of the Conference on Software Engineering Education and Training, pp. 179–188. IEEE (2013)
38. Meerbaum-Salant, O., Hazzan, O.: An agile constructionist mentoring methodology for software projects in the high school. ACM Trans. Comput. Educ. **9**(4), 1–29 (2010)
39. Missiroli, M., Russo, D., Ciancarini, P.: Learning agile software development in high school: an investigation. In: Proceedings of the 38th International Conference on Software Engineering, pp. 293–302. ACM (2016)
40. Missiroli, M., Russo, D., Ciancarini, P.: Una didattica agile per la programmazione. Mondo Digitale **15**(64), 1–10 (2016)
41. Missiroli, M., Russo, D., Ciancarini, P.: Cooperative thinking, or: computational thinking meets agile. In: Proceedings of the Software Engineering Education and Training. IEEE (2017)
42. Missiroli, M., Russo, D., Ciancarini, P.: Agile for millennials: a comparative study. In: Proceedings of the 1st International Workshop on Software Engineering Curricula for Millennials, pp. 47–53. IEEE Press (2017)
43. Popper, K.: The Logic of Scientific Discovery. Routledge, Abingdon (2005)
44. de Raadt, M.: A review of Australasian investigations into problem solving and the novice programmer. Comput. Sci. Educ. **17**(3), 201–213 (2007)
45. Rico, D., Sayani, H.: Use of agile methods in software engineering education. In: Agile Conference, AGILE 2009, pp. 174–179. IEEE (2009)
46. Ringle, C., Wende, S., Becker, J.M.: SmartPLS 3. Boenningstedt: SmartPLS GmbH (2015). http://www.smartpls.com

47. Rittel, H.W., Webber, M.M.: 2.3 planning problems are wicked. Polity **4**, 155–169 (1973)
48. Russo, D., Missiroli, M., Ciancarini, P.: A conceptual model for cooperative thinking. In: Proceedings of the 40th International Conference on Software Engineering, pp. 157–158. ACM (2018)
49. Russo, D., Stol, K.J.: Soft theory: a pragmatic alternative to conduct quantitative empirical studies. In: Proceedings of the Joint 7th International Workshop on Conducting Empirical Studies in Industry and 6th International Workshop on Software Engineering Research and Industrial Practice, pp. 30–33. IEEE (2019)
50. Sarstedt, M., Henseler, J., Ringle, C.: Multigroup analysis in partial least squares (PLS) path modeling: alternative methods and empirical results. In: Measurement and Research Methods in International Marketing, pp. 195–218. Emerald Group Publishing Limited (2011)
51. Schwaber, K.: Agile Project Management with Scrum. Microsoft Press (2004)
52. Sharma, G., Stol, K.J.: Exploring onboarding success, organizational fit, and turnover intention of software professionals. J. Syst. Softw. **159**, 110442 (2020)
53. Steghöfer, J.P., Knauss, E., Alégroth, E., Hammouda, I., Burden, H., Ericsson, M.: Teaching Agile: addressing the conflict between project delivery and application of Agile methods. In: Proceedings of the 38th International Conference on Software Engineering Companion, pp. 303–312. ACM (2016)
54. Trytten, D.: Progressing from small group work to cooperative learning: a case study from computer science. In: 29th Annual Frontiers in Education Conference, FIE 11999, vol. 2, pp. 13A4-22. IEEE (1999)
55. Urbach, N., Ahlemann, F.: Structural equation modeling in information systems research using partial least squares. J. Inf. Technol. Theory Appl. **11**(2), 5–40 (2010)
56. Wang, F.H.: On the relationships between behaviors and achievement in technology-mediated flipped classrooms: a two-phase online behavioral PLS-SEM model. Comput. Educ. **142**, 103653 (2019)
57. Wing, J.: Computational thinking. Commun. ACM **49**(3), 33–35 (2006)
58. Wohlin, C., Runeson, P., Höst, M., Ohlsson, M., Regnell, B., Wesslén, A.: Experimentation in Software Engineering. Springer, Heidelberg (2012). https://doi.org/10.1007/978-3-642-29044-2

Tools and Automation

Analysis of Development Tool Usage in Software Engineering Classes

Shokhista Ergasheva, Vladimir Ivanov, Artem Kruglov$^{(\boxtimes)}$, Andrey Sadovykh, Giancarlo Succi, and Evgeny Zouev

Innopolis University, Innopolis, Russia
a.kruglov@innopolis.ru

Abstract. In this paper, the survey, dedicated to the usage of software systems in a software development process, is analysed. The survey was conducted among the students of Innopolis University. Based on the result of the survey, the following conclusions were made: (1) Windows, macOS and Linux-based operating systems have almost equal share of usage among future software developers (2) the most popular IDE is IntelliJ IDEA, however, to the end of the studying process students the diversity of IDEs usage increases (3) the mostly used code management system by far is Github, with almost 100% share (4) Trello and Jira are the most popular project management software for lightweight and complex industrial projects respectively. The obtained results will be used for the prioritization of the development of integration agents for InnoMetrics project, as well as for the adaptation of a studying process in academic institutions to make it more relevant to the given trends and for the market analysis of software engineering environment.

Keywords: Non-invasive measurement · Software engineering · Computer science education · Software system · Operating system · IDE · Project management software

1 Introduction

One of the most important factors in determining system quality is the quality of individual objects composing this software system. Measurement is a mechanism of adaptation and control of the software quality referring to the received feedback from its environment (set of software systems used in a software development process). The feedback taken within the environment is collected as a set of metrics derived from the software development process and software product analysis [40,42]. Moreover, metrics can help uncovering interesting relationships and properties of software systems and the processes used to develop

---

This research project is carried out under the support of the Russian Science Foundation Grant №19-19-00623.

J.-M. Bruel et al. (Eds.): FISEE 2019, LNCS 12271, pp. 295–309, 2020.
https://doi.org/10.1007/978-3-030-57663-9_19

them, as repeatedly confirmed throughout the years [26,27,30,33,37,41,44–47,50,51,56,59–63], also borrowing from models of machine learning and computational intelligence [48].

One of the obvious drawbacks of the process metrics (e.g. active time tracking) is the high overhead that it entails. Developers must switch between development tasks and metric collection tasks, that places a large cognitive burden on developers. To reduce the metrics collection cost, non-invasive way of collecting metrics can be used for the automatic gathering of metrics without requiring personal involvement of a developer. Non-invasive software measurement techniques are emerging as an effective and solid mechanism to collect software measurement data, forming the basis of software process improvement [35].

The InnoMetrics project [9] aims at building and validating a quantitative framework to assess and guide a software development team using a variety of process and product metrics collected non-invasively throughout the life cycle of software systems, from the initial concept to the deployment, execution, and maintenance. The idea is then to deliver a core portion of it as Open Source [34,38,49,52].

Automated In-process Software Engineering Measurement and Analysis systems (AISEMA) are the ones, which collect automatically data from software development process using non-invasive software measurement techniques [28,39,53–55,57]. The data typically represents fine-grained measurements from a software development processes that are collected automatically without intervention from developers. InnoMetrics is an example of an AISEMA system. It allows developers and managers to be aware of the process strength and weaknesses from several perspectives, including energy efficiency assessment, based on the data from the developers' workstations. The crucial insights are visualized with the help of metrics for a dedicated analysis. This system manifests several benefits including real-time process analysis on a daily basis, the system can be customized to different levels of company sizes and audits of software development process. Moreover, the development itself can be monitored at the same time.

The main objectives of the project are the following:

– To identify existing and easily-collectible measures, if possible, in the early phases of software development, for predicting and modeling both the traditional attributes of software systems and attributes specifically related to their efficient use of resources and to create new metrics for such purposes.
– To create ways to collect these measures during the entire lifecycle of a system, using minimally-invasive monitoring of design-time processes, and consolidate them into conceptual frameworks able to support model building by using a variety of approaches, including statistics, data mining and computational intelligence.
– To create models and tools to support design-time evolution of systems based on design-time measures and to empirically validate them. The models will support designers by providing suggestions with the idea of realizing an experience factory based on the analysis of the available measures e.g. by using

a model, which identifies a vulnerability in the source code and suggests the need for refactoring.

2 Methods

In order to achieve the declared goals of the project, the framework for the non-invasive reconstructing and analysis of the development process has to be developed, which consists of:

- agents for collecting data from different OS types and software systems
- models for quantitative and qualitative analysis of the obtained data and further representation of information based on the purpose of the team assessment
- dashboard for the representation of obtained metrics about the development process

There are a number of software systems used in the software development process. In order to maximize the efficiency of the developing InnoMetrics framework, we have to assign priority on agents and data collectors being implemented within the project. Thus a number of questions have to be answered in the context of this research to justify the project strategy:

RQ 1: What is the most popular operating system at the moment?
RQ 2: What are the most popular IDEs?
RQ 3: What are software engineering tools used in a development process?

To answer these questions, the survey among the students of Innopolis University was conducted. Innopolis University is a Russian higher education institution focused on education and research in the field of IT. Students of Innopolis University get modern education and take on independent research projects in the sphere of IT [10]. At the end of their studies, students implement an industrial project, that is counted toward a thesis. Students and academic staff actively cooperate with representatives of the industry. As students and faculty are in close contact with the industry working in collaborative projects, the knowledge on current practice is naturally spread in the Innopolis community. That is why we consider the Innopolis University's students for our research: they combine up-to-date industry approaches and well-proven practices in their software engineering process, so we can assume this study reflects reality to high extend.

The added benefit of the survey is that its results could be used to align the practical part of the curriculum for software engineering courses with current demand from the industry.

The survey was based on a questionnaire, which consists of the following questions (see Table 1).

The 229 students participated in the survey. One of the aims of the survey was to analyze the differences and trends among the different generations of developers. Thus, the 2–4 year bachelor students and 1 year master students took part in the study. The distribution by year of studying is given in Table 2.

Table 1. Questionnaire

#	Question	Options
1	What operating system are you using?	Windows, macOS, Linux
2	What is your preferable IDE?	IntelliJ IDEA, Eclipse, Visual Studio, Android Studio, Xcode, Qt Creator, pyCharm, other (open-ended choice)
3	What tools are you using in the development process	Github, GitLab, BitBucket, YouTrack, Cloudforge, Trello, Jira, Slack, Mural, Toggl, Atom, Asana, Redmine, Mercurial, other (open-ended choice)

Table 2. The distribution by the year of study

Year	Number of students
2 bachelors	129
3 bachelors	47
4 bachelors	27
1 masters	26

3   Results

It has to be mentioned, that the survey was focused on those who study in the Software Engineering program and do not cover students from Data Science, Robotics, and Cyber Security programs [10]. That is because the aim of the survey is to understand trends in general software development avoiding being biased to specific areas of information technologies. That is why there is so great difference in the number of respondents between 2nd and 3rd year bachelors: in Innopolis University the specialization is performed after 2nd year of study. Also, we do not conduct a survey for the 1st year bachelors, since they rarely have any relevant experience in programming at this stage.

For the preferable operating system, the distribution is the following (see Fig. 1, multiple choice was possible): 89 respondents use Windows OS, 63 respondents use macOS, 91 respondents mentioned different Linux-based system, among which the most popular ones are Ubuntu (specified 30 times) and Arch (specified 7 times).

In respect to the year of study distribution the usage of a particular operating system by the students is the following (see Fig. 2)

The most popular IDE, according to the survey (see Fig. 3), is IntelliJ IDEA [11] (161 references). It followed by pyCharm [12] (116 references), Visual Studio [20] (67 references) and Android Studio [1] (34 references). Less popular are Atom [3] (25 references), VS code [21] (19 references), Xcode [23] (14 references), Qt Creator [13] (13 references), Vim [19] (9 references), WebStorm [22] (8 references), Emacs [8] (7 references), Sublime [16] (6 references), Clion [5] (6

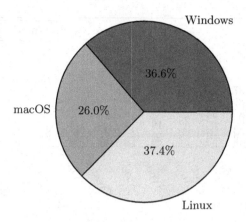

Fig. 1. Usage of the operating systems

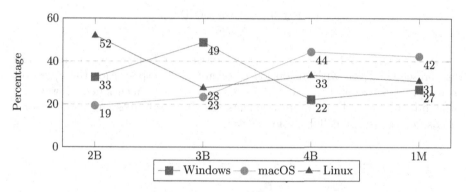

Fig. 2. Usage of operating systems

references). Other IDEs are mentioned 36 times and no one of them mentioned more than two times.

The relative popularity of specific tools, divided by the groups as code management systems (repository + version control software + bug tracker), project management tools, trackers, and corporate messengers is given in Fig. 6, 7, 8 and 9.

The analysis of the most popular IDEs shows the following trend by year (Fig. 4).

In the last category, we did not distinguish the software engineering tools by their purpose. Thus, we have version control systems, project management software, trackers, and other tools in one place, and respondents were free to choose or specify any of them. As a result, the most popular tool in a software development process is Github [6], which is used by almost everyone (213 references). Other popular systems are Trello [18] (129 references), GitLab [7] (103 references), Toggl [17] (62 references) and Slack [15] (58 references). Overall result is shown in Fig. 5.

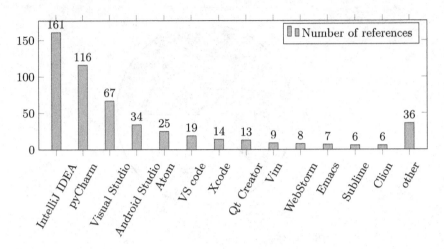

Fig. 3. Usage of the IDEs

In our survey, only one time-tracking software and one corporate messenger are presented. Even with an option of open-ended response for this question, no other tools except Trello and Slack respectively were mentioned. However, it should be mentioned that all respondents used Telegram messenger for personal needs and teamwork collaboration as well.

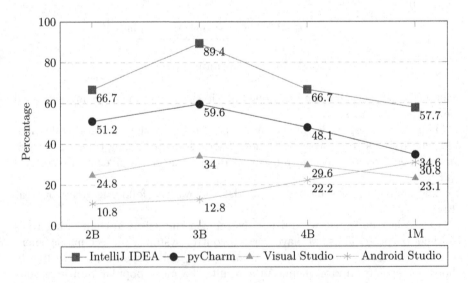

Fig. 4. Relative popularity of the IDEs

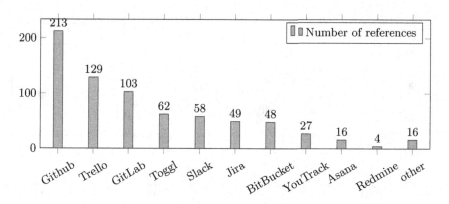

Fig. 5. Usage of the software engineering tools

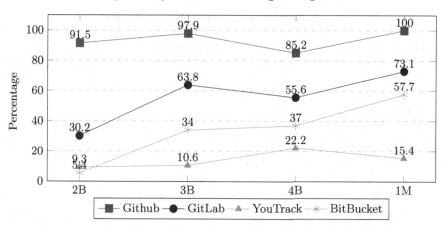

Fig. 6. Relative usage rate of the code management systems

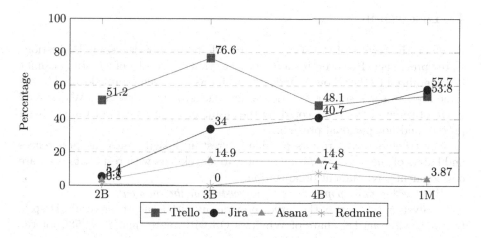

Fig. 7. Relative usage rate of the project management tools

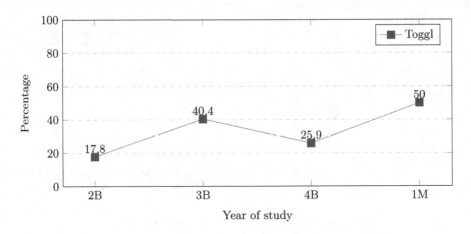

Fig. 8. Relative usage rate of the time tracker

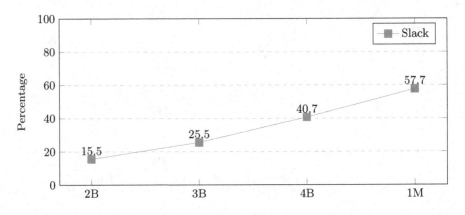

Fig. 9. Relative usage rate of the messenger

4   Discussion

Based on the results of the survey we are able to answer the research questions
stated previously. However, it should be clear that the results of the study cannot
be generalized to the whole IT industry, as far as the given sample located in the
same area and has similar experience and background knowledge. Widespread
usage of some of the tools could be the result of requirements of the studying
process and not personal preferences.

Nevertheless, given results provide interesting insights into the preferences
and habits of the next generation of software developers with respect to software
development environment organization.

What is the most popular operating system at the moment?

Analysis of this part of the survey provides us with a surprising result. Despite
the worldwide market share of Windows OS with more than 77% [58], for the

analyzed group, we have a completely different distribution. For the overall population, we have almost equal shares for Windows and Linux-based systems (Ubuntu, Debian, Arch, Mint, etc.) leaving the Mac system in third place with 26% users.

However, the analysis by the studying year shows that Windows is the less popular operating system for the older students - last year's bachelors and masters. For them, macOS is the most popular system with more than 40%share.

One more interesting fact is that for the new generation (2nd-year bachelors) the most popular are Linux-based systems. The least usage of the Mac system for this year could be explained by the fact that not everyone can afford to purchase Apple products at this stage.

In respect to the InnoMetrics framework, it could be concluded that no one system can be excluded in the data collector development, as far as each of them has a significant share.

What are the most popular IDEs? Even if the preferences of an IDE can be biased due to specific of the study process, we think that, in general, it reflects the actual popularity of the IDEs. Most of the students prefer IntelliJ IDEA with more than a 50% share (up to 89% for 3rd-year bachelors). One important fact that almost no one uses Eclipse, an open source solution and mostly focused on java development as well. According to the worldwide IDEs popularity based on Google searches frequency [25], Eclipse is the second popular IDE after Visual Studio with a decreasing trend (-3.7%). This study can predict a further decline in Eclipse popularity, and it should be taken into account for curriculum updates in Innopolis University, as far as many courses make heavy use of Eclipse in assignments.

For the rest IDEs the most interesting is trend analysis. Thus, pyCharm, having more than 50% share for 2nd and 3rd-year bachelors, decreasing to 34.6% users for master students. That can be the result of software developers' specialization and diversity of applying frameworks. If at the beginning of studying process students are focused on educational tasks and projects, later they meet with industrial projects and such areas as mobile development and cross-platform development [29,31,32].

Thus, with respect to InnoMetrics project, the results of the survey indicate that the development of a plugin for IntelliJ IDEA has the utmost priority. Behind this task, it is much harder to choose one particular framework. We suggest that additional plugins for IDEs should be developed simultaneously to cover most popular programming languages and platforms [43].

What are software engineering tools used in a development process?

Among a huge amount of software engineering tools that can support the software development process within our study, we can derive two primary groups: code management and project management tools. The former related to the organization of a shared repository, version control, and bug tracker functionality, while the letter is about organizing and monitoring development process.

There is one obvious candidate for the code management system - Github. It is used by almost every student in the software engineering course. However, its competitor - GitLab, is also quite popular with increasing share from 30% for the 2nd-year bachelors up to 73% for master students. BitBucket [4] also demonstrate steady growth, starting from 5.4% for 2nd year bachelors up to 57.7% for master students but, in general, it is used much less than GitLab.

Based on the results, GitHub should be considered the top priority for the development of the agents to be integrated into InnoMetrics. Integrating agents with GitLab and BitBucket will cover the majority of developers' activity. YouTrack [24] is the least popular system in this group and its share is relatively small, thus the development of the agent for this system is questionable and should be considered as "could have" but not "must have" feature [36].

The analysis of the survey in the context of project management tools demonstrates that Trello is the most popular task management tool among the students due to its lightweight and intuitive mechanics. More than half of the respondents use this tool in their software development process. By looking at the relative popularity of the project management software (PMS), it can be seen the positive trend of Jira towards the year of study. This tool even competes with Trello in the case of older students - 4th-year bachelors and masters. That could be a result of the increasing complexity of the projects (and development processes) and getting experience in the industry. Thus, this trend could be extrapolated to the graduates - when they will start working in the industry they will prefer one of these two tools with more or less equal probability. Asana [2], being one of the leader in project management tools over the world, demonstrates very low usage rate with only 16 users among all courses which is a quite surprising result. With regard to Redmine [14], it was predictable that this software would be the least popular since it is being displaced from the market by more convenient modern counterparts.

Thus, for InnoMetrics framework the agents for Trello and Jira software should be developed as the ones with the highest usage rate.

Regarding the other tools which were mentioned during the survey, the following facts can be stated. Firstly, it looks like the time tracker Toggl is used mostly due to the requirements of the studying process. Nevertheless, this tool in some aspects could be considered as a competitor for developing InnoMetrics framework - in terms of time tracking of developer's activities. Thus there is no reason to develop the agent for integration with this software. Secondly, for Slack, despite the fact that it is a quite popular tool with a trend on increasing usage rate, the development of the agent is unreasonable. That is due to ambiguous criteria for which activities should be hooked in respect to messenger. It would be more efficient to track time spent in Slack using data collector of the operating system.

One more interesting result of the survey is the level of similarity between 4th-year bachelors and 1st-year master students. In Innopolis University the majority of master students are not graduated bachelors, but those who come from other universities and industry, from different parts of the world. That means, that background of these students is completely different from the one which bachelors have, and it should be reflected in the results of the survey. However, the correlation coefficient between 4th-year bachelors and masters is 0.91, which means that the results of the survey can be extrapolated to other areas despite geography or cultural peculiarities and based only on the experience of the developers.

5   Conclusion

In this paper, an attempt to analyse trends in the usage of certain software systems in a software development process is done. For this purpose the survey among the students of Innopolis University was conducted. The result of the survey provides insights into the most popular tools and frameworks used by the students in their software development process.

This information helps us to form a strategy for InnoMetrics project by assigning a priority to the development of data collectors and agents to external systems. The following decisions were made:

1. Windows, macOS and Linux-based operating systems have an almost equal share of usage, thus data collectors for all three types of systems should be developed. The problem is in the Linux collector development, as far as it is represented by a number of operating systems, among which Ubuntu is the most popular, but Debian, Arch, and Mint also have significant number of users.
2. In respect to the IDE plugins, the most popular one is IntelliJ IDEA, but the trend demonstrates increasing diversity of IDEs usage to the end of education. However, as far as laboratory testing of InnoMetrics is planned to be conducted within the university, it is possible to focus on IntelliJ IDEA, pyCharm, Visual Studio, and Android Studio agents (in this order of priority).
3. In respect to the external software systems, the development team should be focused first of all on Github and GitLab agents to cover code management systems and Trello and Jira for project management tools.

As for the impact on educational process, we can suggest following actions to be taken to make it consistent and align it with up-to-date trends in industry:

1. For any task, students should be provided with cross-platform tools, as far as major operating systems demonstrate equal popularity.
2. For practical tasks, the choice of the IDE and programming language should be provided, at least between Java, Python, and C# (if the particular language is not a subject of the course).
3. In the context of project management tools, students should get experience with both Trello and Jira. For now the former is implicitly promoted in the educational process, while the latter becomes more popular with introducing industrial internship and industrial projects.

We hope, that the result of this study can be useful not only for the InnoMetrics project itself but for analysis and adoption of studying process in Innopolis

University, as well as market analysis and prediction of the upcoming trends in industrial software development.

Acknowledgments. This research project is carried out under the support of the Russian Science Foundation Grant №19-19-00623.

References

1. Android studio. https://developer.android.com/studio. Accessed 25 Mar 2020
2. Asana. https://asana.com/. Accessed 25 Mar 2020
3. Atom text editor. https://atom.io/. Accessed 25 Mar 2020
4. BitBucket. https://bitbucket.org/. Accessed 25 Mar 2020
5. Clion. A cross-platform IDE for C and C++. https://www.jetbrains.com/clion/. Accessed 25 Mar 2020
6. Github. https://github.com/.Accessed 25 Mar 2020
7. GitLab. https://about.gitlab.com/. Accessed 25 Mar 2020
8. GNU Emacs text editor. https://www.gnu.org/software/emacs/. Accessed 25 Mar 2020
9. InnoMetrics project website. https://innometrics.ru/. Accessed 25 Mar 2020
10. Innopolis university. https://university.innopolis.ru/en/about/. Accessed 25 Mar 2020
11. IntelliJ IDEA. https://www.jetbrains.com/idea/. Accessed 25 Mar 2020
12. pyCharm. https://www.jetbrains.com/pycharm/. Accessed 25 Mar 2020
13. Qt Creator. https://www.qt.io/product. Accessed 25 Mar 2020
14. Redmine. https://www.redmine.org/. Accessed 25 Mar 2020
15. Slack. https://slack.com/. Accessed 25 Mar 2020
16. Sublime text editor. https://www.sublimetext.com/. Accessed 25 Mar 2020
17. Toggl - free time tracking software. https://toggl.com/. Accessed 25 Mar 2020
18. Trello. https://trello.com/. Accessed 25 Mar 2020
19. Vim text editor. https://www.vim.org/. Accessed 25 Mar 2020
20. Visual studio. https://visualstudio.microsoft.com/ru/vs/. Accessed 25 Mar 2020
21. Visual studio code. https://code.visualstudio.com/. Accessed 25 Mar 2020
22. WebStorm javascript IDE. https://www.jetbrains.com/webstorm/. Accessed 25 Mar 2020
23. Xcode. https://developer.apple.com/xcode/. Accessed 25 Mar 2020
24. YouTrack. The issue tracker designed for agile software teams. https://www.jetbrains.com/youtrack/. Accessed 25 Mar 2020
25. Carbonnelle, P.: Top IDE index. https://pypl.github.io/IDE.html. Accessed 04 Mar 2020
26. Clark, J., Clarke, C., De Panfilis, S., Granatella, G., Predonzani, P., Sillitti, A., Succi, G., Vernazza, T.: Selecting components in large cots repositories. J. Syst. Softw. **73**(2), 323–331 (2004)
27. Coman, I.D., Robillard, P.N., Sillitti, A., Succi, G.: Cooperation, collaboration and pair-programming: field studies on backup behavior. J. Syst. Softw. **91**, 124–134 (2014)
28. Coman, I.D., Sillitti, A., Succi, G.: A case-study on using an automated in-process software engineering measurement and analysis system in an industrial environment. In: Proceedings of the 31st International Conference on Software Engineering, ICSE 2009, 16–24 May 2009, Vancouver, Canada, pp. 89–99. IEEE (2009)

29. Corral, L., Georgiev, A.B., Sillitti, A., Succi, G.: A method for characterizing energy consumption in android smartphones. In: 2nd International Workshop on Green and Sustainable Software (GREENS 2013), pp. 38–45. IEEE, May 2013

30. Corral, L., Georgiev, A.B., Sillitti, A., Succi, G.: Can execution time describe accurately the energy consumption of mobile apps? an experiment in Android. In: Proceedings of the 3rd International Workshop on Green and Sustainable Software, pp. 31–37. ACM (2014)

31. Corral, L., Sillitti, A., Succi, G.: Software assurance practices for mobile applications. Computing **97**(10), 1001–1022 (2015)

32. Corral, L., Sillitti, A., Succi, G., Garibbo, A., Ramella, P.: Evolution of mobile software development from platform-specific to web-based multiplatform paradigm. In: Proceedings of the 10th SIGPLAN Symposium on New Ideas, New Paradigms, and Reflections on Programming and Software, Onward! 2011, pp. 181–183. ACM, New York (2011)

33. Di Bella, E., Sillitti, A., Succi, G.: A multivariate classification of open source developers. Inf. Sci. **221**, 72–83 (2013)

34. Fitzgerald, B., Kesan, J.P., Russo, B., Shaikh, M., Succi, G.: Adopting Open Source Software: A practical guide. The MIT Press, Cambridge (2011)

35. Janes, A., Succi, G.: Lean software development in action. Lean Software Development in Action, pp. 249–354. Springer, Heidelberg (2014). https://doi.org/10.1007/978-3-642-00503-9_11

36. Khan, J.A., Rehman, I.U., Khan, Y.H., Khan, I.J., Rashid, S.: Comparison of requirement prioritization techniques to find best prioritization technique. Int. J. Mod. Educ. Comput. Sci. **7**(11), 53–59 (2015)

37. Kivi, J., Haydon, D., Hayes, J., Schneider, R., Succi, G.: Extreme programming: a university team design experience. In: Proceedings of the2000 Canadian Conference on Electrical and Computer Engineering. Conference . Navigating to a New Era (Cat. No.00TH8492), vol. 2, pp. 816–820, May 2000

38. Kovács, G.L., Drozdik, S., Zuliani, P., Succi, G.: Open source software for the public administration. In: Proceedings of the 6th International Workshop on Computer Science and Information Technologies, October 2004

39. Marino, G., Succi, G.: Data structures for parallel execution of functional languages. In: Odijk, E., Rem, M., Syre, J.-C. (eds.) PARLE 1989. LNCS, vol. 366, pp. 346–356. Springer, Heidelberg (1989). https://doi.org/10.1007/3-540-51285-3_51

40. Maurer, F., Succi, G., Holz, H., Kötting, B., Goldmann, S., Dellen, B.: Software process support over the internet. In: Proceedings of the 21st International Conference on Software Engineering ICSE 1999, pp. 642–645. ACM, May 1999

41. Moser, R., Pedrycz, W., Succi, G.: A comparative analysis of the efficiency of change metrics and static code attributes for defect prediction. In: Proceedings of the 30th International Conference on Software Engineering ICSE 2008, pp. 181–190. ACM (2008)

42. Moser, R., Pedrycz, W., Succi, G.: Analysis of the reliability of a subset of change metrics for defect prediction. In: Proceedings of the Second ACM-IEEE International Symposium on Empirical Software Engineering and Measurement ESEM 2008, pp. 309–311. ACM (2008)

43. Musienko, Y.: Outstanding devs: top programming languages to learn in 2020. https://merehead.com/blog/most-popular-programming-languages-2020/. Accessed 25 Mar 2020

44. Musílek, P., Pedrycz, W., Sun, N., Succi, G.: On the sensitivity of COCOMO II software cost estimation model. In: Proceedings of the 8th International Symposium on Software Metrics METRICS 2002, pp. 13–20. IEEE Computer Society, June 2002

45. Paulson, J.W., Succi, G., Eberlein, A.: An empirical study of open-source and closed-source software products. IEEE Trans. Softw. Eng. **30**(4), 246–256 (2004)

46. Pedrycz, W., Russo, B., Succi, G.: A model of job satisfaction for collaborative development processes. J. Syst. Softw. **84**(5), 739–752 (2011)

47. Pedrycz, W., Russo, B., Succi, G.: Knowledge transfer in system modeling and its realization through an optimal allocation of information granularity. Appl. Soft Comput. **12**(8), 1985–1995 (2012)

48. Pedrycz, W., Succi, G.: Genetic granular classifiers in modeling software quality. J. Syst. Softw. **76**(3), 277–285 (2005)

49. Petrinja, E., Sillitti, A., Succi, G.: Comparing OpenBRR, QSOS, and OMM assessment models. In: Ågerfalk, P., Boldyreff, C., González-Barahona, J.M., Madey, G.R., Noll, J. (eds.) OSS 2010. IAICT, vol. 319, pp. 224–238. Springer, Heidelberg (2010). https://doi.org/10.1007/978-3-642-13244-5_18

50. Ronchetti, M., Succi, G., Pedrycz, W., Russo, B.: Early estimation of software size in object-oriented environments a case study in a cmm level 3 software firm. Inf. Sci. **176**(5), 475–489 (2006)

51. Rossi, B., Russo, B., Succi, G.: Modelling failures occurrences of open source software with reliability growth. In: Ågerfalk, P., Boldyreff, C., González-Barahona, J.M., Madey, G.R., Noll, J. (eds.) OSS 2010. IAICT, vol. 319, pp. 268–280. Springer, Heidelberg (2010). https://doi.org/10.1007/978-3-642-13244-5_21

52. Rossi, B., Russo, B., Succi, G.: Adoption of free/libre open source software in public organizations: factors of impact. Inf. Technol. People **25**(2), 156–187 (2012)

53. Scotto, M., Sillitti, A., Succi, G., Vernazza, T.: A relational approach to software metrics. In: Proceedings of the 2004 ACM Symposium on Applied Computing SAC 2004, pp. 1536–1540. ACM (2004)

54. Scotto, M., Sillitti, A., Succi, G., Vernazza, T.: A non-invasive approach to product metrics collection. J. Syst. Architect. **52**(11), 668–675 (2006)

55. Sillitti, A., Janes, A., Succi, G., Vernazza, T.: Measures for mobile users: an architecture. J. Syst. Architect. **50**(7), 393–405 (2004)

56. Sillitti, A., Succi, G., Vlasenko, J.: Understanding the impact of pair programming on developers attention: a case study on a large industrial experimentation. In: Proceedings of the 34th International Conference on Software Engineering ICSE 2012, pp. 1094–1101. IEEE Press, Piscataway, June 2012

57. Sillitti, A., Vernazza, T., Succi, G.: Service oriented programming: a new paradigm of software reuse. In: Gacek, C. (ed.) ICSR 2002. LNCS, vol. 2319, pp. 269–280. Springer, Heidelberg (2002). https://doi.org/10.1007/3-540-46020-9_19

58. Statcounter: Desktop operating system market share worldwide. https://gs.statcounter.com/os-market-share/desktop/worldwide. Accessed 25 Mar 2020

59. Succi, G., Benedicenti, L., Vernazza, T.: Analysis of the effects of software reuse on customer satisfaction in an RPG environment. IEEE Trans. Softw. Eng. **27**(5), 473–479 (2001)

60. Succi, G., Paulson, J., Eberlein, A.: Preliminary results from an empirical study on the growth of open source and commercial software products. In: EDSER-3 Workshop, pp. 14–15 (2001)

61. Succi, G., Pedrycz, W., Marchesi, M., Williams, L.: Preliminary analysis of the effects of pair programming on job satisfaction. In: Proceedings of the 3rd International Conference on Extreme Programming (XP), pp. 212–215, May 2002

62. Valerio, A., Succi, G., Fenaroli, M.: Domain analysis and framework-based software development. SIGAPP Appl. Comput. Rev. **5**(2), 4–15 (1997)
63. Vernazza, T., Granatella, G., Succi, G., Benedicenti, L., Mintchev, M.: Defining metrics for software components. In: Proceedings of the World Multiconference on Systemics, Cybernetics and Informatics, vol. XI, pp. 16–23, July 2000

Applying Test-Driven Development for Improved Feedback and Automation of Grading in Academic Courses on Software Development

Dragos Truscan$^{(\boxtimes)}$ ⓘ, Tanwir Ahmad ⓘ, and Cuong Huy Tran ⓘ

Faculty of Science and Engineering, Åbo Akademi University, Turku, Finland
{dragos.truscan,tanwir.ahmad,huy.tran}@abo.fi

Abstract. Grading student assignments and projects in software development courses is a time-consuming task. The lecturer has to download individually each assignment, compile it and manually check that the implementation satisfies the requirements. In addition, the students would like to get early feedback on their solutions, not only as guidelines on whether their solution meets the expectations of the lecturers, but also a way to estimate the current number of points their solution deserves. In this work, we propose the use of the test-driven development process as an approach to both guide the students during the implementation of their projects and as a way to speed up and make the grading process more scalable. Furthermore, we show how we take advantage of community-based software development tools such as GitHub to support our approach. We evaluate the proposed approach by applying it to an academic course for developing web applications. The results show that the approach reduces the grading effort by 60% and that the early feedback it provides was appreciated by students.

Keywords: Test-driven development · Test automation · Academic course · Software development · Course self-evaluation

1 Introduction

Evaluating student projects in academic courses on software development can be a tedious and time-consuming task. In such projects, a software application is typically developed either individually or in groups by students. Lecturers formulate the requirement of the application and then students develop it before the deadline of the task. Then the students submit their project for grading, typically by uploading the project files to a course management system such as Moodle. After the deadline, the lecturers download the project, execute it, and check that the application requirements are satisfied. Then, the lecturers provide feedback for the solution and a grade for the project.

There are two issues with the above approach. First, the students receive feedback and a grade for their project only after the submission deadline and evaluation period needed by the lecturers. Receiving earlier feedback, during the development of the project, would

© Springer Nature Switzerland AG 2020
J.-M. Bruel et al. (Eds.): FISEE 2019, LNCS 12271, pp. 310–323, 2020.
https://doi.org/10.1007/978-3-030-57663-9_20

allow students to evaluate better their work and efforts needed to complete the project. The second issue is related to the time needed by the lecturers to check the project of all the students in the course. For a large number of student projects, it may take several days or weeks before all the submissions are evaluated.

As a concrete example, in a course on developing Web applications at our university, the size of a completed project is between 1500 and 2000 lines of code. On average, grading a project takes around 20 min. The course has a variable number of students each year, ranging between 50 and 100, which can result in a high workload for evaluating all projects and providing feedback by the teaching personnel.

Based on previous experience, following an incremental software development approach for the projects would be beneficial for students in receiving feedback faster, but will increase the amount of work of the lecturers compared to checking the project at the end of the course. This is because the features implemented in past versions have to be rechecked in case they may have been updated. So for every increment of the project more time has to be allocated per student and, in the end, in the last increment the complete project will have to be checked anyway.

Test-driven Development (TDD) is a software development process that promotes the development of software based on short iteration cycles. The starting point is a set of tests that are created, typically from the requirements of the system, before the implementation of the system is available. During each cycle, one or several features of the product are implemented to make one or several of the tests pass. When all the provided tests pass, the development of the software is considered complete.

The proposed approach applies TDD for evaluation and grading of student projects. We create a set of acceptance tests that are provided to students at the beginning of the project. These tests are used as a reference by both the students during the implementation of their projects and by lecturers to evaluate the solutions implemented by students. The approach allows the students to receive continuous feedback during their work on the quality of their solutions and simplifies the grading process by the lecturers. To automate our approach, we use the Github repository hosting service and a set of custom scripts. Using our approach, the lecturers can save time from the grading process and allocate it to providing more in-class feedback during the course.

The work presented in this chapter is an extension of the work published in (Tran, et al. 2020). We extend the previous work with a more thorough introduction of the software development concepts and more details on the approach. Moreover, we provide more details on the case study and its evaluation.

The structure of this chapter is as follows. We start by introducing different concepts of the software engineering field that are relevant for this chapter. Section 3 introduces a generic approach in which TDD is employed for grading student projects and discusses the design decisions and the benefits of the approach. Section 4 presents a case study on how we have applied the approach in practice. We analyze the results in Sect. 5. Finally, we draw conclusions in Sect. 6.

2 Software Development Concepts

Traditionally software is developed in phases starting from the requirements of the application, then its design and implementation. When the implementation is completed, it is tested to see if it satisfies the requirements. In software testing, the implementation (code) is executed with different *test inputs* and the *test outputs* are checked if they correspond to the *expected outputs*. The latter are typically derived from the requirements or specification of the software. Whenever the test outputs correspond to the expected outputs we assign a *passed* verdict to the test, otherwise a *failed* one.

The development phases are typically combined into different software development processes such as waterfall, agile, etc. depending on the characteristics of the application to be developed and of the structure of the development team.

2.1 Test-Driven Development

Originating from Extreme Programming practices, Test-Driven Development (TDD) (Beck 2003) is a software development process that requires tests to be written before the implementation of the code is started. The TDD process is a cycle that is repeated over and over until all the tests pass (Beck 2003), as shown in Fig. 1.

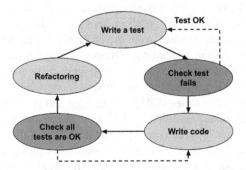

Fig. 1. Test-driven development cycle.

- **Write a test.** Every new feature begins with writing a test. The test should be brief and clearly expressed. Writing a test before the code is implemented motivates the developers to think first about the requirements, the design of the system and the way it should work.
- **Run and check if the test fails.** The test is expected to fail since the application code does not exist yet. This step emphasizes the target feature for the developers. If the test passes, it must be re-written to fail.
- **Write code.** Write just enough production code to fulfill the test. Programmers need to be careful not to implement further than the functionality of the test.
- **Run all tests.** If all tests pass, it means the new code does not break any existing features and the new test is satisfied. If they fail, the new code has to be modified until all tests pass.
- **Refactor code.** In this step, the code is refactored, by cleaning it up, removing duplication, or improving its readability and maintainability. The test cases are re-run frequently to ensure the refactoring code does not alter unrelated features.

The main benefit of TDD is that when writing new code, the test cases can act as a guideline, so the developers can conveniently follow, resting assured that they are on track and no feature's specification is missing IBM (n.d.). Additionally, by running tests throughout the development process, feedback is given regularly and no code left untested. Moreover, developers spend less time on debugging and fixing errors. Although TDD is not a miracle solution to eliminate all bugs, more tests mean better code coverage, and that will reduce the cost of maintenance and a large number of bugs IBM (n.d.). Combined with a version control system, when a test fails, TDD helps to identify the error quickly and more productively. TDD can also lead to more clean, modularized, and extensible code because of the constant refactoring. The code is tidier, well documented, which allows other team members to understand it. This makes the application under development more suitable for future enhancement or expansion.

TDD also has some limitations. Different authors report that TDD's slow learning curve makes it difficult to adopt. In addition, the final product may be too biased by the way the tests were created and the requirements provided may not be complete or well-specified. Furthermore, if the project specifications and requirements are not studied and analyzed well enough, passing tests could cause a false sense of safety. Due to the nature of TDD, it has a long learning curve. Additionally, writing and maintaining an overwhelming number of tests costs time and resources, particularly for small teams. It takes approximately as much as 16% more development time than that of the traditional approach where tests are created after the implementation is completed (George and Williams 2004).

2.2 Software Version Control System

A version control system (VCS) (Spinellis 2005) is a tool that helps developers to manage changes to source code over time so that they can recall them later if needed. VCS keeps track of every modification from add or edit to move or delete in a special kind of database. The types of file VCS can track are not only source code, but also images, audio files, movies, or any other type of digital asset.

For almost all software projects, the source code is the most critical central part, and the teams are responsible for protecting it. A VCS, which is updated frequently during the development, can also act as a backup storage. If some files are lost due to accidents or human error, the team can quickly recover them from VCS.

There are two popular types of version control systems: centralized and distributed. Centralized version control systems store all files and the full version history in one shared server. The developers retrieve some of the source files from the central location, modify it and store it back to the central location. In contrast, in distributed VCSs, the developers completely mirror the project or repository, including the full version history. Then they make changes locally to the files and submit them later to the centralized location.

Git is one of the most popular open-source versioning control systems and several deployment servers are available for public use. For instance, *github.com* is a Git repository hosting service where developers can version and share their software. It provides services for both public and private repositories. It offers several additional functionalities, such issue tracking system, wiki pages, etc.

One interesting feature of github.com is that it is free to use for educational purposes via the GitHub Classroom initiative. GitHub Classroom allows lecturers to create assignments for which students submit code via the VCS, track student progress, and integrate with useful third-party tools. It also scales up for courses with a large number of students.

3 Approach

The proposed solution is to apply the concepts of TDD to evaluating and grading student projects. We provide students with a set of acceptance tests at the beginning of the project to be used as a reference by both the students during the development of the project and by lecturers to evaluate and grade the project after the deadline. The students are not allowed to modify the provided acceptance tests, but they can add additional tests if they consider them helpful for their implementation.

The approach is illustrated in Fig. 2. The requirements of the project are first specified. Then, the lecturers implement a reference project (similar to the one expected to be delivered by students). The set of tests is created from the requirements of the project by the lecturers. However, in order to execute the tests against the implementations created by the students, lecturers need to decide and clearly specify the interface of the application in advance. The tests are executed to verify the implementation of the project. This is an iterative process which ends when tests for all requirements have been implemented.

The requirements specification, interface specification and the tests are used to create a GitHub Classroom assignment. The assignment link is provided to students. Whenever a student accesses the link, a new source code repository is automatically created on GitHub, to which both the student and the lecturers of the course have access. If a starter code is provided in the initial assignment repository, it will be copied to the newly created student repository. When students download (clone) their assignment repository to their computer, they receive a copy of the started code, including the tests, and they can start the implementation of their projects.

The first time the tests are run against the project they will all fail since the project is not yet implemented. The students will proceed with developing their project and can run the tests regularly. As more features are implemented, the tests will start passing. The tests serve as self-evaluation to the students on the progress of their project. At the same time, the students should push their project regularly to the repository for versioning and backing up the code.

When the deadline of the project is over, the code is already available in the repository and the lecturers can evaluate the projects by pulling all student projects from their corresponding repositories and running the tests to check the progress and the completeness of the projects. In our approach, the last two activities are performed automatically using a set of scripts and the Application Programming Interface (API) of GitHub.

When the deadline of the project is over, the code is already available in the repository. Lecturers can pull students' projects and run acceptance tests to evaluate their progress and completeness. In our approach, pulling and running tests are performed automatically using a set of scripts and the Application Programming Interface (API) of GitHub. Based

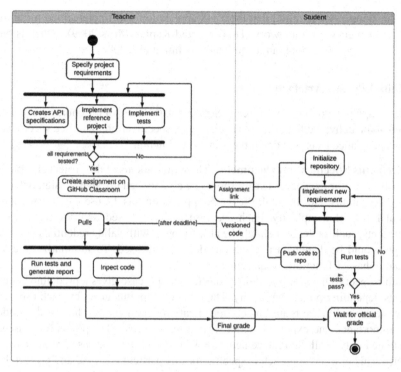

Fig. 2. Workflow of the proposed approach

on the result of the tests, lecturers can create an overview report including the grades. Manual inspection of the code can still take place if lecturers consider it necessary.

4 Case Study

As an example of our approach, we show how we have applied it in practice in an academic course on the development of web applications. In this course, the students have to develop a web application, called YaaS (Yet Another Application) similar to ebay.com, in which different users (sellers) can create auctions to sell products, whereas other users (buyers) can make bids on ing auctions. When the deadline for a given bid passes, the auction is adjudicated to the highest bidder and the seller, buyer and other bidders are notified.

A Web Application is a computer program that provides dynamically created content to be displayed in a web browser (Shklar and Rosen 2003). The information between the client (i.e., the web browser) and the server is exchanged via the HyperText Transfer Protocol (HTTP) (Fielding and Reschke 2014). HTTP is a stateless request/response protocol. In a typical interaction, the client submits a request to a server, the server processes the request and returns a response to the client, most often formatted using the HyperText Markup Language (HTML) (Krause 2016).

In this course, we required that the YaaS application was implemented by students using the Django Web framework (Holovaty and Kaplan-Moss 2009), which is based on the Python programming language (van Rossum et al. 2008).

4.1 Initial Project Artefacts

In order to apply the process proposed in Sect. 3, the lecturers of the course created three artefacts to be delivered to students: requirements specification, interface specification, and the acceptance tests. We detail them in the following.

Requirements Specification Document. The requirements of the project are specified using use cases, for instance, the user should be able to sign up, sign in, sign out, create items, delete items, etc. In total, the YaaS application has 12 use cases, each having different levels of complexity. Each use case is decomposed into several functional requirements, such as the user should be able to log in with valid credentials or an error message should be displayed if invalid credentials are used. To summarize, the YaaS application has 41 functional requirements.

With respect to the grading of the project, each use case gives a predefined number of points depending on its complexity. The number of points given by each use case is clearly mentioned in the requirements specification document as a hint to the students on the importance and expected complexity of the use case. The points for a use case are obtained only if all the requirements associated with the use case are implemented correctly. This grading approach is specific for this particular course and project, but it can be customized in other courses.

Interface Specification. An interface specification is created to reflect all the requirements of every use case in terms of the interface of the application. The interface specification file describes what are the URLs used by each user case, what HTTP requests can be sent to those URLs, what parameters they require, and what is the expected response. An example of interface specification for use case UC1-Create user account is given in the following Table 1.

Acceptance Tests. In order to verify that different project requirements are implemented successfully by students, we create one or several tests for each requirement. Since each requirement belongs to one use case, we group the tests belonging to requirements of the same use case under one test case (see Fig. 6). The tests are implemented based on the given interface specification. For convenience we have implemented them in the Python programming language, using the Python unit testing library. However, other programming languages can be considered because the application interface is clearly specified and the acceptance tests are not dependent on the programming language used for the implementation of the application.

For instance, use case UC1 has five requirements. One of the tests for one of the requirements is shown in Fig. 3 as a test method. The test verifies requirements REQ 1.1 (lines 2–3) by sending an HTTP POST request to the signup/URL (line 9) and providing a set of parameters via the context variable defined at lines 4–8. The test expects (line 10) that the application will return an HTTP response message with status code 302, in which case the test will be marked as PASS otherwise as FAIL.

Table 1. Example of interface specification for UC1

Use case	UC1 - Create a user account
URI	/signup/
Allowed HTTP methods	GET – get a signup form, return code 200 POST – create a user with username and password • Sign up without a password, means invalid data, return status code 200 • Sign up with an already taken username, return status code 400, and an error message is present in the response content (HTML) • Sign up with an already taken email, return status code 400, and an error message is present in the response content (HTML) • Sign up with valid data, return status code 302 because the page would redirect to the index page after a successful signup
Example request:	HTTP1.1 POST/signup

Example expected response:	HTTP1.1 302 Redirect
	{
	"username": "user1",
	"password": "Password1",
	"password1": "Password1",
	"password2": "Password1",
	"email": "user1@mail.com"
	}

```
1    def test_sign_up_with_valid_data(self):
2    # REQ1.1 Sign up with valid username, password and
3    password confirmation, should return status code 302
4        context = {
5            "username": "testUser3",
6            "password": "!@ComplicatedPassword123",
7            "email": "user1@mail.com"
8        }
9        response = self.client.post("signup/", context)
10       self.assertEqual(response.status_code, 302)
11       # calculate points
12       self.class.number_of_passed_tests += 1
```

Fig. 3. Example of a test of requirement REQ 1.1

When the test is successful (PASS verdict), line 12 will be executed and the number of points scored by the entire project will be increased by 1.

4.2 Support for Automatic Grading

Every test case corresponding to a use case has some class-level variables to track and show the number of tests, passed tests, and points of the test case, as shown in Fig. 4.

```
1   number_of_passed_tests = 0 # passed tests in this test case
2   tests_amount = 5 # number of tests in this suit
3   points = 1 # points granted by this use case if all test pass
```

Fig. 4. Example of points awarded for a given use case

When a test case completes its execution, a global method is invoked to calculate points aggregated from the individual tests. The method in Fig. 5 checks if all tests of the test case are passed (line 3). If there is a failed test, the system will prompt a failure message (line 4). Otherwise, the method adds the points of this use case to the total number of points of the project (line 6–7) and the system will print a success message (line 11) to the user.

```
1    def calculate_points(number_of_passed_tests, amount_of_tests,
2                          points_of_the_use_case, use_case_name):
3        if number_of_passed_tests < amount_of_tests:
4            print("{} fails!".format(use_case_name))
5        else:
6            global current_points
7            current_points += points_of_the_use_case
8            msg = """{} passed, {} points,
9                Current points: {}/30""".format(use_case_name,
10               points_of_the_use_case, current_points)
11           print(msg)
```

Fig. 5. Code for calculating the points of the project

4.3 Feedback to Students

During the course, the students receive three types of feedback:

- From the execution of the acceptance tests, students receive feedback when a feature is implemented or not (if its tests pass or not). In addition, we have tried to implement the tests to provide informative error messages. As mentioned in the paper, after each execution of the tests, the students get an automated evaluation of the grade of the project. This is a continuous process.
- Throughout the course, during lectures and labs, the students can ask questions on different aspects related to the teaching material, coding practice or the project implementation from course assistants and lecturers. This is also a continuous process.
- When their project is evaluated, besides checking the project with automated tests, the lecturers also inspect the code and provide the final feedback on the project.

In the following, we will focus on the first type of feedback that is an outcome of our proposed method.

At the beginning of the project implementation, all acceptance tests will fail, since no implementation is yet available. A simplified example of a test report where all the tests fail is shown in Fig. 6.

By having the acceptance tests readily available, the students can check at any moment the status of their implementation. After each execution of the acceptance tests,

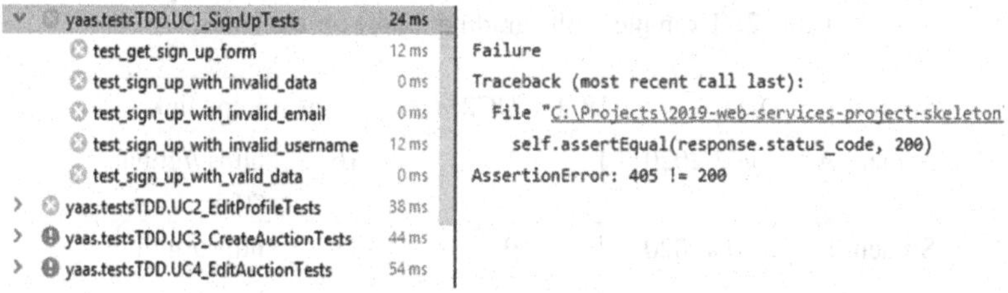

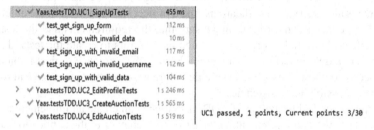

Fig. 6. Example of failed tests.

a report will show what tests have failed or passed and how many points a project has currently earned. Students can inspect the test failure in more detail. Figure 7 shows the test report for the same tests as in Fig. 6, when the functionality of the web application satisfies the requirements of the project.

Fig. 7. Example of passed tests.

The students should frequently commit their projects to the GitHub for backup and versioning purposes. When the deadline for project submission has passed, the latest version in the repository will be considered for grading.

4.4 Support for Automatic Grading by Lecturers

In order to automate the grading process, a set of scripts has been implemented to automate different steps performed by the lecturers. The scripts, written in Python, use the GitHub API to download all student projects from GitHub Classroom and store them in a local folder. Then, they execute the tests on each project and save the test report results in a grading report file with the structure presented in Table 2. For each student, the report includes: name of the student, date of running the script, points received by each use case, the total number of points earned by the student, and the link to the repository of the project.

These scripts can be run not only at the end of the course after the deadline for project submission has passed, but also regularly (e.g., weekly) to check the progress of the students during the course. This allows them to provide additional support or change the pace of the lectures according to the needs of the students.

Table 2. Example of the grading report for the course

Student	Date	UC1	UC2	...	Total	Repo link
Student A	25/03/2020	1	1	...	16	https://github.com/...
Student B	25/03/2020	1	0	...	18	https://github.com/...
Student C	25/03/2020	0	1	...	15	https://github.com/...

5   Discussion and Evaluation

As discussed earlier in this work, TDD brings some benefits but it may also have some limitations. In order to cope with the slow learning curve, we have provided detailed requirements and interface specifications, and a project skeleton to facilitate quick adoption of TDD concepts. In order to make sure that the requirements and the tests were well-specified, the initial effort was allocated by lecturers to create the tests, the reference project, and the interface specification. Having the reference project implemented in advance, also allowed us to make sure that all requirements are testable and to detect and remove possible inconsistencies.

Another perceived limitation of TDD, is that one can create an implementation that passes the tests without implementing the expected behavior of the application and thus providing a false level of confidence. In our approach, this risk is reduced by the way the tests were designed. Some tests were inherently dependent on each other and sharing data. For instance, one test checked if the user can create an account, another test checked if the user can log in with the specified account which should have been created by the previous tests. This is not a complete bullet-proof approach, and for that reason, the lecturers also inspect the code manually to detect possible problems practices.

Additional effort has been required to specify the application interface, but this was a tradeoff for having automated tests for the project. When creating the interface several design decisions had to be made which limited the implementation freedom of the students, in our opinion, but that was an acceptable compromise and we consider that it still satisfied the learning objectives of the course.

For the YaaS application, we have implemented 41 tests in total. We have evaluated the approach in one edition of the course in which 60 students submitted projects. After the deadline, we were able to run the automated tests on all 60 projects submitted by students in around 110 min on a Windows 10 laptop featuring an Intel i7-7500U CPU with two cores at 2.90 GHz and 16 GB of RAM. This means less than two minutes per project. Roughly 5 min of additional time was allocated on average for manual code inspection. This activity was largely performed for giving feedback and recommendations to the students. Overall, we have observed a reduction of more than 65% in the grading time.

The submitted student projects, which received the highest grade, had more than 90% of the project requirements implemented and between 1490 and 2050 lines of code. The acceptance tests we provided achieve between 77% and 91% coverage of the source code, which shows that the acceptance tests give a good metric for the overall quality of the project.

The feedback from the students, collected via interviews and course feedback forms, was in general positive. Most of them liked the approach and considered useful to have the acceptance tests available from the beginning. In addition, they appreciated not only the fact that they could estimate the grade in advance, but they can also utilize the tests as guidelines during the development of their project. However, there were some students that considered that the TDD approach and the use of GitHub for versioning required a different mindset and new technical skills. Nonetheless, we consider that these technical skills are useful and mandatory for any computer engineering student.

Based on this preliminary evaluation, we plan to re-apply the approach in the next editions of the course and, in addition, to extend it to other software development courses at our university.

6   Related Work

Automatic grading of assignments is not a novel topic and several researchers have already addressed this topic in the past with similar approaches.

Edwards (2003a, b) presents his vision and tool support for automatic grading in which TDD should be used in all programming assignments starting from the first year of the Computer Science education. Differently from our approach, Edwards suggests that the students are required to create their own tests to accompany the code that they write, and these tests are evaluated against a reference implementation. Similar to our approach, he proposes an automated assessment tool to which the students submit their code, with the difference the tool is assessing both the correctness of the student tests and of the application. In addition, the tool provides static checks and feedback on the coding style which in our approach is performed manually in class and at the end of the course.

Janzen and Saiedian (Janzen and Saiedian 2006) propose *test-driven learning* as a way of using TDD for teaching both testing and programming. In practice, they suggest that different programming examples and small assignments are accompanied by tests (*assert* statements) that would indicate to students both the expected interface and the expected behavior of the program. The main benefits perceived from their approach is that they can improve the teaching of programming via examples accompanied by tests. Differently from their approach, the goal of our work is automated acceptance testing of student programming projects as a way of guiding the students during their work.

Pilla (Pilla 2017) utilized GitHub and Travis CI, a continuous integration (CI) service that integrates with GitHub, to build an automatic testing environment for students. Although the work was conducted on some simple C-code assignments, the preliminary results showed great potential. Comparably, Cai and Tsai (Cai and Tsai 2019) applied a similar solution to an Android application development course with improved security.

However, neither of them used a starter repository in their solution. Our approach is also different from theirs because we follow TDD to create a starter repository. Students should download the repository and start working immediately. We do not use any continuous integration (CI) service; instead, we have implemented our approach to automatically download student projects, grade them and generate a detailed course-level report. From our experience, a continuous integration does not provide a global view on all student repositories, and it requires students to commit code frequently to be relevant. With our approach, we can retrieve student projects at any time we want and have all the information about those projects in the report. Our approach also allows lecturers to update the starter repository and even student repositories.

7 Conclusions

This chapter introduced an automated approach for evaluating student projects by employing the concepts of the test-driven development approach and by taking advantage of community-based tools such as GitHub. We have applied and evaluated the approach in an academic course on developing web applications. Even though we used a specific development framework in that course such as Django, the approach can be easily adapted and applied with other tools and development environments.

The approach required some extra efforts in the beginning, when creating the tests and the interface specification and developing the scripts used for automatic grading and reporting of all student projects. But these artefacts were created only once and they can be reused in future editions of the course.

Depending on the course settings, the implementation of the reference project can be omitted, which will be in the true spirit of TDD. However, to make sure that the expectations from student projects are realistic we consider it advisable.

The evaluation showed benefits with respect to both the early feedback that the approach provides to students, but also in speeding up the course grading process. The latter makes the approach a good candidate for online courses with a large number of participants.

In future work, we plan to evaluate the approach in future editions of the course and to measure its impact on the grades of the students. To this extent, we plan to run controlled experiments in which a part of the students will use the TDD approach and the other part the manual approach. In addition, we plan to reapply the approach in other courses on software development in order to evaluate its benefits and limitations.

Last but not least, we consider that by having an automatic grading approach, we are not aiming at minimizing the lecturer-student interaction, but by providing clear quantifiable expectations on the course goals and in automating tedious tasks.

Acknowledgements. This work has received partial funding from the Electronic Component Systems for European Leadership Joint Undertaking under grant agreement No 737494. This Joint Undertaking receives support from the European Union's Horizon 2020 research and innovation programme and Sweden, France, Spain, Italy, Finland, the Czech Republic.

References

Beck, K.: Test-Driven Development: By Example. Addison-Wesley, Boston (2003)

Cai, Y.-Z., Tsai, M.-H.: Improving programming education quality with automatic grading system. In: Rønningsbakk, L., Wu, T.-T., Sandnes, F.E., Huang, Y.-M. (eds.) ICITL 2019. LNCS, vol. 11937, pp. 207–215. Springer, Cham (2019). https://doi.org/10.1007/978-3-030-35343-8_22

Tran, C.H., Truscan, D., Ahmad, T.: Applying test-driven development to evaluating student projects. In: 6th International Conference on Higher Education Advances (HEAd'2020) 2020

Edwards, S.: Using test-driven development in the classroom: providing students with automatic, concrete feedback on performance. In: Proceedings of the International Conference on Education and Information Systems: Technologies and Applications EISTA, Vol. 3 (2003a). http://web-cat.org/publications/Edwards-EISTA03.pdf

Edwards, S.H.: Rethinking computer science education from a test-first perspective. In: Companion of the 18th Annual ACM SIGPLAN Conference on Object-Oriented Programming, Systems, Languages, and Applications - OOPSLA 2003 (2003b). https://doi.org/10.1145/949 344.949390

Fielding, R., Reschke, J.: Hypertext transfer protocol (HTTP/1.1): message syntax and routing. RFC 7230 (2014)

George, B., Williams, L.: A Structured Experiment of Test-Driven Development. Inf. Softw. Technol. **46**(5), 337–342 (2004)

Holovaty, A., Kaplan-Moss, J.: The definitive guide to django (2009). https://doi.org/10.1007/978-1-4302-1937-8

IBM. Test-driven development (n.d). https://ibm.com/garage/method/practices/code/practice_test_driven_development/. Accessed 20 Apr 2020

Janzen, D.S., Saiedian, H.: Test-driven learning. In: Proceedings of the 37th SIGCSE Technical Symposium on Computer Science Education - SIGCSE 2006 (2006). https://doi.org/10.1145/1121341.1121419

Krause, J.: HTML: hypertext markup language. Introducing Web Development, pp. 39–63. Apress, Berkeley, CA (2016). https://doi.org/10.1007/978-1-4842-2499-1_3

Pilla, M.L.: Teaching computer architectures through automatically corrected projects: preliminary results. Int. J. Comput. Archit. Educ. **6**(1), 62–67 (2017)

Guido van, R., Hettinger, R., Coghlan, N., Diedrich, J., Beazley, D., Mertz, D.: The python programming language. Prentice Hall Open Source Software Development Series. Prentice Hall PTR (2008)

Shklar, L., Rosen, R.: Web Application Architecture: Principles, Protocols and Practices. Wiley, Hoboken (2003)

Spinellis, D.: Version control systems. IEEE Softw. **22**(5), 108–109 (2005)

Globalization of Education

Internationalization Strategy of Innopolis University

Iouri Kotorov, Yuliya Krasylnykova, Petr Zhdanov$^{(\boxtimes)}$, and Manuel Mazzara

Innopolis University, Innopolis, Republic of Tatarstan, Russian Federation
pe.zhdanov@innopolis.ru

Abstract. Since the establishment of Innopolis University, there was an emphasis placed on the importance of internationalization and international cooperation for its further development, especially in terms of teaching in the English language only, recruiting staff from different cultures and regions of the world, enrollment of students from different countries and educational systems, as well as developing study abroad and joint teaching and research initiatives. Being an English-speaking university in a non-English-speaking country, Innopolis University and its International Relations Office, in particular, as it is responsible for the internationalization strategy of Innopolis University, managed to achieve what might be considered as a significant degree of its internationalization. This paper describes the course of actions taken by Innopolis University towards its internationalization, the strategy adopted and the instruments applied. The definition of internationalization, in general, is briefly discussed and it is suggested that the strategy of internationalization has to be individually considered by every higher education institution as the term is relatively broad. The instruments are described as they were applied by Innopolis University and as they were applied at the time of writing this paper and therefore, there might be certain limitations if adopted.

1   Introduction

Globalization leads to the creation of a unified educational space and market dominated by international rankings where Universities now have to compete [1]. This trend is likely to affect even the countries that are known for their traditional model of cooperation, for example, Nordic European countries [2]. International rankings often become a strategic objective while higher education becomes a global commodity [3]. Russian education has a well-known reputation for its fundamental science, which represents a strong selling point on international markets. In 2012, Russian government proclaimed internationalization as one of the major objectives of higher education development [4] and supported this claim launching the '5top100' project [5] aimed at "maximizing the competitive position of a group of leading Russian universities in the global research and education market." A group of leading Russian universities received additional funding in order to facilitate their international attributes and increase

© Springer Nature Switzerland AG 2020
J.-M. Bruel et al. (Eds.): FISEE 2019, LNCS 12271, pp. 327–340, 2020.
https://doi.org/10.1007/978-3-030-57663-9_21

their positions in the world university rankings (QS World University Rankings, Times Higher Education, Shanghai Ranking of World Universities). A high position of a university in the world university rankings typically means high-quality teaching, research and well-established technological infrastructure. The factors that attract larger flows of best students worldwide [6].

Innopolis University is a young ambitious university located in the Republic of Tatarstan of the Russian Federation. The University is strongly focused on education and scientific research in the fields of IT and robotics. It is located in the founded in 2012 Innopolis City (near the capital city of the Republic of Tatarstan Kazan) which also comprises ICT companies and the Innopolis Special Economic Zone. Innopolis aims to be the major Russian IT hub. In its development, the University is trying to follow the main trends of IT education borrowed from the world's leading higher education institutions. One of these trends is internationalization. In the middle of 2018, the Vice-Rector for Academic Affairs - Head of the Department of Academic Policy and Organization of Educational Activities Sergei Masiagin proclaimed the importance of the internationalization of Innopolis University after securing a solid position and reputation of the University in the Russian Federation. This resulted in a brand new approach to internationalization and the development of a number of innovative solutions.

Historically, universities have always been interested in recruiting students from other countries and even more so today [7], partially as a response to globalization that leads higher education institutions to incorporate 'an international, intercultural or global dimension into the purpose, function or delivery of post-secondary education' [8]. Innopolis University not being an exception since the very foundation tried to attract international students as well as to hunt international faculty members. Additionally, the University has been developing various international initiatives including mobility programs, internships, conferences, etc. Existing for seven years, it could be claimed that the University and its International Relations Office, as it is responsible for the internationalization strategy, succeeded in creating a truly international environment on campus. Besides internationalization at home, Innopolis University considers community building, especially computer science community building, as an integral part of internationalization [9].

In this article, we discuss the internationalization strategy of Innopolis University during its seven years of existence. After this introduction the paper is structured as follows: Sect. 2 (Strategy and Objectives) defines the strategy adopted to reach the objectives of internationalization; Sect. 3 (Instruments) describes the instruments that are used to support the strategy and Sect. 4 (Conclusion) draws some conclusions on the story of the university and the issue of internationalization.

2   Strategy and Objectives

Since the establishment of Innopolis University, there was an emphasis placed on the importance of internationalization and international cooperation for its further development, especially in terms of teaching in the English language only, recruiting staff from different cultures and regions of the world, enrollment of students from different countries and educational systems, as well as developing study abroad and joint teaching and research initiatives. Currently, Innopolis University employs 216 faculty members and research staff from 22 countries and 771 students at undergraduate, graduate and doctoral levels more than 20 per cent of whom are international students.

Many universities across the world claim their 'international' status, but yet there is no agreement on what the internationalization of a higher education institution actually means [10]. In particular, Innopolis University defines its approach to internationalization in line with Knight's [8] definition as 'the international process of integrating an international, intercultural or global dimension into the purpose, functions and delivery of post-secondary education, in order to enhance the quality of education and research for all students and staff, and to make a meaningful contribution to society'. Even though such definition of internationalization is quite popular among higher education institutions, we consider it as relatively wide for our purposes and therefore it can be referred to as an umbrella concept with many different dimensions. That is why to practically use the concept of internationalization, especially in higher education we argue that higher education institutions have to move beyond the umbrella concept and consider application of only certain dimensions of it that we are going to discuss further.

The mission and vision of Innopolis University 'to develop a global university' are supported by its internationalization strategy that aims to increase the international presence across a wide range of activities and to ensure the regarded reputation of the University is maintained and positively developed. It is worth to point out that the growing number of agreements is not an indicator of the internationalization, the viewpoint that is shared by the majority of the partners of Innopolis University, and is definitely not a priority for Innopolis University unlike the high-quality and high level of engagement with partners. As a result Innopolis University conceives increased opportunities for the internationally-minded and mobile academics to conduct internationally co-authored and globally impactful research with a greater propensity for high citation rates, for the internationally engaged and skilled students to be considered highly employable worldwide and for the university to have a world-renowned profile and to attract prominent staff and talented students from all over the world.

Central to the process of the internationalization of Innopolis University is the imperative of developing the University's international profile and promotion of its reputation in education and research as the internationalization strategy is a constituent part of the Innopolis University Strategic Plan 2024. The internationalization strategy of Innopolis University is shaped and informed by the globalization and worldwide interconnectedness within which higher education operates and reflects the understanding of the importance of actively embedding global values into the development of all activities on a 'whole university basis'. The pervasive nature of internationalization is thus embedded across all three main pillars of (1) teaching and learning, (2) research and (3) engagement from the Innopolis University's Strategic Plan. Implementation of the internationalization strategy across the strands is based on the same principles of development, review and enhancement of activities in two distinct domains: 'at home', e.g. internationalization of the curriculum, recruitment of international academic staff and students, integration of international students [10] etc. and 'abroad', e.g. joint ventures with global academic partners, joint research platforms, cotutelles, etc.

Besides being as previously mentioned a constituent part of the Innopolis University Strategic Plan the internationalization strategy integrates with the individual faculty strategies, teaching and learning, research and innovation, external engagement and student experience strategies. Together they form a comprehensive set of mission-driven interventions that support, deepen and enhance the development of Innopolis University during the lifetime of its strategic plan.

The main objectives which Innopolis University seeks to achieve through the next phase of internationalization are to:

1. Advance Innopolis University's leadership in the field of global IT education and improve the visibility and international esteem of the University and its research by reforming academic mobility processes and strengthening and/or expanding partnerships in which Innopolis University has a strategic interest.
2. Deepen and enhance Innopolis University's unique position as the English-speaking IT university in Russia by adding a global intercultural dimension to the University's curriculum and designing study programs offering global labor market-driven expertise and competencies.
3. Internationalize campus, curriculum and services to students and staff to enhance the University's diversity and intercultural understanding by increasing and supporting the number of international students and staff members on campus and by embracing cultural diversity.
4. Facilitate the development of international research projects by building mutually beneficial relationships with key strategic partners and improving national and international cooperation through joint applications and participation in international research projects.

3   Instruments

The internationalization of higher education distinguishes many various strategies and approaches. Committed to its previously described objectives and strategy, Innopolis University uses several instruments in order to promote internationalization, develop intercultural understanding and foster international sensibility. Among them, the following four instruments of internationalization, that include (1) global academic partnerships, (2) international academic mobility, (3) internships, (4) joint research platforms, and (5) cotutelles, are suggested to be essential for the universities that would like to develop and maintain a sustained reputation of an internationally oriented and renowned university. Although these instruments might be of essential value to the internationalization of higher education, it does not mean that the establishment of one of them or even all of them automatically equals the complete internationalization of a university. In other words, the four instruments presented in this paper are merely the means for promoting internationalization and not the goals. As the number of competitors of universities in teaching and research is growing [11], the instruments are supposed to support and develop the knowledge transfer to the students as the initial purpose of universities in which knowledge can be defined as 'information that is relevant, actionable, and based at least partially on experience' [12]. The five instruments discussed in this paper are chosen based on the probability to meet fewer barriers towards the internationalization of the knowledge transfer in human, organizational, strategic and financial dimensions [6].

3.1 Global Academic Partnerships

In higher education, there are several benefits that global partnerships and well-established networks of academic and industry partners can bring to a higher education institute. For instance, a university with a well-established network of academic and industry partners is more likely to achieve a higher position in global rankings as reputation represents a key factor in most of the rankings. What is even more important than the position in rankings, reputation certainly reflects an estimate of the quality of services an institution provides including teaching and learning, research and engagement. Additionally, a network of partners, especially international partners, might serve as a good sign of a significant degree of internationalization of its members. Members of such networks almost automatically are considered as higher education institutes where international students, faculty members, and staff will always receive a warm welcome. Therefore, it could be argued that global academic partnerships developed into established networks of partners may bring not only greater reputation but also recognition through exposure and visibility of its members.

In general, an academic partnership can be defined as a formal collaboration arrangement in which two or more institutions or organizations work together to get mutual benefits in such areas as teaching and learning or research. The activities developed through academic partnerships may include course delivery, course articulation, staff and student mobility, internships, joint research, joint Ph.D. supervision, and many others. In this paper, we understand global academic partnership as the term of the Global Learning Partnership that is successfully used in the healthcare and medicine sectors [13]. As Lees and Webb [13] argue, such partnerships have to have as their goals the intentions not only to create international learning opportunity, develop cultural competence and global-minded workforce, but also to build capacities, create opportunity for academic resource sharing, include students in host countries and create benefits for the bigger community. Using this model it conceives to be easier for the participating institutions to mutually benefit from the global academic partnerships and also to benefit as a partnership entity that builds capacities and expertise in particular aspect of education and international aspect of it that institutions can later capitalize on the global market. The need for global academic partnerships is conceived today even bigger as national economies become more intertwined and increasingly interdependent [11].

To qualitatively improve the internationalization of a university using global academic partnerships a higher education institution though should not only consider establishing the partnerships as such but establishing selection criteria based on which a university will prioritize or choose partners. To ensure the high quality of partnerships, the International Relations Office of Innopolis University selects its partners primarily based on the strategic fit of institutions concerning curricula, research activities, and geographic region. The quality of potential partner institutions is estimated by checking their national and/or international accreditation, research output, and faculty qualification. The geographic area of partners can also play a major role in the partner selection process as geographical proximity can significantly help to develop close cooperation within the framework of a partnership, especially in terms of international academic mobility. Such regionalization or clustering of higher education is an emerging approach that is likely to foster greater regional competition and cooperation across international boundaries [14]. As such, global academic partnerships can bring a significant if not an essential contribution to the development of the internationalization of a higher education institution.

Innopolis University values especially the establishment of high-quality academic partnerships that create routes for international research collaborations, promote international recruitment, provide enhanced student experiences through student mobility, potentially enhance employability prospects, assist in internationalizing the curriculum, strengthen research developments and funding opportunities, and fundamentally enhance the reputation of the universities in such partnerships. At Innopolis University, the establishment of a new academic partnership with a foreign higher education institution normally involves a proposal and a three-stage approval process. A proposal can originate from a range of sources including but not limited to students, faculty members, and staff of Innopolis University or external entity. Global academic partnership proposals are firstly reviewed and approved by the International Relations Office of Innopolis University. The process of approval includes the assessment of a partner proposed and estimation of risks and resource commitment entering the partnership. The operating framework established by the International Relations Office of Innopolis University for the selection and formation of global academic partnerships is intended to help to focus on the most valuable academic partnerships and proceed confident that there is a system of checks and balances to ensure quality and to protect the University's reputation. On the second stage the negotiated agreement undergoes the approval by the Legal Department and lastly the academic partnership is approved on the whole-university level.

Discussing global academic partnerships, we mainly consider two types of official agreements, in particular, memoranda of understanding (MOUs) and inter-institutional agreements (IIAs). Typically, MOUs as legal documents cover general academic activities, such as exchange of best practices and innovative experience, exchange of faculty members and students for lectures, visits, joint experiments, internships and implementation of other collaborative projects, development, and realization of joint educational initiatives and organization of events of common interest and generally lack the binding power of a contract. While IIAs are written contracts between parties to work together on an agreed-upon project or meet an agreed-upon often quantitatively measurable objective, for example, international academic mobility and/or joint laboratories, and as a result are legally binding.

3.2   International Academic Mobility

An act of students, faculty members and staff of one higher education institution (typically known as 'home institution') going to a foreign higher education institution (typically known as 'host institution') for the purpose of learning or teaching is commonly referred to as international academic mobility (IAM). At Innopolis University, IAM is a cornerstone of internationalization, especially considering the overall close relationship between IAM and innovation in different areas, like highly qualified human capital, research networks and publications [15]. On the individual level, students greatly benefit from IAM through the accumulation or enhancement of their productive capacities, such as knowledge, understandings, talents, and skills as well as through the realization of international dimensions of them [16]. Furthermore, coming out of the comfort zone through traveling to new destinations might be a transformative journey of self-discovery where the participants are forced to test themselves in terms of resourcefulness and self-awareness [17]. On the institutional level, partner universities that have regular incoming and outgoing traffic build trust between each other that might serve as a proxy for further cooperation in forms of joint research, joint publications, joint research platforms, and cotutelles. Globally, international academic mobility is of a special value as it offers a competitive advantage in a global knowledge economy in the current fierce battle for brains [18].

Establishing IAM, especially for those universities that are located in non-English speaking countries, might take significant consideration and planning as the English language currently has a status of an 'academic lingua franca' and students normally expect the courses to be taught in English. Being an English-speaking university in a non-English speaking country Innopolis University had though fewer barriers to its internationalization. The fact of having the whole curriculum taught in English even in a non-English speaking country is likely to significantly raise the chances not only to attract foreign applicants as full-time students but also to attract students from partner universities within the framework of IAM. Furthermore, English-medium education provides better chances for Innopolis University to attract prominent foreign faculty members and visiting professors. The foreign faculty members and visiting professors can surely expect the same level of student engagement as they would've expected in the English-speaking countries as the students have proven sufficient English skills. Thus, it may even be argued that English was one of the 'enablers' to the University's IAM development and overall internationalization.

Even though the opportunity of IAM at Innopolis University is offered to students, faculty member and staff, the student mobility is considered as the most important part of IAM as it is typically larger at scale and serves as a groundwork for further general cooperation. Staff and faculty mobility, on the other hand, have other functions within the mobility framework to share and integrate best practices in the administration of higher education and to further research and research practices, respectively. The student mobility at Innopolis University is taking place on a voluntary basis at all levels of studies, including undergraduate, graduate and post-graduate. For the better accommodation to the world practice of IAM, the curricula at Innopolis University are theme and competence-based. The learning outcomes of courses are defined as degree-specific and general competences so that they could be easily matched with the courses offered at the host university by the students who are willing to go on exchange. The general competence may include learning skills, ethical competence, work competence, internationalization competence, and development competence. As Douglas et al. argue [9] the students even of computer science must develop awareness of other cultures and one's own cultural point of view. As a result, mobility programs equip students with necessary skills and international experience, hence enabling them to better perform in a globalized and internationally networked working environment.

In the current age of living in a globalized and interconnected world, IAM is likely to be an increasingly important part of higher education that improves the multicultural and cross-cultural capabilities of its participants. Moreover, considering how social networks as structures and new connections made through travel and communication might define norms and shape decisions, IAM might become a taken for granted part of studies that most of the students will experience [19]. Within the framework of IAM, the International Relations Office of Innopolis University considers its mission to ensure the quality of the IAM experience alongside the commitment to share and integrate the best practices. To fulfill this obligation, the International Relations Office of Innopolis University has implemented a procedure with the selection criteria that are based on merit and without regard to any other factor protected by applicable law (e.g. race, nationality, religion, race, etc.). The women are particularly encouraged to participate as they might have more obstacles than men combining work and family [20]. Addressing inequalities is important issue in higher education as higher education institutions because of their significant involvement in the interdependent national labour markets and overall social life might be a good subject to study the reasons for inequalities production and reproduction [21]. The procedure is open for the access of applicants and is being communicated to every mobility target group within the promotion period of every mobility call.

The applicants are being evaluated based upon academic performance, foreign language skills, involvement in extracurricular activities, interest in learning a new culture and other factors, therefore, increasing chances for the individual to gain the most from the IAM and for the University to build further trust with the partner. Throughout the process of the mobility, namely on the pre-departure, post-arrival, and repatriation stages, the participants receive support and advice from the International Relations Office in terms of professional, cultural and personal challenges that they meet or may meet [22]. Even though it is commonly believed that the success of the overall internationalization of a higher education institution can be expressed in such quantifiable aspects of it as the number of international students, the number of education abroad programs offered, or the proportion of students engaged in education abroad, it is important to remember that IAM is just one of the instruments and typically serves as a proxy for further development of internationalization [23].

3.3 Internships

Having commitment to share and integrate the best practices Innopolis University promotes research internships at its laboratories that provide an opportunity for undergraduate and graduate students to work collaboratively with the members of the computer science faculty of the University on industry and academic projects. The goals of such internships are (1) to provide experience of application of the skills learned during classes to the real-world or close to the real-world projects; (2) to build research capacities among students; (3) to produce new knowledge; and (4) to promote Innopolis University as an English-speaking university and a place to continue your studies. Internships usually have a workload between 10 and 60 ECTS depending on the duration and hours per week dedicated to the work for the laboratory. The internships as a research mobility are likely to experience an increase in scope globally due to the rise of the knowledge economy and the impact of globalization [11].

Acknowledging the fact that students might be resistant to go study or do the internship in a non-English speaking country, Innopolis University offers several types of internships, including onsite, virtual and combined. The onsite internships are carried out on the campus of Innopolis University with the research facilities and equipment provided by the University. Virtual internships though are meant to be carried out remotely what might happen due to several reasons ranging from the fear to come to a different especially non-English speaking country, disability to other personal reasons that do not let the intern leave his/her country including the outbreaks of the viruses such as the recent COVID-19. And finally, combined internships are the combination of both with the virtual part of the internship preceding or succeeding the onsite part. Applications for any type of the internship are accepted from undergraduate and graduate students from any university, not necessarily from partner universities. However, it may be preferable to review the applications from partner universities as the quality of the students from those universities might be already known as high. After the application is received there would be typically two interviews scheduled with one of the members of faculty and a representative of the International Relations Office. At first, the candidate needs to fulfill the requirements of the laboratory that he or she applies to, after what the International Relations Office helps to decide on the way and the period of internship delivery and also helps to solve administrative problems. Unlike IAM that is typically carried out between partner universities, regular internships can lead to an academic partnership, especially if any student from any university can apply for an internship position throughout the year as it is established at Innopolis University.

3.4   Joint Research Platforms

Despite the fact that higher education institutions face growing competition even in research, they remain to be the biggest accumulators of scientific human capital and hubs of scientific networks [11]. In higher education, the joint research platform might be referred to differently, for instance, joint laboratory, double laboratory, mirror laboratory or virtual laboratory. Fundamentally, they all represent research-based cooperation between two or more institutions. For the inexperienced in this type of international cooperation institutions, it might be more beneficial to establish a joint research platform of two partner institutions at first. The International Relations Office of Innopolis University considers establishing joint research platforms as a further development of existing partnerships between higher education institutions. In other words, there must be some form of cooperation between particular professors and/or faculties, for instance, joint research, joint publications, joint course delivery or articulation, preceding the establishment of a joint research platform. Normally, those professors become the heads of the joint research platform established. Based on the trust of the previous cooperation we argue it is easier to create such platforms that will allow participating institutions to develop grander mutual research projects, attract funding from complementary sources and build a multidisciplinary team around those projects with the potential to attract visiting scientists and trainees from Ph.D., Master's and Bachelor's level students.

After the establishment of a joint research platform, its team assigned to the mission of a new project, obtain several key opportunities that otherwise would not occur, for example, (1) inter-institutional cooperation with postdoctoral researchers, interns, graduate and undergraduate students that could result in joint publications and participation in conferences (particular interest should be placed on those students that are oriented on the future academic career); (2) platform creation for the work with postdoctoral researchers; (3) platform creation for the work with Ph.D. students and a further selection of elite candidates for cotutelle; (4) experience of coordinating an international project for the team and other attracted participants.

On the initiation stage, the costs of establishing a joint research platform can be as low as nearly zero, especially if it is based on the existing partnership between professors and/or faculties and if the partner universities have certain already existing research capacities dedicated to the research area of the joint project. The further development and expansion of research resources though can be funded by not only the participating institutions but also by taking grant or commercial projects and research opportunities. The research opportunities of the involved in the projects institutions and research cooperation with other organizations offer a chance to raise awareness about the issue and increase the citation rate of the institutions as the research and publications with a larger number of participants are likely to get bigger exposure.

Based on the successes of a joint research platform, the partners might build further initiatives such as a joint learning platform that could serve as an instrument for (1) the development of double degree programs for Master's and Bachelor's level students; (2) development of unique courses to be taught at partner institutions; (3) development of unique study programs to be taught at partner institutions; (4) development of intensive study and research programs to bring together students and researchers from the partner institutions; (5) establishment of dedicated and mutually taught summer schools that might take place on the campuses of different universities during the year.

Procedurally, if the proposal of a joint research platform gets the green light from the administrations of the participating institutions, the heads of the platform are to set and prioritize goals, define deliverables with the milestones, establish and assign responsibilities for the team members, create a project schedule and complete a risk assessment. Typically, the planning stage provides a well-formulated, data-informed and mutually agreed upon strategy with goals and objectives, with solid resource and/or fiscal plan to support the strategy and each goal and objective and accountability process to monitor the progress on further stages of implementation and control. The practical experience of Innopolis University shows that the establishment and planning processes of such projects will face fewer bureaucratic procedures and less resistance from the administrations of the participating institutions if the joint research platform uses as little additional resources as possible.

As it is regulated at Innopolis University, the role of the International Relations Office is to select the partners for the establishment of a joint research platform based on the strategy and objectives of the internationalization of the University. Upon selection, the largest part of the involvement of the International Relations Office belongs to the first stage of the initiation of cooperation. The main tasks are to initiate, negotiate and define agreements required for the establishment of a joint research platform. After the official documents are signed by all partner institutions, the International Relations Office of Innopolis University has to make sure that the strategy sessions are carried out and a proposal of strategy and goals for the joint research platform as a result of those sessions is submitted for approval by the Faculties and administrations of partner universities. Upon mutual approval of the strategy, the International Relations Office's primary job becomes to track the project progress in terms of milestones and goals. The heads of the platform are responsible for tracking the activities and resources the reports of which they normally submit to the International Relations Office to keep the paperwork of the project at one place. Typically, the team working at the joint research platform reports the results 2 times per year for the assessment by the heads of the platform and the International Relations Offices of every partner. The purpose of involvement of the International Relations Office throughout the whole process of establishing and operating a joint platform is to have a third party that is not directly benefitting from the partnership but can serve the partner universities as an enforcer of the strategy approved. The process of initiation, planning and implementation described in this section is as it is used at Innopolis University when considering an establishment of a joint research platform. However, the process can be adjusted to certain regulations and requirements of the partner universities.

3.5 Cotutelles

A cotutelle agreement is an inter-institutional agreement that allows two partner higher education institutions to co-supervise a Ph.D. candidate that after successful evaluation of his/her doctoral degree dissertation receives a diploma from each of the partner institutions. A term 'cotutelle' originates from French practice of 'co-tutoring'. Establishing a cotutelle means not only benefit for the student who will manage to get two diplomas but it can also create a 'triple win' situation where the student, his home university and the cotutelle partner university win. It may be more beneficial to consider this type of partnership when the study program that a Ph.D. candidate as a result of this type of agreement gets could not be delivered otherwise. Also, such research training might be the first time when the student is exposed to international research networks [11]. In general, such agreement must regulate the procedures for enrollment, supervision and the evaluation of the candidate's doctoral degree dissertation and the international cooperation within the agreement.

When entering cotutelle agreements, especially with European higher education institutions, Innopolis University gets an opportunity to offer its students a chance to get a degree recognized worldwide. The European institutions though get the access to the best candidates as Innopolis University only considers top performing students for the co-supervision opportunities. Moreover, to ensure that only the top performing students are enrolled into a double degree program Innopolis University introduces a program of excellence at the graduate level with the future incentive to be enrolled into a double Ph.D. program.

Such partnership is an attempt to solve the issue of inequalities derived from the non-recognition of qualifications by certain national educational and labour market systems [21]. Furthermore, the non-recognition of degrees and different legislations may create certain challenges for cotutelle. The establishment of cotutelle agreements might be challenging as the terms that such agreements use are likely to differ from country to country. Failure in matching the bureaucratic constrains might result in failure of the partnership. Furthermore, as cotutelle is a prolonged partnership for at least 3 years, there is always a risk of legislation change that will hinder the implementation of the program. Besides being a long and a complex engagement the co-supervision can always be restrained by a lack of interested students, dedicated faculty or continuous financial support.

4   Conclusion

Despite being an internationally oriented university from the very beginning, one and a half years ago, Innopolis University has reconsidered its approach to internationalization and revitalized all its international activities. With the dedication to its newly advised mission and vision, the university and internationalization strategies Innopolis University successfully gained the experience of development of the internationalization of a higher education institution and international cooperation in such forms as global academic partnerships, student and staff mobility including Erasmus+ programs, internships, joint research platforms, joint Ph.D. supervision and other international joint projects. Although the instruments of the internationalization described in this paper helped significantly Innopolis University, they have their limitations and should be adopted according to the policies of a particular university. The limitations of those instruments and their universality can be a subject for further research. It is also recommended that a comprehensive examination of risk management of internationalization be undertaken as the situation with COVID-19 demonstrated that there are circumstances that might significantly hinder the efforts of higher education institutions to internationalize their activities. With the extensively developed network of international higher education institutions, established student and staff mobility programs, collaboration with such organizations as CERN [24], collaborative supervision of Ph.D. students with the University of Toulouse - Jean Jaures II, the University of Southern Denmark and the University of Messina, Innopolis University is aiming at maximizing the benefits of global trends without compromising on the excessive emphasis on the market needs from higher education and avoiding the risks of losing the fundamental academic values in favor of a higher position in the global rankings [25].

References

1. Gao, Y., Baik, C., Arkoudis, S.: Internationalization of Higher Education, pp. 300–320. Palgrave Macmillan, London (2015)
2. Kristensen, K.H., Karlsen, J.E.: Strategies for internationalisation at technical universities in the Nordic countries. Tert. Educ. Manag. **24**(1), 19–33 (2017). https://doi.org/10.1080/13583883.2017.1323949
3. Soliman, S., Anchor, J., Taylor, D.: The international strategies of universities: deliberate or emergent? Stud. High. Educ. **44**(8), 1413–1424 (2019)
4. Decree of the president of the russian federation. http://www.kremlin.ru/acts/bank/35263. Accessed 23 Aug 2018
5. Project 5top100. https://5top100.ru/en/. Accessed 23 Aug 2018
6. Pagani, R.N., Ramond, B., Silva, V.L.D., Zammar, G., Kovaleski, J.L.: Key factors in university-to-university knowledge and technology transfer on international student mobility. Knowl. Manag. Res. Pract. 1–19 (2019)
7. Baker, W.: English as an academic lingua franca and intercultural awareness: student mobility in the transcultural university. Lang. Intercultural Commun. **16**(3), 437–451 (2016)
8. Knight, J.: Updating the definition of internationalization (2003)

9. Douglas, S., Farley, A., Lo, G., Proskurowski, A., Young, M.: Internationalization of computer science education. In: Proceedings of the 41st ACM Technical Symposium on Computer Science Education, pp. 411–415 (2010)
10. Robson, S., Almeida, J., Schartner, A.: Internationalization at home: time for review and development? Eur. J. High. Educ. **8**(1), 19–35 (2018)
11. Jacob, M., Meek, V.L.: Scientific mobility and international research networks: trends and policy tools for promoting research excellence and capacity building. Stud. High. Educ. **38**(3), 331–344 (2013)
12. Leonard, D., Sensiper, S.: The role of tacit knowledge in group innovation. Calif. Manag. Rev. **40**(3), 112–132 (1998)
13. Lees, J., Webb, G.: A review of the literature to inform the development of a new model of global placement: the global learning partnership. Phys. Ther. Rev. **23**(1), 40–49 (2018)
14. Gao, Y., Baik, C., Arkoudis, S.: Internationalization of higher education. In: Huisman, J., de Boer, H., Dill, D.D., Souto-Otero, M. (eds.) The Palgrave International Handbook of Higher Education Policy and Governance, pp. 300–320. Palgrave Macmillan, London (2015). https://doi.org/10.1007/978-1-137-45617-5_17
15. Siekierski, P., Lima, M.C., Borini, F.M., Pereira, R.M.: International academic mobility and innovation: a literature review. J. Glob. Mobility Home Expatriate Manag. Res. **6**, 285–298 (2018)
16. Cao, C., Zhu, C., Meng, Q.: A survey of the influencing factors for international academic mobility of chinese university students. High. Educ. Q. **70**(2), 200–220 (2016)
17. Brown, L.: The transformative power of the international sojourn: An ethnographic study of the international student experience. Ann. Tourism Res. **36**(3), 502–521 (2009)
18. Riaño, Y., Van Mol, C., Raghuram, P.: New directions in studying policies of international student mobility and migration. Globalisation Soc. Educ. **16**(3), 283–294 (2018)
19. Beech, S.E.: International student mobility: the role of social networks. Soc. Cult. Geogr. **16**(3), 332–350 (2015)
20. Nikunen, M., Lempiäinen, K.: Gendered strategies of mobility and academic career. Gend. Educ. pp. 1–18 (2018)
21. Bilecen, B., Van Mol, C.: Introduction: international academic mobility and inequalities. J. Ethnic Migr. Stud. **48**, 1241–1255 (2017)
22. Conroy, K.M., McCarthy, L.: Abroad but not abandoned: supporting student adjustment in the international placement journey. Stud. High. Educ. 1–15 (2019)
23. Green, M.F.: Measuring and assessing internationalization. In: NAFSA: Association of International Educators, vol. 1, pp. 1–26 (2012)
24. Bauer, R., et al.: The biodynamo project: experience report. In: Advanced Research on Biologically Inspired Cognitive Architectures, pp. 117–125. IGI Global (2017)
25. Jibeen, T., Asad Khan, M.: Internationalization of higher education: potential benefits and costs. Int. J. Eval. Res. Educ. (IJERE) **4**, 196–199 (2015)

Finding the Right Understanding: Twenty-First Century University, Globalization and Internationalization

Iouri Kotorov, Yuliya Krasylnykova, Petr Zhdanov$^{(\boxtimes)}$, and Manuel Mazzara

Innopolis University, Innopolis, Republic of Tatarstan, Russian Federation
pe.zhdanov@innopolis.ru

Abstract. The "idea of a university" has been a subject of contested discussions for over a century. There is a significant number of different views on what it means to be a university of the twenty-first century as well as on its purpose and primary functions. Today, universities as any other organization experience transformations forced by the current trends, including globalization. As a result, twenty-first century universities have to come up with the strategies and tools such as internationalization strategy that could help them to utilize the advantages that the twenty-first century brings and to minimize the temporary influences of today that could undermine the essence of the "idea of a university". The aim of this paper is to discover the concept of a university in the twenty-first century, the impact of the ever growing globalization and the role of institutional internationalization in today's world. Exploring the interconnected nature of a twenty-first century university, globalization and internationalization this paper seeks to report a neglected aspect of the understanding of the "idea of a university", especially by such university community as professional staff. An implication of this paper is the possibility to popularize the "idea of a university" in order to promote a contribution to its development by communities other than academics and students.

1 Introduction

It is hard to disagree with the claim that in the twenty-first century organizations including universities tend to operate within ever more interconnected regional, national and transnational networks that still might be influenced by the decisions of governments and market forces. Despite the fact that governments do not always take decisions considering the global perspective instead often preferring national interests, the universities can though greatly benefit through the participation in global networks because such networks typically have greater power to lobby, attract larger sources of funding and conduct grander projects [1]. These benefits suggest that universities have to think and research more globally and riskier, in other words, past their local comfort zone [2].

Today, universities build networks not only because of the geographical proximity but also based on their identifications, such as "research-led universities",

© Springer Nature Switzerland AG 2020
J.-M. Bruel et al. (Eds.): FISEE 2019, LNCS 12271, pp. 341–353, 2020.
https://doi.org/10.1007/978-3-030-57663-9_22

"young universities" or universities that have a particular religious standpoint [1]. Development of such networks definitely supports the idea of growing globalization which itself suggests the interconnectedness between countries and organizations [3]. Furthermore, globalization that might have started to influence universities already in the 1970s and 1980s, is also pushing them to change their nature or the "idea of a university" from the classical notion of "a place of teaching universal knowledge" [4] to the tailored for economic utilitarianism organization repurposed to the preferences of transnational organizations [5]. The universities of the twenty-first century as a result had most likely to be transformed not only internally with the "idea of a university" reimagined but also externally coming up with new strategies and tools such as internationalization strategy that could help them to develop their global capacities and facilitate partnerships that would be beneficial for their global development and would not allow to be influenced extensively by the temporary needs of the private sector.

In this article, we explore the nature of universities in the twenty-first century, the impact of challenging external factors such as globalization, competitiveness, and the knowledge-based economy, and examine the internationalization as an intentional answer to external challenges. Following the introduction the paper is structured as follows: Sect. 2 discovers the "idea of a university", Sect. 3 focuses on the factors that led to a change of the universities in the twenty-first century, Sect. 4 describes the importance and advantages of the internationalization process while Sect. 5 provides certain conclusions.

2 The Idea of a Twenty-First Century University

The "idea of a university" as "a place of teaching universal knowledge" [4] is more than a hundred years old. Already in 1810 Humboldt suggested that there should be two types of higher scientific institutions: (1) academies that must be free to choose what and how they are going to research and (2) universities that are supposed to develop practical knowledge to transfer it to its students [6]. The second type might though mislead the reader into believing that the universities have to basically serve the industries and organizations that their students are going to be employed in. Contrary to this belief the Humboldtian idea of such universities indicates that the science was meant to develop autonomously from the political agenda and economic tendencies and the ultimate goals of science were supposed to intrinsically demonstrate the excellence and the highest scientific and academic aspirations [5]. Acknowledging the importance of science and scientific discoveries, Newman [4] also supported the idea of the importance of knowledge transfer for the universities arguing that there would be no need for students if science was a primary concept for the "idea of a university".

Since the original publications of the works by Wilhelm von Humboldt in 1810 and Will John Henry Cardinal Newman in 1899, the concept of the "idea of a university" has most certainly evolved. Nowadays, Salisbury and Pesete [7] argue that the discourse over the previous century was historically restricted to academics and students and thus might have left certain university communities out of the conversation but whose role might be of an essential value especially for the university as an institute. Being disengaged such communities as professional staff of a university might not even fully grasp the "idea of a university" and therefore might be able to contribute much less to its development and the development of a university as an institute [7]. The "idea of a university" itself has always been a multidisciplinary phenomenon with no clear borders between history, philosophy of education and sociology [8]. Barnett claims that the meaning of "being a university" becomes increasingly inclusive over the years: from the years of the orientation on knowledge, truth and understanding to the focus on financial, societal and power expansion and finally to the recent development of such areas as rules, regulations, risks, audits, procedures, systems and processes [8].

In the twenty-first century when organizations can have extremely complex organizational structures and mixed functions, it might be critical to differentiate: (1) a university as an idea and (2) a university as an institute. The former suggests the general purpose and functions of a university while the latter represents the form or organizational structure. One of the major characteristics of the idea of a twenty-first century university is the so-called 'third mission', the concept that has already been discussed for over two decades [9]. The 'third mission' is an attempt to formalize the socio-economic role of universities in addition to their classic functions of teaching and research. It can be argued that a twenty-first century university may be found being pressured simultaneously by (1) government regulations to accept the new mission and obligations to contribute to the development of the society and (2) industry demands to follow the trends of market forces in teaching and research, especially the current trend of digitalization. As Jongbloed [10] suggests government regulations and market forces turn the universities of the twenty-first century into hybrid organizations that have to adjust their objectives in teaching, research and contribution to society. Depending on which pulling force between government and private sector a university relies to a greater extent, it will produce greater number of either professional or academic publications [10]. Even though generating a higher share of funding from the private sector may seem to liberate a university from the government, it is likely to limit teaching and research to the current trends of the market forces and force a university to almost forget the Humboldtian idea of the highest scientific and academic aspirations. For a twenty-first century university as an institution, Nelles and Vorley [9] suggest that the 'third-mission' pushes them to design and build entrepreneurial architecture meaning establishing departments that will be responsible for the commercialization of the research. It is worth to point out that the degree of the changes brought to a university by the 'third-mission' is likely to differ depending on the type of a university: public or private, local or global, liberal or conservative. In general, such evolution of the "idea of a university" and university as an institute is likely to be caused not only by the development of the discourse as such but by certain external factors, as well.

Also, it is worth noting that there are two approaches to higher education. The initial 'university' approach was originally introduced during the times when the world was seen as a coherent whole and the word, a 'university', itself meant "a whole unit or a single community—whether of fishmongers or scholars (both masters and students)" [11]. It was only later when the meaning of the word became strongly associated with a scholar community as it is now. In the 1960s though Clark Kerr introduced a new approach namely "multiversity" that reflected a new form of higher education institution which combined traditional undergraduate colleges, professional schools, and graduate research scholarship, in other words, it represented a community of communities with mixed and potentially conflicting interests [12]. Even though this approach "glorified a truly American model, infusing the best of British and German traditions" [12], it was also meant to especially stress the connection between certain groups of scholars and external patrons meaning that the multiversities almost became the retailers of knowledge [11]. Today, this term might characterize what is known as 'research universities' that are engaged in teaching, research and knowledge transfer [13]. In the twenty-first century, it is even argued that we have moved into yet another face of academic development, suggesting the appearance of new approach of 'transversity' which reflects the current trends of continuous rather than episodic learning and education delivery through the Internet as if the higher education of the twenty-first century transcends one place, population and purpose [12].

3   Globalization, Competitiveness and the Knowledge-Based Economy in the Twenty-First Century

The external circumstances that the universities operate in have drastically changed over the last century. Even though the universities internally might operate based on the previously mentioned strong idealistic principles as defined by the classic scholars, they can barely allow themselves to ignore the trends and the changes of the twenty-first century and moreover are often pushed by the government to respond and develop certain policies accordingly. As several scholars [5,14] suggest there are three major narratives that have significantly affected the development of the "idea of a university" and a university as an institution at the end of the twentieth century and the beginning of the twenty-first century: (1) globalization, (2) competitiveness and (3) the knowledge-based economy.

Globalization is likely to be a phenomenon that is the largest in scope among those three. Even though it is a complicated and multi-faceted process, as a whole it is not a new phenomenon and has already influenced the world for over the past three decades. With its great power and broad effects on almost every aspect of our lives it has certainly been a subject of many debates and grabbed significant attention in the scholar community. Due to the still increasing trend of globalization, transforming not only higher education but all areas of the organization and cooperation in the world, investigating the impact of economic globalization on higher education is prominent and as a result it is worth understanding what is meant by economic globalization per se. As it is defined by Babones [15], the economic globalization is:

"one of the three main dimensions of globalization commonly found in countries, academic literature, with the two others being political globalization and cultural globalization, as well as the general term of globalization."

Having found the place of economic globalization among other dimensions it is important to point out to the definition of the United Nations [16] that suggests the economic globalization refers to:

"the increasing interdependence of world economies as a result of the growing scale of cross-border trade of commodities and services, flow of international capital and wide and rapid spread of technologies. It reflects the continuing expansion and mutual integration of market frontiers, and is an irreversible trend for the economic development in the whole world at the turn of the millennium."

Since the process as it is described above is irreversible, the effects of economic globalization need to be discovered more closely. Samimi and Jenatabadi [17] argue that economic globalization effects:

"flows of goods and services across borders, international capital flows, reduction in tariffs and trade barriers, immigration, and the spread of technology, and knowledge beyond borders."

In higher education, globalization is not a new trend either, but what might be new in the twenty-first century is its form and intensity [2]. The definitions of globalization and internationalization are sometimes used interchangeably, but for the purpose of this paper the globalization will be referred to as the economic and academic trends of the twenty-first century and internationalization as the policies and practices developed by universities to stay ideologically and institutionally up to date with the global academic environment [18]. Although globalization means that several global trends influence the universities across the world, it does not equal to standardization as the responses might significantly differ. As Tight [2] argues the number of general approaches to globalization might be limited to: (1) pragmatic using which universities desperately attracting international students and staff and thus project power globally and (2) idealistic with the universities openly critique the international practices and only adapt those that can enhance student experience and curriculum.

The other two factors of competitiveness and the knowledge-based economy are most likely the products of the influence of the twenty-first century on higher education and the proliferation of neoliberalism. With the growth of economy becoming prevailing concern of states, governments are likely to push local universities to their economic success intending to increase their productivity and obtaining of a larger world "market share" in higher education and research [14]. To fully grasp the idea of competitiveness the concept of a world-leading university must be discussed. If in the twentieth century the leading universities were likely defined by the number of staff with outstanding awards, the twenty-first century brought the complex systems of quantitative evaluations that help to rank universities. To compare the universities in their key activities today there are ranking agencies such as QS World University Rankings, Times Higher Education and Shanghai Ranking. Based on these annual rankings the administration of universities, governments and other stakeholders in higher education often take decisions. While the economic growth might become the most significant quantitative result for the governments to evaluate their successes, the management of the private companies leverage more influence on universities through their direct or indirect participation in international organizations and state bureaucracies almost dictating what skills the students have to have when graduated and what research is needed by the industry [5]. Even though universities have to maneuver among such actors in higher education as governments, global governance institutions, ranking agencies and transnational corporation, universities as a unique educational form have to remember their primary goal of promoting the common learning of mankind [5].

The third factor of the knowledge-based economy became certainly of an extraordinary intensity in the twenty-first century with its growing digitalization and extreme demand in particular types of experts such as computer science specialists. According to Chochliouros et al. [19], the knowledge-based economy is

"a form of modern economy referring to a specific structural transformation, where the fast creation of new knowledge and the improvement of access to various knowledge bases increasingly constitute the main resource for greater efficiency, novelty and competitiveness."

It is worth to note though that already at the start of the post-industrial era the role of knowledge might have become even more pervasive than the role of capital and land [20]. The increasing since then importance of knowledge and knowledge-based professions has definitely changed the landscape of teaching and research, the two primary functions of a university. Pugh et al. [21] argue that the emergence of the knowledge-based economy has pushed universities to the commercialization and maximization of their economic application. The universities as the commonly recognized accreditors of professional knowledge and guarantor of the knowledge base may thus have become less ideological in their pursuits but rather a market-driven organization [20]. Being the engines of the knowledge-based economy it is clear that the twenty-first century universities obtained a unique opportunity to gain substantial funding from the industry that is suffering from the insufficient number of the experts and research in their industry.

As a consequence of all these fast changes, the profile of a modern university looks very different from even a couple of decades ago. However independent the universities across the world are, staying aside from the globalization, competitiveness and the knowledge-based economy they might lose significant advantages that these factors bring but they also always should consider if those changes will bring them further away and how far away from their primary missions.

4 What Is Internationalization?

As the twenty-first century unfolds and globalization brings unprecedented changes into economy, politics and society, internationalization of the university has become a strategic priority for numerous universities. With the growing pace of globalization, competitiveness and the knowledge-base economy, universities of the twenty-first century could not stay ideologically and institutionally unchanged and had to begin to adapt to the changing circumstances. Moreover, as argued by the American Council on Education [22], if a nation wants to prosper in the twenty-first century, its higher education institutions must become borderless. Higher numbers of the mobility of students and staff, full-time international students and international collaborations between researchers and teachers on individual level lead the universities of the twenty-first century to the necessity of an institutional answer that is often named as internationalization. The emphasis within the discourse of internationalization has often been put on the importance of understanding other nations, languages and cultures that historically led to the introduction of various initiatives in higher education, for instance, Erasmus, Camett and Tempus, the student mobility programs in Europe.

Although the internationalization as such is far from a clearly defined and completely understood concept of higher education [23], one of the most encompassing definitions of internationalization may be suggested by Knight [24] who defines it as:

"the process of integrating an international, intercultural or global dimension into the purpose, functions or delivery of post-secondary education."

Analyzing Knight's definition it can be claimed that internationalization is a continuous process that is shaped by the effects of globalization according to which universities need to reconsider their purpose, functions and delivery of their services. In other words, the universities are basically changing the idea of a university and also are changing themselves as institutions. A more detailed definition of internationalization and especially in terms of the institutional changes of universities can be found in the works of Ellingboe [25] who suggests internationalization to be:

"the process of integrating an international perspective into a college or university system. It is an ongoing, future-oriented, multidimensional, interdisciplinary, leadership-driven vision that involves many stakeholders working to change the internal dynamics of an institution to respond and adapt appropriately to an increasingly diverse, globally focused, ever-changing external environment."

It is important to note that Ellingboe points out the role of leadership in the process of internationalization and acknowledges the role of other stakeholders demonstrating the inter-connectedness of today's world. Another definition of internationalization, in particular suggested by Hudzik [26], says that internationalization is:

"a commitment, confirmed through action, to infuse international and comparative perspectives throughout the teaching, research and service mission of higher education [26]."

Unlike previously described definitions, Hudzik suggests that internationalization should be committed to and also can be instilled. Therefore, according to this definition, it can be argued that internationalization is a process of engineering and implementation of particular policies and programs that contribute to the international dimension of a university. Supporting this idea Bartell [23] claims that international literacy is a crucial part of the cultural, technological, economic and political health of mankind in the twenty-first century.

Contrary to the previous relatively broad definitions some of the scholars though define the contribution of internationalization to the international dimension of a university in an extremely specific manner expecting individual students to:

"speak two to three languages in addition to English at the level of 7 or above on a 10 point scale, where zero means no knowledge of the language and 10 refers to native knowledge of the language, and reside in at least two non-English speaking countries, in non-Americanized environments, for at least one year each [27]."

Even though the international experience may now have become less of an exclusive option of the elites, such definition of a student with international competences still seems to be hardly achievable, especially on a scale. Considering the existence of such a specific definition it is worth mentioning that although the internationalization can be expressed in certain quantitative results to be achieved, it might be more beneficial to think of it, as it has been described above, as a conceptualized transformative process that involves several stakeholders and is aimed at the adaptation to the global tendencies and also helps to develop teaching, research and service mission of higher education.

Global competition is most certainly driving universities of the twenty-first century towards the preference of quantitative over qualitative evaluations, especially of those mentioned by ranking agencies. However, such a tendency to have quantitatively comparable results often leads the administrations of universities to fall into believing that the numbers of international agreements, numbers of international staff employed as well as numbers of international mobility can truly reflect the internationalization of a university. It may be understandable that administrations of universities and governments would like to have measurable results from internationalization as it is a relatively new instrument and thus may still need to prove its workability, but the problem is that measurable results do not always reflect the degree and the entirety of the advantages of internationalization. Several of the main advantages of the internationalization are often mentioned as: (1) extensive global cooperation including but not limited to joint research and mobility; (2) the access to the global and typically larger sources of research funding; (3) curriculum innovation; (4) higher quantitative results in the areas defined by the leading ranking agencies that may lead to a higher position in the world university rankings. Even though these types of benefits may seem attractive, especially for the management of a university, it is also important to remember that a university should qualitatively enhance its primary functions of teaching, research and its 'third mission' of socio-economic contribution.

Discussing the advantages that internationalization can bring, it is critical to mention the practically-oriented concept of 'comprehensive internationalization' defined by CIGE [28] as:

"a strategic, coordinated process that seeks to align and integrate international policies, programs, and initiatives, and positions colleges and universities as more globally oriented and internationally connected institutions. This process requires a clear commitment by top-level institutional leaders, meaningfully impacts the curriculum and a broad range of stakeholders, and results in deep and ongoing incorporation of international perspectives and activities throughout the institution."

The main underlying messages of this definition may be that (1) comprehensive internationalization is a process of integration of international policies throughout the whole institution and that (2) it is a complex in its institutional nature process involving institutional leaders, curriculum changes and engagement with various stakeholders. To visualize the idea clearly, CIGE [28] offers a model with six vertical pillars that represent: (1) articulated institutional commitment, (2) administrative leadership, structure, and staffing; (3) curriculum, co-curriculum and learning outcomes; (4) faculty policies and practices; (5) student mobility; (6) collaboration and partnerships. Across those six pillars at the bottom the 'comprehensive internationalization' is depicted as a double arrow linking the pillars and as if simultaneously assisting in their expansion. Such inter-connectedness of individual pillars through the 'comprehensive internationalization' also represents the idea that progress or lack of it in one area can have an impact on the others [28].

As the curriculum is one of the main tools with the help of which students can get international literacy and international competence and as campuses are the locations where the internationalization is supposed to take place, it could be claimed that the internationalization of the curriculum and the internationalization of campuses are the subcategories of the 'comprehensive internationalization'. Curriculum, co-curriculum and learning outcomes, in particular, as one of the six defined by CIGE [28] pillars of 'comprehensive internationalization' represents the obligation:

"of colleges and universities to prepare people for a globalized world including developing the ability to compete economically, to operate effectively in other cultures and settings, to use knowledge to improve their own lives and their communities, and to better comprehend the realities of the contemporary world so that they can better meet their responsibilities as citizens."

To fulfill this obligation a university must explicitly incorporate into the content of its formal and informal curriculum intercultural dimension and intercultural learning objectives as well as learning and assessment activities to be able to measure the progress of intercultural competencies as without designated tasks, attendance sheets, credits and grades it might be difficult to track such development [29]. Even though these solutions might sound easily implementable, especially on paper, in the process of curriculum internationalization a university might face significant challenges as intercultural interactions are intrinsically intense and risky and therefore it can be beneficial if the teaching staff would be trained to obtain certain knowledge and skills in this area [29]. Curricular and co-curricular programs are often influenced by an institutional culture that can be rigid and slow to transform. The internationalized curriculum is supposed to provide tasks and learning activities to the students that could not be completed without them engaging in a meaningful exchange of cultural information [29]. As a result of an internationalized curriculum as proposed by Leask [29], the students are to engage with internationally informed research and cultural and linguistic diversity during their studies and graduate as global professionals and citizens with international and intercultural perspectives.

The development of intercultural competencies of students is also significantly dependent on the campus environment. Therefore, the internationalization of the campus is likely to be another subcategory of 'comprehensive internationalization' that represents a number of interventions for the support and development of international and intercultural interactions on campus and complement the formal program learning [29]. As argued by the British Council [30] the presence of international students on campus does not in itself equals the internationalization of campus pointing out to the importance of integration of international students in communities and classes and considering integration as an integral part of campus internationalization that potentially can help the further promotion of a university and even a nation. Although student mobility is also often highly prioritized as such, for the purpose of this paper it is considered as the cornerstone and the 'face' of internationalization [31] and thus can not be internationalized as such. Spencer-Oatey et al. [32] point out in their study that even though the language barrier is definitely a major aspect of integration and the internationalization of campus, additional factors such as individual preferences of international students, cultural distance, welcoming approach and situational context should be considered as well. In other words, to internationalize a campus requires to develop such campus environment and institutional culture that would acknowledge the individualities of international students, demonstrate the openness to other cultures and reward support of international students and interaction between international and home students in terms of curricular and extra-curricular activities. Such an environment can definitely assist and encourage students in becoming responsible global citizens that can well manage challenging intercultural situations. Culturally diverse and essentially internationalized campus thus can provide opportunities for the students from different cultures to learn form each other and obtain skills that will help them to become a member of a globalized community.

Considering the scope of the overall 'comprehensive internationalization' it becomes clear that to introduce and implement this process a broad range of people of the university community has to be involved from teaching and research staff to service and administrative departments. The amount of resources required for this process is likely to depend on such factors as (1) structure of a university, (2) strategy, (3) field of study, and (4) university culture [23]. For instance, the internationalization of a university that (1) structurally has a department dedicated to international functions such as international relations office, (2) is strategically-oriented to internationalization, (3) is involved into research and teaching in the globalized area, for example, computer science and (4) has intercultural awareness among the staff, could be more successful in the adaptation to environmental changes. Obvious from the discussion of the definition the role of the leadership is central to the process of internationalization and to the question of university culture, in particular. A hierarchically-driven university that is focused on internal maintenance, operations and control will not likely be open to the changes and advantages that internationalization can bring [23]. To implement changes in the previously described six pillars of 'comprehensive internationalization', especially in curriculum and university culture, a university must embrace creativity, innovation and entrepreneurial spirit among its departments. The role of leadership thus becomes to support and reward the diversity of cultures and subcultures of different units that eventually will represent and promote the "meaning and identification with the objectives and strategies of internationalization" [23].

5   Conclusion

As we enter the third decade of the twenty-first century, higher education is facing the influence of intensity of globalization, competitiveness and the knowledge-based economy at an unprecedented level. The noteworthy changes in the global and academic trends might be stirring not only the way how universities operate as institutions but also the "idea of a university", its functions and roles in today's society. On the one hand, globalization exposes universities to a global competition that requires them to demonstrate certain quantitative results and thus to prioritize strategies, policies, programs and audits that help to produce these results. However, it is not clear if such orientation could produce any significant contribution to the essential functions of universities of teaching and research. On the other hand, the inter-connectedness of the globalized world and the knowledge-based economy brings different cultures, sometimes previously totally unexposed to each other, closer with the student mobility being a cornerstone of such a process. International students bring cultural diversity to the campus and provide the home students with the opportunity to learn intercultural competencies and also develop their understanding of what it means to be a global citizen.

Systemic answer of a university to the challenges that the twenty-first century brings would be a well-planned internationalization strategy. The scope of the internationalization needed will likely depend on the analysis of such factors as current structure of a university to define the amount of resources to dedicate to this purpose, current general strategy that might have already included certain aspects of internationalization, current state of a field of study as there are more and less affected by globalization industries, and finally organizational culture of universities that may need to involve cultural awareness to a greater extent. Internationalization strategy today is likely to be the key instrument that can help a university in the twenty-first century to maintain its primary functions and simultaneously use the advantages that the current trends offer. Careful planning and commitment to a qualitative change within the comprehensive internationalization or internationalization of certain aspects such as curriculum or campus can be of an immense value to the international status of a university and even a nation.

References

1. Kirkland, J.: A centenary reflection: challenges for universities and the wider commonwealth. Round Table **103**(3), 323–330 (2014)
2. Tight, M.: Globalization and internationalization as frameworks for higher education research. Res. Pap. Educ. 1–23 (2019)
3. Beech, S.E.: International student mobility: the role of social networks. Soc. Cultural Geograph. **16**(3), 332–350 (2015)
4. Newman, J.H.: The idea of a university, longimans (1986)
5. Patomäki, H.: Repurposing the university in the 21st century: toward a progressive global vision. Globalizations **16**(5), 751–762 (2019)
6. von Humboldt, W.: On the internal and external organization of the higher scientific institutions in berlin. Ger. Hist. Doc. Images **1**, 1648–1815 (1810)
7. Salisbury, F., Peseta, T.: The "idea of the university": positioning academic librarians in the future university. New Rev. Acad. Librarianship **24**(3–4), 242–262 (2018)
8. Barnett, R.: Being a University. Foundations and Futures of Education. Taylor & Francis, Abingdon (2010)
9. Nelles, J., Vorley, T.: From policy to practice: engaging and embedding the third mission in contemporary universities. Int. J. Soc. Soc. Policy (2010)
10. Jongbloed, B.: Universities as hybrid organizations: Trends, drivers, and challenges for the european university. Int. Stud. of Manag. Organ. **45**(3), 207–225 (2015)
11. McCully, G.: Multiversity and university. J. High. Educ. **44**(7), 514–531 (1973)
12. Halfond, J.: In my opinion: from multiversity to transversity: the new uses of the university. J. Continuing High. Educ. **53**(2), 41–42 (2005)
13. Frank, A.I., Sieh, L.: Multiversity of the twenty-first century-examining opportunities for integrating community engagement in planning curricula. Plan. Pract. Res. **31**(5), 513–532 (2016)
14. Sum, N.-L., Jessop, B.: Competitiveness, the knowledge-based economy and higher education. J. Knowl. Econ. **4**(1), 24–44 (2013)
15. Babones, S.: Studying globalization: methodological issues (2007)
16. Shangquan, G., et al.: Economic globalization: trends, risks and risk prevention. Econ. Soc. Aff. CDP Backround Pap. **1** (2000)
17. Samimi, P., Jenatabadi, H.S.: Globalization and economic growth: empirical evidence on the role of complementarities. PLoS One **9**(4), e87824 (2014)
18. Altbach, P.G., Knight, J.: The internationalization of higher education: motivations and realities. J. Stud. Int. Educ. **11**(3–4), 290–305 (2007)
19. Chochliouros, I.P., Spiliopoulou, A.S., Chochliouros, S.P.: Exploitation of public sector information in Europe (2008)

20. Holmwood, J., Servos, C.M.: Challenges to public universities: digitalisation, commodification and precarity. Soc. Epistemol. **33**(4), 309–320 (2019)
21. Pugh, R., Hamilton, E., Jack, S., Gibbons, A.: A step into the unknown: universities and the governance of regional economic development. Eur. Plann. Stud. **24**(7), 1357–1373 (2016)
22. American Council on Education: Washington, Educating Americans for a World in Flux: Ten Ground Rules for Internationalizing Higher Education. American Council on Education (1995)
23. Bartell, M.: Internationalization of universities: a university culture-based framework. High. Educ. **45**(1), 43–70 (2003)
24. Knight, J.: Updated definition of internationalization. Int. High. Educ. (33) (2003)
25. Ellingboe, B.J.: Divisional strategies to internationalize a campus portrait: results, resistance, and recommendations from a case study at a us university. Reforming High. Educ. Curriculum: Int. Campus **1998**, 198–228 (1998)
26. Hudzik, J.K.: Comprehensive Internationalization: From Concept to Action. NAFSA: Association of International Educators, Washington, DC (2011)
27. Dobbert, M.L.L.: The impossibility of internationalizing students by adding materials to courses. Reforming High. Educ. Curriculum: Int. Campus 53–68 (1998)
28. Helms, R.M., Brajkovic, L., Struthers, B.: Mapping Internationalization on US Campuses: 2017 Edition. American Council on Education, Washington, DC (2017)
29. Leask, B.: Using formal and informal curricula to improve interactions between home and international students. J. Stud. Int. Educ. **13**(2), 205–221 (2009)
30. British Council: Integration of International Students - a UK Perspective. British Council (2014)
31. Knight, J.: Student mobility and internationalization: trends and tribulations. Res. Comp. Int. Educ. **7**(1), 20–33 (2012)
32. Spencer-Oatey, H., Dauber, D., Jing, J., Lifei, W.: Chinese students' social integration into the university community: hearing the students' voices. High. Educ. **74**(5), 739–756 (2017)

Tools Workshop: Artificial and Natural Tools (ANT)

Automated Cross-Language Integration Based on Formal Model of Components

Artyom Aleksyuk and Vladimir Itsykson[✉]

JetBrains Research, Peter the Great St. Petersburg Polytechnic University,
Saint Petersburg, Russia
aleksyuk@kspt.icc.spbstu.ru, vlad@icc.spbstu.ru

Abstract. The paper presents the research aimed at development of a new method for integration of software components written in different languages, which allows omitting glue code manual writing. The necessity to write additional project-specific linking logic requires that programmers have at least good knowledge of two languages. Therefore, it is rather difficult to reuse well-tested libraries and other software components written in other languages in spite of the benefits, which they can offer. The paper analyzes advantages and disadvantages of the previously developed methods and tools intended for linking software components. The proposed method is based on the RPC approach, augmented with the LibSL language, previously created by the authors of the research that is designed to describe the software components external interface. The description of the external interface allows generating all the glue code automatically.

Based on the offered method, the tool that supports C, Java, Kotlin, Go, and JavaScript was developed. Applicability and efficiency of the proposed solution was tested by creation of the LibSL descriptions and stubs generation for a set of real-world libraries, such as a Z3 SMT solver.

Keywords: Cross-language integration · Language interoperability · Library models

1 Introduction

Today, it is common to have multiple languages in one software project. Languages differ in their usage areas, approaches to memory control and multithreading, applicability for different tasks. Old languages tend to have longstanding, well tested sets of libraries, though new languages usually provide additional syntactic sugar and safety improvements.

Although there exist several solutions for the cross-language interaction, most of them focus on solving particular tasks or require writing an additional linking code. Another issue with currently existing techniques is that they usually

This research work was supported by the Academic Excellence Project 5–100 proposed by Peter the Great St. Petersburg Polytechnic University.

J.-M. Bruel et al. (Eds.): FISEE 2019, LNCS 12271, pp. 357–370, 2020.
https://doi.org/10.1007/978-3-030-57663-9_23

require that software developers have good knowledge of both languages, which limits their applicability. The aim of this study is to create the method for the cross-language interaction, which allows software developers to use software components written in other programming languages without glue code manual writing and to implement it in a tool. The following tasks were established:

- Study the difficulties that arise when pairing different languages and runtime environments.
- Explore existing solutions to the problem of linking programs written in different programming languages.
- Create the method for the cross-language interaction which does not require glue code manual writing.
- Develop the research tool that implements the proposed method.
- Test the developed tool to verify the applicability of the method.

The rest of the paper is organized as follows. The second section contains the description of the state of the art. In the third section the proposed method for cross-language integration is presented. The fourth section is devoted to the implementation of the tool that proves feasibility of our method. In the fifth section the estimation of the tool applicability and performance is given. In the conclusion the obtained results are analyzed and possible directions of the future research are discussed.

2   State of the Art

The field of cross-language integration has been around for a long time. It is considerably related to the world-wide tendency to maintain already existing software over to develop the completely new [12]. There are a large number of approaches and tools that implement various aspects of cross-language integration.

In order to analyze the achievements in this area it is necessary to establish criteria for evaluating existing tools and approaches.

- Language support—a range of supported programming paradigms, runtimes, and memory models. Example: support for programming languages with a procedural paradigm, support for languages with automatic memory management using garbage collection.
- Difficulty of adaptation to a new language—the number of the components of the approach that should be modified in order to be applied to a new language.
- Difficulty of adaptation to a new project—the number of project components that need to be changed in order to apply the approach to a new project.
- Performance—the amount of additional overhead incurred due to the use of integration tools

We can distinguish the following existing approaches to solving the problem: FFI (Foreign Function Interface), based on function call convention bridging, RPC (Remote Procedure Call), based on data and function call exchange between separate processes, and application-level virtualization, based on creating a unified runtime environment for programs.

FFI is the approach assuming that the reused software component is located in the same virtual address space as the main program. Thus, the main task of FFI is to bridge calling conventions between different languages. Examples of the tools implemented on the top of the FFI approach are libffi and Java JNI [1]. libffi implements a calling convention for several popular operating systems and processor architectures, controls the location of arguments of called functions on the stack and in CPU registers.

Due to the fact that both programs are located in a common address space, data exchange between them is simplified. There is no need to convert data into a special format convenient for transmission (i.e. to perform a serialization). Since both programs from the point of view of the operating system are a single process, data exchange between them does not require a context switch. Switching the context is a resource-intensive operation, therefore, the absence of the need for switching allows increasing the performance of event transmission between programs and reduction of the transmission delay. FFI requires writing an additional code for each call to the reused software component. Also, FFI does not solve the task of adaptation of complex data structures, so it should be solved by a developer. Another drawback of the FFI approach is that it does not support bridging language runtimes. Many implementations of modern programming languages require usage of complex runtimes, which manage memory, process operating system events, and organize an interaction with a debugger. Several runtimes running inside the same process may have problems with gaining an exclusive access to the specified resources [13,18].

Usability of the tools grounded in FFI approach can be improved by application of wrapper programs, which establish all the data transformations necessary for the cross-language integration. Such wrappers can be written manually or generated by some tool. The main disadvantage of the wrapper-based approach is that a separate wrapper should be created for each pair of integrated languages. Also, wrappers are usually unable to solve the problem of bridging language runtimes. FFI and wrapper approach are widely used when it is necessary to reuse software components written in C, C++, and Fortran language, but are rarely used to integrate more high-level languages. The following projects are examples of this approach:

- SWIG [3] is a wrapper generator developed to allow using libraries written in C and C++. To describe libraries, SWIG uses its own language, partially compatible with C and C++. It is enough for the developer to rewrite the header files from C or C++ to the SWIG project language, which does not usually cause much difficulty.
- Lua programming language is specially designed for convenient interaction with C code [8].

- JNA (Java Native Access) utilizes interfaces written in Java language to describe functions and structures in a C library.

Another approach is to use RPC (Remote Procedure Call). Like FFI, it allows calling methods written in different languages, however, in case of RPC, two software components are loosely coupled, have separate virtual address spaces, and the only way to transfer data between them is to serialize it and send over a channel (over some kind of IPC, for example). RPC approach is not affected by the problem of conflicting runtimes and thus it is easy to add support for new languages to it. Examples of modern RPC tools are Google gRPC and Apache Thrift [16].

An RPC system consists of a client-side stub, which encodes a function call request and sends it over a channel, a server-side stub, which decodes a request, and a set of handlers which process the decoded request. To describe types of messages and their content, a special language called IDL (Interface Definition Language) is used. While most of RPC implementations automatically generate client stubs, there is still a need to manually write handlers for the receiving side which call a reused component [5]. Another drawback is the necessity to perform a serialization and synchronization of data. Problems can arise during serialization of objects with cyclic relationships, or when introspection information is not available. The examples of modern RPC systems are Cap'n Proto RPC and gRPC.

A special case of RPC is an approach called ORB (Object Request Broker). In addition to the functionality of calling functions from another language, ORB provides features for creating distributed applications, such as transaction support. One of ORB implementations is CORBA (Common Object Request Broker Architecture), a standard for organizing distributed application development, which can also be used for linking software components written in different languages. Despite its extensive capabilities, CORBA is almost not used for linking components on a single computer, primarily because of its complexity, as well as the need to manually write a glue code. A detailed analysis of the shortcomings of CORBA is available in the research works [7] and [11].

Another approach to solve this problem is to create an application-level virtual machine (VM) that can run programs written in different programming languages internally. The VM unifies the data types, the way data structures are stored in memory, and the calling convention. The VM also includes a runtime environment that is responsible for memory management. Using a common environment for multiple languages makes it easier to organize interaction between software components. An example of this approach is the Java Virtual Machine (JVM), which was originally created for one language, but later became used for other languages, such as Python (using Jython), Ruby (using JRuby), Kotlin (using Kotlin/JVM), and others. The development of JVM ideas is the GraalVM virtual machine [6]. The .NET CLR runtime was originally created to support multiple languages. The disadvantage of this approach is the need to develop a new environment, which is a time-consuming task, and can cause possible incompatibility of the existing software with the new environment.

There are several research papers with the analysis of the considered approaches applied to the specific areas of cross-language integration. Despite the specifics, as a rule, the findings can be reused in other areas. For example, the research work [4] covers the field of integration in relation to bioinformatics, while the article [17] considers the current situation in the field of aerospace.

Of the approaches considered, RPC is the easiest to adapt for new languages and new projects, but none of the tools considered based on RPC allows linking components written in different programming languages without manual glue code writing. This complicates the pairing procedure, depriving the developer of the advantages that the code reuse gives them.

3 The Proposed Method

To overcome the limits of the listed solutions, a new method for cross-language integration called LibraryLink was developed. The method in based on the RPC approach and extends it with automatically generated server and client stubs and several other additions, which allow reusing the existing software components without manual code writing.

The components of the method split into two categories: components that make a link between two programs (run time components) and components that generate a code (generator components). The scheme demonstrating relations between the runtime components is shown on Fig. 1.

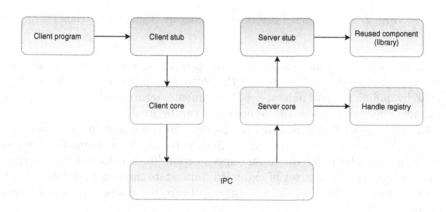

Fig. 1. The scheme of run time components

- **Client program** and **reused component** are the existing software components that should be linked.
- **Client-side stub** is a library written in a *client program*'s language which has the same external interface as the *reused component*. This library doesn't contain any business logic of the *reused component*, it only receives calls and redirects them to another components.

- **Client core** is a module that encodes method calls and data exchanges to the form suitable for the transfer to another process via an **IPC**.
- **Server core** decodes messages received from the *client core.*
- **Server-side stub** is a module written in *reused component*'s language which translates messages into the actual calls to the *reused component.*

Modules marked in orange are independent of the specific library, so they can be developed once. Modules marked in red are dependent to the specific library, so they need to be written manually or generated automatically. The scheme which demonstrates generator components is presented on Fig. 2.

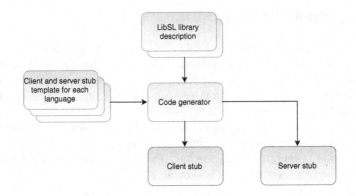

Fig. 2. The scheme of generator components (Color figure online)

To generate those modules, a description of the library's external interface is necessary. An external interface of the software component includes its class hierarchy, public method names, list of arguments, return value types and other elements, which define how the components can be used.

In this research the LibSL language [10] was chosen for description of an external interface of software components. LibSL is based on the formalism created earlier by the authors for the library specification [9]. The formalism describes software components as a set of extended finite state machines (EFSMs). Each EFSM reflects the life cycle of the entire software component or its individual entity.

The model of the program library in the LibSL language is a formal description of the external interface of the library available to the programmer for the use in software projects, as well as a description of the behavior of the library, abstracted from the specific implementation. LibSL description language is not tied to a specific programming language. LibSL is already used in other projects, such as Library Migration [2], so the description of a software component in LibSL allows solving a number of tasks.

The library model description in LibSL consists of the following sections:

- List of library modules and header files.
- Description of entities and data types used by the library.
- Description of automata.
- Declaration of functions and methods of a software component.

The data types section describes all semantic data types that are contained in or used by the library. Semantic data types are classes, structures, enumerations, and primitive data types in case they have a special meaning in the library, such as file descriptors or sockets. The section describing automata defines extended finite state machines (EFSM), which describe the behavior of library entities. The definition of a finite state machine includes the list of its states, as well as possible transitions between them (the transition function).

For the developed method, the most important transitions are the transition to the `Constructed` state (corresponds to calling the object constructor or initializing the structure) and the transition to the finished state marked with the `finishstate` keyword (corresponds to closing the resource and freeing the memory). Thus, if the client program is written in a language with automatic garbage collection and the reused component is written in a language with manual memory management, the developed method can intercept the garbage collection event in the client program and translate this event into a specified resource release operation in the reused component. Similarly, a call to the constructor in the client program is translated into a call to the initialization function in the component.

The functions and methods declaration section includes the description of the function/method signature of the software component, as well as the description of the properties of the function being described. The signature includes the function name, the list of function arguments (the argument name and its semantic type), and the value returned by the function. Each function is bound to a semantic type or entity. Listing 1 contains a fragment of Requests library description in LibSL. For more information about the LibSL syntax see [10].

```
types {
  Requests (Requests);
  Response (Response);
  StatusCode (Int);
}

automaton Requests {
  state Constructed;
  shift Constructed -> self (get);
}

fun Requests.get(url: URL, headers: Dict): Response;
```

List. 1. A fragment of Requests library description in LibSL

While developing the method, the LibSL language was expanded with a number of new constructions. The keyword `extendable` means that the library user can adjust the operation of the entity. The specific meaning depends on the programming language for which the libraries are described. If there is an inheritance mechanism in the language, this flag means that the entity can be inherited. If there is a callback mechanism or other mechanism in which the code is a data type, the flag extendable means that developers can set their own callback function. A description fragment that uses the keyword `extendable` is shown in Listing 2.

```
types {
  ErrorHandler (Z3_error_handler);
}

automaton ErrorHandler {
  shift Constructed -> self (invoke);
  extendable;
}

fun ErrorHandler.invoke(c: Z3_context, e: Int);
```

List. 2. A fragment of Z3 library specification illustrating a callback function

One of the tasks solved when developing the method was to eliminate the difficulties associated with serialization of data structures. The need to serialize transmitted structures is associated with the following difficulties:

- Need to track and synchronize changes in the client program and in the reused component.
- Requirement for an introspection programming interface in the programming language.
- Need to handle circular references when synchronizing changes.

The method uses the approach that eliminates the need for serialization of data structures. To do this, the interaction between components is organized using so-called handle objects. The client program works with handle, not with the objects of the reused component itself. Handles correspond to library objects and contain the same methods as the library objects. The handle method calls are translated into calls to the library methods. The actual data transfer is performed only when the main program requests data for transmission to other parts of the program and is limited only to primitive data types. This solution is similar to object references used in CORBA, promises used in Cap'n Proto RPC, and the proxy design pattern, but is applied not only to objects but also to the data structures and primitive types. Handles are stored in the **Handle registry**, see Fig. 1.

LibraryLink requires that not only the reused component be described but also its environment, in particular, the standard library of the language and its type system. To do this, separate LibSL descriptions are prepared and attached to the description of the reused component. For common data structures such as array, list, text string, and map, special reserved types were added to LibSL with a set of basic functions for operating these data structures. If necessary, other data structures can be specified in the description of language's standard library.

To improve performance, LibraryLink uses semantic information about the software component that is being reused. In particular, on the basis of the automata-based model and information about semantic actions it is determined whether it is possible to prefetch data from the component to the client code. More information about semantic actions can be obtained from the description of formalism [9]. For example, if a getter call is linked to a transition in an automata-based model, the model allows this transition at the next step, and this transition has no associated semantic actions, then we can assume that the transition has no side effects, and therefore the getter can be called in advance to forward data to the client program. This mechanism can be disabled if there is a possibility that data will be modified from another thread of the reused component.

The developed method involves developing *client core*, *server core*, and *IPC* for each supported language, as well as preparing a set of templates for generating *client stub* and *server stub*. The advantage of this method is that there is no need to develop components for each pair of languages. The method does not require serialization of the transmitted data. By using semantic information about the library, in particular, information about transitions in the automata-based model, the method allows coordinating memory management in the linked languages and prefetch data from the reused component in advance. To summarize the information, the comparison of LibraryLink to the basic approaches, such as RPC or FFI, is presented in Table 1.

Table 1. Comparison of cross-language integration methods and approaches

Solution	Glue code	Language support code	Serialization required	Memory management coordination	Caching and prefetching
FFI	Manually written	For each pair of languages $(\sim N^2)$	No	Manual	Manual
RPC	Manually written	For each language (N)	Yes	Manual	Manual
LibraryLink	Generated	For each language (N)	No	Inferred from a semantic model	Inferred from a semantic model

4   Tool Development

Based on the developed method, a research tool was developed[1]. The structure of the tool follows the structure of the method illustrated in Fig. 1 and Fig. 2.

Client core and Server core are written from scratch based on a custom IPC layer. The IPC layer employs Unix sockets because of their good performance [14] and wide support in different programming languages. However, the tool can be adapted to use an existing message exchange system like ZeroMQ. The developed tool is multithreaded since it is intended for modern object-oriented and procedural languages. A data exchange in one thread does not block an ability to transfer data in another thread.

To parse library descriptions written in LibSL, the ModelParser component was developed, which is placed in a separate library[2]. ModelParser is written in Kotlin and allows getting the library description in the form of AST. The ANTLR 4 parser is used to build the syntax tree. In addition, there is support for converting AST back to text (pretty printing).

Currently the tool allows generating *server stubs* for Java, Kotlin, Python, Go, and C programming languages. For Python, a universal stub is used that does not require adaptation for specific libraries and uses introspection and reflection, for other languages stubs are generated from the descriptions of specific libraries. In the case of *client stubs*, Java, Kotlin, and JavaScript programming languages are supported. The tool is able to generate Kotlin stubs that can be used from both Kotlin and Java programs, special Kotlin annotations are used for this purpose to establish compatibility with Java. A universal client stub was implemented for JavaScript using the Proxy API.

The first versions of the tool used separate libraries for each language, for example, JavaParser - for generating a code in Java and Jennifer - for generating code in Go. Stub AST was being constructed, which then was being converted into a code using the pretty printing component. The main disadvantage of this approach is a large amount of duplicate codes, since the stub generation process is structurally similar for different languages, but it still has enough differences to extract common code blocks. In addition, libraries for building AST are often written in the same language that they generate. Although it was possible to use these libraries with the tool being developed, the process known as bootstrapping was necessary.

The current version of the tool uses a template-based system. StringTemplate4 [15] is used as a template engine, which was initially developed for generating a program code. Although the new implementation has no drawbacks in code duplication, there is a issue of lack of conditional operators in the ST4 template language. To resolve this problem, an additional and more detailed intermediate representation of the library model is created during the stub generation. As possible ways to develop further the code generation component, we can consider switching to a template engine with more functionality. Another

---

[1] https://github.com/h31/LibraryLink.
[2] https://github.com/h31/ModelParser.

possible development direction is to abandon the code generation approach and switch to using introspection and reflection for all languages that support it.

A distinctive feature of our tool is an ability to release memory when objects become unused. The *client core* communicates with a garbage collector, and when a handle in the client program has no references pointing to it, the tool sends a message to the *server core* to remove all references on the actual object from the inner structures of the tool. A library description may contain information about how to properly delete an object and the tool is able to use this information. This feature is disabled by default for languages with manual memory management, but can still be enabled.

When using callback functions, the event initiator is the server. Therefore, the entire infrastructure for receiving and processing requests should be implemented on the client side. When the client code sets a callback function, a stub should be passed to the reused component that would translate the call back to the client part. In addition to the call event, arguments should be passed to the client program, which may require creating additional handles. If the client code sets several different callback functions, then several different stubs should be generated for the reused component so that the resulting events could be distinguished and dispatched to different handlers on the client side. Since it is impossible to determine in advance how many functions there will be, the dynamic generation of trampoline stub functions is used.

5   Evaluation

To test the applicability of the method several tests were performed using a tool developed on the basis of the method.

To test the completeness of support for syntactic constructions in the library description language, examples of using the Z3 library were rewritten in Kotlin (the file `examples/c/test_capi.c` from the Z3 source code tree). The result of rewriting can be found in the repository of the developed tool. The code written in Kotlin calls the Z3 library written in C++ (with C external interface) using the developed tool. The example of the source code in C and a rewritten version in Kotlin are shown in Listing 3 and Listing 4 respectively.

During this test, functions of the Z3 library are called, text strings and arrays are processed, data structures are selected in memory and deleted, and custom callback functions are installed. The check shows that the result of executing the original and rewritten versions coincides, and the programs output identical information to the standard output stream.

```
Z3_config cfg;
Z3_context ctx;
Z3_ast x, y, not_x, not_y, x_and_y;
Z3_ast args[2];

cfg            = Z3_mk_config();
ctx            = Z3_mk_context(cfg);
```

```
Z3_del_config(cfg);
x                     = Z3_mk_const(ctx, symbol_x, bool_sort);
y                     = Z3_mk_const(ctx, symbol_y, bool_sort);

not_x                 = Z3_mk_not(ctx, x);
not_y                 = Z3_mk_not(ctx, y);
args[0]               = x;
args[1]               = y;
x_and_y               = Z3_mk_and(ctx, 2, args);
```

List. 3. Fragment of C code using Z3 library

```
LibraryLink.runner = CRunner()
val cfg = Z3Kotlin.Z3_config();
val args = cArray<Z3Kotlin.Z3_ast>(2);
val ctx = cfg.Z3_mk_context();
x = ctx.Z3_mk_const(symbol_x, bool_sort);
y = ctx.Z3_mk_const(symbol_y, bool_sort);
not_x = ctx.Z3_mk_not(x);
not_y = ctx.Z3_mk_not(y);
args[0] = x;
args[1] = y;
x_and_y = ctx.Z3_mk_and(2, args);
```

List. 4. Fragment of Kotlin code using Z3 library

To test the correctness of the *server stub* implementations in Python and Go, we have prepared examples of using Requests and Jennifer libraries from the Kotlin language. The test showed that the created examples were working correctly. To test the *client stub* in JavaScript, an example of program using the Z3 library was created.

Despite the improvement of performance characteristics of cross-language integration was not specified as the main objective of research, performance testing was conducted. The results are shown in Table 2. All tests were run for 60 seconds with extra 10 seconds for warm up. Confidence level is 99.9%.

For performance testing, the JMH library (Java Microbenchmark Harness) was employed. Since we were interested only in a rough estimation of overhead added by tool, the test consisting a single function call which returns integer was developed. The client side was a module in Kotlin language, and the server side was a module in Go. The proposed test was run multiple times on Intel i7-4790 CPU and Linux with kernel version 5.3. The speed of call transfer was 57438 calls per second. With prefetch of up to 16 calls enabled, the speed increased to 194552 calls per second. Garbage collector was enabled during the test.

To conduct an illustrative performance comparison for LibraryLink and JNI methods the standard wrapper for the Z3 library (Z3 JNI) was utilized and several tests, containing different commonly used library calls, were developed. It takes 138.73 µs to create an object of the Context class, which is comparable to the results shown by LibraryLink (160.84 μs). However, it took 1.06 microsecond to make a simple `Context.mkBoolSort` call using JNI, and 25.6 microseconds to make a call using LibraryLink.

Table 2. Performance characteristics of LibraryLink and JNI

Payload	Tool	Calls/s	Av. time (μs)	St. dev	Confidence interval
No-op func	LibraryLink	57438	17.41	2.12	[15.99, 18.82]
No-op func w/ prefetch	LibraryLink	194552	5.14	2.82	[4.19, 6.10]
new Context	JNI	7208	138.73	28.98	[135.71, 141.76]
	LibraryLink	6217	160.84	13.36	[156.31, 165.37]
mkBoolSort	JNI	943396	1.06	0.85	[≈ 0, 2.37]
	LibraryLink	39062	25.6	0.87	[24.05, 26.68]

6   Conclusion

The aim of the presented research is to develop the cross-language integration method that allows developers to use software components written in other programming languages with a minimum amount of manual work. The new method called LibraryLink was created to solve this task. The developed method utilizes formal library models to generate the necessary glue code and does not require modifying reused components. The key features of LibraryLink are inheritance support and bridging of memory management between languages. The method was implemented in a tool supporting Kotlin, Java, C, Go, JavaScript and Python. The developed tool was successfully tested on a set of real-world libraries, which proves the applicability of the method.

The key direction of the future work is to adapt the developed tool for less popular languages where the library shortage issue is more substantial than in the mainstream ones including functional languages.

References

1. Adler, D.: Dynamic language bindings for C libraries with emphasis on their application to R. Ph.D. thesis, Niedersächsische Staats-und Universitätsbibliothek Göttingen (2013)
2. Aleksyuk, A.O., Itsykson, V.M.: Semantics-driven migration of Java programs: a practical application. Autom. Control Comput. Sci. **52**(7), 581–588 (2018)
3. Beazley, D.M., et al.: Swig: an easy to use tool for integrating scripting languages with C and C++. In: TCL/TK Workshop, vol. 43 (1996)
4. Bonnal, R.J.P., et al.: Sharing programming resources between bio* projects. In: Anisimova, M. (ed.) Evolutionary Genomics. MMB, vol. 1910, pp. 747–766. Springer, New York (2019). https://doi.org/10.1007/978-1-4939-9074-0_25

5. Grechanik, M., Batory, D., Perry, D.E.: Design of large-scale polylingual systems. In: Proceedings of 26th International Conference on Software Engineering, pp. 357–366 (2004)
6. Grimmer, M., Schatz, R., Seaton, C., Würthinger, T., Luján, M., Mössenböck, H.: Cross-language interoperability in a multi-language runtime. ACM Trans. Program. Lang. Syst. **40**(2), 8:1–8:43 (2018). http://doi.acm.org/10.1145/3201898
7. Henning, M.: The rise and fall of CORBA. Commun. ACM **51**(8), 52–57 (2008). https://doi.org/10.1145/1378704.1378718
8. Ierusalimschy, R., de Figueiredo, L.H., Celes, W.: The evolution of Lua. In: Proceedings of the 3rd ACM SIGPLAN Conference on History of Programming Languages, pp. 2-1 (2007)
9. Itsykson, V.M.: Formalism and language tools for specification of the semantics of software libraries. Autom. Control Comput. Sci. **51**(7), 531–538 (2017). https://doi.org/10.3103/S0146411617070100
10. Itsykson, V.: LibSL: language for specification of software libraries. Softw. Eng. **9**, 209–220 (2018)
11. Kaplan, A., Ridgway, J., Wileden, J.C.: Why IDLs are not ideal. In: Proceedings Ninth International Workshop on Software Specification and Design, pp. 2–7 (1998)
12. Krikhaar, R., Postma, A., Sellink, A., Stroucken, M., Verhoef, C.: A two-phase process for software architecture improvement. In: Proceedings IEEE International Conference on Software Maintenance - 1999 (ICSM 1999). Software Maintenance for Business Change (Cat. No.99CB36360), pp. 371–380 (1999)
13. Li, D., Srisa-an, W.: Quarantine: a framework to mitigate memory errors in JNI applications. In: Proceedings of the 9th International Conference on Principles and Practice of Programming in Java, PPPJ 2011, pp. 1–10. Association for Computing Machinery, New York (2011). https://doi.org/10.1145/2093157.2093159
14. Nambiar, M.K., Samudrala, S., Narayanan, S.: Experiences with UNIX IPC for low latency messaging solutions. In: International CMG Conference (2009)
15. Parr, T.J.: Enforcing strict model-view separation in template engines. In: Proceedings of the 13th International Conference on World Wide Web. WWW 2004, pp. 224–233. Association for Computing Machinery, New York (2004). https://doi.org/10.1145/988672.988703
16. Slee, M., Agarwal, A., Kwiatkowski, M.: Thrift: scalable cross-language services implementation. Facebook White Paper **5**(8) (2007)
17. Snyder, R.D.: A cross-language remote procedure call framework. In: 18th AIAA/ISSMO Multidisciplinary Analysis and Optimization Conference, p. 3822 (2017)
18. Tan, G.: JNI Light: An Operational Model for the Core JNI. In: Ueda, K. (ed.) APLAS 2010. LNCS, vol. 6461, pp. 114–130. Springer, Heidelberg (2010). https://doi.org/10.1007/978-3-642-17164-2_9

Scalable Thread-Modular Approach
for Data Race Detection

Pavel Andrianov$^{(\boxtimes)}$ and Vadim Mutilin

Ivannikov Institute for System Programming of the RAS,
Moscow Institute of Physics and Technology, Moscow, Russia
andrianov@ispras.ru

Abstract. Most of the state-of-the-art verifiers do not scale well on complicated software. Concurrency benchmarks from SV-COMP based on Linux device drivers cause significant difficulties for any software model checker tool.

We suggest a method, which is based on the Thread-Modular approach and Configurable Program Analysis theory. It overapproximates a potential thread iteration by a "worst case" assumption, that the threads may change the shared data in any way. The suggestion allows to avoid construction of a precise thread environment and simplifies the analysis.

For data race detection we use an extension of the Lockset algorithm based on compatibility of partial states. A BnB memory model allows to deal with complicated data structures without a precise alias analysis.

The approach was evaluated on benchmarks set, based on Linux device drivers. The approach allows verifying industrial software, as it was shown on the Linux drivers benchmarks. Predicate abstraction keeps false alarms rate on a reasonable level.

Keywords: Data race · Thread-modular approach · Linux kernel

1 Introduction

Verification of a multithreaded program is always a much more complicated task then verification of sequential program. Precise computation of all possible interleavings leads to a state explosion. Thus, most of the verification tools try to perform different kinds of optimizations: partial order reduction [1,2], counter abstraction [3] and others. Anyway, most state-of-the-art tools do not scale well on real-world software. That is confirmed by the software verification

The research was carried out with funding from the Ministry of Science and Higher Education of the Russian Federation (the project unique identifier is RFMEFI60719X0295).

J.-M. Bruel et al. (Eds.): FISEE 2019, LNCS 12271, pp. 371–385, 2020.
https://doi.org/10.1007/978-3-030-57663-9_24

competition [4]. Concurrency benchmarks based on Linux device drivers[1] cause significant difficulties for any software model checker tool.

Software model checkers usually have the following two stages for data race detection algorithm:

1. Constructing of a set of reachable states.
2. Checking a property over the set of the reached states.

The two steps may be performed sequentially or in parallel and even the reached set construction may be driven by the checked property. The most complicated task is considered to be an efficient construction of a reached set. However, finding a pair of states, which forms a data race is also a nontrivial task for a complicated software.

Regarding the construction of a reached set, our tool is based on a thread-modular approach [5,6], which is an efficient technique for analysis of multi-threaded software. The thread-modular approach considers each thread separately, that allows avoiding cartesian product of thread states, which is common for model checking. As a result, an abstract state is not a complete one anymore and represents only a state of a single thread as a partial state. Usually, analysis of a single thread without any other interactions is more efficient, than an analysis of all together. However, considering only partial states, the analysis loss information about transitions in other threads, which are strongly required for the soundness of the analysis.

The classical thread-modular approaches construct a thread environment, which overapproximates the potential thread effect. However, the construction of a precise environment is a difficult task. In the paper we describe an approach, which is invariant to thread effects, and thus avoids much effort for environment construction. Also, we describe a specific optimization for reached set construction based on Block Abstraction Memoization [7,8].

An implementation on the top of the CPAchecker framework allows combining different approaches to strengthen their advantages. For example, together with the thread-modular approach, we use CEGAR algorithm [9] and predicate abstraction [10]. The level of the abstraction may be flexibly adjusted.

Considering options to detect data races, static data race detectors usually use a Lockset algorithm [11]. We use a more intelligent way to detect data races: a potential data race is a pair of two compatible abstract states with corresponding transitions, which modifies the same memory. Compatibility here means the two partial abstract states may be a part of a single global state. Thus, the precision of such definition corresponds to a level of abstraction. So, for a single lock analysis, which tracks acquired locks, compatibility check corresponds to a classical Lockset algorithm.

We evaluated our approach on a set of benchmarks, based on Linux device drivers. They are prepared by Klever, a framework for verification of large software systems [12,13] which divides a large codebase into separate verification tasks (usually, one or two Linux modules) and prepares an environment model.

---

[1] sv-benchmarks/c/ldv-linux-3.14-races/directory.

Our contribution is:

- an extension of CPA theory to be able to describe thread-modular approach;
- an approach for data race detection, based on the extended theory;
- a tool, which was successfully evaluated on benchmarks, based on Linux device drives.

The rest of the paper is organized as follows. In Sect. 2 we present an overview of the approach. The Sect. 3 introduces a program model and basic definitions. The Sect. 4 describes an extension of the general CPA theory. The Sects. 5 and 6 contain two extended CPAs for thread modular approach: predicate analysis and lock analysis. In the Sect. 7 we discuss some specifics of data race detection with our approach. The Sect. 8 describes the Block Abstraction Memoization optimization. The Sect. 9 presents the results of our approach on a benchmark set, based on Linux device drivers.

2 Overview of the Approach

Consider a simple program, which has only two threads (Fig. 1). This is a model example, which contains accesses to a shared data, which are protected by a lock. Thus, there is no data race.

```
volatile int d = 0;
Thread1 {
    lock();                    Thread2 {
    if (d > 0) {                   lock();
        d = d + 1;                 d = 2;
    }                              unlock();
    unlock();                      ...
    ...                        }
}
```

Fig. 1. An example of code

Classic model checking approaches have to consider all possible interleavings, and possible values of shared data. It leads to a high consumption of resources: memory and time. Figure 2 presents a potential Abstract Reachability Graph (ARG), which may be computed by a precise software model checker tool.

To identify a potential data race, it is necessary to find an abstract state which has two potential transitions in both threads, and the transitions should modify the same variable. Each state marked as $\#1, \#2, \#3$ has an outgoing transition, which modifies the global variable, but there is no transition from the other thread. Thus, the model checker confirms that the example has no data race.

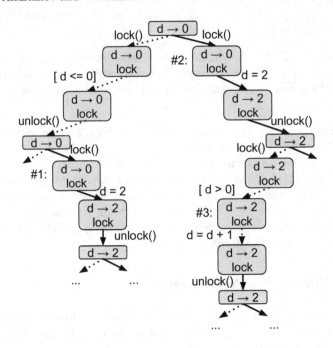

Fig. 2. ARG with interleaving analysis

In the paper we suggest an approach based on a well-known idea of thread-modular approach. In this case threads are analyzed separately in a special environment. The environment may be computed in a different way, and its precision strongly affects on precision of the whole analysis. However, construction of a precise environment takes a lot of time for complicated benchmarks. So, to consider a thread interaction we overapproximate possible thread effects and suppose that any thread may affect shared data in any way. That means, that value of shared data may be changed arbitrary at any moment. This is a very strong overapproximation, but it allows to consider every thread without any interaction, as we have already supposed the worst case.

Let us show, how thread-modular approach works.

Figure 3 shows a part of abstract reachability graph (ARG) for both threads. This is an imaginary analysis, which tracks only acquired locks. Values of a shared variable d is totally ignored in both threads. So, this part of ARG totally corresponds to the source code (or CFA), as if the threads are executed separately.

To check if there is a data race we need to find a pair of states, which start a transitions over the same shared data. Then we should check a *compatibility* of the states. Compatible partial states mean that they may be a part of a single global state. In the example there are states, which are followed by transitions with accesses to a global variable. Consider those ones, which modify a global variable d: #1 and #2. The states are not compatible, as both have the same

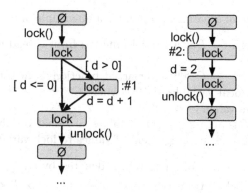

Fig. 3. ARG with thread-modular analysis

lock acquired. There can not be a global state, where two threads acquired the same lock simultaneously. In other words, the sets of the acquired locks of the sates must be disjoint. As the states are not compatible, they can not form a data race. For other accesses the reasoning are the same, thus there are no data races in the example.

The number of states are less than for classical model checker approach. It is achieved by two main reasons: the interaction of thread was omitted and the states become more abstract due to abstraction from shared variables. Thus, there are less resources consumed.

3   Preliminary Definitions

In this section, we present preliminary definitions of a parallel program and reachable concrete states in the program.

We restrict the presentation to a simple imperative programming language, where all operations are assignments, assumptions, acquire/release synchronization operations and thread creates. We denote all operations in a program as Ops.

A parallel program is represented by a Control Flow Automaton (CFA) [14], which consists of a set L of program locations (modeled by a program counter, pc), and a set $G \subseteq L \times Ops \times L$ of control-flow edges (modeling the operation that is executed when control flows from one program location to another). There is a thread create operation in Ops which creates a thread with an identifier from the set T and the thread starts from some location in L. The set of program variables that occur in assignment and assumption operations from Ops is denoted by X having values from $\mathbb{Z}$. The parts of X, containing local and global variables, are denoted by X^{local} and X^{global} respectively. Acquire/release operations are defined over a set of lock variables S having values from $T \cup \{\perp_T\}$, where $t \in T$ means that the lock is acquired by a thread t and $\perp_T$ means that the lock is not acquired.

A *concrete state* of a parallel program is a quadruple of (c_{pc}, c_l, c_g, c_s), where

1. A mapping $c_{pc} : T \to L$ is a partial function from thread identifiers to locations.
2. A mapping $c_l : T \to C^{local}$ is a partial function from thread identifiers to assignments to local variables C^{local}, where $C^{local} : X^{local} \to \mathbb{Z}$ assigns each local variable its value.
3. $c_g : X^{global} \to \mathbb{Z}$ is an assignment of values to global variables.
4. $c_s : S \to T \cup \{\perp_T\}$ is an assignment of values to lock variables.

A set of all concrete states of a program is denoted by C.

We define a (labeled) transition relation $\xrightarrow{\subseteq} C \times G \times T \times C$. We will write $c \xrightarrow{g,t} c'$ instead of $(c, g, t, c') \in \longrightarrow$

We denote $Reach_{\longrightarrow}(c) = \{c' \mid \exists c_1, \ldots, c_n \in C.c \longrightarrow c_1 \longrightarrow \ldots \longrightarrow c_n = c'\}$

We skip a complete definition of the semantics of all operators.

4   Extension of Configurable Program Analysis

The CPA theory was suggested in [14,15]. Basically, the main concepts of the theory remain the same. In our theory, an abstract state is a partial one, so it may not represent any concrete state of a program. That is why the concretization function in our theory differs from the original one. Our concretization function is defined on a set of elements. However, this change does not affect operator definitions. One more change is introduction of a new operator for checking compatibility of states.

Now define the *Configurable Program Analysis* $\mathbb{D} = (D, \Pi, merge, stop, prec, \leadsto, compatible)$. It consists from an abstract domain D of abstract elements, a set of precisions Π, a merge operator *merge*, a termination check *stop*, a precision adjustment function *prec* and transfer relation $\leadsto$ and compatibility check *compatible*. The operator *compatible* is a new operator for CPA theory, which is used for checking if the two partial states can represent parts of a single concrete state.

1. The *abstract domain* $D = (C, \mathcal{E}, \llbracket \cdot \rrbracket)$ is defined by the set C of concrete states, the semi-lattice $\mathcal{E}$ of abstract states and a concretization function $\llbracket \cdot \rrbracket$. The $\mathcal{E} = (E, \top, \perp, \sqsubseteq, \sqcup)$ consists of the (possibly infinite) set E of abstract domain elements, a top element $\top \in E$, a bottom element $\perp \in E$, a partial order $\sqsubseteq \subseteq E \times E$ and a function $\sqcup : E \times E \to E$ (join operator). The function $\sqcup$ yields the least upper bound for two lattice elements, and symbols $\top$ and $\perp$ denote the least upper bound and greatest lower bound of the set E respectively. The concretization function $\llbracket \cdot \rrbracket : 2^E \to 2^C$ assigns to each set of abstract states $R \subseteq E$ its meaning, i.e. the set of concrete states that it represents. Note, that we use concretization on sets of state instead of a single state. Thus we have
$$\forall R \subseteq E : \llbracket R \rrbracket \supseteq \bigcup_{e \in R} \llbracket \{e\} \rrbracket$$

meaning that the summary knowledge for the set of partial states may be bigger than union of knowledge for the single (partial) transition.

For thread-modular analyses a concretization function $[\![\cdot]\!]$ means all possible compositions of partial states:

$$\forall R \subseteq E : [\![R]\!]_P =$$

$$\bigcup_{k=1}^{\infty} \quad \bigcup_{\substack{e_0, e_1, \ldots, e_k \in R \\ t_0, t_1, \ldots, t_k \in T}} \quad \bigoplus_I \left(\left\{ \begin{pmatrix} e_0 \\ t_0 \end{pmatrix}, \ldots, \begin{pmatrix} e_k \\ t_k \end{pmatrix} \right\} \right) \qquad (1)$$

So, an analysis is required to define not a concretization function $[\![\cdot]\!]$, but a composition operator $\bigoplus$ because the thread-modular approach requires unified schema for calculation of concrete states.

As we have already discussed all states are partial, so they may not be directly related to concrete states. To get a complete state we should get a composition of a set of partial states, which represent all available threads. Compatible partial states can be composed into a complete concrete state with an operator $\bigoplus : 2^{E \times T} \to 2^C$. It returns a set of concrete states, which is represented by given partial states.

2. The *transfer* relation $\leadsto : E \times \Pi \times E$ assigns to each partial state $\hat{e}$ with precision π possible new abstract state e' which is abstract successor of $\hat{e}$. The transfer relation must overapproximate the concrete transitions:

$$\forall R \subseteq E, \pi \in \Pi$$

$$[\![\bigcup_{e \in R} \{e' \mid (e, \pi) \leadsto e'\} \cup R]\!] \supseteq \bigcup_{c \in [\![R]\!]} \{c' \mid c \longrightarrow c'\} \qquad (2)$$

The requirement 2 generalizes the requirement on *transfer* operator in the classical CPA theory, because of change in concretization function.

3. For data race detection we need one more operator: *compatible* : $E \times E \to \{true, false\}$. It defines if the two partial states may be a part of a single concrete state. If so, the corresponding transitions may be executed in parallel from different threads. The operator is used not in main CPAAlgorithm, but for data race detection after construction of reached set.

The precision domain Π, termination check *stop*, merge operator *merge*, precision adjustment *prec* are the same as in the original CPA theory. The main algorithm, which computes a set of reached abstract transitions, also stays the same.

The main Theorem 1 may be proven for the algorithm with extended operators as well as for classical version.

Theorem 1 *(Soundness). For a given configurable program analysis with thread abstractions $\mathbb{D}$ and an initial abstract state e_0 with precision π_0, Algorithm CPA computes a set of abstract states that overapproximates the set of reachable concrete states:*

$$[\![CPA(\mathbb{D}, e_0, \pi_0)]\!] \supseteq Reach_{\longrightarrow}([\![\{e_0\}]\!])$$

5   Predicate Analysis

In the section, we describe a commonly used Predicate Analysis [16] in a thread-modular version. To satisfy the requirement 2 the analysis has to be invariant to possible changes in other threads. That means, the predicate abstract state should not contain any information about shared data, considering that it may be changed at any moment by some other thread.

Let $\mathscr{P}$ be a set of formulas over program variables in a quantifier-free theory $\mathscr{T}$. Let $P \subseteq \mathscr{P}$ be a set of predicates. Let $v : X \to \mathbb{Z}$ is a mapping from variables to values. Define $v \models \varphi$, where v is called model of φ.

Define $(\varphi)^\pi$ – the boolean predicate abstraction of formula φ.

Define $SP_{op}(\varphi)$ – strongest postcondition of φ and operation op, regarding the specifics of shared data.

We define Predicate Analysis $\mathbb{P} = (D_P, \Pi_P, \rightsquigarrow_P, merge_P, stop_P, prec_P)$ which can track the validity of predicates over program variables.

It consists of the following components.

1. The abstract domain $D_P = (C, \mathcal{E}_P, \bigoplus_P)$.
   $\mathcal{E}_P = (E_P, \top_P, \bot_P, \sqsubseteq_P, \sqcup_P)$. $E_P = \mathscr{P}$, so a state is a quantifier free formula. The top element $\top_P = true$, and bottom element $\bot_P = false$. The partial order $\sqsubseteq_P \subseteq E_P \times E_P$ is defined as $e \sqsubseteq_P e' \Leftrightarrow e \implies e'$. The join $\sqcup_P : E_P \times E_P \to E_P$ yields the least upper bound according to partial order.

$$\forall e_0, \ldots, e_n \in E_P, t_0, \ldots, t_n \in T, t_i \neq t_j, \hat{v}_i \models e_i :$$

$$\bigoplus_P \left(\left\{ \begin{pmatrix} e_0 \\ t_0 \end{pmatrix}, \ldots, \begin{pmatrix} e_n \\ t_n \end{pmatrix} \right\} \right) = \left\{ c \in C \, \middle| \, \begin{matrix} \forall 0 \leq i \leq n \\ c_l(t_i) = \hat{v}_i \end{matrix} \right\} \quad (3)$$

   The definition of $\bigoplus_P$ means that the abstract partial states are combined using only information about local variables. So, any model $\hat{v}_i$ for every local state e_i may produce a corresponding local part of a global state $c_l(t_i)$. There is no limitations about global part c_g as the analysis has no information about values of global variables.

2. The set of precisions $\Pi_P = 2^P$ models a precision for an abstract state as a set of predicates.

3. For $g \in G$ we have the transfer $(e, \pi) \rightsquigarrow_P e'$ with $g = (\cdot, op, \cdot)$, if $e' = SP_{op}(e)$.

4. Merge operator may have several modifications, for example,
   (a) $merge_{Join}$ merges both parts of the transition:

$$\forall e, e' \in E_P, \pi \in \Pi_P :$$

$$merge_P(e, e', \pi) = e \lor e' \quad (4)$$

   (b) $merge_{Sep}$ does not merge elements.

5. The *stop* checks if e is covered by another state in the reached set: $stop_P(e, R, \pi) = \exists e' \in R : (e \sqsubseteq e')$.
6. The precision adjustment function constructs predicate abstraction over predicates in precision π: $prec_P(e, \pi, R) = e^\pi = (s^\pi, q)$.
7. Compatibility check is trivial, because PredicateCPA does not track the values of global variables: $compatible(e_1, e_2) \equiv true$.

6   Lock Analysis

We define Lock Analysis $\mathbb{S} = (D_S, \Pi_S, \leadsto_S, merge_S, stop_S, prec_S)$ which tracks the set of acquired locks (synchronization variables) for each thread.
   It consists of the following components.

1. The abstract domain $D_S = (C, \mathcal{E}_S, \bigoplus_S)$ uses semi-lattice $E_S = 2^S \cup \{\top^E, \bot^E\}$ is a superset of synchronization variables, $\bot_S \sqsubseteq ls \sqsubseteq_S \top_S$ and $ls \subseteq ls' \Rightarrow ls \sqsupseteq_S ls'$ for all elements $ls, ls' \subseteq S$ (this implies $\bot_S \sqcup_S^S ls = ls$, $\top_S^S \sqcup ls = \top_S$, $ls \sqcup_S ls' = ls \cap ls'$ for all elements $ls, ls' \subseteq S, ls \neq ls'$),

$$\forall e_1, \ldots, e_n \in E_S :$$

$$\bigoplus_S \left(\left\{ \begin{pmatrix} e_0 \\ t_0 \end{pmatrix}, \ldots, \begin{pmatrix} e'_n \\ t_n \end{pmatrix} \right\} \right) =$$

$$= \begin{cases} \{c \in C \mid \hat{s} \in s_i \implies c_s(\hat{s}) = t_i\}, & \text{if } \forall i \neq j : compatible(e_i, e_j) \\ \emptyset, & \text{otherwise} \end{cases}$$

The definition of $\bigoplus_S$ means that the partial states may be combined into global ones if any acquired lock is acquired only in a one state. Then, in a corresponding global states the acquired lock appears in a c_s.
2. There is only one empty precision: $\Pi_S = \{\{\emptyset\}\}$.
3. The *transfer* increases the number of stored locks in case it goes via *acquire* operator and decreases in case of *release*. Formally, the transfer relation $\leadsto_S$ has the transfer $(e, \pi) \overset{g}{\leadsto}_S e'$, $g = (\cdot, op, \cdot')$ if
   - $op = acquire(s)$ and $s \notin e \wedge e' = e \cup \{s\}$, $g' \in G$.
   - $op = release(s)$ and $e' = e \setminus \{s\}$, $g' \in G$.
   - $op = thread\_create(l_\nu)$ and $ls' = \emptyset$, $g' \in G$.
   - otherwise, $ls = ls'$, $g' \in G$.
4. The merge operator does not combine elements: $merge_S(e, e', \pi) = e'$.
5. The termination check is true if exists state which contains less locks: $stop_S(e, R, \pi) = (\exists e' \in R \wedge e \sqsubseteq e')$.
6. The precision is never adjusted: $prec_S(e, \pi, R) = (e, \pi)$.
7. $\forall e_1, e_2 \in E_S : compatible_S(e, e') = (ls \cap ls' = \emptyset)$. The compatibility check is very close to basic Lockset algorithm. If there is the same lock in both threads, the operations can not be composed into the concrete one, as two threads can not acquire the same lock.

7   Data Race Detection

Usually, data race is considered to be a situation where simultaneous accesses to the same memory takes place from different threads, and one of the accesses is a write one. Here are two main issues: how to detect the same memory in a static way and how to detect simultaneous accesses. Further, we will discuss the two features of our approach.

To detect data race conditions, we construct an abstract reachability graph of possible abstract states. Then, we search for two compatible states, which are followed by transitions, modifying the same memory. Our approach for static race detection is a generalization of Lockset [11], which claims data race as two accesses with disjoint sets of locks. One of the limitations of the Lockset approach is the absence of support of other synchronization primitives. We use *compatible* operator to identify the potentially parallel operations. As compatibility check is based on different kinds of analyzes, including Lock analysis, it is more precise, than the Lockset.

The presented theory supports shared data, which are expressed only by global variables. In a real-world software, there are a lot of operations with pointers, structure fields and so on. We are using BnB memory model, which divides memory into a disjoint set of regions [8,17,18]. The region corresponds to a special data type or to a special structure field in case of the field was not addressed. The memory model has a certain number of limitations. First of all, it does not support address arithmetic and casting, which reduces the soundness. Then, there may be false alarms for general data types, like integer, as there are a lot of accesses to it.

The data race detection algorithm consists of the following steps:

1. compute a complete set of reached abstract states (ARG);
2. for every reached state extract a memory region it accesses to;
3. for every memory region try to find a compatible pair of transitions, which form a race condition;
4. check every potential data race for feasibility and refine a predicate abstraction if necessary [16];

8   Utilizing Block Abstraction Memoization

Block Abstraction Memoization (BAM) implements an optimization, which is based on caching the results of the analysis. Caching is performed on border of blocks, which are usually function bodies. So, at block entry an abstract state is remembered as starting state and at block exit an abstract states are remembered as final states. And at the next block entry with the same starting state the analysis reuse the final state without reconstruction of the reached states inside the block.

To increase the number of cache hits a transformation of states is applied. An operator *reduce* remove irrelevant part of the starting state, generalizing it. So, two different starting states may be reduced into the same one, and there is a cache hit. A missed information is returned at the block exit with *expand* operator. The operators are defined by every CPA.

Reached states inside an abstract block are combined into a nested reached set. The nested reached set may be reused several times if there are multiple entries into the corresponding abstract block. It allows to significantly reduce memory consumption, as a single copy is stored.

```
int global;
...
1: int f(int a) {
2:   int r = a + 1;
3:   return r;
4: }

5: int main(){
6:    int l = nondet_int();
7:    l = f(l);
8:    lock();
9:    l = f(l);
10:   unlock();
11:}
```

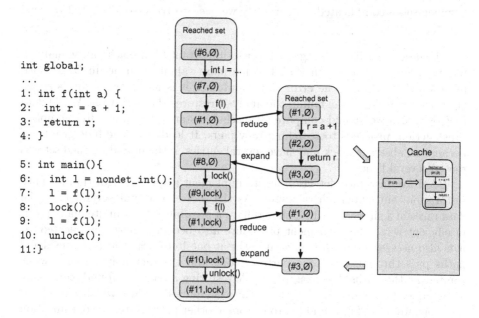

Fig. 4. An example of BAM work

Figure 4 presents an example of analysis with BAM. At the first entry in function f, operation *reduce* does not change the state. At the second entry in function f, operation *reduce* removes a lock and after that the reduced states becomes equal to the first reduced state. Thus, BAM gets the result of analysis of function f from the cache. After that it expands the resulting state and returns the omitted lock.

Using reduction of states and a cache, BAM allows to reduce exploring state space using a cache. However, the optimization has a number of disadvantages.

1. A set of reached states becomes incomplete. Due to *reduce* operation the reached set may not contain those states, which are reachable in analysis without BAM. As the reduced states are generalization of expanded ones, that does not mean the analysis becomes unsound, but it becomes imprecise. Although *reduce* operation should save all relevant information for analysis, missed details may be necessary for some post-analysis, for example, data race detection.

2. A set of reached states becomes distributed between different abstract blocks. For every abstract block its own reached set is created, which contains all states reachable in the particular block. The copy is used to convenient work with the cache.
3. The previous issues lead to problems with path computation, as the path goes through different reached sets and potentially reduced states.
4. All modifications of reached set, for example, removing a part of ARG, become much more complicated, as currently we need to traverse all nested reached sets.

The described disadvantages are not so important for a reachability analysis, but for data race detection they become more valuable. In origin BAM optimization there is only one error state, and once it is found the analysis stops. So, if the error state was found, the analysis restores the path to it. While data race detection we should compute all reachable states, and only after complete construction, proceeds to searching racy pairs. It leads to some indeterminacy, because an abstract block may have several entries, if the nested reached set was reused several times.

BAM for data race detection has to implement a specific algorithm for path restoration, and subgraph removing. As the tool can output several potential data races in a single launch, it should have a possibility to compute many paths in efficient way. The refinement procedure also becomes more complicated, as it is also necessary to refine several paths at one iteration. Many of considered paths pass through the same parts of code and the fact may be used while computing the paths. For example, while restoring a path, we found, that there are a sequence of states, which is the same as in infeasible path, which was refined just now, we may skip it and try to restore another path. Note, the optimization does not lead to unsoundness, as if the data race is true, it will appear on the next iteration of the analysis.

9 Evaluation

We have evaluated CPALockator tool in the following configuration:

- Location Analysis (tracks program locations),
- Callstack Analysis (tracks function callstack),
- Thread Analysis (tracks tread creation points to detects happens-before dependencies),
- Lock Analysis (Sect. 6),
- Predicate Analysis (Sect. 5)
- BAM optimization (Sect. 8)

The benchmark sets were launched on a set of machines with a GNU/Linux operating system (x86_64-linux, Ubuntu 18.04), Intel Xeon E3-1230 v5, 3.40 GHz. We used default SV-COMP limits: 15 min of CPU time and 15 GB of memory.

The set of benchmarks, based on Linux device drivers, was prepared by Klever tool, a framework for verification of large software systems [12,13]. It divides a large codebase into separate verification tasks. For the Linux kernel, a verification task consists of one Linux module. Then Klever automatically prepares an environment model, which includes a thread model, a kernel model, and operations over the module. After the preparation of a verification task, Klever calls a verification tool via a common interface – BenchExec [19].

We chose the *drivers/net/* subsystem of Linux kernel 4.2.6, for which Klever prepared 425 verification tasks[2]. We compared the following configurations:

1. **Base**. The default configuration without BAM and without Predicate analysis.
2. **WithBAM**. A configuration with BAM optimization.
3. **WithPredicate**. A configuration with Predicate analysis.
4. **Both**. A configuration with both BAM and Predicate analysis.

Table 1 presents the results.

Table 1. Comparison on benchmarks *drivers/net/*

Approach	Base	WithBAM	WithPredicate	Both
False verdicts	135	158	5	38
correct	85	85	3	29
confirmed	1	2	3	29
incorrect	50	73	2	9
True verdicts	246	246	248	256
correct	246	246	248	256
incorrect	0	0	0	0
Unknown	44	21	172	131
CPU time (c)	14 300	13 100	70 500	98 600

Discussion. A false verdict means, that there is at least one potential data race condition. Note, the potential race condition may be not correct one, for example, due to infeasible paths. We denote modules with feasible data races as *confirmed*. So, without predicate analysis most of the warnings have contradictions in variable values along the path. They are false alarms even though the final verdict is correct, because corresponding paths are infeasible.

Base configuration works very fast because of absence of precise predicate analysis. However, it also leads to imprecision and lots of false alarms (not confirmed). **WithBAM** improves the situation a bit, but new verdicts are mostly incorrect. **WithPredicate** improves the precision, but losing the speed.

---

[2] https://gitlab.com/sosy-lab/software/ldv-benchmarks.git, directory *linux-4.2.6-races*.

Enabling BAM in **Both** configuration significantly improves the situation. Note, the increasing CPU time for the configuration **Both** in comparison to **With-Predicate** is related to a number of out of memory results in the latter. For these cases BAM allows to reduce memory consumption and works longer. The evaluation confirms the efficiency of BAM optimization.

We reported most of the true race conditions and they were confirmed by Linux maintainers. However, most of the bugs were found in ancient drivers and nobody wants to fix it. Only a couple of patches are applied to the upstream as a part of Google Summer of Code project.

10   Conclusion

The paper presents an approach for practical data race detection in complicated software. We extended an existing CPA theory and implemented it in a new tool. The experiments show the benefit of the approach on large examples. On the other hand, small and complicated benchmarks are better solved with other approaches. Anyway, the approach is sound and may be improved and optimized in the future.

One of the possible directions is to implement a precise thread-modular approach, which can compute thread environment efficiently. It will help to increase the precision of the whole analysis.

References

1. Abdulla, P., Aronis, S., Jonsson, B., Sagonas, K.: Optimal dynamic partial order reduction. SIGPLAN Not. **49**(1), 373–384 (2014)
2. Godefroid, P.: Partial-Order Methods for the Verification of Concurrent Systems: An Approach to the State-Explosion Problem. Springer, Heidelberg (1996). https://doi.org/10.1007/3-540-60761-7
3. Basler, G., Mazzucchi, M., Wahl, T., Kroening, D.: Symbolic counter abstraction for concurrent software. In: Bouajjani, A., Maler, O. (eds.) CAV 2009. LNCS, vol. 5643, pp. 64–78. Springer, Heidelberg (2009). https://doi.org/10.1007/978-3-642-02658-4_9
4. Beyer, D.: Automatic verification of C and Java programs: SV-COMP 2019. In: Beyer, D., Huisman, M., Kordon, F., Steffen, B. (eds.) TACAS 2019. LNCS, vol. 11429, pp. 133–155. Springer, Cham (2019). https://doi.org/10.1007/978-3-030-17502-3_9
5. Henzinger, T.A., Jhala, R., Majumdar, R., Qadeer, S.: Thread-modular abstraction refinement. In: Hunt, W.A., Somenzi, F. (eds.) CAV 2003. LNCS, vol. 2725, pp. 262–274. Springer, Heidelberg (2003). https://doi.org/10.1007/978-3-540-45069-6_27
6. Gupta, A., Popeea, C., Rybalchenko, A.: Threader: a constraint-based verifier for multi-threaded programs. In: Gopalakrishnan, G., Qadeer, S. (eds.) CAV 2011. LNCS, vol. 6806, pp. 412–417. Springer, Heidelberg (2011). https://doi.org/10.1007/978-3-642-22110-1_32

7. Friedberger, K.: CPA-BAM: block-abstraction memoization with value analysis and predicate analysis. In: Chechik, M., Raskin, J.-F. (eds.) TACAS 2016. LNCS, vol. 9636, pp. 912–915. Springer, Heidelberg (2016). https://doi.org/10.1007/978-3-662-49674-9_58

8. Andrianov, P., Friedberger, K., Mandrykin, M., Mutilin, V., Volkov, A.: CPA-BAM-BnB: block-abstraction memoization and region-based memory models for predicate abstractions. In: Legay, A., Margaria, T. (eds.) TACAS 2017. LNCS, vol. 10206, pp. 355–359. Springer, Heidelberg (2017). https://doi.org/10.1007/978-3-662-54580-5_22

9. Clarke, E.M., Grumberg, O., Jha, S., Lu, Y., Veith, H.: Counterexample-guided abstraction refinement. In: Emerson, E.A., Sistla, A.P. (eds.) CAV 2000. LNCS, vol. 1855, pp. 154–169. Springer, Heidelberg (2000). https://doi.org/10.1007/10722167_15

10. Graf, S., Saidi, H.: Construction of abstract state graphs with PVS. In: Grumberg, O. (ed.) CAV 1997. LNCS, vol. 1254, pp. 72–83. Springer, Heidelberg (1997). https://doi.org/10.1007/3-540-63166-6_10

11. Savage, S., Burrows, M., Nelson, G., Sobalvarro, P., Anderson, T.: Eraser: a dynamic data race detector for multi-threaded programs. SIGOPS Oper. Syst. Rev. **31**(5), 27–37 (1997)

12. Novikov, E., Zakharov, I.: Towards automated static verification of GNU C programs. In: Petrenko, A.K., Voronkov, A. (eds.) PSI 2017. LNCS, vol. 10742, pp. 402–416. Springer, Cham (2018). https://doi.org/10.1007/978-3-319-74313-4_30

13. Novikov, E., Zakharov, I.: Verification of operating system monolithic kernels without extensions. In: Margaria, T., Steffen, B. (eds.) ISoLA 2018. LNCS, vol. 11247, pp. 230–248. Springer, Cham (2018). https://doi.org/10.1007/978-3-030-03427-6_19

14. Beyer, D., Henzinger, T.A., Théoduloz, G.: Configurable software verification: concretizing the convergence of model checking and program analysis. In: Damm, W., Hermanns, H. (eds.) CAV 2007. LNCS, vol. 4590, pp. 504–518. Springer, Heidelberg (2007). https://doi.org/10.1007/978-3-540-73368-3_51

15. Beyer, D., Henzinger, T.A., Theoduloz, G.: Program analysis with dynamic precision adjustment. In: 2008 23rd IEEE/ACM International Conference on Automated Software Engineering, pp. 29–38, September 2008

16. Beyer, D., Keremoglu, M.E., Wendler, P.: Predicate abstraction with adjustable-block encoding. In: Formal Methods in Computer-Aided Design, FMCAD 2010 (2010)

17. Bornat, R.: Proving pointer programs in hoare logic. In: Backhouse, R., Oliveira, J. (eds.) MPC 2000. LNCS, vol. 1837, pp. 102–126. Springer, Heidelberg (2000). https://doi.org/10.1007/10722010_8

18. Burstall, R.M.: Some techniques for proving correctness of programs which alter data structures. Mach. Intell. **7**, 23–50 (1972)

19. Beyer, D., Löwe, S., Wendler, P.: Reliable benchmarking: requirements and solutions. Int. J. Softw. Tools Technol. Trans. **21**(1), 1–29 (2017). https://doi.org/10.1007/s10009-017-0469-y

On the Development of the Compiler from C to the Processor with FPGA Accelerator

Anton Baglij[✉], Elena Metelitsa, Yury Mikhailuts, Ruslan Ibragimov, Boris Steinberg, and Oleg Steinberg

Southern Federal University, Rostov-on-Don, Russia
{abagly,metelica,mihayluc,ribragimov,
byshtyaynberg,obshtyaynberg}@sfedu.ru

Abstract. This work describes the further development of the compiler project for CPU with FPGA-accelerator. This compiler is based on the Optimizing Parallelizing System (OPS) of the Southern Federal University. There is a structure of the considered compiler briefly described in the article. Some specific parts of OPS internal representation for pipelines and automats to control pipelines are described in more detail. Examples of programs that are compiled by an experimental compiler are given, as well as high-level program transformations of OPS that can be used in this compiler.

Keywords: HDL · FPGA · Compiler · Pipeline generation · Program transformations

To the famous developer of compilers, Andrey Nikolaevich Terekhov is devoted

1 Introduction

Field-programmable gate arrays (FPGA) deliver performance advantages for a wide class of problems as well as relatively low energy consumption. This makes FPGAs more appealing for use in unmanned vehicles, especially flying ones, as well as in supercomputers. However, FPGA development is set back by a lack of high-level programming language compilers. This work is continuing the authors' previous work dedicated to the development of the compiler for a reconfigurable computational architecture. Target computer is either a system on chip that contains a processor core along with a reconfigurable logic block matrix [1] or a standard processor with FPGA accelerator.

This compiler's structure was described in previous work [2], This project's relevance is proved by the fact that a reconfigurable architecture accelerator is

Supported by organization Southern Federal University x.

J.-M. Bruel et al. (Eds.): FISEE 2019, LNCS 12271, pp. 386–400, 2020.
https://doi.org/10.1007/978-3-030-57663-9_25

able to adjust to the structure of high-level programs and reach higher performance than universal accelerators.

Computers with programmable and reconfigurable pipeline architectures are being developed for a wide range of applications and show high efficiency [3,4]. Multi-pipeline architectures are described in works [5–8].

It should be noted that there are a lot of tools for high-level synthesis. Examples of commercial products are: Catapult C, Vivado Design Suite, Impulse CoDeveloper, Altium Designer, HDL Coder for MATLAB. Academic research projects: C-to-Verilog [9], THE [10] and Parallel Intellectual Compiler [11]. Here we can also mention the system described in [12], which contains a Converter from high-level language to electronic circuit design. The Trident Compiler [13] system requires a user to manually split the code into software and hardware parts.

There are a set of tools for lower-level synthesis as well. Mitrion C [14], Handel-C [15], and HaSCoL [16] systems use specially designed language constructs to describe hardware elements and commands that are not present in traditional programming languages (operations with individual bits, synchronization tools, etc.). This makes such languages lower-level. For example, the paper [17] proposed a generalization of data flow graph under the name bit-flow graph. In [18], Autocode is a low-level FPGA language, but higher than Verilog or VHDL.

This paper proposes a compiler from C to a processor with an FPGA accelerator. The compiled code is partially run on the CPU and on the FPGA. This approach is very close to one from the Altera C2H compiler project for the NIOS2 processor. This compiler became obsolete as it requires to write a lot of architecture-specific pragmas along with the program code in the C language. However, this requirement destroys the idea of high-level languages, because the programmer must know the features of the target architecture. In addition, transferring code from this processor to other processors or, conversely, from other processors to this one is also very time-consuming.

Let us note the works of a group of authors that preceded this article. Previously, this group of authors described the C2HDL converter from C to the HDL language [2,19–23]. It has made several versions of this converter. This converter creates an HDL description of the pipeline matching a one-dimensional program loop written in C. HDL-code generation is performed from the OPS IR (internal representation of Optimizing parallelizing system), which allows you to use the high-level program transformations implemented in the OPS [24]. The advantages for generating HDL descriptions of a high-level OPS intermediate representation compared to register-based internal representations were described in [25]. An internal representation of pipeline [26] has been included to the OPS as a subclass of the OPS internal representation. We consider an algorithm for creating a tree that covers several trees in [27]. This algorithm replaces two pipelines with one that is slightly more complex. This transformation solves the problem of minimizing the reconfiguration time of the FPGA when it is necessary to perform calculations sequentially by different pipelines. The drivers' generator is proposed for mapping programs to a CPU with an FPGA accelerator in [28]. If the body of the pipelined loop contains few operations, the generated pipeline will use few FPGA resources and will not be efficient enough. To increase efficiency, it is proposed to make a sweep of the pipelined loop. In this case, it will be necessary to generate a multi-pipeline instead of a pipeline [29–31]. This will require creating multiple memory modules for each array on FPGA (in order to read multiple array elements simultaneously). This leads to the problem of placing arrays in distributed memory which was discussed in [21].

We propose the following new compiler elements for a CPU and FPGA accelerator in this paper. When the HDL pipeline code is generated automatically, the innermost loop of a nest is pipelined. However, if this loop is inside another loop, then for different values of the outer loop counter, the pipeline must be generated with some differences for the inner loop. Therefore, in this paper we propose the generation of a state machine that controls the generated pipeline. Program transformations implementations for OPS "circular shift" and "retiming" [32,33], which allows regrouping operations in a one-dimensional loop. This paper suggests using these transformations to optimize the generated pipeline and provides examples to illustrate their advantages. We consider that accelerator can be effectively applied to the loop nests called singular. A function that recognizes singular loop nests has been developed based on the OPS.

2   Automatic Pipeline Creation and the State Machine that Controls This Pipeline

Pipeline inner representation (PIR) – abstract structure, which represents a pipeline architecture along with some specific information about pipeline nodes. Pipeline nodes can be divided into two types: buffers and cores. Together, they allow using the power of DataFlow architecture in pipeline design.

The core is a simple processor, which is capable of processing a single operator within an exact amount of time. The core can be of various arity, still binary cores are the most common. Moreover, it contains a special signal aggregator to provide DataFlow capability. This aggregator takes *ready* signals from core data sources, processes them and returns true or false. As soon as the aggregator returns true, the core starts operating. The most common type of aggregator is simple conjunction, which means that an operation begins as soon as all its data sources are ready.

The buffer is a data container. It stores data after core processing and serves as a data source for further cores. Every core stores its results to a single buffer, but, in general, a buffer can be a source for multiple cores simultaneously. Therefore, it is designed as an outgoing oriented tree of memory cells. Each tree branch serves as a data source for a single core. Various branch lengths are to delay data for some ticks in order to balance data threads and minimize core downtime. As soon as the datum in the leaf is used by the core, it is replaced by the datum from its ancestor cell, and so on towards the tree root. This is a basic buffer behaviour, but there are some cases when the same value should be read multiple times, e.g. a variable referenced inside a loop body. Moreover, there is a possibility to store a constant literal in a buffer permanently.

Some buffers serve as a pipeline interface. To emphasize this, special tags called ports are applied to these buffers. A port contains a reference to the buffer and a reference to the data, e.g. the array, which should be transferred to or read from the buffer. As the pipeline is based on for loop body, it is possible to calculate an exact order of array elements to transfer to the buffer, using loop iteration borders and a loop step.

Considering the node types above, the pipeline can be represented as a bipartite oriented graph. One part is formed by buffers, another one - by cores. Pipeline construction can be performed while traversing calculation graph with DFS. In order to make this process handy, there is a set of dynamic construction methods, which allow to add a buffer, a core, or a literal to the pipeline.

As soon as the pipeline is designed, it needs data to process. As for loop with arrays references inside its body is of most interest for us, special mechanism of data arrays transfer from RAM to pipeline is necessary. To fulfill this purpose, a special autogenerated driver is designed. It uses information about data from pipeline ports and sends or receives array elements in exact order, which pipeline requires. Thus, entire pipelined for loop can be replaced in the source code with a single driver access statement.

The workflow described above works quite well considering one dimensional for loops. However, as soon as we try to increase loop dimensions, we face a dramatic performance deterioration. The case can be revealed studying the example in the Fig. 1. Here, the inner loop was pipelined and all the data referenced inside its body should be transferred to the pipeline via its driver on each outer loop iteration. It results in multiple transmissions of the same array elements, which has a bad impact on the overall performance. To overcome this issue, FPGA inner storage should be used to store processed arrays in case of multidimensional loops. This gives a rise for further problems with transmission array elements to the pipeline in exact order inside FPGA. Considering all these, we came up with an idea of driver hardware implementation and extension, which is called pipeline FSM (finite-state machine) inner representation.

Pipeline FSM inner representation – abstract structure, which represents a loop nest as a pipeline for the most inner loop using PIR and a FSM, which controls the iteration order of all the other nested loops and serves as a hardware driver for the pipeline, calculating the exact order of array elements for each iteration and transferring them to the pipeline. As FSM, it has a set of states as a Cartesian multiplication of the sets of all possible loop counter values for each loop except for the most inner one, which was pipelined. Thus, a single state is a set of loop counters values, or an exact nest iteration. Signal to change the state is sent by the pipeline when it has finished operating. Next state is picked while trying to increment each loop counter if it is possible, or reset it otherwise, from inner to outer loops, until a single counter is incremented. This is a total analogy to the process of for loop nest next iteration. After each state change, the exact order of the array elements to be sent to the pipeline is recalculated as a function of loop counters. The whole process is finished as soon as the state became initial again (all the counters have been reset while picking the next state). Quite similarly to single-loop case, the entire pipelined loop nest can be replaced with a single driver access statement, but in this case a driver will avoid repeatable data sending.

3   The HDL Modules Generation and the Drivers Generation

3.1   The Compiler Structure Scheme

The compiler was implemented based on OPS. It uses OPS high-level internal representation Reprise for C and VHDL. Some VHDL language constructions, that are not presented in Reprise, were implemented as an extension of the standard internal representation. The process of the compilation can be divided into 4 phases using different classes:

1. The phase of source code parsing when a parser class converts C source files to OPC internal representation Reprise.
2. The phase of pattern searching. Each pattern is searched by the corresponding transformation class. An instance of the class is created for each piece of code satisfying one of the patterns. This instance provides an abstract description of the algorithms of the corresponding pattern to be later transferred to FPGA.
3. The phase of pattern processing. During this phase driver code instances are created in the internal representation, and HDL module instances are created for algorithms that are transferred to FPGA.
4. The output phase. During this phase the results of the previous step are written to the output files.

The structure scheme that shows the interactions of compiler modules at all phases is presented at Fig. 1.

3.2   The Structure of HDL-Generator

Now the compiler has two HDL generators of pattern implementation - for pipelines and for state machines. In addition to HDL generators for patterns, the compiler contains generators of utility modules, such as buffers. Moreover, the compiler has a library of predefined utility modules on SystemVerilog, such as a queue, a counter, a memory cell with parameterized address alignment.

3.3   Pipeline HDL Code Generator

The algorithm of pipeline HDL code generation can be divided into three phases:

1. Generation of structures described by the main pattern class.

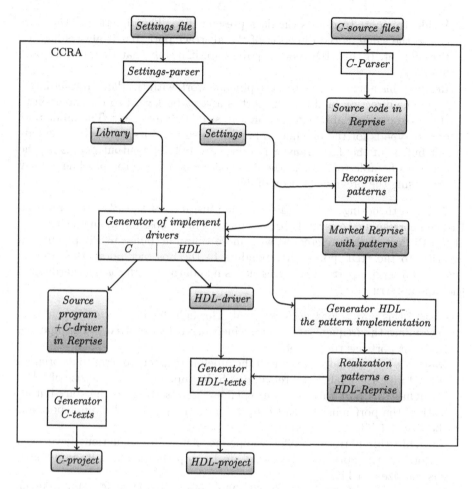

Fig. 1. The Compiler Structure Scheme. The classes or the groups of classes performing certain transformations or analyses are lightened out. The classes or the groups of classes that are responsible for data storage are grayed out. The arrows indicate the information dependencies of blocks.

2. Traversing of the pipeline graph and generation of structures that describe the edges between nodes.
3. The generation of utility modules - buffers and operations.

During the first phase the main HDL module that describes the pipeline body and its ports and declarations of some related signals is generated. Three HDL ports are created for each abstract port:

– Data—this port passes the payload directly. Its direction coincides with the direction of the abstract port and its size is equal to the size of the corresponding data type.

- Valid—this port transmits the data presence flag. The direction of this port is also the same as the direction of the abstract port, but it always has the size of 1 bit. If this HDL port is pulled up, it means that the abstract port has data.
- Ready—this port synchronizes the pipeline work with the data transfer interface. The direction of this HDL port is always backward to the direction of the corresponding abstract port and its size is always 1 bit. The input port of this type is for the pipeline to be able to suspend its work when the output buffers of the data transfer interface are full. The output port is for the driver to be able to suspend the data submission while the pipeline is busy processing the previous portion of data.

It is worth noting that in this case one instance of the PLPort class from PIR can correspond to several abstract ports. This is possible when one instance of the PLPort class is referenced with more than one buffer in the pipeline In addition to the HDL ports corresponding to the abstract ports, the pipeline generates 5 service ports. Their presence is mandatory in all cases, regardless of the pipeline structure:

- Clock—this port is for the clock signal. Through this port a clock signal that determines the frequency of the pipeline work is transmitted to the pipeline. Its input port has the size of 1 bit.
- Reset—it is a vent port. It is for all the pipeline registers to reset to its original state during the enable and reload of VS. Its input port has the size of 1 bit.
- TurnOn—this port turns on the pipeline. After setting up the start initialization, the port must be pulled up to start the pipeline. Its input port has the size of 1 bit.
- TurnOff—this port turns off the pipeline. After all calculations have been performed, the port must be pulled up to stop the pipeline. Its input port has the size of 1 bit.
- IsOn—the sign of the pipeline work. This port is pulled up if and only if the pipeline is active. It allows the driver to get information about the current state of the pipeline. Its output port has the size of 1 bit.

3.4   The Generator of State Machine HDL Code

The algorithm of state machines generation can be divided into four phases:

1. The generation of ports and service structures.
2. The generation of counters that implement the state and the function of the state machine state.
3. The generation of distributed memory blocks and the construction of switching circuitries.
4. The generation of the controlled pipeline.

The list and the purpose of service ports that are created at the first phase of the state machine's HDL code generation coincide with the list and the purpose of the ones for single-pipeline case: Clock, Reset, TurnOn, TurnOff, IsOn. But the list of HDL ports corresponding to the abstract ports of the state machine is constructed differently. Thus, one instance of the PLPort class always corresponds exactly to one abstract port and generates the following HDL ports:

- Data—the port of the data. Its direction coincides with the direction of the abstract port and its size is the same as the data bus capacity of the target architecture in all cases.
- Address—the address port. It is always an input port and its size is equal to the target architecture address bus bit set.
- Valid—this port transmits the data presence flag. It is always pointed in the same direction as the abstract port that has generated it; it has a size of 1 bit.
- Keep—this port allows the driver to point the Data port bytes that have the payload. This is necessary when the Data port contains data that is smaller than the size of the bus data. This port is always input, it can be generated only for the input abstract port. It has a size equal to the size of the Data port divided by the size of the smallest data type. At the moment, this type of data has the size of one byte that is equal to 8 bits.
- ReadEnable—this port allows the driver to report to the state machine about the necessity of reading the data of the corresponding output port. It is an input port and can be generated only by an output abstract port. It has a size of 1 bit.

The state function of the state machine is built in the form of counters; each of them corresponds exactly to the counter of one of the external (in relation to the innermost loop, that was transformed to pipeline) loops of nest. Currently, the start value, the step and the final value of such counters can be only a compile-time constant.

During the memory blocks generation, the number of blocks is considered equal to the number of the managed pipeline's abstract ports. Moreover, for each abstract port of the pipeline, a so-called "Selector" is generated; it actually is the same counter as the counters that are part of the state function of the state machine. The only difference of the selector is that its start value, step and final value are not set by constants, but by affine expressions, the arguments of which are the values of the counters that form the state of the automaton. At the same time, some memory blocks and abstract ports can be combined into one group if they all correspond to the same state machine abstract port. In the case of such combining, there may be a situation where, under different states of the control state machine, the same abstract port of the pipeline must read or write data to different blocks of distributed memory. In this case, an additional switch is generated as part of the state machine that is parameterized by the index expressions of the corresponding abstract ports. The placement of data in distributed memory occurs according to the scheme proposed in [34].

4 Finding Singular Loop Nests with OPS

While mapping a source code to a heterogeneous system with CPU and FPGA accelerator, it is important to choose fragments of an input program that would be mapped onto FPGA. Usually such fragments should be of limited size and performing large amount of computations. We consider loop nests to be the most typically chosen fragments with the mentioned characteristics. However, not all loop nests are suitable for optimization and translation onto FPGA.

Modern processors require an order of magnitude less time to perform simple arithmetic operations than to read their operands from memory. Because of this, code regions that have a lot more computational operations in relation to the number of memory accesses are more suitable to be mapped onto FPGA accelerator. Shared memory access is the bottleneck of many algorithms. In such algorithms, using the local memory (processor cache) would be more efficient, as its performance is significantly higher than operative memory's. This creates a necessity for data locality. Without it, accelerators cannot give a significant performance boost.

For a subset of C programs, it is possible to approximate amount of memory accesses inside a loop nest in relation to the number of basic arithmetic operations. The number of operations inside a loop nest is proportional to the number of vertices in the iterations space of that loop nest. The number of operations in a loop nest, which has k loops with N iterations each, is proportional to N^k. The amount of data required to compute a loop nest is usually proportional to N^m, where m is the maximum dimension of the arrays used in the loop nest. Mapping a loop nest to an accelerator is potentially more beneficial if the inequality $m < k$ holds true. We define a singular loop nest as a loop nest in which the number of indices for each variable occurrence is less than the number of loops in the nest.

E.g. a singular loop nest that has two loops can only have one-dimensional arrays and scalar variables. Choosing singular loop nests to be run on accelerator is very likely to lead to overall speedup.

For example, the loop nest that calculates a convolution is a singular loop nest.

```
for(i = 0; i < M; i++)
  for(j = 0; j < N; j++)
    X[i] = A[i+j]*B[j];
```

The next loop nest is singular, but is very unlikely to be sped up by an accelerator, because it has $O(M \cdot N)$ operators and $O(M \cdot N)$ array entries.

```
for(i = 0; i < M; i++)
  for(j = 0; j < N; j++)
    A[i*N+j] = B[i] + C[j]*D[i+j];
```

The above loop nest is equivalent to the following one-dimensional loop.

```
for(i = 0; i < M*N; i++)
  A[i] = B[i div N] + C[i mod N]*D[(i div N)+(i mod N)];
```

The fact that a loop nest is singular does not necessarily mean that it could be sped up. However, it could be done with higher probability. The acceleration potential depends on data dependencies and target computer architecture.

5 Loop Unrolling and Array Distribution in Distributed Memory

Example of convolution program source code that is used to test target architecture performance.

```
for ( j = 0;  j < CONV_LEN ;  j += 1)
   for  ( i = 0;  i < CORE_LEN ;  i += 1)
      a0 [ j ] = a0 [ j ] + c [ j + i ] * b [ i ];
```

If CORE_LEN is divided by 8, then the loop unrolling looks as follows

```
for ( j = 0;  j < CONV_LEN ;  j += 1)
   for  ( i = 0;  i < CORE_LEN ;  i += 8)
      a0 [ j ] = a0 [ j ] +
                 c [ j + i + 0] * b [ i + 0] + c [ j + i + 1] * b [ i + 1] +
                 c [ j + i + 2] * b [ i + 2] + c [ j + i + 3] * b [ i + 3] +
                 c [ j + i + 4] * b [ i + 4] + c [ j + i + 5] * b [ i + 5] +
                 c [ j + i + 6] * b [ i + 6] + c [ j + i + 7] * b [ i + 7];
```

Loop unrolling reduces the number of iterations of the loop that is to be transformed to pipeline. After the loop unrolling each occurrence of the array is repeated several times with different index expressions. For the efficiency of the pipeline all the data are to be read simultaneously. Therefore, the elements of each array must be placed in a special way in several memory blocks. Such placements are described in [34].

The figure shows how to speed up the calculations by loop unrolling (Fig. 2).

6 Loop Statements Regrouping to Save Time the Initial Load and Buffer Memory Pipeline

This transformation changes the order of loop body operator execution. Similar transformations include retiming [33, 35] and round-robin loop body shift [32]

We will examine how loop operator regrouping is working on an example.

For example, consider a loop which data dependency graph is a tree:

```
for ( i =0;  i<N;  ++i) {
    a [ i +1] = b [ i +2] * c [ i ];
    d [ i ] = a [ i ] + e [ i ];                    (1)
    b [ i ] = f [ i ] - g [ i ];
}
```

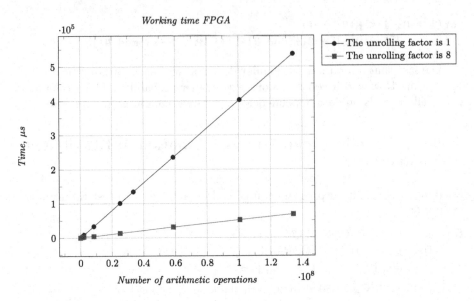

Fig. 2. The dependence of the convolution computation time on FPGA on the number of arithmetic operations for the unrolling factors that are equal to 1 and 8.

Different index expressions for the variable occurrences "a" and "b" lead to a necessity for synchronization buffers inside the pipeline and preliminary (before pipeline start) loading of some of these buffers. Preliminary loading requires FPGA elements that are used only once before the pipeline start. Because of this, lowering the volume of preliminary loading raises FPGA efficiency (Fig. 3).

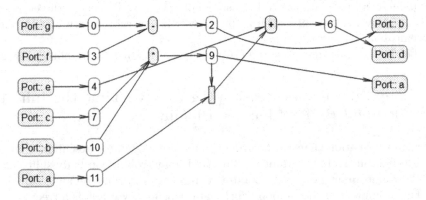

Fig. 3. Diagram of a pipeline created for a loop (1) by OPSDemo

After application of "loop operator regrouping" transformation to loop (1) the following code fragment is created:

```
d[0]  = a[0] + e[0];
b[0]  = f[0] - g[0];
b[1]  = f[1] - g[1];
for ( i =0;  i<N-2;  ++i ) {
     a[i+1]  = b[i+2] * c[i];
     d[i+1]  = a[i+1] + e[i+1];                    (2)
     b[i+2]  = f[i+2] - g[i+2];
}
a[N-2]  = b[N-2] * c[N-2];
a[N-1]  = b[N-1] * c[N-1];
d[N-1]  = a[N-1] + e[N-1];
```

Computing "prologue" (three assignment operators before loop (2)) and "epilogue" (three assignment operators after loop (2)) could be carried out on the CPU.

It is worth to point out that after performing "loop regrouping" transformation in loop (2) the variable occurrences "a" and "b" have identical index expression. This means that it is no longer necessary to perform initial pipeline loading for these variables. Apart from that, pipeline would now require less buffer memory for data movement synchronization (Fig. 4).

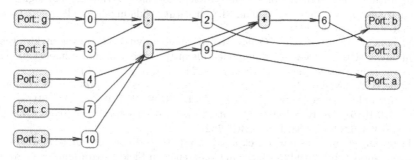

Fig. 4. Diagram of a pipeline created for a loop (2) by OPSDemo

7   Conclusion

This article takes a new step towards building a compiler from a high-level language to a processor with a FPGA-accelerator. The compiler built Pipeline computing systems for loops with several assignment operators, and there may be information dependencies between operators. Together with the pipeline, an automaton is created to control this pipeline. There is presented the optimizing loops transformation, which simplifies the generated HDL-code of the pipeline, it saves FPGA resources. This transformation is implemented in the Optimizing Parallelizing System on the basis of which the compiler is developed. The OPS function is developed, which looks for program code fragments that could be transferred to the accelerator.

References

1. Preliminary Product Specification/XILINX/Zynq-7000 All Programmable SoC Overview (2018). http://www.xilinx.com/support/documentation/data_sheets/ds190-Zynq-7000-Overview.pdf. Accessed 21 July 2019
2. Steinberg, B.Y., Dubrov, D.V., Mikhailuts, Y., Roshal, A.S., Steinberg, R.B.: Automatic high-level programs mapping onto programmable architectures. In: Malyshkin, V. (ed.) PaCT 2015. LNCS, vol. 9251, pp. 474–485. Springer, Cham (2015). https://doi.org/10.1007/978-3-319-21909-7_46. ISBN 978-3-319-21909-7
3. Bondalapati, K.K.: Modeling and mapping for dynamically reconfigurable hybrid architectures. Ph.D. thesis. University of Southern California, California (2001)
4. Kalyaev, A., Levin, I.: Modulno-narashchivaemye mnogoprotsessornye sistemy so strukturno-protsedurnoi organizatsiei vychislenii. (Russian) [Modularly multiprocessor systems with structurally-procedural organization of computations]. "Ianus-K", p. 380 (2003)
5. Korneev, V.: Arkhitektura vychislitelnykh sistem s programmiruemoi strukturoi. (Russian) [Programmable Computer Architecture]. Nauka, Novosibirsk (1985)
6. Kalyaev, I., Levin, I.: Rekonfiguriruemye multikonveiernye vychislitelnye struktury. (Russian) [Reconfigurable multi-pipeline computing structures] ed. by I. Kaliaeva, Izdatelstvo IuNTs RAN, Rostov-n/D, p. 344 (2009)
7. Yadzhak, M.: Vysokoparallelnye algoritmy i metody dlia resheniia zadach massovykh arifmeticheskikh i logicheskikh vychislenii. (Russian) [Highly parallel algorithms and methods for solving problems of mass arithmetic and logical calculations]: Ph.D. thesis, Yadzhak, M.S. Institut prikladnykh problem mekhaniki i matematiki, Lvov (2001)
8. Samofalov, K., Lutskii, G.: Osnovy teorii mnogourovnevykh konveiernykh vychislitelnykh sistem. (Russian) [Fundamentals of the theory of multidimensional conveyor computing systems]. Radio i sviaz, Moskva, p. 272 (1989)
9. Yosi, B.-A., Nadav, R., Eddie, S.: Finding the best compromise in compiling compound loops to Verilog. J. Syst. Arch. **56**(9), 474–486 (2010). https://doi.org/10.1016/j.sysarc.2010.07.001. http://www.sciencedirect.com/science/article/pii/S1383762110000688. ISSN 1383-7621
10. Esko, O., et al.: Customized exposed datapath soft-core design flow with compiler support. In: 2010 International Conference on Field Programmable Logic and Applications, pp. 217–222 (2010). https://doi.org/10.1109/FPL.2010.51
11. Polyakov, G., Lysykh, V.: A formal method of functional SNS-synthesis of problem-oriented parallel-pipelined devices. In: Proceedings of the National Supercomputer Forum (NSCF-2013). Pereslavl-Zalessky, Russia (2013)
12. Cardoso, J., Diniz, P.: Compilation Techniques for Recongurable Architectures (2009)
13. Tripp, J.L., Gokhale, M., Peterson, K.: Trident: from high-level language to hardware circuitry. Computer **40**(3), 28–37 (2007). https://doi.org/10.1109/MC.2007.107. ISSN 0018-9162
14. Kindratenko, V.V., Brunner, R.J., Myers, A.D.: Mitrion-C application development on SGI Altix 350/RC100. In: Proceedings of the 15th Annual IEEE Symposium on Field-Programmable Custom Computing Machines, FCCM 2007, pp. 239–250. IEEE Computer Society, Washington, DC (2007). https://doi.org/10.1109/FCCM.2007.45. ISBN 0-7695-2940-2
15. Self, R.P., Fleury, M., Downton, A.C.: Design methodology for construction of asynchronous pipelines with Handel-C. IEE Proc. Softw. **150**(1), 39–47 (2003). https://doi.org/10.1049/ip-sen:20030206. ISSN 1462-5970

16. Boulytchev, D., Medvedev, O.: Hardware description language based on message passing and implicit pipelining. In: 2010 East-West Design Test Symposium (EWDTS), pp. 438–441 (2010). https://doi.org/10.1109/EWDTS.2010.5742095
17. Zhang, J., et al.: Bit-level optimization for high-level synthesis and FPGA-based acceleration. In: Proceedings of the 18th Annual ACM/SIGDA International Symposium on Field Programmable Gate Arrays, FPGA 2010, pp. 59–68. ACM, Monterey (2010). https://doi.org/10.1145/1723112.1723124. http://doi.acm.org/10.1145/1723112.1723124. ISBN 978-1-60558-911-4
18. Lacis, A., Dbar, S.: Sistema programmirovaniia Avtokod HDL i opyt ee primeneniia dlia skhemnoi realizatsii chislennykh metodov v FPGA. (Russian) [Programming system Autocode HDL and experience of its application for circuit implementation of numerical methods in FPGA], Nauchnyi servis v seti Internet: masshtabiruemost, parallelnost, effektivnost: Trudy Vserossiiskoi nauchnoi konferentsii (21–26 sentiabria 2009 g., g. Novorossiisk). Izd-vo MGU, p. 237 (2009)
19. Dubrov, D., Roshal, A.: Generating pipeline integrated circuits using C2HDL converter. In: East-West Design Test Symposium (EWDTS 2013), pp. 1–4 (2013). https://doi.org/10.1109/EWDTS.2013.6673108
20. Dubrov, D., Roshal, A.: Avtomaticheskoe otobrazhenie programm na protsessor s PLIS-uskoritelem. (Russian) [Automatic mapping of programs on a processor with FPGA accelerator], Vestnik Iuzhno-uralskogo gosudarstvennogo universiteta. Seriia "Vychislitelnaia matematika i informatika", vol. 3, no. 2, pp. 117–121 (2014)
21. Steinberg, B.Y., et al.: A project of compiler for a processor with programmable accelerator. Procedia. Comput. Sci. **101**(1), 435–438 (2016). https://doi.org/10.1016/j.procs.2016.11.050. https://www.sciencedirect.com/science/article/pii/S1877050916327193
22. Steinberg, B.Y., et al.: Developing a high-level language compiler for a computer with programmable architecture. In: Proceedings of the 12th Central and Eastern European Software Engineering Conference in Russia on - CEE-SECR 2016, pp. 1–6. ACM Press, New York (2016). https://doi.org/10.1145/3022211.3022226. http://dl.acm.org/citation.cfm?doid=3022211.3022226. ISBN 9781450348843
23. Steinberg, B.Y., et al.: Classification of loops with one statement for executing on the processor with programmable accelerator. Prog. Syst. Theory Appl. **8**(3), 189–218 (2017). https://doi.org/10.25209/2079-3316-2017-8-3-189-218. ISSN 2079-3316
24. Optimizing parallelization system (2013). www.ops.rsu.ru. Accessed 21 July 2019
25. Gervich, L.R., et al.: How OPS (optimizing parallelizing system) may be useful for clang. In: ACM International Conference Proceeding Series Association for Computing Machinery (2017). https://doi.org/10.1145/3166094.3166116. ISBN 9781450363969
26. Alymova, E.V.: On the intermediate program representation for automatic generation of pipeline compute units. University News. North-Caucasian Region. Technical Sciences Series, no. 3, pp. 22–28 (2017). https://doi.org/10.17213/0321-2653-2017-3-22-28. ISSN 03212653
27. Steinberg, B.Y., et al.: Pipeline circuits to compute several expressions. In: Proceedings of the 14th Central and Eastern European Software Engineering Conference Russia on ZZZ - CEE-SECR 2018, pp. 1–7. ACM Press, New York (2018). https://doi.org/10.1145/3290621.3290632. http://dl.acm.org/citation.cfm?doid=3290621.3290632. ISBN 9781450361767

28. Mikhajluts, J., et al:. Drajvery dlja obespechenija vzaimodejstvija uskoritelja s rekonfiguriruemoj arhitekturoj i central'nogo processora vychislitel'noj sistemy. (Russian) [Drivers for the interaction of the accelerator with the reconfigurable architecture and the central processor of the computing system]. Jazyki programmirovanija i kompiljatory. Trudy Vserossijskoj nauchnoj konferencii pamjati A.L. Fuksmana. Publishing house of the southern federal university, Rostov-on-Don,, pp. 205–208 (2017)

29. Steinberg, R.: Vychislenie zaderzhki v startakh konveierov dlia superkompiuterov so strukturno protsedurnoi organizatsiei vychislenii. (Russian) [Calculation of delay in pipeline starts for supercomputers with structurally procedural organization of calculations]. Iskusstvennyi intellekt. Nauchnoteoreticheskii zhurnal, no. 4, pp. 105–112 (2003)

30. Steinberg, R.: Ispolzovanie reshetchatykh grafov dlia issledovaniia mnogokonveiernoi modeli vychislenii. (Russian) [The Use of Lattice Graphs to Research the Multi-Pipeline Computation Model]. Izvestiia VUZov. Severokavkazskii region. Estestvennye nauki, no. 2, pp. 16–18 (2009)

31. Steinberg, R.: Otobrazhenie gnezd tsiklov na mnogokonveiernuiu arkhitekturu. (Russian) [Mapping Loop Nests to a Multi-Pipeline Architecture] Programmirovanie 36(3), 177–185 (2010)

32. Steinberg, O.B.: Circular shift of loop body-programme transformation, promoting Parallelism. Vestnik Iuzhno-Uralskogo gosudarstvennogo universiteta. Seriia: Matematicheskoe modelirovanie i programmirovanie 10(3) (2017)

33. Steinberg, O.B., Ivlev, I.A.: Primenenie preobrazovaniia tsiklov "Retiming" s tseliu umensheniia kolichestva ispolzuemykh registrov. (Russian) [Using "Retiming" loop transformation to reduce the number of registers used]. Izvestiia vysshikh uchebnykh zavedenii. Severo-Kavkazskii region. Tekhnicheskie nauki. 3(195) (2017)

34. Steinberg, B.: Blochno-affinnye razmeshcheniia dannykh v parallelnoi pamiati. (Russian) [Block-affine Parallel Memory Locations]. Informatsionnye tekhnologii, no. 6, pp. 36–41 (2010). https://elibrary.ru/item.asp?id=14998775. ISSN 1684–6400

35. Liu, D., et al.: Optimally maximizing iteration-level loop parallelism. IEEE Trans. Parallel Distrib. Syst. 23(3), 564–572 (2012)

Author Index

Printed in the United States
by Baker & Taylor Publisher Services

Printed in the United States
by Baker & Taylor Publisher Services